INTERNATIONAL INVESTMI

The updated edition of this acclaimed book offers a critical overview of the law of foreign investment, incorporating a thorough analysis of the principles and standards of treatment available to foreign investors in international law. It is authoritative and multi-layered, offering an analysis of the key issues and an insightful assessment of recent trends in the case law, from both developed and developing country perspectives.

A major feature of the book is that it deals with the tension between the law of foreign investment and other competing principles of international law. In doing so, it proposes ways of achieving a balance between these principles and the need to protect the legitimate rights and expectations of foreign investors on the one hand, and the need not to restrict unduly the right of host governments to implement their public policy on the other, including the protection of the environment and human rights, and the promotion of social and economic justice within the host country.

Many of the pioneering ideas that were advanced in the first edition of this book in 2008 have been taken up by governments and international organisations in their attempts to reform the investor-State dispute settlement mechanism and strike a balance between different competing principles in developing international investment law. Accordingly, this fourth edition captures the essence of the ongoing multiple reform processes – either planned or envisaged – currently underway.

International Investment Law

Reconciling Policy and Principle

Fourth Edition

Surya P Subedi

QC (Hon), OBE, DCL & DPhil (Oxford)

Professor of International Law, University of Leeds, United Kingdom

Member, Institute de Droit International

Barrister, Three Stone Chambers, Lincoln's Inn, London

·HART·

OXFORD · LONDON · NEW YORK · NEW DELHI · SYDNEY

HART PUBLISHING

Bloomsbury Publishing Plc

Kemp House, Chawley Park, Cumnor Hill, Oxford, OX2 9PH, UK

1385 Broadway, New York, NY 10018, USA

HART PUBLISHING, the Hart/Stag logo, BLOOMSBURY and the Diana logo are
trademarks of Bloomsbury Publishing Plc

First published in Great Britain 2020

A catalogue record for this book is available from the British Library.

Library of Congress Cataloging-in-Publication data

Names: Subedi, Surya P., 1958- author.

Title: International investment law : reconciling policy and principle / Surya P Subedi, O.B.E., DPhil (Oxford),
Barrister (Middle Temple), Professor of International Law, University of Leeds, United Kingdom,
Member, Institut de Droit International.

Description: Fourth edition. | Oxford ; New York : Hart Publishing, 2020. |
Includes bibliographical references and index.

Identifiers: LCCN 2020015065 (print) | LCCN 2020015066 (ebook) | ISBN 9781509936366 (pb) |
ISBN 9781509936373 (ePDF) | ISBN 9781509936380 (EPub)

Subjects: LCSH: Investments, Foreign (International law)

Classification: LCC K3830 .S88 2020 (print) | LCC K3830 (ebook) | DDC 346/.092—dc23

LC record available at https://lccn.loc.gov/2020015065

LC ebook record available at https://lccn.loc.gov/2020015066

ISBN: PB: 978-1-50993-636-6
ePDF: 978-1-50993-637-3
ePub: 978-1-50993-638-0

Typeset by Compuscript Ltd, Shannon
Printed and bound in Great Britain by CPI Group (UK) Ltd, Croydon CR0 4YY

To find out more about our authors and books visit www.hartpublishing.co.uk.
Here you will find extracts, author information, details of forthcoming events
and the option to sign up for our newsletters.

Preface to the Fourth Edition

The objective of this book is to present a panoramic picture of the evolution and current state of affairs within international investment law. In doing so, it presents an analysis of the current law and recent trends within this area of law and suggests measures to develop it to address the challenges of the 21st Century in governing economic relations among States and between foreign investors and host governments. The central theme running through this work is the challenge and the need to reconcile the law on the protection of foreign investment with other competing principles of international law. In this book, I have attempted to bring to bear my knowledge of the law both as a generalist international lawyer and a specialist in international investment law. It has benefitted from my experience of working as a government lawyer, practitioner, academic and an international diplomat.

International investment law is a rapidly developing and fast changing area of inter-national law. Momentous changes are taking place in this area. As I write, proposals for reform of the investor-state dispute settlement mechanism to settle investment disputes are being discussed and negotiated within both the International Centre for Settlement of Investment Disputes and the United Nations Commission on International Trade Law, a subsidiary body of the UN General Assembly. Thus, it is a challenge to cover all of these ongoing changes and proposals for reform of both the law and the institutions administering the law in a work of this nature. However, I have attempted to capture the essence of these changes and proposals for reform in this edition.

I have been humbled by the impact this work has had on the development of international investment law since the publication of its first edition in 2008. It has 'undoubtedly contributed to the reform of the sector that is now being seriously addressed by various States', the judges on the Oxford University panel stated in 2019 in their recommendation to award me the highest degree – the Doctor of Civil Law (DCL) – by Oxford where I had obtained my DPhil (PhD) in International Law in 1993. They highlighted that I was 'one of the first scholars to analyse the tension that exists between protecting the interests of investors and the obligations of States to address other core policy concerns'. Similar complimentary remarks were made by reviewers of my book in nine leading international law journals such as the *European Journal of International Law* and the *NYU Journal of International Law and Politics*. It is indeed gratifying that many of the ideas that were advanced in the first edition of this book way back in 2008 are now being implemented by States and international organisations.

This book, along with the other seven of my books and around 60 published journal articles of mine seem to have been taken into consideration leading to my appoint-ment as a Queen's Counsel, QC (Hon) in the UK in 2017, in recognition of, among other things, my 'contribution to the development of international law'. Furthermore, this book has been translated into Chinese and Farsi (Persian) by international law professors of renown and published in a number of countries. I hope the fourth edition of this book continues to enthuse students and practitioners alike in this area of law and serves as a useful source of reference for policy and decision makers within governments and international organisations involved in the reform of the relevant law and institutions. I thank the superb team at Hart Publishing for their excellent cooperation in publishing this book.

Surya P Subedi
London, January 2020

Contents

List of Abbreviations

AALCO	Asian-African Legal Consultative Organisation
ACP	African, Caribbean and Pacific Group of States
AJIL	American Journal of International Law
APEC	Asia-Pacific Economic Cooperation
ASEAN	Association of Southeast Asian Nations
BEE	Black Economic Empowerment
BIPPA	Bilateral Investment Promotion and Protection Agreement between India and Nepal
BITs	Bilateral Investment Treaties
BLIHR	Business Leaders' Initiative for Human Rights
BYIL	British Yearbook of International Law
CAFTA	Central-American Free Trade Agreement
CARICOM	Caribbean Community
CERD	Charter of Economic Rights and Duties of States
CERES	Coalition for Environmentally Responsible Economies
CETA	Comprehensive Economic Trade Agreement
CIA	Central Intelligence Agency
CIS	Commonwealth of Independent States
CNRP	Cambodian National Rescue Party
COMESA	Common Market for Eastern and Southern Africa
CPTPP	Comprehensive and Progressive Agreement for Trans-Pacific Partnership
CSD	Commission on Sustainable Development
CTC	Commission on Trans-national Corporations
DSB	Dispute Settlement Body of the WTO
EC	European Communities

ECOSOC	Economic and Social Council
EITI	Extractive Industries Transparency Initiative
EU	European Union
FCN	Friendship, Commerce and Navigation Treaties
FDI	Foreign Direct Investment
FET	Fair and Equitable Treatment
FTAA	Free Trade Agreement of the Americas
FTAs	Free Trade Agreements
G-20	Group of Twenty
GATS	General Agreement on Trade in Services
GATT	General Agreement on Tariffs and Trade
GRI	Global Reporting Initiatives
GSB	Growing Sustainable Businesses
HMSO	Her Majesty's Stationary Office
HRC	Human Rights Council
IBA	International Bar Association
IBRD	International Bank for Reconstruction and Development
ICC	International Chamber of Commerce
ICCPR	International Covenant on Civil and Political Rights
ICJ	International Court of Justice
ICLQ	International and Comparative Law Quarterly
ICSID	International Centre for the Settlement of Investment Disputes
ICTSD	International Centre for Trade and Sustainable Development
IFC	International Finance Corporation
IIAs	International Investment Agreements
IIMS	International Investment Mediation Service
IISD	International Institute of Sustainable Development
ILA	International Law Association
ILC	International Law Commission
ILM	International Legal Materials

ILO	International Labour Organization
ILR	International Law Reports
IMF	International Monetary Fund
IOE	International Organization of Employers
ISDS	Investor-State Dispute Settlement
ITO	International Trade Organisation
IWG	Intergovernmental Working Group
JWT	Journal of World Trade
LCIA	London Court of International Arbitration
LNTS	League of Nations Treaty Series
MAI	Multilateral Agreement on Investment
MDGs	Millennium Development Goals
MERCOSUR	Southern Common Market
MFN	Most-Favoured Nation Treatment
MIC	Multilateral Investment Court
MIGA	Multilateral Investment Guarantee Agency
MNEs	Multinational Enterprises
NAFTA	North American Free Trade Agreement
NGOs	Non-Governmental Organisations
NIEO	New International Economic Order
NILR	Netherlands International Law Review
NPM	Non-Precluded Measures
ODI	Overseas Development Institute
OECD	Organisation for Economic Cooperation and Development
PCIJ	Permanent Court of International Justice
PSI	Pre-Shipment Inspection
PSNR	Permanent Sovereignty of States over their Natural Resources
RIAA	Reports of International Arbitral Awards
RTAs	Regional Trade Agreements
TNCs	Trans-national Corporations

TPP	Trans-Pacific Partnership
TRIMs	Trade-Related Investment Measures
TRIPs	Trade-Related Intellectual Property Rights
TTIP	Transatlantic Trade and Investment Partnership
UN	United Nations
UNASUR	Union of South American Nations
UNCITRAL	United Nations Commission on International Trade Law
UNCTAD	United Nations Conference on Trade and Development
UNDP	United Nations Development Programme
UNEP	United Nations Environmental Programme
UNGA	United Nations General Assembly
UNTS	United Nations Treaty Series
USMCA	United States-Mexico-Canada Agreement
WRAP	World-Wide Responsible Apparel Production
WTO	World Trade Organization

Table of Cases

Table of Legislation

France

Germany

Iran

Mexico

Peru

South Africa

United Kingdom

United States

Venezuela

Table of Conventions, Treaties, Agreements etc

Bilateral Investment Treaties (BITs)

Model BITs

Freedom of Commerce and Navigation Treaties

UN Resolutions

Arbitration Rules

Introduction

Momentous changes are currently underway in the world of international investment law and arbitration. The landscape of investor-state dispute settlement is changing for the better, thanks to the endeavours made by various actors over the past two decades. These are exciting times to be practising, studying, researching and writing about this area of law. States are forging ahead with the negotiation and conclusion of investment treaties or free trade agreements with substantial chapters on investment that have innovative provisions to protect foreign investment while safeguarding their sovereign rights and protecting societal values. Older generation regional treaties, such as the North American Free Trade Agreement (NAFTA), are being replaced by new treaties such as the United States-Mexico-Canada Agreement (USMCA) and the Comprehensive and Progressive Agreement for Trans-Pacific Partnership (CPTPP). New bilateral investment treaties (BITs) and model BITs have included innovative provisions designed not only to protect foreign investment but also to protect other societal values such as human rights, the environment and sustainable development. For instance, the new Model Dutch BIT goes on to establish, inter alia, a link between gender equality and investment. Whether it is the Model Indian BIT, the Dutch Model BIT or the Nigeria-Morocco BIT of 2016 they are comprehensive in their scope, signify change in emphasis and seek to rebalance the competing interests and principles within international investment law. International investment tribunals sitting under the International Centre for the Settlement of Investment Disputes (ICSID) or United Nations Commission on International Trade Law (UNCITRAL) rules have made ground-breaking awards that have brought more clarity to the law and contributed to the development of international investment law. Leading cases such as *Salini*, *Methanex* and *Philip Morris* have sought to define differently the nature and scope of certain core principles of the law, have tried to reconcile competing principles of international law and influenced the decision-making by subsequent tribunals.

The changes in the law and the institutions administering the law suggested by scholars and by civil society organisations such as those advanced by the present author in the first edition of this book way back in 2008 seem to be having an impact. As stated by Kaufmann-Kohler and Potesta, 'Growing criticism over investor-state arbitration has triggered demands for reforms of the existing framework from countries, international organizations and civil society groups'.[1] Indeed, efforts are underway both within the ICSID and UNCITRAL to reform the investor-state dispute settlement (ISDS) mechanism. ICSID has carried out a number of procedural reforms three times in the past and the fourth round is currently underway in which some innovative

---

[1] Gabrielle Kaufmann-Kohler and Michele Potestà, 'Challenges on the road toward a multilateral investment court', *Columbia FDI Perspectives*, no 201, 5 June 2017.

proposals for procedural reform are on the table for negotiations. As summed up by the Secretary-General of ICSID, 'the fourth update to its procedural rules, and the changes envisioned are the most extensive to date. They cover arbitration, conciliation, fact-finding, and mediation' under the various ICSID instruments.[2] It is hoped that the 'extensive' changes proposed will go a long way to satisfy some of the concerns of different stakeholders. Institutions such as the ICSID are needed and should be strengthened and not condemned or side-lined. Yet, they should be reformed to make them work in accordance with the demand of time so that they can command the trust and confidence from all sides of the equation needed to strengthen the rule of law at the international level. While some States are withdrawing from ISDS mechanisms new ones such as Mexico have decided to join them. In 2017, Mexico became 162nd country to sign the ICSID Convention testifying to its usefulness for States seeking to attract foreign investment offering incentives. At the time of revising this book for its fourth edition in January 2020, Working Group III of UNCITRAL was convened in Vienna to work on possible ISDS reform. The Working Group, which is charged with developing multilateral reforms to the current ad hoc system of ISDS, focussed its work in its Vienna session on designing permanent adjudicative institutions for the resolution of investment disputes, including a standing appellate mechanism and a Multilateral Investment Court (MIC).

It has also identified a wide range of concerns relating to ISDS, grouping them into four general categories: (1) costs and duration of proceedings; (2) inconsistency, incoherence, unpredictability and incorrectness of decisions; (3) arbitrators and decision-makers; and (4) third-party funding.[3] Different delegates have identified a set of cross-cutting issues for inclusion in the deliberations and they are: means other than arbitration to resolve investment disputes as well as dispute prevention methods; exhaustion of local remedies; implications for third parties and the role of third-party participation; investor obligations and counterclaims; regulatory chill; and damages.[4]

United Nations Conference on Trade and Development (UNCTAD) is also engaged in the reform process of investment treaty regime. It has identified the following core international investment treaty regime reform objectives: preserving the right to regulate while providing protection; reforming investment dispute settlement; promoting and facilitating investment; and ensuring responsible investment.[5]

The ISDS reform process within these various institutions, which is currently underway, was possible when even governments that had been staunch supporters of

---

[2] Meg Kinnear, 'Moving with the Times: amending the ICSID rules', *Columbia FDI Perspectives*, no 233, 27 August 2018.

[3] See N. Bernasconi-Osterwalder and Lise Johnson, 'What to Expect in the January 2020 Session of UNCITRAL Working Group III on ISDS Reform', *Investment Treaty News*, 17 December 2019, available at https://www.iisd.org/itn/2019/12/17/what-to-expect-in-the-january-2020-session-of-uncitral-working-group-iii-on-isds-reform-nathalie-bernasconi-osterwalder-lise-johnson (accessed on 20 January 2020).

[4] Ibid.

[5] Elisabeth Tuerk Diana Rosert, 'UNCTAD's 2019 High-level IIA Conference: A new momentum for Phase 2 reform', *Investment Treaty News*, 17 December 2019, available at https://www.iisd.org/itn/2019/12/17/unctads-2019-high-level-iia-conference-a-new-momentum-for-phase-2-reform-elisabeth-tuerk-diana-rosert (accessed on 20 January 2020).

the ISDS mechanism (such as European Union Member States and the United States) decided to change course. They were joined enthusiastically by developing countries and supported by many civil society organisations. While the reform process within the ICSID framework is focussed on modernising procedural aspects of the ISDS mechanism, many States including the EU, have aspired to a more ambitious reform including the creation of a MIC with an appellate mechanism.

The international legal order established in the post-Second World War period to promote international peace and security, human rights and economic development has provided stability for peace and economic growth over the past 75 years. No third World War has taken place largely due to the existence of the United Nations (UN) and other institutions such as ICSID. The ground rules of international law, such as the principles of sovereignty, sovereign equality and non-interference, have allowed countries to achieve economic development, peace and prosperity. States have benefitted a great deal from the principle of economic sovereignty and other rules of international trade and investment to harness their natural resources and to engage in cross-border transactions.

However, the political and economic architecture developed in the aftermath of the Second World War has come under pressure due to the rise in resource nationalism, excesses of capitalism, lack of reform of international institutions and unilateralism in international affairs. This worrying trend in international affairs is undermining the ethos of multilateralism, weakening the global institutions and corroding people's confidence in these global institutions and rules of international law. Now the question is – where do we go from here? What can be done to revive the faith in multilateralism and reform the global institutions? What are the current challenges to the international legal order and possibilities for the future? The current situation offers both challenges and opportunities, but what are they? These and other associated issues are what this book seeks to examine within the context of international investment law and arbitration.

Although the law of foreign investment is one of the oldest branches of international law, as recently as the early 1970s the International Court of Justice (ICJ) described it as a relatively underdeveloped area of international law.[6] Indeed, at that time, the number of bilateral investment treaties (BITs) as well as the body of jurisprudence of international arbitral tribunals sitting under BITs was small. These arbitrations had been mainly state-to-state rather than investor-state arbitrations. According to published reports available, it was only in 1987 that the first such investment arbitration under a BIT took place.[7] Prior to this, investment disputes referred to

---

[6] The ICJ made the following remarks in 1970 about the state of development of the law of foreign investment in the *Barcelona Traction* case: 'Considering the important developments of the last half-century, the growth of foreign investments and the expansion of international activities of corporations, in particular of holding companies, which are often multinational, and considering the way in which the economic interests of states have proliferated, it may at first sight appear surprising that the evolution of the law has not gone further and that no generally accepted rules in the matter have crystallized on the international plane.' *Barcelona Traction, Light and Power Co (Belgium v Spain)*, ICJ Reports 1970, 3, 46–47.

[7] This was a case brought against the government of Sri Lanka by a Hong Kong investor using a UK BIT for losses arising out of a conflict between the security forces of Sri Lanka and the Tamil rebel groups. *Asian Agricultural Products Ltd v Sri Lanka*, ICSID Case No ARB/87/3 (registered in 1987).

international tribunals were either brought by private parties pursuant to contractual agreements or by one state against another. Investment arbitration had traditionally been considered to be a private commercial matter between two disputants. The BITs themselves were basically a construct of the postcolonial era and developed in the context of an escalation in the Cold War.

However, within a short period of time this area of law has witnessed a phenomenal growth and has now become one of the fastest changing areas of international law with exciting and far-reaching implications for both investment-receiving and investment-exporting countries, thanks to enterprising claimants and innovative interpretations and expansive approaches adopted by international investment tribunals. These changes are taking place in both state practice and jurisprudence – the total number of international investment agreements (IIAs) is now more than 5,600 (including some 3,000 BITs and a number of other regional, bilateral and interregional agreements to this effect),[8] and the number of investment cases referred to international investment tribunals has recently seen a massive growth. This rapid growth has often been described as an 'explosion' or 'revolution' in foreign investment law. International investment arbitration itself has acquired a new currency, ie from a private commercial dispute settlement mechanism to a more mainstream international law dispute settlement mechanism resolving disputes involving even public international law and general public law questions.

As stated by UNCTAD:

> [A]t the international level, countries and regions continue their efforts to negotiate and conclude international investment agreements (IIAs). With the addition of 31 agreements, the regime had grown to 3,271 agreements (2,926 bilateral investment treaties and 345 other IIAs) by the end of 2014. While the annual number of BITs continues to decline, more and more countries and economies are engaged in IIA negotiations at regional and sub-regional levels. For example, the four ongoing negotiations on the 'Transatlantic Trade and Investment Partnership (TTIP)', the 'Regional Comprehensive Economic Partnership (RCEP)', the 'Tripartite Free Trade Area (TFTA)', and the 'Pacific Agreement on Closer Economic Relations (PACER) Plus' agreements involve close to 80 economies.[9]

Negotiations on the Trans-Pacific Partnership (TPP) agreement were concluded in October 2015 between the US, Japan and 10 other Pacific Rim states, creating the largest regional trading bloc in history. Although the US decided not to proceed with this agreement, other States decided to proceed with it in an amended form.

The BITs or the IIAs themselves have not only reiterated certain customary international law principles of foreign investment law advanced largely by developed countries of the West but also have extended the scope of such rules to a great extent. They contain provisions designed to offer as much protection as possible to foreign investors to attract, retain, manage and protect foreign investment. The very notion of customary international law has been perceived in many quarters in the

---

[8] See UNCTAD, 'Systematic Issues in International Investment Agreements (IIAs)', IIA Monitor No 1 (2006), International Investment Agreements, UNCTAD/WEB/ITE/IIA.2006/2 (New York, United Nations, 2006) 1.

[9] UNCTAD, *World Investment Report 2015: Recent Policy Developments and Key Issues* (UNCTAD, Geneva, 2015) ch III.

developing world as a means of restricting the freedom of action of developing countries and continuing the imposition of the will of Western countries on the rest of the world. However, this perception is changing due to some of the leading countries, such as China and India, becoming themselves investor countries and needing the same investment protections abroad already enjoyed by investors from the developed countries. The BITs are being followed by a new generation of ambitious and comprehensive free trade agreements (FTAs) with more expansive and elaborate provisions on foreign investment. Most of these FTAs contain innovative provisions dealing, inter alia, with foreign investment. The investment arbitration tribunals have gone even further by extending the scope of application of various provisions of BITs or FTAs into a new terrain in their interpretation of these international instruments. The vast majority of disputes referred to the International Centre for the Settlement of Investment Disputes (ICSID) or other international investment tribunals under BITs involve an allegation of host-state responsibility for some form of indirect expropriation without compensation or breach of the principle of fair and equitable treatment.

However, there is now a growing concern that the changes in this area of law have not been managed well and are squeezing the policy space of the host countries as some investment tribunals have gone too far in limiting or disregarding the sovereign rights of host countries. Traditionally, BITs were regarded as instruments designed to assist developing countries to attract foreign investment so that the capital, managerial know-how and technology needed for economic development could flow from developed to developing countries. However, due to the recent developments within the international law of foreign investment, the perception is that neither the institution of a BIT nor foreign investment law itself is serving either the interests of developing countries or the higher policy objectives of the international community such as promoting economic and social justice or sustainable development. For instance, under BITs many developing countries have been required to 'outsource' the adjudication of key elements of their public policy to international investment tribunals. However, the growing perception is that the 'outsourcing' of the settlement of investment disputes is not working well and the time has come to review the investment dispute settlement mechanism itself. Accordingly, both the ICSID and UNCITRAL have embarked on a process of reform of the mechanisms for the settlement of investment disputes.

There seems to be a certain unease on the part of many developing countries and some developed countries about the recent trend in jurisprudence of international investment tribunals. This is especially so in relation to the awards made against countries such as Argentina in a number of cases by international investment tribunals arising out of the financial crisis the country experienced in 2000–01. Many investment tribunals rejected the argument based on the doctrine of necessity or legitimate public interests advanced by Argentina to defend the emergency measures it took in the face of the financial crisis in the country around the turn of the 20th century. Thus, the question as to whether foreign investment law should become the law of investment protection or rather remain simply foreign investment law capable of reconciling itself with other competing extant and evolving principles of international law has become a pertinent one.

As the number of investment cases referred to international investment tribunals has increased, concern has also been expressed that some of the decisions of such tribunals may have gone too far or become too creative in interpreting the rules of foreign investment law, such as those concerning indirect expropriation or fair and equitable treatment in favour of foreign investors, at the expense of the legitimate sovereign rights of host states including the regulatory or 'police powers' of states or other environmental or human rights considerations. Indeed, a number of decisions of international investment tribunals, which have sought to provide protection to foreign investors by resorting to creative interpretations of the rules of foreign investment at the expense of national and international public policy, have come under heavy public scrutiny.

Thus, pressure is growing on international investment tribunals from civil society organisations, states and academics to reconcile private interests with public interests or to reconsider the fairness of the investor-state dispute settlement (ISDS) system altogether. This is because under the current ISDS mechanism only investors enjoy a private right to action when seeking redress under the majority of IIAs, BITs and FTAs. Host countries do not enjoy such a choice; only investors can initiate the ISDS mechanism when disputes between investors and host countries arise.

One of the reasons given by Bolivia for its withdrawal from ICSID in 2007 was the alleged lack of balance between public and private interests by ICSID tribunals in delivering their ruling in investment cases. Venezuela, too, withdrew from ICSID.[10] Indeed, there seems to be a greater realisation that increasing numbers of decisions by international investment tribunals of private character are producing an adverse impact on both national and international public policy objectives of the disputing states, especially developing countries. This also appears to be one of the reasons why Ecuador notified ICSID in 2007 that it would not consent to having disputes over non-renewable resources arbitrated at the Centre. Not only have states such as Bolivia and Ecuador taken a strong stance against ICSID, but also countries such as India[11] Indonesia[12] and South Africa[13] appear reluctant to include clauses in trade and investment pacts that permit foreign investors to sue a host country at an international dispute settlement agency.

Specifically, Indonesia has actually decided to discontinue its existing IIAs. As of July 2015, 17 out of 64 such treaties had been discontinued by the country and the rest placed under review.[14] This change in policy seems to be prompted by a desire to strike a balance between investor protection and national sovereignty in order to protect the country's policy space to implement its own development objectives, and to express its concerns regarding the ISDS mechanism. While many Latin American states seem to

---

[10] See generally, C Titi, 'Investment Arbitration in Latin America' (2014) 30 *Arbitration International* 357.

[11] B Dhar, 'India's Experience with BITs: Highlights from Recent ISDS Cases', *Investment Policy Brief*, no 3, July 2015.

[12] A Jailani, 'Indonesia's Perspective on Review of International Investment Agreements', *Investment Policy Brief*, no 1, July 2015.

[13] X Carim, 'International Investment Agreements and Africa's Structural Transformation: A Perspective from South Africa', *Investment Policy Brief*, no 4, August 2015.

[14] Jailani (n 7).

be seeking to establish a regional alternative for dispute settlement under the Union of South American Nations (UNASUR),[15] other states seem to be exploring international alternatives to the current ISDS mechanism dominated by ICSID.

In addition to developing countries, developed countries such as Australia and New Zealand have also started to adopt a policy against international arbitration for investment disputes, and are insisting on according national treatment to foreign investors, which means settlement of investment disputes by national courts. Moreover, states such as South Africa are looking to renegotiate BITs that provide international arbitration of investment disputes. Proposals have also been made for the use of local judicial remedies as the most appropriate tools to address investment disputes in various free trade negotiations.

Furthermore, states have started to include provisions in BITs, FTAs or other IIAs designed to protect the environment, promote human rights, reduce poverty and implement certain elements of corporate social responsibility. An ever-increasing number of cases referred to international investment tribunals by foreign investors include allegations of an array of 'regulatory takings', 'indirect expropriations' or 'regulatory expropriations' or breach of the principle of fair and equitable treatment by host states. More and more tribunals are perceived to be giving their rulings in favour of foreign investors, and in doing so they mainly rely on commercial considerations of the dispute involved or on the expanded interpretation of the principles of international foreign investment law, and disregard other competing principles of public law, public international law or the fundamentals of the global order that sustains and underpins foreign investment law itself. This is one reason why, as stated by the United Nations Conference on Trade and Development (UNCTAD),

> [C]ountries and regions [are] consider[ing] new approaches to investment policymaking. Reacting to the growing unease with the current functioning of the global IIA regime, together with today's sustainable development imperative and the evolution of the investment landscape, at least 50 countries and regions have been engaged in reviewing and revising their IIA models and formulating new IIA strategies.[16]

Consequently, this body of law is attracting the attention of not only legal scholars[17] and practitioners but also a wide spectrum of national and international civil society

---

[15] See Carim (n 8) 6.

[16] UNCTAD (n 4). According to UNCTAD, there were 42 new ISDS cases in 2014, bringing the total number of known treaty-based claims to 608. Although developing countries continue to bear the brunt of these claims as defendants, the share of developed countries is on the rise.

[17] See generally, Sir R Jennings and Sir A Watts (eds), *Oppenheim's International Law*, 9th edn (Harlow, Longman, 1992) vol I, parts 2–4, 911–27; G Schwarzenberger, *Foreign Investment and International Law* (New York, Praeger, 1969); DW Bowett, 'State Contract with Aliens' (1988) 29 *British Year Book of International Law* 49; R Higgins, 'The Taking of Property by the State' (1982-III) 176 *Recueil des Cours* 259; M Sornarajah, *The International Law on Foreign Investment* (Cambridge, Cambridge University Press, 2010); G van Harten, *Investment Treaty Arbitration and Public Law* (Oxford, Oxford University Press, 2007); S Montt, *State Liability in Investment Treaty Arbitration: Global Constitutional and Administrative Law in the BIT Generation* (Oxford, Hart Publishing, 2011); UNCTAD, *Investor–State Disputes: Prevention and Alternatives to Arbitration*, UNCTAD Series on International Investment Policies for Development (New York and Geneva, United Nations, 2010); C McLachlan et al, *International Investment Arbitration: Substantive Principles* (Oxford, Oxford University Press, 2007); R Dolzer and C Schreur, *Principles of International Investment Law* (Oxford, Oxford University Press, 2008); P Muchlinski et al, *The Oxford*

organisations working in the areas of foreign investment protection, the environment, sustainable development, human rights, global poverty reduction, and international economic and social justice.

Various public and private institutions have made attempts to address certain aspects of investment regulation. For instance, Professor John Ruggie was appointed by the UN as the Special Representative of the Secretary-General to develop a set of principles to deal with issues surrounding business and human rights and concluded his work by recommending a set of principles.[18] Amnesty International itself is concerned about these issues and is involved in an international campaign to adopt a set of principles or guidelines for foreign investors.[19] The Canada-based International Institute of Sustainable Development (IISD) is at the forefront of the debate on balancing investment protection with environmental protection and has proposed a Model International Agreement on Investment for Sustainable Development to this effect.[20] Such campaigns in favour of the environment and other societal values seem

---

Handbook of International Investment Law (Oxford, Oxford University Press, 2008); I Tudor, *The Fair and Equitable Treatment Standard in International Foreign Investment Law* (Oxford, Oxford University Press, 2008); P Muchlinski, *Multinational Enterprises & the Law*, 2nd edn (Oxford, Oxford University Press, 2007); JW Salacuse, *The Law of International Investment Treaties* (Oxford, Oxford University Press, 2010); C Binder et al (eds), *International Investment Law for the 21st Century: Essays in Honour of Christoph Schreuer* (Oxford, Oxford University Press, 2009); AF Lowenfeld, *International Economic Law*, 2nd edn (Oxford, Oxford University Press, 2008); LT Wells and R Ahmad, *Making Foreign Investment Safe, Property Rights and National Sovereignty* (Oxford, Oxford University Press, 2006); C Schreuer, *The ICSID Convention: A Commentary* (Cambridge, Cambridge University Press, 2001); R Dolzer, 'Fair and Equitable Treatment: A Key Standard in Investment Treaties' (2005) 39(1) *International Lawyer* 87; S Vasciannie, 'The Fair and Equitable Treatment Standard in International Investment Law and Practice' (1999) 70 *British Year Book of International Law* 99; P Muchlinski, '"Caveat Investor"? The Relevance of the Conduct of the Investor under the Fair and Equitable Treatment Standard' (2006) 55 *ICLQ* 527; M Klein Bronfman, 'Fair and Equitable Treatment: An Evolving Standard' (2006) 10 *Max Planck Yearbook of United Nations Law* 609; AS Weiner, 'Indirect Expropriations: The Need for a Taxonomy of "Legitimate" Regulatory Purposes' (2003) 5 *International Law Forum du droit international* 166–75; T Waelde and A Kolo, 'Environmental Regulation, Investment Protection and "Regulatory Taking" in International Law' (2001) 50 *ICLQ* 811–48; ILA Committee on International Law on Foreign Investment, 'Final Report', International Law Association (ILA), *Report of the Seventy-Second Conference, Toronto 2006* (London, ILA, 2006) 407–55; R Dolzer and F Bloch, 'Indirect Expropriation: Conceptual Realignments?' (2003) 5 *International Law Forum du droit international* 155; F Orrego Vicuna, 'Regulatory Authority and Legitimate Expectations: Balancing the Rights of the State and the Individual under International Law in a Global Society' (2003) 5 *International Law Forum du droit international* 188; OECD, 'Indirect Expropriation' and the 'Right to Regulate' in International Investment Law', OECD Working Papers on International Investment, 2004/4 (Paris, OECD Publishing); SF Puvimanasinghe, *Foreign Investment, Human Rights and the Environment: A Perspective from South Asia on the Role of Public International Law* (The Hague, Martinus Nijhoff, 2007); Martins Paparinskis (ed), *Basic Documents on International Investment Protection* (Oxford, Hart Publishing, 2012); M. Sornarajah, *Resistance and Change in the International Law of Foreign Investment* (Cambridge, Cambridge University Press, 2015).

[18] Report of the Special Representative of the Secretary-General on the issue of human rights and transnational corporations and other business enterprises, J Ruggie, 'Guiding Principles on Business and Human Rights: Implementing the United Nations "Protect, Respect and Remedy" Framework', UN Doc A/HRC/17/31.

[19] See eg Amnesty International, United Kingdom Business Group, *Human Rights Guidelines for Companies* (London, Amnesty International, 1998). See also a public statement of Amnesty International on the UN initiatives concerning business and human rights, AI Index: IOR 41/044/2005, News Service No 104, 21 April 2005.

[20] International Institute for Sustainable Development (IISD), 'Model International Agreement on Investment for Sustainable Development', April 2005. Available at: www.iisd.org/investment.

to be having a certain impact on new BITs and FTAs as well as on certain principal areas of commercial law. The inclusion of provisions on regulatory measures in the Canada–Peru BIT and the African, Caribbean and Pacific (ACP)–EU Agreement on Economic Partnership and Nigeria-Morocco BIT of 2016 are notable examples. Similarly, the inclusion in the UK's Companies Act 2006 of a duty to pay attention to the environment in the list of a company director's duties is another example.[21]

It is in this context that this book aims to analyse the fundamental principles of foreign investment law and the manner in which these principles have been interpreted and applied by international investment courts and tribunals. It will examine the extent to which the jurisprudence of arbitral decisions interpreting the rules of foreign investment law and state practice, including BITs and FTAs, has taken into account other competing principles of public law or public international law embodied in other international treaties in developing this area of law and in providing protection to foreign investors. The aim is to examine how foreign investment law has changed over time in response to the economic and political realities of the world, and what impact this new trend in foreign investment law is having on the public policy objectives of investment-exporting and investment-receiving countries. In doing so, it will analyse the challenges this body of law is facing at present and how these can be addressed within the overall framework of international law.

Accordingly, Chapter 1 will present the current trends in international investment law. Chapter 2 will provide a historical account of the evolution of foreign investment law. Chapter 3 will analyse the successes and failures of international efforts in developing the law of foreign investment since the establishment of the United Nations (UN) in 1945 and in regulating foreign investment in the interests of both developed and developing countries. Chapter 4 will examine the substantive principles of foreign investment law, including the principles constituting the minimum international standards of protection available to foreign investors under general customary international law, and how they have been interpreted in jurisprudence. Next, will be an examination, in Chapter 5, of the treatment of foreign investors under BITs and FTAs. How the jurisprudence of international courts and tribunals has fleshed out the protection available to foreign investors under foreign investment law will be assessed in Chapter 6.

Chapter 7 will evaluate the impact that foreign investment law is having on the public policy objectives of the international community in general and developing host countries in particular. Chapter 8 will explore various ways and means of addressing the challenges within foreign investment law. This study will conclude by presenting some overarching conclusions regarding the role of foreign investment law in a broader framework of global governance designed to achieve the higher objectives of the international community.

---

[21] For an analysis of this provision, see: A Keay, 'Section 172(1) of the Companies Act 2006: An Interpretation and Assessment' (2007) 28 *Company Lawyer* 106.

1

International Investment Law in a Changing World

Introduction

A fundamental change is underway in the landscape of international investment law. There seems to be a new trend in state practice which has been characterised by various scholars as the revival of the Calvo doctrine or the return of the 'new international economic order' (NIEO), considered long dead by many. Whether the new trend is described as 'the end of history', the return to the Calvo doctrine or the advent of 'neo-NIEO', the world is witnessing an attempt to reform the investor-state dispute settlement (ISDS) mechanism both within the International Centre for Settlement of Investment Disputes (ICSID) and United Nations Commission on International Trade Law (UNCITRAL) and to strike a balance between different competing principles of international law in developing international investment law. Therefore, this chapter attempts to capture the essence of these developments in international investment law and analyse various trends and attempts in this direction.

A New Turn in International Investment Law

International investment law is currently undergoing an exciting phase in its development and taking a new turn for four reasons. First, foreign investors have started to sue host governments over the exercise of their regulatory powers and international investment tribunals have come under pressure to take a greater account of the policy space of sovereign states to address the backlash against the ISDS mechanism not only in developing countries but also in some developed countries. Secondly, there has been a rethink on the part of many States about the very institution of BITs or IIAs, around which international investment law has developed in recent decades. Thirdly, some of the leading states which have traditionally stood as staunch supporters of the traditional regime of investment protection seem now to be retrenching and accommodating some of the concerns raised by academics, civil society and other stakeholders to make BITs or IIAs more balanced in favour of other societal values.

These concerns centre around two main areas: the perceived excessive protection accorded to foreign investors, and the creative and expansive trend in jurisprudence in favour of foreign investors. The examples of this shift in attitude are the provisions in the 2012 US Model BIT, and the European Commission's proposal in September 2015 to create a new World Trade Organization (WTO) Dispute Settlement Body-style Investment Court with an appellate body in relation to the negotiations with the US over a Transatlantic Trade and Investment Partnership (TTIP). The 2012 US Model BIT, which contains a number of provisions designed to strike a balance between investment protection and public interest, has set a trend in this direction. It is an admission that international investment law should not exist in isolation but rather as a part of the broader international legal order. As such, it should thus accommodate competing interests.

Fourthly, the division between pro-status quo scholars and practitioners and reformists has become sharper in academic discourse. In particular, the rift often involves those who are opposed to any major reform of the BIT/IIA regime or the ISDS mechanism and those who have championed reforms such as the creation of an international investment court or an appellate mechanism. The reformists especially advocate the revising of BIT/IIA framework by completely removing or carrying out a major reform of the ISDS mechanism. As a result, this polarisation has made the study of international investment law ever more interesting. The issues relating to the international investment regime has started to receive attention far beyond the confines of a small group of investment negotiators, practitioners and academics, as well as the sporadic involvement of non-governmental organisations. Different stakeholders from various walks of life are increasingly interested in investment law matters, especially the ISDS mechanism. The main concern for these stakeholders seems to be with the ISDS mechanism due to the apparent inconsistencies in arbitral decision-making, insufficient regard by some arbitral tribunals to the host state's right to regulate in interpreting IIAs, BITs or FTAs, charges of bias of the system in favour of foreign investors, concerns about the lack of independence and impartiality of arbitrators, and the absence of an appellate mechanism to ensure the correctness of their decisions.

Reform of the Investor-State Dispute Settlement Mechanism

States were traditionally insulated from certain kinds of lawsuits by foreign private entities, whether natural or juridical, by the principle of sovereign immunity.[1] But an

---

[1] See generally, H Fox and P Webb, *The Law of State Immunity*, 3rd edn (Oxford, Oxford University Press, 2013).

exception or a limitation to that immunity was voluntarily accepted by states when they concluded BITs or IIAs with an ISDS mechanism. Such exception allows foreign investors to sue the host governments before international courts and tribunals on alleged breaches of BITs or IIAs.[2] This was a radical move in the development of international law in general and international investment law in particular.

The first generation of BITs was concluded in the post-World War Two era when the Cold War made the political environment unstable in many parts of the developing world. This instability was particularly manifested by various coups d'état or other political upheavals resulting in frequent changes of government through undemocratic means and the left-leaning and anti-investor tendencies of many of these governments. During this period, few international human rights treaties protecting the right to property of foreign investors were in existence, although the volume of cross-border trade and business activity was increasing. Accordingly, investor states sought additional protection in international law for the investors from their countries who were investing abroad, especially in politically unstable but resource-rich countries. This was also the political context that led to the enshrinement of ISDS mechanisms in international treaties, specifically the 1965 adoption of ICSID.

However, after nearly 50–60 years of concluding BITs or IIAs, a momentous change is taking place within this body of law, characterised by the call for a major overhaul of the ISDS mechanism and change in the approach to BITs and other IIAS. This is partly because some international investment tribunals started according a meaning to certain provisions in the treaties that differed significantly in scope and breadth from what the states had originally intended them to mean. The view held in certain quarters was that by being creative and adopting an expansive approach to treaty interpretation, these tribunals were encroaching upon the policy space of states. The issues of legitimacy, accountability, transparency and fairness associated with the workings of such tribunals, the propriety of the selection process of the arbitrators and their integrity as well as the absence of an appeal mechanism against their decisions have contributed to the growing opposition to the existing ISDS mechanism.

According to Schultz and Dupont, a backlash is raging against investment arbitration.[3] In their view, investment arbitration was mainly used until the mid-to-late 1990s as a neo-colonial instrument to strengthen the economic interests of developed states and as a means to impose the rule of law in non-democratic states with a weak law-and-order tradition. But the backlash against the current ISDS mechanism in general, and the ICSID in particular, began with a number of Latin American countries withdrawing from ICSID. These were the states that had opposed the adoption of ICSID in the first place in Tokyo in 1964, known as the 'Tokyo No'.[4] ICSID was adopted to protect foreign investment – the right to property in general and foreign investment in particular – in the wake of the wave of expropriation by

---

[2] See C de Stefano, 'Arbitration Agreements as Waivers to Sovereign Immunity' (2014) 30 *Arbitration International* 59.

[3] T Schultz and C Dupont, 'Investment Arbitration: Promoting the Rule of Law or Over-Empowering Investors? A Quantitative Empirical Study' (2014) 25 *European Journal of International Law* 1147, 1147.

[4] C Titi, 'Investment Arbitration in Latin America: The Uncertain Veracity of Preconceived Ideas' (2014) 30 *Arbitration International* 357, 361.

newly independent states in different parts of the world and the threat from communist states and their satellites to the international legal order.

Many developing countries came to the realisation that much of international investment law had been written by Western countries and that the notion of customary international law had strengthened the practice of largely Western countries, which tended to favour maximising the protection of foreign investors. Essentially, customary international law standards regarding the treatment of foreign investors meant Western standards.[5] Having woken up to this reality, many developing countries began to assert themselves and challenge certain norms that they perceived to be detrimental to their interests.

The momentum against ISDS in its current form is gathering pace not only within the developing world but also in the developed world, especially in relation to the debate on the draft TTIP agreement with an ISDS mechanism between the EU and the US.[6] The EU, rather than its individual Member States, is negotiating such a treaty after the Lisbon Treaty reformed EU policies by transferring the power to enter into international investment agreements from the Member States to the EU under the common commercial policy of the organisation.[7] Since the rules of the Lisbon Treaty gave powers to the European Parliament to approve new investment treaties, negotiations for an IIA by the EU with other states or entities, the EU has been subject to public scrutiny in this respect. After being given competence for negotiating IIAs under the Lisbon Treaty, the EU itself has been rethinking the traditional approach to IIAs in general and BITs in particular. In January 2014, the European Commission announced its intention to pause investment treaty negotiations with the US under the TTIP Agreement in order to address what it termed 'unprecedented public interest' within the EU Member States on the matter of IIAs.[8] The announcement identified some of the critical issues at stake, including the need to reaffirm the right of governments to regulate in the public interest and to revisit the ISDS mechanism under IIAs.

As stated by Kaufmann-Kohler and Potesta, 'Growing criticism over investor-state arbitration has triggered demands for reforms of the existing framework from

---

[5] See generally, K Miles, *The Origins of International Investment Law: Empire, Environment, and the Safeguarding of Capital* (Cambridge, Cambridge University Press, 2013).

[6] It was in July 2013 that the EU and the US launched negotiations for a Transatlantic Trade and Investment Partnership Agreement (TTIP) with a view to reaching a comprehensive economic agreement between these two major global trading. Its proponents have argued that it offers great opportunities for liberalising trade and investment and regulatory convergence. See R Geiger, 'The Transatlantic Trade and Investment Partnership: A Critical Perspective', *Columbia FDI Perspectives*, no 119, 14 April 2014.

[7] Art 207 Lisbon Treaty defines the scope of the common commercial policy of the EU, [2007] OJ C306, available at http://eur-lex.europa.eu/legal-content/EN/ALL/?uri=OJ:C:2007:306:TOC. See generally on this topic, R Dolzer, 'Remarks', [2011] *ASIL Proceedings* 339. On 28 August 2014, Regulation No 912/2014 of the European Parliament and of the Council of 23 July 2014 establishing a framework for managing financial responsibility linked to investor-to-state dispute settlement tribunals established by international agreements to which the EU is party was published in the OJ.

[8] European Commission, Press Release, 'Commission to Consult European Public on Provisions in EU–US Trade Deal on Investment and Investor–State Dispute Settlement', Brussels, 21 January 2014, as cited in X Carim, 'International Investment Agreements and Africa's Structural Transformation: A Perspective from South Africa', *Investment Policy Brief*, no 4, August 2015, 5.

countries, international organizations and civil society groups'.[9] Indeed, changes are underway in State practice in this area. For instance, EU-Canada Comprehensive Economic and Trade Agreement (CETA) and EU-Vietnam Free Trade Agreement (FTA), the contracting parties replaced the ad hoc system of investment arbitration with standing bilateral bodies composed of first-instance and appellate tribunals. The European Commission launched its own public consultation in December 2016 on a 'multilateral reform of investment dispute resolution' with a view to establishing a multilateral investment court. With the departure of the UK from the EU known as Brexit in 2020, the country will be free to negotiate investment treaties on its own accord. It remains to be seen what approach the UK will take on ISDS matters in its treaty negotiations. There are a number of both developed and developing countries that seek to do away with the existing ISDS mechanism or narrow down its scope. For instance, New Zealand's Prime Minister, Jacinda Ardern, has stated that investor-state dispute settlement (ISDS) must not be a part of any future trade agreements signed by New Zealand. In the case of the Trans-Pacific Partnership (TPP, which is now renamed as Comprehensive and Progressive Agreement for Trans-Pacific Partnership (CPTPP)), the scope of ISDS is much narrower, with many conditions attached to it. According to the Prime Minister: 'There has been a narrowing of [investor-state dispute settlement clauses (ISDS)] provisions in three areas. One, ISDS no longer applies to investor screening. The second, anyone who takes up a contract with a Government is no longer able to sue through ISDS, but must go through domestic procedures instead. The third relates to financial services.'[10]

Likewise, when the US, Mexico and Canada signed in December 2019 an agreement the United States-Mexico-Canada Agreement (USMCA)[11] that replaces the North America Free Trade Agreement (NAFTA) they opted for a narrower access to the ISDS mechanism for foreign investors with a limited and a varying degree of bilateral ISDS mechanism between the parties. That is one reason why Cabrera states that:

> In the current investment arbitration crisis, USMCA presents a new gold standard to enforce investment protection. First, under general investment, USMCA reduces states' risk exposure by precluding investors' access to ISDS for claims of alleged breaches to indirect expropriation and fair and equitable treatment standards, and national treatment and most-favored-nation standards at the investment's pre-establishment phase. Governments concerned with regulatory chill and the exercise of police powers should adopt the USMCA model, as it reduces the risk of ISDS claims related to the regulation of health, national security, morals, and the environment. Philip Morris, which questioned the 'plain packaging' and 'single presentation' policies adopted by Australia and Uruguay, would have had no grounds to advance a claim under USMCA. Also, with the Covered Government

---

[9] Gabrielle Kaufmann-Kohler and Michele Potestà, 'Challenges on the road toward a multilateral investment court,' Columbia FDI Perspectives, No. 201, June 5, 2017.

[10] As quoted in 'The "Ardern Clause" in TPP: A Novel Approach to Curbing Investment-State Dispute Settlement', posted by Rob Howse and Simon Lester in International Economic Law and Policy Blog – 5 of 12 November 2017, available at FeedBlitz <feedblitz@mail.feedblitz.com> (accessed on 17 January 2020).

[11] BBC News, 'USMCA: Agreement reached on Nafta trade deal replacement', 10 December 2019, available at https://www.bbc.co.uk/news/business-50733120 (accessed on 19 January 2020).

Contracts, governments will continue protecting the most sensitive sectors in which ISDS cases frequently arise.[12]

It remains to be seen whether other states would follow suit or opt for the creation of a multilateral investment court as proposed by the European Union and an idea advanced by the present author in the First Edition of this book way back in 2008 or dispense altogether with the ISDS mechanism, opting for other options such as a speedy, effective, and independent commercial tribunals within the national judiciary.

Public View on the Investor-State Dispute Settlement Mechanism

Whether it is in the context of the TTIP or another IIA or BIT, the general public, academics, journalists and civil society organisations have all expressed their concern about including an ISDS mechanism in its traditional form in such treaties. For instance, both the left-leaning and right-leaning leading newspapers in the UK cautioned against the conclusion of the TTIP in the draft form published. *The Economist*, a right-wing British publication, stated the following about ISDS:

> If you wanted to convince the public that international trade agreements are a way to let multinational companies get rich at the expense of the ordinary people, this is what you would do: give foreign firms a special right to apply to a secretive tribunal of highly paid corporate lawyers for compensation whenever a government passes a law to, say, discourage smoking, protect the environment or prevent a nuclear catastrophe. Yet this is precisely what thousands of trade and investment treaties over the past half-century have done, though a process known as 'investor-state dispute settlement', or ISDS
>
> ...
>
> Multinationals have exploited woolly definitions of expropriation to claim compensation for changes in government policy that happen to harm their business.[13]

The Guardian, a left-leaning British newspaper, published an article that characterises ISDS as 'a full frontal assault on sovereignty and democracy'.[14] In spite of such opposition to IIAs or to an ISDS mechanism, the EU in September 2014 concluded a far-reaching economic integration agreement with Canada, the Comprehensive Economic Trade Agreement (CETA), which uses an ISDS mechanism, albeit with some reforms.

However, when the EU began its consultation process on the draft TTIP agreement more than one million people signed petitions against it.[15] According to an article

---

[12] Orlando F Cabrera C, 'The US-Mexico-Canada Agreement: the new gold standard to enforce investment treaty protection?', *Columbia FDI Perspectives*, no. 269 13 January 2020.

[13] 'Investor–State Dispute Settlement: The Arbitration Game', *The Economist*, 11 October 2014, 82.

[14] G Monbiot, 'The Real Threat to the National Interest from the Rich and Powerful', *The Guardian*, 15 October 2013.

[15] Public consultations by the European Commission in the context of the TTIP Agreement yielded nearly 150,000 replies on investment protection and ISDS issues alone. See European Commission, Press Release,

entitled 'Free Trade Should Not Put Democracy in the Dock' in the *Financial Times*, those in Britain who thought the agreement would be bad for the country outnumbered those who thought it would be beneficial by three to one.[16] Of the 149,399 submissions received by the European Commission in response to its consultation process on the draft TTIP agreement, 97% expressed their opposition to the agreement in general or to the ISDS provision in particular. This led the EU Trade Commissioner Cecelia Malmstrom to conclude that 'the consultation clearly shows that there is a huge scepticism against the ISDS instrument'.[17] Consequently, the European Commission identified four areas to be further developed: the protection of the right to regulate; the establishment and functioning of arbitral tribunals; the relationship between domestic judicial systems and ISDS; and the review of ISDS decisions for legal correctness through an appellate mechanism.[18]

Adding his voice to the concerns raised about the ISDS mechanism in general and the TTIP in particular, Martti Koskenniemi stated that the ISDS provisions in TTIP would be 'a transfer of power from public authorities to an arbitration body, where a handful of people would be able to rule whether a country can enact a law or not and how the law must be interpreted'.[19] Speaking in a debate in the UK House of Commons, a backbencher for the Conservative Party, Zac Goldsmith, asked his government: 'Why do we need these tribunals for a country where the rule of law is adhered to, more or less across the board?'[20] This is precisely the point that many states seem to be making in relation to the need for an ISDS mechanism.

Various independent UN human rights experts too have intervened in the matter and presented their critical views of the ISDS mechanism. For instance, the UN independent expert on the promotion of a democratic and equitable international order, Alfred de Zayas, stated in his report submitted to the UN Human Rights Council in September 2015 that the ISDS mechanism

> has mutated into a privatized system of 'justice', incompatible with Article 14(1) of the International Covenant on Civil and Political Rights, whereby three arbitrators are allowed to override national legislation and the judgments of the highest national tribunals, in secret and with no possibility to appeal. This constitutes a grave challenge to the very essence of the rule of law.[21]

Similarly, scholars within the US have voiced their concern about the negative impact that the current ISDS regime is having on the development, enforcement and application of US domestic law. For instance, Lise Johnson, Lisa Sachs and Jeffrey Sachs have stated that expanding ISDS 'by including it in new trade and investment agreements

---

'Report Presented Today. Consultation on Investment Protection in EU–US Trade Talks', Strasbourg, 13 January 2015, available at http://europa.eu/rapid/press-release_IP-15-3201_en.htm.

[16] J Kay, 'Free Trade Should Not Put Democracy in the Dock', *Financial Times*, 4 February 2015, 11.

[17] 'European Commission Consultation Shows Public Rejection of Investor–State Dispute Settlement', *Investment Treaty News*, 19 February 2015.

[18] Ibid.

[19] As quoted in J Kleinheisterkamp, 'Who Is Afraid of Investor–State Arbitration? Unpacking the Riddle of "No Greater Rights in the TTIP"', *Investment Treaty News*, 18 November 2014.

[20] Ibid.

[21] News Release of the UN Office of the High Commissioner for Human Rights, 'UN Expert: UN Charter and Human Rights Treaties Prevail Over Free Trade and Investment Agreements', 17 September 2015.

such as the [TTIP and TPP] will expose the US government to new claims and liabilities challenging government action and inaction at all levels of government – local, state and federal'.[22]

Changing State Practice

Apparently heeding many of these concerns, the European Commission released in September 2015 a revised draft Chapter II of the TTIP containing a proposal for a new and transparent system for resolving disputes between investors and states – the Investment Court System. If the Commission's proposals are accepted, the new Investment Court System will replace the existing ISDS mechanism in all ongoing and future EU investment negotiations, including the TTIP.[23]

Concurrently, there is similar momentum gathering pace in other parts of the world. For instance, a bloc of a dozen Latin American states agreed in September 2013 to take collective action against the ISDS mechanism under the IIAs and explore alternatives to the current ISDS mechanism. Beginning with Bolivia's denouncement of ICSID in 2007, other Latin American countries have since followed suit. Notably, Ecuador has not signed any BIT since 2001, has terminated many of its existing BITs and attempted to terminate many others, including those with France, Germany and the UK.[24] It was reported in 2017, that Ecuador had unilaterally withdrawn from its remaining 16 BITs, including those signed with the Netherlands, Germany, Great Britain, France, Spain, Italy, Sweden, Switzerland, Canada, the United States, China, Argentina, Bolivia, Peru, Venezuela and Chile.[25] As summed up by Roberts, the trend to exclude or narrow down the scope of the ISDS in BITs or other IIAS is gathering momentum and the following are the notable examples:

— Brazil, which has never ratified an investment treaty providing for ISDS. More recently, it has started signing Cooperation and Investment Facilitation Agreements that encourage the use of alternative dispute resolution mechanisms, such as conciliatory settlement of disputes through Ombudsmen that are subject to a Joint Committee of the treaty parties, and ultimately permit state-to-state arbitration but not investor-state arbitration.

— South Africa, which began a process of terminating its investment treaties in 2012 and in their place has passed the Protection of Investment Act 22 of 2015, which

---

[22] L Johnson, L Sachs and J Sachs, 'Investor–State Dispute Settlement, Public Interest and US Domestic Law', Columbia Centre on Sustainable Development, Policy Paper, May 2015, 1.

[23] European Commission, Press Release, 16 September 2015, available at: http://europa.eu/rapid/press-release_IP-15-5651_en.htm (accessed 24 September 2015). The draft of the Commission of Chapter II on Investment is available at: http://trade.ec.europa.eu/doclib/docs/2015/september/tradoc_153807.pdf (accessed 24 September 2015).

[24] C Titi, 'Investment Arbitration in Latin America: The Uncertain Veracity of Preconceived Ideas' (2014) 30 *Arbitration International* 357.

[25] Daniel Uribe, Ecuador withdraws from its remaining investment treaties', *SOUTH NEWS*, a publication of the South Centre, no 155, 23 May 2017.

gives primacy to domestic remedies, including mediation and domestic courts. This Act provides that South Africa may consent to international arbitration over an investment dispute, but this would be subject to exhaustion of domestic remedies and would also take place on a state-to-state, rather than an investor-state, basis.

— India, which radically revised its Model BIT in 2015, to significantly limit access to ISDS. Before an investor can bring an investor-state claim under the Indian Model, it must first seek to exhaust domestic remedies for a period of up to five years. It may then proceed to arbitration, subject to a six-month negotiation period, provided that it brings the claim within six years of knowing about the measure that it is complaining about. These tribunals are also not permitted to review the merits of a decision made by domestic courts.

— Australia, which has adopted some FTAs (e.g., with the United States and Japan) that do not include ISDS clauses.

— Ecuador, which recently terminated 16 of its investment treaties, following the recommendation of a national Commission that Ecuador pursue new treaties which exclude investor-state dispute settlement mechanism and instead provide investors with access to national courts.[26]

It is some of these states that have gone to the UN Human Rights Council seeking a binding international agreement on business and human rights adopted so that foreign investors could be held accountable for violations of human rights in host countries. Unsurprisingly Latin American countries have been the focus of around half of all investor-state lawsuits referred to the ICSID.

The growing opposition to BITs or ISDS is partly due to the confidence that many largely democratic countries in the developing world, such as India, Indonesia and South Africa, have in their own national legal and judicial systems. They appear to imply that foreign investors should be comfortable with the protection of the right to property under their individual constitutions and under the international human rights treaties ratified by them. Compounding this confidence is their dissatisfaction with some of the rulings of ICSID panels, both initial and annulment, and other UNCITRAL arbitration panels in the face of their ostensible failure to balance private interests with public interests and between competing principles within international law in general and international investment law in particular.

The Investor-State Dispute Settlement Mechanism at a Cross Roads

The main reasons why the public in many countries and many developing states oppose the ISDS mechanism are as follows: the arbitrators sitting on an ICSID or

---

[26] Anthea Roberts, International Economic Law and Policy Blog – 'A Turning of the Tide against ISDS?' of 20 May 2017, available at FeedBlitz feedblitz@mail.feedblitz.com (accessed on 27 January 2020).

UNCITRAL panel apply treaty standards which are typically drafted in very vague, broad terms, giving arbitrators in each case substantial latitude to determine what the standards mean in practice while having limited checks on arbitrators' power of interpretation; they do not have to meet any qualification threshold to get appointed as arbitrators, unlike the judges of the International Court of Justice (ICJ), they are neither elected nor accountable to anyone; they are private arbitrators appointed on a case-by-case basis; some of them may not even have a background in international law, but they apply treaty law as interpreted by them; there are limited avenues to challenge their awards; and the procedures of the ICSID or UNCITRAL panels do not have to meet the tests of transparency, legitimacy and accountability.[27]

As stated by Johnson, Sachs and Sachs, the above-mentioned and other aspects of ISDS

> create a privileged and powerful avenue through which foreign investors can challenge the actions of host governments whether at the local, state, or federal level, and whether taken by the executive, legislative, or judicial branch. ... investors can use the mechanism to contest a virtually unlimited range of actions (or inactions), including measures relating to taxation, environmental regulation, tariffs for water and electricity, health insurance regulation, and health and safety regulations of pharmaceutical imports, among others.[28]

Furthermore, a number of such awards, including those against Argentina, have proved controversial and several of them have been annulled. As observed by Titi, some of these awards 'were found to contain errors of law and annulment committees concluded that the tribunals had entirely failed to apply the applicable law'.[29]

It is not only developing countries, but also developed countries that have become increasingly vigilant about the ISDS mechanism. As Roberts has stated:

> [W]hen capital-exporting states originally drafted investment treaties, they viewed them as exclusively or primarily aimed at protecting the rights of their investors abroad and thus demonstrated little concern about the breadth of interpretative authority being delegated to investment tribunals or the absence of clear language protecting regulatory powers.[30]

However, a number of cases have been brought against developed states themselves, including the United States, Canada, Australia and Germany.

This trend has engendered an increasing appreciation for the need to protect the regulatory freedom of host states and limit arbitral discretion.[31] Indeed, some high-profile regulatory disputes, such as Germany being sued over its decision to phase out nuclear power[32] and Australia being sued over its tobacco packaging regulations, have

---

[27] Johnson, Sachs and Sachs (n 18) 2.

[28] Ibid.

[29] Titi (n 20) 382 (footnotes omitted).

[30] A Roberts, 'Clash of Paradigms: Actors and Analogies Shaping the Investment Treaty System' (2013) 107 *American Journal of International Law* 45, 78.

[31] Ibid, 78.

[32] *Vattenfall v Germany*, ICSID Case No ARB/12/12. After the 2011 nuclear disaster in Fukushima, and as the culmination of a decades-long public debate, the German parliament decided to amend the Atomic Energy Act to speed up the phase-out of nuclear energy, which entailed the immediate shutdown of some of Germany's oldest reactors. Vattenfall, an energy company wholly owned by the Swedish state, operated and owned two of those reactors: the Krümmel (66.7% ownership) and Brunsbüttel (50% ownership)

made capital-exporting countries themselves cautious about the ISDS mechanism in its current form. There is concern that these cases could be a foretaste of what may be to come. Furthermore, states are concerned that international investment tribunals of ad hoc character and consisting of arbitrators chosen by disputing business organisations have started to hold host states accountable for judicial activities of the supreme courts. The *White Industries v India*[33] case is a notable example.[34]

The Impact of Change in State Practice

Several new examples of state practice are having a profound impact on the traditional norms of international investment law. For example, recently there have been more balanced IIAs or FTAs with an investment chapter that strengthen the public policy space of the host states. Simultaneously, there is a gradual rejection of the older generation of BITs by leading developing countries from India to Indonesia and South Africa. Other trends include the denunciation of ICSID by a growing number of states, public opposition to the ISDS mechanism within both developed and developing countries,[35] the adoption of new model investment treaties by a growing number of states accepting the notion of non-compensable regulatory expropriation and a gradual acceptance of the idea of an appellate mechanism for investor-state disputes by states, including a proposal by the European Commission itself for the creation of such a mechanism in relation to the debate on the draft TTIP Agreement.

This new pattern of state practice is likely to contribute towards creating new rules or modifying the existing rules of customary international law concerning investor protection or the regulation of foreign investment. The era of traditional BITs seems gradually to be drawing to a close, and the world of international investment law seems to be entering a new phase. Some commentators have even speculated that the new developments in the world of international investment law may represent 'the end of history', so far as the era of traditional BITs or the IIAs is concerned.[36] Whether it is 'the end of history' or history repeating itself by returning to the Calvo doctrine or the advent of 'neo-NIEO', fundamental change is underway within the landscape of international investment law.

---

power plants. According to Vattenfall, the shutdown of the two reactors resulted in a loss of expected revenues of 10.5 billion Swedish kroner (US$1.5 billion) in 2011 alone. Seeking to 'obtain fair compensation for the financial losses', Vattenfall and the two power plant companies (collectively, 'Vattenfall') initiated arbitration proceedings against Germany before ICSID, and also filed a lawsuit before the Federal Constitutional Court of Germany. See N Bernasconi-Osterwalder and MD Brauch, 'The State of Play in Vattenfall v Germany II: Leaving the German Public in the Dark', Briefing Note, International Institute for Sustainable Development, December 2014.

[33] *White Industries v Republic of India*, Final Award, UNCITRAL, 30 November 2011.

[34] See P Ranjan, 'Can BIT Claims be Made against India for the Actions of the Indian Judiciary?' (2013) 1(1) *National Law University Jodhpur Law Review* 87.

[35] J Stiglitz, 'South Africa Breaks Out', in Project Syndicate, available at: http://justinvestment.org/2013/11/south-africa-breaks-out (accessed on 29/01/2014).

[36] J Karl, 'The "Spaghetti Bowl" of IIAs: The End of History?', *Columbia FDI Perspectives*, no 115, 17 February 2014.

Commenting on the recent trend in international investment law and especially the content of the US Model BIT of 2012 and the opposition to the ISDS mechanism in its present form coming from different quarters, Brower and Melikian have stated that what we are witnessing is a 'neo-NIEO' or a 'Northern neo-NIEO'.[37] For instance, states such as Bolivia, Ecuador and South Africa have enacted domestic laws to provide protection to foreign investors instead of relying on BITs or IIAs for this purpose. These laws contain standards of protection similar to those contained in BITs that these states have terminated or plan to terminate. The new Bolivian Investment Promotion Law, for example, establishes that any disputes will have to be resolved under Bolivian law.

In much the same way, Ecuador has enacted its own laws for the protection of foreign investors.[38] The Constitutional Court of Ecuador has gone further and declared that all BITs are unconstitutional.[39] As stated by the Ecuadorian Minister of Knowledge and Human Talent:

> Ecuador has established a domestic law to protect investments. Ecuador now signs investment contracts with regional (ie Latin American) arbitration allowed, so long as it is based on national laws and regulations, excludes regulatory and tax policy space from the ambit of arbitration, and requires that domestic jurisdiction be exhausted. These contracts also include performance requirements for the investors and are balanced. They include rights and duties for both parties – unlike BITs that are blank checks for the investor.[40]

Attempts to Reconcile Competing Principles

Many disadvantaged developing countries have come to regret signing BITs in the past and have sought to reassert themselves by freeing themselves from the clutches of these BITs. They have started to reject BITs with imprecise principles concerning the protection of foreign investors. Likewise, the general public in both developed and developing countries also seems to have woken up to the drawbacks of the current ISDS mechanism. As a result of such pressures coming from different directions there seems to be a paradigm shift taking place within international investment law in favour of a more equitable, more just and fairer system. As stated by the South African ambassador to the WTO in Geneva, 'Rebalancing the relationship between investor protection and government's right to regulate in the public interest has moved to the centre of the debate on the future of IIAs.'[41] The future discourse on international investment law is likely to be characterised by this attempt at rebalancing of

---

[37] CN Brower and S Melikian, 'We Have Met the Enemy and He Is Us! Is the Industrialised North "Going South" on Investor–State Arbitration?' (2015) 31 *Arbitration International* 19, 25.

[38] G Andres Arauz, 'Ecuador's Experience with International Investment Arbitration', *Investment Policy Brief*, no 5, August 2015.

[39] This is partly due to the fact that many BITs, including the Ecuador–US BIT, and the ICSID Convention do not seem to have fulfilled the constitutional and legal ratification processes.

[40] Andres Arauz (n 32) 4.

[41] Carim (n 8), 1–2.

competing interests, whether it is in relation to the conclusion of new IIAs, an international framework agreement[42] or any WTO-style plurilateral agreements.

Indeed, a growing number of model BITs or IIAs themselves have started to include provisions designed to admit non-compensable regulatory expropriation. The 2012 US Model BIT is an example. A draft Indian Model BIT released in March 2015 goes significantly further than other model BITs in narrowing down the definition of investment by excluding portfolio investment and intellectual property, omitting altogether the troublesome principles of fair and equitable treatment and most-favoured-nation treatment, incorporating the notion of non-compensable regulatory expropriation, and requiring the exhaustion of local remedies before resorting to international arbitration and limiting the scope for ICSID-style arbitrations.[43] This draft Model BIT requires foreign investors to contribute to the development of the host country and to operate by recognising the rights, traditions and customs of local communities in order to benefit from treaty provisions on investor protection. As a result, it gives host countries the right to initiate counterclaims in international arbitration, allows the possibility of bringing civil action against foreign investors in their home countries for wrongs committed abroad, and places restrictions on the discretion of arbitral tribunals when interpreting substantive principles in a BIT or IIA.[44]

Another example of state practice in this direction is the 2011 India–Nepal BIT which defines in Article 5(2) the nature and scope of regulatory expropriation.[45] The definition of regulatory expropriation in this BIT is an attempt to reconcile the law on foreign investment protection with other competing principles of international law. It respects the sovereignty of states and enables them to fulfil their commitments flowing from other international treaties or to pursue bona fide economic, environmental, health- and safety-related policies in the greater interest of the native residents in the host countries. If the trend of accepting legitimate or bona fide governmental measures undertaken in a non-discriminatory manner for environmental, health or safety causes as non-compensable regulatory expropriation continues, bona fide governmental measures to protect core human rights will soon be subsumed under the definition of regulatory expropriation as well.

With the demise of the bipolar world and the resurgence of the multipolar world, more and more states have become cautious and sceptical about the ISDS mechanism.

---

[42] G Hufbauer and S Stephenson, 'The Case for a Framework Agreement on Investment', *Columbia FDI Perspectives*, no 116, 3 March 2014.

[43] Model text for the Indian BIT, available at https://mygov.in/group-issue/draft-indian-model-bilateral-investment-treaty-text/ (accessed 17 August 2015).

[44] S Jandhyala, 'Bringing the State Back In: India's 2015 Model BIT', *Columbia FDI Perspectives*, no 154, 17 August 2015.

[45] Art 5(c) of the 2011 Indian–Nepal BIT reads as follows: 'Non-discriminatory regulatory measures by a Contracting Party that are designed and applied to protect legitimate public welfare objectives including the protection of health, safety and environment do not constitute expropriation or nationalization; except in rare circumstances, where those measures are so severe that they cannot be reasonably viewed as having been adopted and applied in good faith for achieving their objectives. (d) Actions and awards by judicial bodies of a Contracting Party that are designed, applied or issued in public interest including those designed to address health, safety and environmental concerns, do not constitute expropriation or nationalization.' See SP Subedi, 'India's New Bilateral Investment Promotion and Protection Treaty with Nepal: A New Trend in State Practice' (2013) 28 *ICSID Review: Foreign Investment Law Journal* 384.

Consequently, they have started systematically terminating BITs that provide for access to ICSID for foreign investors. Instead, various civil society organisations are now leading the campaign against the ISDS mechanism both within the EU and elsewhere, and they seem to command the support of the public.[46] Recent developments such as those challenging regulatory powers of states in favour of public health or other public good have exposed the flaws inherent in the current ISDS system and brought many valid issues into the fore. For instance, the tobacco giant Philip Morris challenged Australia's decision to adopt its Tobacco Plain Packaging Bill of 2011 through its Hong Kong subsidiary. It relied on the Hong Kong–Australia BIT by initiating arbitration against Australia in the Permanent Court of Arbitration under the UNCITRAL Arbitration Rules, alleging expropriation of investment.[47] In 2010, Philip Morris Products S.A. and related entities launched an arbitration under the 1998 Switzerland–Uruguay BIT against Uruguay's tobacco control measures. In 2011, Philip Morris Asia Limited brought claims under the 1993 Australia-Hong Kong BIT against Australia's mandatory 'plain' packaging of tobacco products. In the end Philip Morris lost both disputes. The ICSID tribunal demonstrated how international investment law can accommodate public health and other domestic policy objectives. The award of July 2016 in *Philip Morris v. Uruguay* accorded appropriate weight to sovereign regulatory objectives: 'investment tribunals should pay great deference to governmental judgments of national needs in matters such as the protection of public health'.[48] This is a landmark ruling because it supports regulatory powers of not only Uruguay but of States in general to adopt laws and regulations to protect public health.

An earlier example of a similar attempt to seek compensation against a public policy initiative of the host government was the series of cases challenging South Africa's Black Economic Empowerment (BEE) policy. In 2007 investors from Luxembourg and Italy brought a claim against South Africa under the ICSID additional facility rules, arguing that South Africa's Mining and Petroleum Resources Development Act as part of the BEE programme contained provisions that effectively expropriated their

---

[46] For instance, M Perez and S Trew write that NAFTA gave multinational corporations the right to sue governments to block regulations that they do not like, and undermine democracy and local sovereignty. See fpif.org, 14 January 2014 (accessed 1 February 2014). Likewise, R Broad and J Cavanagh write that activities are challenging rules that grant corporations the right to sue government, see 'The Global Fight against Corporate Rule', thenation.com, 14 January 2014 (accessed 1 February 2014).

[47] *Philip Morris Asia Limited v The Commonwealth of Australia*, UNCITRAL, PCA Case No 2012-12. See more at: http://www.italaw.com/cases/851#sthash.71JYrBNP.dpuf. On 1 December 2011, the Tobacco Plain Packaging Act 2011 had received Royal Assent and became law in Australia, as part of a comprehensive range of tobacco control measures to reduce the rate of smoking in Australia. Australia had stated that tobacco plain packaging was a legitimate public health measure. Philip Morris Asia challenged the tobacco plain packaging legislation under the 1993 Agreement between the government of Australia and the government of Hong Kong for the Promotion and Protection of Investments (the Hong Kong Agreement). Philip Morris Asia argued that (1) Australia's tobacco plain packaging measure constituted an expropriation of its Australian investments in breach of Art 6 of the Hong Kong Agreement; (2) the tobacco plain packaging measure was in breach of Australia's commitment under Art 2(2) of the Hong Kong Agreement to accord fair and equitable treatment to Philip Morris Asia's investments; and (3) tobacco plain packaging constituted an unreasonable and discriminatory measure and that Philip Morris Asia's investments had been deprived of full protection and security in breach of Art 2(2) of the Hong Kong Agreement.

[48] *Philip Morris Brands Sàrl v Uruguay*, ICSID No ARB/10/7, Award (8 July 2016), para 399.

mineral rights. Although the parties settled the claim, it triggered a process of review by South Africa of its BITs with other states and termination of its BITs with Belgium and Luxembourg and later with Spain and Germany, etc. The termination of the BIT with Germany was of great significance because this European economic powerhouse was South Africa's third most important trading partner (after China and the US), and the fourth biggest holder of foreign investment in South Africa (after the UK, the Netherlands and the US).[49] Although the protection provided under the treaty with Germany would remain effective for existing investors for a period of 20 years under the notion known as the 'sunset clause', new investments would not receive such protection under a BIT. Rather, they will be protected by a new investment law enacted by South Africa whose provisions mirror those in a BIT with the exception of an ISDS provision.

The Inherent Weaknesses of International Investment Law

Unlike in international human rights law or international human rights law where there is a group of core treaties which constitute the corpus of the law in the area, there is no single global treaty on international investment law. Various attempts to codify the rules concerning international investment law have not been successful. It is a patchwork of IIAs, BITs and FTAs and some WTO agreements such as the General Agreement on Trade in Services (GATS) and the Agreement on Trade-related Investment Measures (TRIMs) that deal with the treatment of international investors by host countries. In the absence of a global comprehensive treaty these agreements are supplemented by a number of voluntary, soft laws and instruments that address various aspects relating to international investors. Therefore, since the law itself is not clear in international investment law, this area of law has been a 'goldmine' for international investment lawyers. In particular, third party funding has fuelled the temptation to use international investment arbitration to sue governments for alleged breaches of all sorts of trade and investment law rules.

One of the other flaws in the current regime of international investment law is that the very body of law that seeks to protect corporations does not deal with corporate conduct or corporate liability. As Appleton states, the 'current situation is ripe for bad decision-making. It facilitates inconsistency rather than enhancing stability and predictability from a consistent meaning and application of international investment treaty norms.'[50] Therefore, it has become necessary to bring clarity in international

---

[49] S Woolfrey, 'Hot Seat Comment: Another BIT Bites the Dust', tralac.org, 30 October 2013 (accessed 29 January 2014).

[50] B Appleton, 'The Song Is Over: Why it's Time to Stop Talking about an International Investment Arbitration Appellate Body' (2013) 107 *Proceedings of the Annual Meeting of the American Society of International Law* 23, 25.

investment law and address the imbalances within this body of law in general and the ISDS mechanism and ICSID and UNCITRAL in particular. For this, it would be necessary to look at the principles, institutions and processes involving international investment law.

However, given the nature of negotiations over the Trans-Pacific Partnership (TPP)[51] concluded in October 2015 with some revisions two years later and the stalled negotiations on the TTIP agreement or the attempts made within other international forums to reform the ISDS system, it seems unlikely that a substantive reform will be carried out in the near future.

The most likely scenario seems to be an incremental reform of the system and a gradual return to the Calvo doctrine. Nevertheless, change is coming, and it is coming faster than expected in the world of international investment law and arbitration.

Indications for the Future

The absence of clarity in the law has oftentimes given investment tribunals the freedom to declare what the law is on the basis of the arbitrators' understanding of the law. The arbitrators are called upon to adjudicate on a given dispute even though many of them may not necessarily possess the requisite qualifications. Since many of the arbitrators have interpreted the law according to their understanding of the law, they have frequently been creative and expansive in the interpretation of the principles concerning the standards of investment protection in deciding cases before them. If no discipline and coherence is imposed on international investment arbitration, this expansive trend may continue ceaselessly and eventually tempt business organisations to use international investment arbitration to sue host governments for violations of WTO law.[52] This is because private actors such as business organisations have no access to the WTO dispute settlement mechanism, as it is an inter-state dispute settlement mechanism. Therefore, there would be every temptation to bring WTO law disputes within the ambit of international investment arbitration, whether it is invoking the all-encompassing fair and equitable treatment principle, the umbrella clause or other international investment law principles.

As stated by Alford, parallel proceedings witnessed in cases such as Philip Morris illustrate 'a willingness by multinational corporations to pursue all possible avenues of relief in response to onerous government regulation'.[53] Alford goes on to state that: 'An arbitration panel liberally construing a broad umbrella clause could transform

---

[51] R Bhala, 'Trans-Pacific Partnership or Trampling Poor Partners? A Tentative Critical Review' (2014) 11 *Manchester Journal of International Economic Law* 2.

[52] SP Subedi, 'WTO Dispute Settlement Mechanism as a New Technique for Settling Disputes in International Law', in D French, M Saul and ND White (eds), *International Law and Dispute Settlement: New Problems and Techniques* (Hart Publishing, Oxford, 2010) 173.

[53] RP Alford, 'The Convergence of International Trade and Investment Arbitration' (2013) 12 *Santa Clara Journal of International Law* 35, 50.

how WTO obligations are adjudicated.' Furthermore, 'umbrella clauses in BITs could create a private right of action for resolving WTO disputes. Investment arbitration circumvents the traditional barrier to initiating a WTO dispute.'[54] He concludes that 'the convergence of trade and investment has taken hold with investment chapters in preferential trade agreements. Convergence of the two disciplines with respect to dispute resolution is a nascent development.'[55]

Even if the current regime of investment protection through BITs or IIAs or FTAs were to be restricted, international human rights standards will remain applicable. The concepts such as such as the denial of justice[56] under regional and international human rights treaties and the rule of law in its broadest sense[57] are likely to be invoked by foreign investors to sue host governments for compensation for their failings in protecting foreign investors under these human rights standards. Supposing that the traditional ISDS mechanism were to cease to exist in its current form, there is nothing to prevent foreign investors for suing host governments before other human rights mechanisms, such as the European Court of Human Rights, or in national courts themselves in the host countries. Thus, the issues associated with business and human rights are likely to be the growth areas, heralding an interesting new phase of development in international investment law.[58] The award made by an UNCITRAL tribunal in *White Industries v India* is an example of how the denial of justice could be interpreted, invoked and applied in favour of a foreign investor. Furthermore, as experienced in this case, there are indications that business organisations will not hesitate to challenge the activities of domestic courts, including supreme courts, before international investment tribunals of an ad hoc character.

Conclusions

Recent trends in state practice demonstrate that, in the absence of fundamental reform, neither the BIT/IIA regime nor the ISDS mechanism may survive for long in their present form. Therefore, it seems imperative to bring discipline and coherence to international investment arbitration and the European Commission's proposal for a new and transparent system for resolving disputes between investors and states – the Investment Court System – seems to be a measure in this direction. Under these

---

[54] Ibid, 59.

[55] Ibid, 62.

[56] J Paulsson, *Denial of Justice in International Law* (Cambridge, Cambridge University Press, 2005).

[57] For example, see: The Bingham Centre for the Rule of Law and Investment Treaty Forum, 'Risk and Return: Foreign Direct Investment and the Rule of Law' (London, British Institute of International and Comparative Law, 2015) 17; and SP Subedi, 'The Universality of Human Rights and the UN Human Rights Agenda: The Impact of the Shift of Power to the East and the Resurgence of the BRICS' (2015) *Indian Journal of International Law*.

[58] See generally, UE Ofodile, 'Foreign Investment in Land and the Clash of Regimes: Mapping the Role of International Law and International Human Rights Law' (2013) 7 *Human Rights and International Legal Discourse* 56.

proposals, the new investment law court system will include a public Investment Court System composed of a first-instance Tribunal and an Appeal Tribunal; their judgments would be made by publicly appointed and highly qualified judges, comparable to those required for the members of permanent international courts such as the ICJ and the WTO Appellate Body; the new Appeal Tribunal would operate on similar principles to the WTO Appellate Body; and governments' right to regulate would be enshrined and guaranteed in the provisions of the trade and investment agreements.

2

Evolution of International Investment Law

Introduction

Although modern international investment law and policy regime is a relatively young construct, this field of law has been in existence for a long time. Before arriving at its present form, this field evolved significantly whether under the scope of state responsibility for internationally wrongful acts or the protection of aliens in international law generally or the protection of the right to property of foreigners under human rights related treaties. The aim of this chapter is to provide an understanding as to how foreign investment law has evolved in response to the changing economic and political situation of the world. In doing so, it will also look at the impact that the traditional developed–developing country tension has had on the evolution of international foreign investment law.

The Early Years

Since time immemorial people have gone abroad to invest and to engage in business. When European traders first visited Asia, Africa and Latin America to trade with the local communities, it was held that the local law did not apply to them since they were already subject to the law of their home country. Early scholars such as Grotius[1] and Vattel[2] lent their support to such a position. This argument was based on the assumption that these businessmen carried the law of the country of their nationality with them wherever they went and were thus not subject to local law. These European

---

[1] H Grotius, *De Jure Belli ac Pacis Tres* (rev edn, 1946), reprinted in (1925) 3 *The Classics of International Law* 385 (trans F Kelsey), as cited in TM Franck, *Fairness in International Law and Institutions* (Oxford, Clarendon Press, 1995) 457, n 11.
[2] E de Vattel, *The Law of Nations* (ed J Chitty, 1852) 174, as cited in Franck (n 1) 457.

foreigners sought special and superior treatment from the local population in much of Asia, Africa and Latin America. The implication of this idea was that their assets could not be expropriated or nationalised through legislation enacted by the local population. Since the local law was inferior, it could not apply to the foreigners, who were subject to the superior body of law of their home country.

As noted by Sutton, many treaties concluded by European powers with Asian and African states stated that the Europeans remained under the jurisdiction of their home states and that their consuls exercised jurisdiction over their fellow nationals.[3] For instance, the treaty concluded between the Sheikhdom of Bahrain and the British government in 1861 stated in Article 4 that the British subjects and the dependants in Bahrain shall receive the treatment and consideration of the most favoured people: 'All offences which they may commit or which may be committed against them, shall be reserved for the decision of the British Resident, provided the British agent of Bahrain shall fail to adjust them satisfactorily.'[4]

Thus, in the early years of the development of foreign investment law it was understood that no state could expropriate or nationalise foreign assets. Arising from the notion of an international minimum standard, states could not invoke national laws as a reason for avoiding their international obligations. It was only in the next phase of development when the number of independent states grew that it came to be accepted that states could expropriate the assets of foreigners under narrowly defined conditions and against the payment of compensation.

Foreign investment law has its origins in the international law concerning the protection of aliens – a legal regime based on both the international human rights law and the public international law principles of fairness, equity, justice and non-discrimination.

National Treatment versus International Minimum Standard

When colonial territories began to gain independence they started to challenge the concept that foreigners residing and doing business in those countries could not be governed by the law enacted by the local population. Relying on the doctrine of sovereignty and sovereign equality, they asserted that every sovereign state had the right to expropriate or nationalise foreign assets within their jurisdiction provided that the foreign investor was provided with compensation. The very notion of sovereignty meant that foreigners residing within the national borders of the country were subject to the law of the land. For instance, Article 9 of the Convention on the Rights and

---

[3] SD Sutton, '*Emilio Augustin Maffezini v Kingdom of Spain* and the ICSID Secretary-General's Screening Power' (2005) 21(1) *Arbitration International* 113, 119.

[4] As quoted in Sutton, ibid.

Duties of States, one of the first international instruments to support the idea of national treatment, signed at the Seventh Pan-American Conference, provided that:

> The jurisdiction of States within the limits of national territory applies to all the inhabitants. Nationals and foreigners are under the same protection of the law and the national authorities and the foreigners may not claim rights other or more extensive than those of the nationals.[5]

The Latin American countries were the first group of states to gain independence from their colonial rulers. These newly independent states began to assert that foreign investors were not entitled to any greater protection than those accorded to the nationals of the country under the law of the land. If the host states treated foreign investors on a par with the nationals of the country, the host states were acting within the norms of international law. Consequently, the right to expropriate the assets of foreign companies with compensation was accepted as an appropriate corollary to state sovereignty.

However, it was submitted that if the local law were considered inferior, not well developed or failed to meet the standards of justice and equity, the international minimum standard rather than national law would apply to foreign investors. The assertion was that international law provided for the international minimum standard and all states had to accept the international minimum standard by bringing their national laws up to this standard. Consequently, the focus was on interpreting what constituted the international minimum standard.[6]

One of the advocates of the application of an international minimum standard to the treatment of aliens, including foreign investors, was Elihu Root, a leading American international lawyer, who argued in 1910 that there was a standard of justice which formed a part of international law. Any national law dealing with the treatment of aliens had to conform to this general international standard:

> If any country's system of law does not conform to that standard, although the people of the country may be content or compelled to live under it, no other country can be compelled to accept it as furnishing a satisfactory measure of treatment to its citizens.[7]

Schwarzenberger added his voice in support of this argument in the following words:

> [T]he national standard cannot be used as a means of evading international obligations under the minimum standard of international law. Even if the standard of national treatment is laid down in a treaty, the presumption is that it has been the intention of the parties to secure to their nationals in this manner additional advantages, but not to deprive them of such rights as, in any case, they would be entitled to enjoy under international customary law or the general principles of law recognised by civilised nations.[8]

---

[5] The Convention on the Rights and Duties of States (Montevideo Convention, 1933), text in (1976) 70 *AJIL* 445.

[6] Sir R Jennings and Sir A Watts (eds), *Oppenheim's International Law*, 9th edn (Harlow, Longman, 1992) vol I, parts 2–4, 931.

[7] E Root, 'The Basis of Protection to Citizens Residing Abroad' (1910) 4 *American Journal of International Law* 517, 521–22. See also G Schwarzenberger, 'The Standard of Civilization in International Law' (1955) VII *Current Legal Problems* 220.

[8] G Schwarzenberger, *International Law as Applied by International Courts and Tribunals* (London, Stevens, 1957) 248.

Those scholars who articulated the notion of an international minimum standard drew on the doctrine of state responsibility, which provided protection against injury to aliens and alien property.[9] States were not legally bound to admit aliens into their territory but once admitted they had to be accorded a certain standard of decent treatment. The concept of national treatment would entitle foreign investors to the same rights and privileges as those enjoyed by the nationals of a country, but it would not provide adequate protection to foreign investors if the nationals and foreign investors were treated equally badly. As stated by Asante, according to the doctrine of state responsibility,

> host States are enjoined by international law to observe an international minimum standard in the treatment of aliens and alien property. The duty to observe this standard – objective international standard – is not necessarily discharged by according to aliens and alien property the same treatment available to nationals. Where international standards fall below the international minimum standard, the latter prevails. Breach of the minimum standard engages the responsibility of the host State, and provides a legitimate basis for the exercise by the home State of the right of diplomatic protection of the alien, a right predicated on the inherent right to protect nationals abroad.
>
> ...
>
> The development of the law of State responsibility was inspired by Western *laissez-faire* ideas and liberal concepts of property. From the juristic standpoint, one of the underlying principles is the duty of the host State to display fair and equitable treatment or good faith in its conduct towards aliens.
>
> The Law of State Responsibility, which was originally conceived for the purpose of protecting individual aliens, was subsequently extended to foreign companies and other foreign business concerns.[10]

In the *Barcelona Traction* case, the ICJ stated that:

> When a State admits into its territory foreign investments of foreign nationals, whether natural or juristic persons, it is bound to extend to them the protection of the law and assumes obligations concerning the treatment to be afforded them.[11]

In the *Roberts* claim, the General Claims Commission held that:

> Facts with respect to equality of treatment of aliens and nationals may be important in determining the merits of a complaint of mistreatment of an alien. But such equality is not the ultimate test of the propriety of the acts of authorities in the light of international law. That test is, broadly speaking, whether aliens are treated in accordance with ordinary standards of civilization.[12]

---

[9] See generally EM Borchard, 'The Minimum International Standard in the Protection of Aliens' (1939) 33 *ASIL Proceedings*; AA Fatouros, 'Transnational Enterprises and in the Law of State Responsibility', in RB Lillich (ed), *The International Law of State Responsibility for Injuries to Aliens* (Charlottesville, University Press of Virginia, 1983) ch VIII.

[10] SKB Asante, 'International Law and Foreign Investment: A Reappraisal' (1988) 37 *ICLQ* 588, 590.

[11] *Barcelona Traction, Light and Power Co Case (Belgium v Spain)*, ICJ Reports 1970, 3, para 33.

[12] The Roberts, Hopkins, and British Claims in the Spanish Zone of Morocco cases (1926), RIAA, iv.41; (1926) RIAA iv.411; and (1925), RIAA ii.617, respectively, as cited in JC Thomas, 'Reflections on Article 1105 of NAFTA: History, State Practice and Influence of Commentators' (2002) 17 *ICSID Review: Foreign Investment Law Journal* 21, 33.

However, since there was no internationally negotiated treaty outlining the terms and conditions of protection of foreign investment, one had to look at other sources of international law, mainly customary international law, in order to ascertain what constituted international law on the subject matter or the international minimum standard.[13] Thus, normally, the practice of investor countries had to be relied upon to determine what constituted customary international law. The same is true of the general principles of law or of the subsidiary sources of international law because whatever writing existed on international law or whatever case law existed on the subject matter was based on the law hitherto in existence and the practice of investor countries. Furthermore, the law hitherto in existence was the law made by the investor countries designed to protect foreign investment abroad. Therefore, once it was agreed that international law or an international minimum standard would apply to foreign investment, this meant, for all practical purposes, applying the law of investor countries. This is one reason why the classic doctrinal tension that existed with regard to foreign investment law was the tension between those who preferred to apply national law to regulate foreign investment and those who preferred to apply international law, meaning customary international law made by investor countries.

When it was submitted that the international minimum standard[14] rather than national law was applicable to foreign investment, an attempt was made to define the international minimum standard not only in light of the general principles of justice and equity and the practice of states on the treatment of foreign investment, but also in light of the existing rules of both the conventional and customary international law of human rights. In other words, human rights principles, including the right to property, were also invoked to define what constituted the international minimum standard. Under the evolving principles of international human rights law, every individual, both physical and juridical and whether national or alien, residing within any country, was entitled to their basic human rights, including property rights, protected by law. Consequently, when it came to defining what constituted the international minimum standard, not only foreign investment law, but also human rights law, including the property rights of the individuals, whether national or alien, had to be taken into account. Thus, in effect, the international human rights agenda, which supplemented and complemented foreign investment law, would extend the application of the national property law of investor countries to foreign investors doing business abroad. This meant that individual property belonging to either nationals or aliens could not be expropriated or nationalised by a state without compensation.[15]

Accordingly, the right of states to regulate foreign investment under their national law in exercise of their sovereign rights had to be balanced with the principles of international human rights law. Consequently, one of the benefits seen by many states

---

[13] See Hussein Haeri, 'A Tale of Two Standards: 'Fair and Equitable Treatment' and the Minimum Standard in International Law', 27 (1) *Arbitration International* (2011), pp 27–45.

[14] E Borchard, 'The Minimum Standard of Treatment of Aliens' (1940) 38 *Michigan Law Review* 445; A Roth, *The Minimum Standard of International Law as Applied to Aliens* (thesis, Geneva, 1949).

[15] CF Amerasinghe, *State Responsibility for Injuries to Aliens* (Oxford, Clarendon Press, 1964); C Eagleton, *The Responsibility of States in International Law* (New York, New York University Press, 1928); Lillich (n 9).

in the promotion of the human rights agenda and in supporting the universality of human rights was the protection of the investment made by their nationals abroad. Thus, the cumulative effect of all customary and conventional rules of international law was that foreign investors were entitled to the protection accorded under the notion of international minimum standard, which was based on both foreign investment law and international human rights law. Accordingly, one of the requirements of this international minimum standard was that the taking of private property by a state had to be non-discriminatory, for a public purpose, against the payment of appropriate compensation and in accordance with the due process of law. For instance, a provision in the Central American Free Trade Agreement (CAFTA) states that the provisions concerning expropriation and compensation in Article 10.7 are 'intended to reflect customary international law concerning the obligation of States with respect to expropriation'.[16]

The Era of Gunboat Diplomacy

Prior to the introduction of state-to-state arbitration or inter-state claims commissions, particularly in the nineteenth century, influential individuals and corporations would persuade their governments to send a small contingent of warships to moor off the coast of the host states until reparation was forthcoming. This was practised frequently by the major trading nations of Europe. This kind of 'gun-boat' diplomacy sought to protect the interests of those nationals who invested abroad by the government of their home country. For instance, in 1902 the governments of Great Britain, Germany and Italy sent warships to the Venezuelan coast to demand reparation for the losses incurred by their nationals caused by Venezuela defaulting on its sovereign debt.[17] However, the provision for the settlement of international disputes between states by peaceful means by the Second International Peace Conference of The Hague in 1907, which adopted the Convention on the Peaceful Resolution of International Disputes, opened the possibility of state-to-state arbitration on investment disputes.

Diplomatic Protection and the Treatment of Aliens
in International Law

Once it was established that foreign investors enjoyed the international minimum standard of protection under international law, the home states invoked the law to

---

[16] Annex 10-C on 'Expropriation' of CAFTA, www.ustr.gov/new/fta/cafta/text.
[17] A Redfern et al, *Law and Practice of International Commercial Arbitration*, 4th edn (London, Sweet & Maxwell, 2004) 562–63.

provide protection to their citizens doing business abroad and sought remedy for them under the notion known as 'diplomatic protection'. This meant that the government of the home country would take up cases on behalf of its nationals and engage in negotiations or arbitration with the foreign government on their behalf. This notion is an integral part of the subject of 'treatment of aliens' in traditional international law which prescribes the rules governing the treatment of the person and property of aliens. Breaching such rules gives rise to responsibility to the state nationality of the injured person, whether natural or juridical. As stated in a commentary to the Draft Articles on Diplomatic Protection prepared by the International Law Commission, diplomatic protection 'is traditionally a mechanism designed to secure reparation for injury to the national of a State premised largely on the principle that an injury to a national is an injury to the State itself'.[18] Diplomatic protection must be exercised through lawful and peaceful means such as diplomatic action. The state itself would intervene on behalf of its citizens abroad and demand protection and compensation from the host states alleged to have breached the international minimum standard of protection, which included the principles concerning the treatment of aliens in international law. The right of a state to protect its citizens abroad had been admitted as early as the middle of the eighteenth century by jurists such as Vattel. He wrote:

> Anyone who mistreats a citizen directly offends the State. The sovereign of that State must avenge its injury, and if it can, force the aggressor to make full reparation or punish him, since otherwise the citizen would simply not obtain the goal of civil association, namely security.[19]

Other scholars such as Borchard have since endorsed and expounded on the notion of diplomatic protection. In a monograph published in 1915 Borchard stated that:

> Diplomatic protection is in its nature an international proceeding, constituting an appeal by nation to nation for the performance of the obligations of the one to the other, growing out of their mutual rights and duties.[20]

The Permanent Court of International Justice (PCIJ) pronounced its justification for the right of states to resort to diplomatic protection in the following manner in the *Mavrommatis Palestine Concessions* case:

> It is an elementary principle of international law that a State is entitled to protect its subjects, when injured by acts contrary to international law committed by another State, from when they have been unable to obtain satisfaction through the ordinary channels. By taking up the case of one of its subjects and by resorting to diplomatic action or international judicial proceedings on his behalf, a State is in reality asserting its own rights – the right to ensure, in the person of its subjects, respect for the rules of international law.[21]

---

[18] UN Doc A/61/10, 2006; (2006) II *Yearbook of the International Law Commission*, Part Two.

[19] E de Vattel, *Le droit des gens ou les principes de la loi naturelle* (vol I, 1758) 309, as translated and cited in Z Douglas, 'The Hybrid Foundations of Investment Treaty Arbitration' (2003) 74 *British Year Book of International Law* 151, 165.

[20] E Borchard, *The Diplomatic Protection of Citizens Abroad or the Law of International Claims* (New York, Banks Law Publishing, 1915) 354.

[21] PCIJ Reports Series (1924) A No 2.

This ruling has since found its expression and endorsement in other decisions of the PCIJ and its successor, the ICJ.[22] The doctrine of diplomatic protection finds its expression in various manifestations. The right of foreign investors to sue a state before an international tribunal under a BIT can, in fact, be regarded as an extension of diplomatic protection by states because it is states that have created this right for foreign investors through a BIT. For instance, in *The Republic of Ecuador v Occidental Exploration & Production Co*, Aikens J of the English High Court of Justice stated that:

> It is a long-standing principle of public international law that States owe duties to other States to protect their citizens. This is known as the 'doctrine of diplomatic protection'. Effectively, BITs are treaties that acknowledge this principle of public international law, apply it to particular circumstances between two States and develop the protection of investors by giving them 'standing' to pursue a State directly in 'investment disputes' between an investor and a State Party in ways that are set out in the BIT.[23]

Although the traditional form of diplomatic protection is no longer necessary in today's world where aggrieved foreign investors can resort to various international tribunals under BITs and regional trading agreements (RTAs), states can always avail themselves of this well-recognised tool of international law when it becomes necessary.[24] Many of the inter-state investment disputes referred either to the ICJ or to other international courts and tribunals are manifestations of the exercise of powers under the institution of diplomatic protection. Whether or not there is a BIT or some other treaty between the states concerned, a home state can always invoke the principles of public international law concerning the treatment of aliens and protect its citizens, both natural and juridical, abroad.[25] Thus, the protection available to foreign investors under the international law minimum standard of treatment of aliens is the foundation of modern foreign investment law. This level of treatment is part of customary international law and is thus binding on all states except for persistent and subsequent objectors under narrowly defined conditions. An attempt has been made in the recent past by both States and international investment tribunals to expand this customary international law protection to foreign investors through a BIT or some other treaty of a similar nature.

The Calvo Doctrine

Those who were opposed to accepting the law of investor countries, in the name of the international minimum standards, were of the view that no state should be

---

[22] Eg, *Reparation for Injuries Suffered in the Service of the United Nations* case (Advisory Opinion), ICJ Reports 1949, 181 and *Barcelona Traction, Light and Power Co (Belgium v Spain)*, ICJ Reports 1970, 3.

[23] *The Republic of Ecuador v Occidental Exploration & Production Co*, High Court of Justice, Queen's Bench Division, Commercial Court, Case No 04/656, 2 March 2006, para 8.

[24] Eg, this issue arose recently in a case between *Sempra Energy v Argentina*, ICSID Case No ARB/02/16, 11 May 2005, para 134.

[25] I Seidl-Hohenveldern, *Corporations in and under International Law*, Hersch Lauterpacht Memorial Lectures (Cambridge, Grotius Publications, 1987).

required to offer more protection to foreign investors than that accorded to its own nationals. There had to be equality of treatment. If the state in question was not discriminating against foreign investors, it was not violating any rules of customary international law. The argument was that it would be difficult for countries that are newly independent and that have not attained the level of economic development required, or acquired a developed legal system, to accord a higher standard of treatment to foreign investors.

At the forefront of the argument in favour of national treatment of foreign investors and the right of states to expropriate the assets of foreign companies was a leading nineteenth-century Latin American jurist, Carlos Calvo of Argentina,[26] who articulated the position of relying on the doctrine of economic sovereignty of states in the following terms:

> It is certain that aliens who establish themselves in a country have the same right to protection as nationals, but they ought not to lay claim to a protection more extended. If they suffer any wrong, they ought to count on the government of the country prosecuting the delinquents, and not claim from the state to which the authors of the violence belong any pecuniary indemnity.
>
> …
>
> The rule that in more than one case it has been attempted to impose on American States is that foreigners merit more regard and privileges more marked and extended than those accorded even to the nationals of the country where they reside.
>
> The principle is intrinsically contrary to the law of equality of nations.[27]

The central element of the Calvo doctrine was to require aliens to submit disputes arising in a country to that country's courts. In other words, it seeks to ensure that foreign companies or other foreign investors would exhaust local remedies prior to resorting to international arbitration or international adjudication. According to Verwey and Schrijver, the Calvo doctrine basically stipulates that the principle of territorial sovereignty of the state entails:

(a) the principle of absolute equality before the law between nationals and foreigners;
(b) the exclusive subjection of foreigners and their property to the laws and juridical regimes of the State in which they reside or invest; and
(c) strict abstention from interference by other governments, notably the governments of the States of which the foreigners are nationals, in disputes arising over the treatment of foreigners or their property (ie, abstention from diplomatic protection.)[28]

The essentials of the Calvo doctrine found their way into numerous Latin American constitutions (such as those of Peru,[29] Venezuela and Mexico), treaties (such as the

---

[26] K Lipstein, 'The Place of the Calvo Clause in International Law' (1945) 24 *British Year Book of International Law* 130; AV Freeman, 'Recent Aspects of the Calvo Doctrine and the Challenge to International Law' (1946) 40 *American Journal of International Law* 131.

[27] Translated and quoted from Calvo's work in Spanish by DR Shea, *The Calvo Clause: A Problem of Inter-American and International Law and Diplomacy* (Minneapolis, University of Minnesota Press, 1955) 17–19.

[28] WD Verwey and NJ Schrijver, 'The Taking of Foreign Property under International Law: A New Legal Perspective?' (1984) XV *Netherlands Yearbook of International Law* 3, 23.

[29] Art 17 of the 1939 Constitution of Peru provided that: 'Commercial companies, national or foreign, are subject, without restrictions, to the laws of the Republic. In every state contract with foreigners, or in the

Pact of Bogota)[30] and investment pacts (such as the Andean Foreign Investment Code).[31] In simple terms, according to the Calvo doctrine, land and other natural resources belong to the state by virtue of the doctrine of sovereignty and no foreign entity can permanently own land in a host state. After the communist revolution in Russia in 1917 and the agrarian revolution in Mexico at around the same time, the governments of these countries proclaimed state ownership of land; and the assets of foreign companies were expropriated and nationalised without proper compensation, through invoking the sovereignty of states. This was an attempt to take the notion of national treatment to its extreme. The actions of the Soviet and Mexican governments were opposed by Western states, who held the view that although sovereign states had the right to expropriate the assets of foreign companies, they could do so only under certain narrowly defined conditions stipulated in international law and the expropriation had to be coupled with prompt, adequate and effective compensation. Through several decrees issued after the Bolshevik revolution, the ownership of land and other natural resources was transferred to the state, all banks were nationalised, and the public debt was repudiated without any compensation. Since the decrees drew no distinction between property owned by Russian nationals and foreign-owned property, Western countries protested against the Russian measures. After years of protests and counter-protests, a form of claims settlement was reached between the US and the USSR in 1933 under the Litvinov Assignment.[32]

Similarly, Article 27 of the Mexican constitution promulgated in 1917 following a revolution, during which agrarian expropriations, including land owned by US nationals, were carried out, reads as follows:

> Ownership of the lands and materials included within the boundaries of national territory belongs to the Nation, which has had and continues to have the right to transmit ownership thereof to private parties, thereby constituting private property.
>
> Expropriations may only be made for reasons of public utility and by means of compensation.
>
> The Nation shall have at all times the right to impose on private property the modalities required by the public interest, as well as the right to regulate the exploitation of natural resources capable of expropriation in order to conserve them and to make equitable distribution of public wealth.[33]

Unlike Russia, Mexico did not deny the duty to compensate foreigners against expropriation of the assets that they owned in Mexico, but the nature of compensation was

concessions which grant them in the latter's favour, it must be expressly stated that they will submit to the laws and courts of the Republic and renounce all diplomatic claims.'

[30] Art 7 of the American Treaty on Pacific Settlement (Pact of Bogota, 1948) reads: 'The High Contracting Parties bind themselves not to make diplomatic representations in order to protect their nationals, or to refer a controversy to a court of international jurisdiction for that purpose, when the said nationals have had available the means to place their case before competent domestic courts of the respective State' (30 UNTS 55).

[31] Art 50 of the Andean Code of 1971 provided that 'Member countries shall not grant to foreign investors any treatment more favourable than that granted to national investors.' Text in (1972) XI ILM 126 et seq.

[32] See for the text of the Assignment contained in a letter to the US President by Litvinov, Soviet People's Commissar for Foreign Affairs, *United States v Pink*, 315 US 203 at 212 (1942). See also JW Garner, 'Recognition by the United States of the Government of Soviet Russia' (1935) 16 *British Year Book of International Law* 171.

[33] The 1917 Constitution of Mexico together with Art 27 is still valid, but in its amended form as amended in 1992. See for the text of the amended article, GH Flanz (ed), *Constitutions of the Countries of the World: Mexico* (release 98–4, issued June 1998) (Dobbs Ferry, NY, Oceana Publications) 17–21.

not necessarily prompt, adequate or effective; it depended on the ability of the state to pay compensation. After years of negotiations, a binational claims commission was established in 1927 between the US and Mexico to consider claims of US foreign investors whose assets, mainly land, had been expropriated by Mexico. However, since not a single claim had been adjusted or paid by 1938, the US intensified its diplomatic efforts. The US Secretary of State, Cordell Hull, began a series of diplomatic exchanges with the Mexican government and the content of these diplomatic exchanges, in which Hull articulated US views on compensation, came to be known in international foreign investment law as the Hull formula.

The Hull Formula

Outlining the US position on the issue of expropriation and the nature of compensation under international law, Hull stated that:

> The taking of property without compensation is not expropriation. It is confiscation. It is no less confiscation because there may be an expressed intent to pay at some time in the future. If it were permissible for a government to take the private property of the citizens of other countries and pay for it as and when, in the judgment of that government, its economic circumstances and local legislation may perhaps permit, the safeguards which the constitutions of most countries and established international law have sought to provide would be illusory. Governments would be free to take property far beyond their ability or willingness to pay, and the owners thereof would be without recourse. We cannot question the right of a foreign government to treat its own nationals in this fashion if it so desires. This is a matter of domestic concern. But we cannot admit that a foreign government may take the property of American nationals in disregard for the rule of compensation under international law. Nor can we admit that any government unilaterally and through its domestic legislation can, as in this instant case, nullify this universally accepted principle of international law, based as it is on reason, equity and justice.[34]

His letter goes on to outline the justifications for his position by drawing on the basic principles of international law governing international relations:

> The whole structure of friendly intercourse, of international trade and commerce, and many other vital and mutually desirable relations between nations indispensable to their progress rest upon the single and hitherto solid foundation of respect on the part of the governments and of peoples for each other's rights under international justice. The right of prompt and just compensation for expropriated property is a part of this structure. It is a principle to which the Government of the United States and most governments of the world have emphatically subscribed and which they have practiced and which must be maintained. It is not a principle which freezes the *status quo* and denies changes in property rights but a principle that permits any country to expropriate private property within its borders in furtherance of public purposes. It enables orderly change without violating the legitimately acquired interests of citizens of other countries.[35]

---

[34] Letter of the US Secretary of State to Mexican Ambassador to the United States, 21 July 1938, as cited in AF Lowenfeld, *International Economic Law* (Oxford, Oxford University Press, 2002) 398.
[35] Ibid, and also (1938) 32 *American Journal of International Law*, Suppl 181–207.

However, the Mexican Foreign Minister disagreed with Hull's views of international law that was applicable to this subject matter. He replied by stating that there was in international law

> no rule universally accepted in theory nor carried out in practice, which makes obligatory the payment of immediate compensation nor even of deferred compensation, for expropriations of a general and impersonal character like those which Mexico has carried out for the purpose of redistribution of the land.[36]

The reply went on to assert that

> there does not exist in international law any principle universally accepted by countries, nor by the writers of treatises on this subject, that would render obligatory the giving of adequate compensation for expropriations of a general and impersonal character. Nevertheless, Mexico admits, in obedience to her own laws, that she is indeed under obligation to indemnify in an adequate manner; but the doctrine which she maintains on the subject, which is based on the most authoritative opinions of writers of treatises on international law, is that the time and manner of such payment must be determined by her own laws.[37]

Hull responded in the following terms:

> The Government of the United States merely adverts to a self-evident fact when it notes that the applicable precedents and recognized authorities on international law support its declaration that, under every rule of law and equity, no government is entitled to expropriate private property, for whatever purpose, without provision for prompt, adequate and effective payment therefor. In addition, clauses appearing in the constitutions of almost all nations today, and in particular in the constitutions of the American republics, embody the principle of just compensation. These, in themselves, are declaratory of the like principles in the law of nations.[38]

In his response the Mexican Foreign Minister rejected Hull's assertion and justified the Mexican expropriations as being a move designed to achieve social justice in the country. However, just before the Second World War spread to the Western hemisphere, Mexico and the US reached an agreement to establish a commission to determine the compensation to be paid to US nationals affected by the Mexican agrarian expropriations which took place after 30 August 1927. The two countries struck a deal designed to compensate these US investors. Moving from agrarian expropriations, the Mexican government issued a decree in March 1938 expropriating British- and American-owned oil companies. Another round of diplomatic exchanges took place between the US and Mexico during which Hull reiterated his position that the US recognised the right of Mexico to expropriate foreign assets for public purposes but that such expropriation had to be 'coupled with and conditioned on the obligation to make adequate, effective and prompt compensation'.[39] He concluded: 'The legality of an expropriation is in fact dependent upon the observance of this requirement.'[40] In the same agreement that was

---

[36] Mexican Minister of Foreign Affairs to US Ambassador, 3 August 1938, as cited in Lowenfeld (n 33) 399.
[37] Ibid.
[38] Ibid, 400.
[39] Secretary Hull to Mexican Ambassador, ibid, 402.
[40] Ibid.

concluded to settle the agrarian claims, the two countries agreed to settle the petroleum claims by each appointing an expert to establish just compensation 'on the basis of common rules of justice and equity'.[41]

Throughout its dealings with the US, the Mexican government maintained the position that as a sovereign state it had the right to expropriate the assets of foreign investors in pursuance of a social policy. Thus, foreign investors had no special rights and privileges when it came to awarding compensation and any compensation had to be determined by applying the national laws of Mexico and the principles of justice and equity rather than those international law standards as claimed by Hull. Although the US and Mexico settled the claims relating to both agrarian and petroleum expropriations, there was no agreement on the law applicable to such expropriations. However, the report of two experts – appointed to establish just compensation for the US owners of the nationalised petroleum properties in Mexico – acknowledged that expropriation and the rights of states to expropriate under the laws of the nations concerned were a recognised feature of the sovereignty of all modern states.

Conclusion

As seen in the preceding sections, by the end of the 1940s the basic conditions under which the assets of foreign companies could be expropriated became clearer in state practice. During this time, foreign investment law started to take a shape as a distinct body of law. The Hull formula, advocated by developed countries in general and the US in particular, became a powerful norm that sidelines much of the tenets of the Calvo doctrine favoured by developing countries. At the same time it also became acceptable in international law, as championed by developing countries, that states had a right to expropriate foreign assets under narrowly defined conditions; however, expropriations had to be accompanied by prompt, adequate and effective compensation.

---

[41] Exchange of Notes of 1941 between Mexico and the US, ibid, para 9.

3

International Efforts to Regulate Foreign Investment

Introduction

Regulation of foreign investment or the activities of multinational enterprises, which are a major vehicle for foreign investment, have been on the international agenda for some time. Consequently, various treaties have been concluded which deal with certain aspects of investment regulation. Some notable examples include the UN convention on the control of corrupt business practices or transparency on international investment and a number of soft law instruments in the form of guidelines or declarations. However, in spite of several attempts, there has been no single comprehensive convention adopted on the subject matter. This chapter aims to examine the efforts made under the auspices of the UN, the World Bank, the WTO and other economic organisations such as the Organisation for Economic Cooperation and Development (OECD) or other private and professional organisations such as the Institut de Droit International and the World Economic Forum in Davos to regulate investment.

The Havana Charter of 1948

A Draft Convention on the Treatment of Foreign Investors was mooted in 1929 under the aegis of the League of Nations.[1] This Draft Convention, prepared by the Economic Committee of the League of Nations, was considered at the

---

[1] Text of the Draft Convention, League of Nations Doc No C.I.T.E.I.C36.M.21, 1992II; see also JW Cutler, 'The Treatment of Foreigners in Relation to the Draft Convention and Conference of 1929' (1933) 27 *American Journal of International Law* 255 and AK Kuhn, 'The International Conference on The Treatment of Foreigners' (1930) 24 *American Journal of International Law* 570.

1929 Paris International Conference on the Treatment of Foreign Nationals. It focused mainly on guaranteeing wide-ranging national treatment rights to foreign investors. However, states were divided in their views on a number of provisions, including those on compensation against expropriation. Consequently, the Draft Convention was not adopted as some countries objected to some of its provisions. Thus, most attempts at international regulation of foreign investment have only been made since the inception of the UN.

With the establishment of the UN, a new world order, both economic and political, was envisaged. While the UN was seen primarily as a political body, the World Bank and the International Monetary Fund (IMF) were established as financial and monetary institutions, respectively. Part of this grand vision for a new world order was the establishment of an international organisation dealing with international trade. Accordingly, a UN Conference on Trade and Employment was held at Havana, Cuba, between 21 November 1947 and 24 March 1948. However, the draft Havana Charter submitted to the Conference contained no provision on the regulation of foreign investment. One of the reasons for this deliberate omission seems to have been the fear on the part of the US that 'investment provisions negotiated at a multilateral conference might express the lowest common denominator of protection to which any of the participants would be willing to agree'.[2] Nevertheless, when a chapter on economic development was added to the initial draft Charter proposed by the US, a number of provisions making reference to foreign investment were included. Articles 11 and 12 of the Havana Charter[3] included the following provisions on investment:

Article 11

Means of Promoting Economic Development and Reconstruction

Progressive industrial and general economic development, as well as reconstruction, requires among other things adequate supplies of capital funds, materials, modern equipment and technology and technical and managerial skills. Accordingly, in order to stimulate and assist in the provision and exchange of these facilities:

...

(b) no Member shall take unreasonable or unjustifiable action within its territory injurious to the rights or interests of nationals of other Members in the enterprise, skills, capital, arts or technology which they have supplied.

Article 12

International Investment for Economic Development and Reconstruction

1.   The Members recognize that:

(a)   international investment, both public and private, can be of great value in promoting economic development and reconstruction, and consequent social progress;

---

[2] C Wilcox, *A Charter for World Trade* [1949] (New York, Arno Press, 1972) 145–46, as cited in AF Lowenfeld, *International Economic Law* (Oxford, Oxford University Press, 2002) 404.

[3] Interim Commission for the International Trade Organization, Final Act and Related Documents of the United Nations Conference on Trade and Employment, Havana, Cuba, E Conf 2/78, April 1948.

   (b)   the international flow of capital will be stimulated to the extent that members afford nationals of other countries opportunities for investment and security for existing and future investments;

   (c)   without prejudice to existing international agreements to which Members are parties, a Member has the right:

       (i)   to take any appropriate safeguards necessary to ensure that foreign investment is not used as a basis for interference in its internal affairs or national policies;

     (ii)   to determine whether and to what extent and upon what terms it will allow future foreign investment;

   (iii)   to prescribe and give effect on just terms to requirements as to the ownership of existing and future investments;

   (iv)   to prescribe and give effect to other reasonable requirements with respect to existing and future investments ...

2.   Members therefore undertake:

   ...

     (i)   to provide reasonable opportunities for investments acceptable to them and adequate security for existing and future investments, and

    (ii)   to give due regard to the desirability of avoiding discrimination as between foreign investments ...

According to Lowenfeld, a provision requiring Member States to make just compensation for property taken into public ownership, subject to various exceptions, was dropped from the final version as adopted at Havana.[4] In the end, the Charter itself never came into effect due, inter alia, to the US decision to abandon it in 1950. The states participating in the Havana Conference had decided, through Chapter VII of the Havana Charter, to establish an International Trade Organization (ITO) whose functions could have included making recommendations for and promoting bilateral and multilateral agreements on measures designed 'to assure just and equitable treatment for the enterprise, skills, capital, arts and technology brought from one Member country to another'.[5] However, the ITO never came into existence and the Charter remained a document of merely historical interest.

An attempt was made in 1959 by the major capital-exporting countries to adopt an international instrument on foreign investment known as the Abs–Shawcross Draft Convention on Investment Abroad to protect the interests of foreign investors. Described as the 'Charter' or 'Magna Carta' of private investors, this Draft Convention included stronger standards for protection for foreign investors, including a broader definition of expropriation and an investor-state dispute settlement (ISDS) mechanism. However, in the face of strong opposition from the capital-importing countries, this Draft Convention was not adopted. Although most of its provisions found their way once again into the 1967 Draft Convention on the Protection of Foreign Property proposed by the OECD, this too was not adopted and remained as a draft.[6]

---

[4] Lowenfeld (n 2) 405.

[5] Art 11(2)(a) Havana Charter.

[6] See G van Harten, *Investment Treaty Arbitration and Public Law* (Oxford, Oxford University Press, 2007) 20–21.

The UN Declaration on Permanent Sovereignty Over Natural Resources

One of the fundamental principles of the UN Charter is the sovereign equality of states, and it was the establishment of the UN that acted as a catalyst for independence movements in the colonial territories of Asia, Africa, the Caribbean and the South Pacific. As states gained political independence, their main priority was to assert economic independence. Gaining economic independence was a tricky task as many of the newly independent states had inherited an economic situation whereby their natural resources were controlled or exploited by foreign companies under concessions or other agreements concluded by the former colonial administration. Therefore, newly independent states sought to rely on the doctrine of economic sovereignty to claim permanent sovereignty over their natural resources; the goal being that once permanent sovereignty of states over their natural resources (PSNR) was acknowledged, sovereign states would be able to negotiate their way out of the old agreements and concessions.

While well-established principles such as the sanctity of contracts and *pacta sunt servanda* of the law of treaties required states to respect the sanctity of the existing agreements, an equally powerful doctrine of international law was evolving to allow states to take back control of their natural resources. To this end, the doctrine of PSNR was invoked by relying on one of the most powerful doctrines of international law: the sovereignty of states. This was not an attempt to rewrite the law completely, but an attempt to give a new direction to foreign investment law on the basis of certain rules of public international law, including economic sovereignty and the right to economic self-determination of states. Indeed, without achieving economic sovereignty, states would not be fully sovereign. Although the states could also invoke the right to expropriate the assets of foreign companies, this right was limited in scope, technical in character and subject to a number of conditions; it would not have allowed states to achieve full economic sovereignty vis-à-vis their natural resources. Rather, the idea was to strengthen and expand, inter alia, not only the right to expropriate the assets of foreign investment but also other rights of states flowing from the doctrine of sovereignty through the principle of PSNR.[7]

Thus, the attempt to articulate the notion that states had permanent sovereignty over their respective natural resources began within the UN at the behest of developing states. Again, it was the Latin American countries, such as Uruguay and Chile, that led the way in introducing the idea of PSNR onto the UN agenda. The first of such initiatives was a General Assembly resolution (Resolution 626 (VII) of 21 December 1952) that supported the concept of economic self-determination.

---

[7] MS Rajan, *Sovereignty over Natural Resources* (Atlantic Highlands, NJ, Humanities Press, 1978); N Schrijver, *Sovereignty over Natural Resources: Balancing Rights over Duties* (Cambridge, Cambridge University Press, 1997).

The notion was developed further when a draft article adopted by the Third Committee of the General Assembly in 1955 on the right of self-determination as part of the Human Rights Covenants sought to articulate the principle of PSNR in the second paragraph in the following words:

> The peoples may, for their own ends, freely dispose of their natural wealth and resources without prejudice to any obligations arising out of international economic co-operation, based upon the principle of mutual benefit, and international law. In no case may a people be deprived of its own means of subsistence.

In 1958, the Commission on Permanent Sovereignty over Natural Resources was established to consider the question of PSNR. As a result of the work done in this Commission, as well in the Economic and Social Council, the General Assembly adopted a resolution (Resolution 1803 (XVII)) on 14 December 1962 on the Permanent Sovereignty of States over their Natural Resources. The resolution provides, inter alia, that:

1. The right of peoples and nations to permanent sovereignty over their natural wealth and resources must be exercised in the interest of their national development and of the well-being of the people of the State concerned;
2. The exploration, development and disposition of such resources, as well as the import of the foreign capital required for these purposes, should be in conformity with the rules and conditions which the peoples and nations freely consider to be necessary or desirable with regard to the authorization, restriction or prohibition of such activities;
3. In cases where authorization is granted, the capital imported and the earnings on that capital shall be governed by the terms thereof, by the national legislation in force, and by international law. The profits derived must be shared in the proportions freely agreed upon, in each case, between the investors and the recipient State, due care being taken to ensure that there is no impairment, for any reason, of that State's sovereignty over its natural wealth and resources; and
4. Nationalization, expropriation or requisitioning shall be based on grounds or reasons of public utility, security, or the national interest which are recognized as overriding purely individual or private interests, both domestic and foreign. In such cases the owner shall be paid appropriate compensation, in accordance with the rules in force in the State taking such measures in the exercise of its sovereignty and in accordance with international law. In any case where the question of compensation gives rise to a controversy, the national jurisdiction of the State taking such measures shall be exhausted. However, upon agreement by sovereign States and other parties concerned, settlement of dispute should be made through arbitration or international adjudication.

Thus, this General Assembly resolution sought to strike a balance between the interests of both the host and the home countries by incorporating in one single instrument the issues of vital concern for both groups of states. For instance, when outlining principles applicable to the nationalisation or expropriation of foreign investment, the resolution conforms fully neither to the Hull formula nor to the Calvo doctrine; rather it contains elements of both of these approaches. While it seeks to limit the conditions under which nationalisation or expropriation can take place, it lists enough conditions to enable a country to embark upon nationalisation and expropriation when necessary. It speaks of appropriate compensation rather than prompt, adequate and effective compensation[8] and in accordance not only with the laws of the country concerned but also with international law.

Although the principle of PSNR represented an attempt to develop certain new rules in favour of developing countries on the basis of the extant and evolving rules of international economic law, it was accepted by the international community without much opposition from any quarter. Indeed, the UN General Assembly resolution to this effect has been regarded as a successful compromise between developed and developing countries and a statement of the law that is acceptable to both sides.

Thus, this UN General Assembly resolution enunciating the PSNR principle became the first international instrument to gain near-universal support for the notion that sovereign states had the right to expropriate the assets of foreign companies under certain conditions, which included appropriate compensation. While the PSNR resolution met the aspirations of the developing countries, it also embraced part of the Hull formula preferred by the developed countries. Consequently, it can be argued that this resolution remains to date the most widely accepted international instrument on foreign investment law and represents an articulation of customary international law principles on the subject matter.[9]

Attempts to Develop the Law Through the New International Economic Order

When the developing countries gained a numerical majority in the UN General Assembly, they sought to use the UN system to introduce fundamental reforms to the laws governing international economic relations among states. Encouraged and influenced by the oil crisis of the early 1970s, and disappointed at the lack of progress in addressing the issues of economic equality and prosperity for all, the developing countries introduced the agenda of a new international economic order (NIEO) within the UN; one of the items on the agenda was the regulation of foreign investment in a manner more favourable to developing countries.[10] Many developing countries were concerned about the rise of corporate power and its ability and willingness to intervene in their internal affairs, both in the pursuit of profit and to further the political agenda of their home countries during the Cold War.

---

[8] Nevertheless, the US made it clear that it understood 'appropriate compensation' as incorporating the 'international minimum standard' of the Hull formula (UN Doc A/C.2/SR.835, para 10). On the other end of the spectrum the following amendment to para 4 proposed by the USSR was defeated: 'The question of compensation to the owners shall in such cases be decided in accordance with the national law of the country taking these measures in the exercise of its sovereignty' (UN Doc A/C.2/L670).

[9] In *Texaco v Libya* the arbitrator held that the 1803 resolution reflects the state of customary international law existing in this field (1977) 53 ILR 389, para 87. See for similar views the *Aminoil* case, *Kuwait v American Independent Oil Co* (1976) 21 ILM, paras 143, 144 and the *Topco/Calasiatic* case (1978) 17 ILM 3.

[10] K Hossain (ed), *Legal Aspects of a New International Economic Order* (London, Frances Pinter, 1980); SR Chowdhury et al (eds), *The Right to Development in International Law* (Dordrecht, Martinus Nijhoff, 1992).

For example, the alleged involvement of a US multinational corporation in the overthrow of the elected Allende government in Chile, the installation of the military dictatorship led by Pinochet and the involvement of the US Central Intelligence Agency (CIA) in the overthrow of the Mossadegh government in Iran in the 1950s – following the expropriation of the Anglo-Iranian Oil Company – had alarmed many developing countries. There was a desire to go one step further from the PSNR resolution and strengthen the hands of developing countries by rewriting foreign investment law. Accordingly, the UN General Assembly adopted a Declaration on the Establishment of a New International Economic Order on 1 May 1974 through Resolution 3201 (S-VI) and a Programme of Action on the Implementation of the Declaration through Resolution 3202 (S-VI).[11]

Article 4 of the Declaration listed the principles on which the NIEO had to be founded, and one of these, included in Article 4(e), relates to the question of PSNR and the issue of expropriation and nationalisation. It recognised '[f]ull permanent sovereignty of every State over its natural resources and all economic activities', and went on to add that:

> In order to safeguard these resources, each State is entitled to exercise effective control over them and their exploitation with means suitable to its own situation, including the right to nationalization or transfer of ownership to its nationals, this right being an expression of the full permanent sovereignty of the State. No State may be subjected to economic, political or any other type of coercion to prevent the free and full exercise of this inalienable right.

The Declaration stressed the need to regulate and supervise the activities of transnational corporations (TNCs) by taking measures in the interest of the host countries. The Programme of Action adopted by the General Assembly for the Implementation of the NIEO Declaration called for the formulation of an 'international code of conduct for the transfer of technology corresponding to needs and conditions prevalent in developing countries'.[12] Article V of the Programme of Action went on to speak of regulation and control over the activities of TNCs in the following terms:

> All efforts should be made to formulate, adopt and implement an international code of conduct for transnational corporations:
>
> (a) To prevent interference in the internal affairs of the countries where they operate and their collaboration with racist regimes and colonial administrations;
>
> (b) To regulate their activities in host countries, to eliminate restrictive business practices and to conform to the national development plans and objectives of developing countries, and in this context facilitate, as necessary, the review and revision of previously concluded agreements;
>
> (c) To bring about assistance, transfer of technology and management skills to developing countries on equitable and favourable terms;

---

[11] See generally, Hossain (n 10); Schrijver (n 7).

[12] Art IV(a) of General Assembly Resolution 3202 (S-VI) of 1 May 1974. The terms 'TNC' and 'MNE' are used interchangeably in this book. However, the term 'TNC' is used in the context of the work of the UN in this area and the term 'MNE' elsewhere.

(d) To regulate the repatriation of the profits accruing from their operations, taking into account the legitimate interests of all parties concerned; and

(e) To promote reinvestment of their profits in developing countries.

As part of the drive to restructure the legal order for the world economy, the Charter of Economic Rights and Duties of States was adopted by the General Assembly on 12 December 1974, ie about six months after the adoption of the NIEO.

The 1974 Charter of Economic Rights and Duties of States

The Charter of Economic Rights and Duties of States is perhaps the most comprehensive international instrument outlining the economic rights and duties of states. However, it is not a 'hard law' instrument, as it was adopted through a resolution[13] of the General Assembly whose powers are limited to making recommendations under the Charter of the UN. Moreover, it was adopted by a vote of 120 in favour, 6 against[14] and 10 abstentions.[15] Thus, it is an instrument of limited legal significance.[16] Nevertheless, it was seen as an instrument with far-reaching practical implications by the vast majority of states who voted in favour of the resolution and has had a measure of influence in the development of international legal order since its adoption. Although adopted as part of the NIEO agenda, it has had an independent status and existence; its significance has not been diminished by its passing into history of the ideas that lay behind the NIEO itself.

With regard to foreign investment law, the relevant provision can be found in Article 2 of the Charter, which reads as follows:

Article 2

Every State has and shall freely exercise full permanent sovereignty, including possession, use and disposal, over all its wealth, natural resources and economic activities.

Each State has the right:

(a) To regulate and exercise authority over foreign investment within its national jurisdiction in accordance with its laws and regulations and in conformity with its national objectives and priorities. No State shall be compelled to grant preferential treatment to foreign investment;

---

[13] Resolution 3281 (XXIX) of 12 December 1974.

[14] Belgium, Denmark, the German Federal Republic, Luxembourg, the UK and the US voted against the resolution.

[15] Austria, Canada, France, Ireland, Israel, Italy, Japan, the Netherlands, Norway and Spain abstained from voting on the resolution.

[16] See B Weston, 'The Charter of Economic Rights and Duties of States and Deprivation of Foreign-Owned Wealth' (1981) 75 *American Journal of International Law* 437; CN Brouwer and JB Tape, 'The Charter of Economic Rights and Duties of States: A Reflection in Rejection of International Law' (1973) 9 *International Lawyer* 295; RCA White, 'A New International Economic Order' (1975) 24 *ICLQ* 542; SK Chatterjee, 'The Charter of Economic Rights and Duties of States: An Evaluation after 15 Years' (1991) 40 *ICLQ* 669.

(b) To regulate and supervise the activities of transnational corporations within its national jurisdiction and take measures to ensure that such activities comply with its laws, rules and regulations and conform with its economic and social policies. Transnational corporations shall not intervene in the internal affairs of a host State. Every State should, with full regard for its sovereign rights, co-operate with other States in the exercise of the right set forth in this sub-paragraph; and

(c) To nationalize, expropriate or transfer ownership of foreign property, in which case appropriate compensation should be paid by the State adopting such measures, taking into account its relevant laws and regulations and all circumstances that the State considers pertinent. In any case where the question of compensation gives rise to a controversy, it shall be settled under the domestic law of the nationalizing State and by its tribunals, unless it is freely and mutually agreed by all States concerned that other peaceful means be sought on the basis of the sovereign equality of States and in accordance with the principle of free choice of means.

These provisions are a reflection of the provisions of the NIEO resolution. Of particular note is that the above-cited provisions make no reference to international law, which is a break with the past and especially with the more balanced provisions of Resolution 1803 of 1962 on PSNR. In particular, the Charter does not require that any regulation of foreign investment, nationalisation or expropriation be in accordance with international law;[17] nor does it impose any conditions under which expropriation or nationalisation can take place.

The Charter takes the situation to a certain extent back to the era of the Calvo doctrine and rejects some of the core elements of the Hull formula. The emphasis is on the application of national law rather than on international law on issues concerning foreign investment and expropriation or nationalisation. This was one reason why many developed countries did not at the time support the Charter.

Nevertheless, the provisions in the Charter are not as radical as the approach taken by the Russians after the 1917 revolution or by the Mexicans during the agrarian expropriations, in which even the requirement to provide compensation to foreign investors who were affected by expropriations and nationalisation was contested. The Charter does require, as does the 1962 PSNR Declaration, the payment of appropriate compensation, despite being in accordance with national law rather than international law, to foreign investors affected by expropriation and nationalisation. However, the Charter departed to a certain extent from the 1962 PSNR declaration with regard to the standard of treatment of foreign investors and especially the provisions relating to expropriation and compensation.

---

[17] In *Texaco v Libya* the arbitrator was not prepared to accept that this provision of CERD reflected customary international law: 'Article 2 of this Charter must be analyzed as a political rather than as a legal declaration concerned with the ideological strategy of development, as such, supported only by non-industrialized States. ... The absence of any connection between the procedure of compensation and international law and subjection of this procedure solely to municipal law cannot be regarded by this Tribunal except as a *de lege ferenda* formulation, which even appears *contra legem* in the eyes of many developed countries. Similarly, several developing countries, although having voted favourably, on the Charter of Economic Rights and Duties of States as a whole, in explaining their votes regretted the absence of any reference to international law' ((1977) 52 ILR 389, para 88).

The UN Draft Code of Conduct for Transnational Corporations

The NIEO resolutions had called for the adoption of two codes of conduct – one on the transfer of technology and another on the regulation of TNCs. One of the achievements of the NIEO process was the establishment of the UN Commission on Transnational Corporations (CTC) in 1974 by the Economic and Social Council to consider proposals for the regulation of multinational enterprises.[18] The decision to establish the CTC was taken in the aftermath of the alleged involvement of a US TNC in the overthrow of the elected government in Chile with the tacit support of the US; high-profile corruption scandals such as the Lockheed affair; and a wave of nationalisation and expropriation in the developing world in the 1960s and 1970s. The activities of the CTC were linked to the efforts to realise the objectives of the NIEO.

Much of the debate throughout the 1970s and 1980s focused on the content of a code of conduct for TNCs and whether this code should be voluntary or mandatory.[19] When the CTC finally formulated a draft code of conduct for TNCs in 1988 it became clear that there remained so many areas of major disagreement among states that the CTC itself seemed resigned to the impossibility of adopting an internationally agreed code. Consequently, through a letter of 31 May 1990 to the President of the ECOSOC,[20] the Chairman of the reconvened special session of the CTC forwarded a draft code of conduct, stating that there remained numerous areas of disagreement among states.[21] With regard to the treatment of TNCs, the UN draft code provided that:

> States have the right to regulate the entry and establishment of transnational corporations including determining the role that such corporations may play in economic and social development and prohibiting or limiting the extent of their presence in specific sectors.[22]

The draft code went on to state that TNCs 'shall receive fair and equitable treatment in the countries in which they operate',[23] and that they should be entitled, with some exceptions designed to maintain public order and to protect national security and other legitimate interests, 'to treatment no less favourable than that accorded to domestic enterprises in similar circumstances'.[24] The provision of the Draft Code on expropriation and nationalisation reads as follows:

> It is acknowledged that States have the right to nationalize or expropriate the assets of a transnational corporation operating in their territories, and that adequate compensation

---

[18] ECOSOC Resolutions 1908 (LVII) of 2 August 1974 and 1913 (LVII) of 5 December 1974.

[19] See generally N Horn (ed), *Legal Problems of Codes of Conduct for Multinational Enterprises* (Deventer, Kluwer, 1980); S Dell, 'The United Nations Code of Conduct on Transnational Corporations', in J Kaufmann (ed), *Effective Negotiation: Case Studies in Conference Diplomacy* (Dordrecht, Kluwer, 1989) 53–74.

[20] UN Doc E/1990/94 of 12 June 1990.

[21] Ibid. See also UN Doc E/1988/39/Add.1.

[22] Ibid, para 48.

[23] Ibid, para 49.

[24] Ibid, para 50.

is to be paid by the State concerned, in accordance with the applicable legal rules and principles.[25]

With regard to the settlement of disputes, the Draft Code provided that they must be submitted to competent national courts or authorities.[26] Similarly, it went on to state that government action on behalf of a TNC operating in another country would be subject to the principle of exhaustion of local remedies provided in such a country.[27]

An Appraisal of the Efforts Made in the UN

The involvement of the UN in the codification and progressive development of foreign investment law and its attempts to adopt a code of conduct on TNCs came to an unsuccessful end in the early 1990s without the adoption of a comprehensive treaty on foreign investment law or a mandatory code of conduct for TNCs. After failing to generate an internationally agreed code of conduct, the CTC was disbanded in 1993, which signalled the end of UN efforts in this area. Although UNCTAD has carried out a number of worthy activities in the area of international investment regulation since then, so far as the attempt to adopt a binding international instrument on the subject is concerned nothing much came out of the efforts made within the UN in the 1980s and early 1990s. As demonstrated in the preceding paragraphs, the UN did make great strides during the 1950s–1980s in declaring and developing the norms applicable to foreign investment and the treatment of foreign investors through some 'soft-law' instruments. Throughout much of the 1970s, and until the mid-1980s, the debate continued within the UN on the ways and means of implementing the principles of the NIEO. However, nothing much could be achieved without the support of the leading developed countries who had opposed the adoption of the NIEO resolution. Since the UN was unable to come up with a final or definitive word on foreign investment law, the stage was left open for other actors. In particular, the World Bank, the OECD and the WTO tried to assert themselves as leaders in the development of foreign investment law.

It was mainly the developing countries that, in an effort to assert economic self-determination and full economic sovereignty, sought to rewrite the law on foreign investment under the auspices of the UN in the 1950s and early 1960s. Their efforts resulted in the adoption of certain fundamental and internationally accepted principles of international economic relations such as the PSNR. However, when the developing countries sought to go beyond the 1962 PSNR Declaration, the consensus reached between the developed and developing countries within the UN was broken and policies such as the NIEO were pursued within the UN mainly by developing countries. In the 1980s, much of the developing world went through a period of economic difficulty due to the failures of their – generally socialist – economic policies, and began to reverse their traditional attitude towards foreign investment, which

---

[25] Ibid, para 55.
[26] Ibid, para 57.
[27] Ibid, para 65.

was now seen as a solution to their economic problems. By the mid-1980s developing countries were competing with each other to attract foreign investment and offering unprecedented incentives to foreign investors rather than seeking tighter regulation on foreign investment.

In the face of the fierce competition for foreign investment, the disintegration of Third World solidarity, the chaos in the communist world that followed the collapse of communism in Europe and the fall of the Berlin Wall, there was no longer the appetite within the UN to push ahead with the adoption of an international instrument to regulate or control the activities of foreign investors. Thus, by the late 1980s the pendulum had begun to swing in the opposite direction, rendering the NIEO and the idea of regulating foreign investment in favour of host countries redundant. At this time, the idea was to offer TNCs or MNEs as many concessions as possible in order to attract foreign direct investment. Encouraged by these developments, the TNCs or MNEs began to demand greater protection for their overseas investments since they were now undertaking large-scale investments in countries with unstable political situations and needed as much protection as possible.

Traditional foreign investment law, referred to by some critics as 'Western' international foreign investment law,[28] came to be accepted as global law by the end of the twentieth century. The law, developed to protect capital and vigorously defended by Western governments, was embraced by almost all states. Many leading developing countries with socialist tendencies such as India and Zambia reversed their policies, as did former socialist states such as China and Vietnam. The Andean countries, known for their collective and rigid position on foreign investment policies, also reversed their position in the 1990s. Those states that had in the past gone down the road to the expropriation and nationalisation of foreign investment now accepted the practice that had evolved in favour of foreign investors in the 1990s through BITs concluded with investor countries and through other regional and international treaties. It was now extremely difficult for any state to resort to traditional methods of outright expropriation or nationalisation without opting out of the international economic legal order developed around the WTO and foreign investment law.

Similar to other political and economic upheavals, the disintegration of the Soviet Union and the emergence of the Commonwealth of Independent States (CIS) had the potential to pose challenges to foreign investment law; however, the triumphant Western countries intervened in such a way that they actually succeeded in securing much better protection for foreign investment from these countries than available hitherto under international law. The conclusion of the Energy Charter Treaty of 1994 is

---

[28] Eg, Huan Xiang, a former Chairman of the Chinese Society of International Law, stated the following: 'Principles and rules of international law since Hugo Grotius' time (in general) reflected the interests and demands of the bourgeoisie, the colonialists and in particular the imperialists. The big and strong powers have long been bullying the small and weak nations, sometimes even resorting to armed aggression. International law has often been used by the imperialists and hegemonists as a means to carry out aggression, oppression and exploitation and to further their reactionary foreign policies. Apologies for aggression and oppression can often be found in the writings on international law.' H Xiang, 'Strive to Build up New China's Science of International Law', in *Selected Articles from the Chinese Yearbook of International Law* (Beijing, 1983) 3, as cited in K Qingjiang, 'Bilateral Investment Treaties: The Chinese Approach and Practice' (2003) 8 *Asian Yearbook of International Law* 108.

an example of such Western success.[29] Taking advantage of the chaotic situation that followed the collapse of the Soviet Union, especially during the presidency of Boris Yeltsin, many individuals and national and international companies engaged in the practice of so-called 'asset grabbing' when the Russian Federation embarked on the road to privatisation of state companies and assets. After the collapse of the Soviet Union, most developing countries came to embrace the idea that foreign investment was a necessity for economic development, and good incentives, including legal protection and tax incentives, had to be offered to attract such investment. Thus, the 1990s can be seen as a 'rosy' or a roaring decade for TNCs or MNEs as foreign investment law was adjusted or modified to suit their needs and aspirations.

The Role of the World Bank

The World Bank, formally known as the International Bank for Reconstruction and Development (IBRD), has had a long-standing interest in promoting foreign investment for economic development and has associated itself with a number of initiatives in this area.[30] Among them is the Convention for the Settlement of Investment Disputes of 1965, the Convention Establishing the Multilateral Investment Guarantee Agency of 1985 (MIGA) and the Guidelines on the Treatment of Foreign Direct Investment of 1992.

International Convention on the Settlement of Investment Disputes

Foreign investors wish to have legal certainty when making investment decisions. One of those certainties is to have a credible mechanism for the settlement of investment disputes. The perceived wisdom is that if foreign private investors are assured that in the event of a dispute between them and the state in question the dispute can be referred to an independent international tribunal, they will view that state as a relatively safe place in which to invest. Foreign investors would generally be unwilling to invest in countries where the judiciary is not fully independent and the political situation is unstable. However, if the state in question has agreed through an international agreement to settle an investment dispute with potential foreign investors, such investors would be encouraged to invest in such states. Accordingly, with the goals of establishing an international centre for the settlement of investment disputes and

---

[29] TW Waelde, 'International Investment under the 1994 Energy Charter Treaty' (1995) 29(5) *Journal of World Trade* 5.
[30] IFI Shihata, *The World Bank in a Changing World: Selected Essays* (Dordrecht, Martinus Nijhoff, 1991).

encouraging states to refer investment disputes with foreign private investors to an international arbitration tribunal, ICSID[31] was concluded in 1965.

The idea of creating such a vehicle for settling investment disputes between private investors and host states was mooted in 1961 by Aaron Broches, then the General Counsel of the World Bank. This was an attempt to advance a more general debate initiated by the OECD in the late 1950s to promote and protect foreign investment.[32] Under ICSID, the Bank is the host of the International Centre for the Settlement of Investment Disputes, which is similar in many respects to other international arbitration centres. The very idea of submitting investment disputes to the Centre ran counter to the ideas behind the Calvo doctrine, and the NIEO, yet no state was obliged to become a party to the Convention or to submit any particular dispute to the Centre or to any conciliation or arbitration body. Rather, the Convention is designed to offer yet another platform for the settlement of investment disputes between a state party to the Convention and private foreign investors, should they wish to avail themselves of this opportunity.

Although an agreement to refer investment disputes to the Centre could be perceived as demonstrating a lack of confidence in the judiciary of the country concerned, the idea behind the Convention is to build confidence in private foreign investors and to provide a credible dispute settlement mechanism for such investors. Of course, states are free to agree to submit investment disputes to international commercial arbitration or other arbitration or conciliation centres, but by becoming a party to the Convention states would, as the perceived wisdom goes, stand a better chance of attracting foreign investment from those investors wary of losing their investment through expropriation, nationalisation or other government actions. Thus, the ratification of ICSID would serve as additional insurance or an assurance to potential investors that they would always have recourse to this independent dispute settlement mechanism should the government of a state undermine the property rights of the foreign investors. Under Article 25(1) the jurisdiction of the Centre would be as follows:

> The jurisdiction of the Centre shall extend to any legal dispute arising directly out of an investment, between a Contracting State (or any constituent subdivision or agency of a Contracting State designated to the Centre by that State) and a national of another Contracting State, which the parties to the dispute consent in writing to submit to the Centre. When the parties have given their consent, no party may withdraw its consent unilaterally.

According to Article 26, consent of the parties to arbitration under ICSID would normally be deemed consent to such arbitration as the sole remedy. Similarly, once a dispute is submitted to the ICSID Centre, diplomatic protection by a contracting state would also be ruled out. The provision in Article 42(1) is perhaps one of the most

---

[31] For a detailed commentary on the ICSID Convention, see CH Schreuer, *The ICSID Convention: A Commentary* (Cambridge, Cambridge University Press, 2001).

[32] This initiative of the OECD resulted in the preparation of a Draft Convention on the Protection of Foreign Property in 1962. However, this Draft Convention did not go much further because of differences of opinion as to the level or standard of compensation payable upon nationalisation or expropriation of foreign investments. See E Lauterpacht, 'Foreword' to Schreuer (n 31) xi.

important ones because this Article stipulates the law applicable to a dispute submitted to the arbitration tribunal of the ICSID Centre:

> The Tribunal shall decide a dispute in accordance with such rules of law as may be agreed by the parties. In the absence of such agreement, the Tribunal shall apply the law of the Contracting State party to the dispute (including its rules on the conflict of laws) and such rules of international law as may be applicable.

Thus, at a time when a vast majority of developing states were asserting within the UN that any dispute arising out of expropriation or nationalisation should be resolved by applying the national laws of the states concerned and by resorting to the local remedies provided for in the national laws and constitutions of the host states, it was quite a major departure from that position to agree to the provisions of ICSID just outlined. The adoption of ICSID under the auspices of the World Bank signalled that developments relating to foreign investment law could also take place outside of the UN framework. Having said this, it should be born in mind that there were a number of states, mainly from Latin America, which were opposed to the creation of the ICSID mechanism at the time of its adoption. In what became known as the 'Tokyo No', 19 Latin American states, including Argentina, Brazil and Mexico – traditional adherents to the Calvo doctrine – and other countries such as Iraq and the Philippines voted against the adoption of the ICSID Convention with its ISDS mechanism at the Tokyo annual meeting of the Board of Governors of the World Bank in 1964, which nevertheless went on to approve the Convention.[33]

The concerns expressed these days about ICSID range widely from structural issues to arbitration weaknesses. For instance, some of its key institutional flaws include its allegedly 'pro-investor' bias as an institution,[34] its umbilical cord with the World Bank,[35] a lack of transparency by arbitration panels, the high cost of arbitration that results from the consultation fees of extremely expensive international law firms,[36] inadequate attention paid by ICSID tribunals to the regulatory powers of states, lack

---

[33] ICSID, *History of the ICSID Convention: Documents Concerning the Origin and the Formulation of the Convention on the Settlement of Investment Disputes between States and Nationals of Other States* (Washington, DC, ICSID) vol II-1, 606–08.

[34] See R Broad, 'Corporate Bias in the World Bank Group's International Centre for Settlement of Investment Disputes: A Case Study of a Global Mining Corporation Suing El Salvador', School of International Service, American University, Washington DC, Working Paper Series, Paper No 2015-3, 25 March 2015.

[35] As alleged by the Ecuadorian Minister of Knowledge and Human Talent, Andres Arauz, 'The geopolitics of ICSID are intertwined with those of the Bretton Woods system because of the World Bank's power to determine the arbitrators. The President of the World Bank designates the arbitral tribunals' president when the parties' arbitrators do not agree on a common name. Likewise, and more gravely, the President of the World Bank designates the three members of the Annulment Committee (a sort of last recourse of an arbitration proceeding) after an award has been made. The President of the World Bank has always been a US citizen, and most commonly, a former high ranking US government official. The US has blocked World Bank loans to states that have ICSID awards pending. During all of ICSID's history, the US has not lost one case as a defendant. Thus, ICSID as a forum for investor-state dispute settlement in the context of the TTIP is dangerous even for European Union Member States.' A Arauz, 'Ecuador's Experience with International Investment Arbitration', *Investment Policy Brief*, no 5, August 2015, 1–2 (footnotes omitted).

[36] With contributions from T Amos and N Buxton, P Eberthardt and C Olivet, 'Profiting from Injustice: How Law Firms, Arbitrators and Financiers Are Fuelling an Investment Arbitration Boom', in H Burley (ed), (Brussels/Amsterdam, Corporate Europe Observatory and the Transnational Institute, 2012).

of diversity in the appointment of members of arbitration panels, and the absence of an appeals process and only a limited annulment procedure, and inconsistency in the awards of different tribunals consisting of three random arbitrators, who may not necessarily be well qualified to deal with the gravity of the matters before them, on very similar facts and issues. In addition, pundits have questioned the failure of many ICSID panels to take into account the need of states to take emergency financial and economic measures in the face of massive economic crises, the repeat appointment of the same arbitrators known for their 'pro-investor' approach to serve on arbitration panels, the failure of various panels to put international investment issues in a wider public international law context, and the inadequacy of the ICSID – as a mechanism designed initially to deal with commercial/contractual disputes of private law character – to adjudicate on big public law or public international law matters affecting the lives of hundreds of millions of people or involving millions or billions of dollars of public money paid in compensation to foreign investors against claims of dubious character against host states. Critics go on to argue that there is no equality of arms in ICSID proceedings as powerful multinational companies can spend huge fortunes against financially poor developing countries.

A 'Silent Revolution' in International Law?

The idea of allowing private companies, not subject to international law, direct access to an international dispute settlement mechanism created under ICSID was an innovative development in international law. It can be compared with the idea of individual petitions against human rights violations developed in the 1960s under the Optional Protocol to the International Covenant on Civil and Political Rights. Although host states can offer foreign investors the opportunity to take investment disputes to international tribunals under domestic legislation, and some countries have done this, it is uncommon for national legislation to do so.

The ISDS mechanism of ICSID[37] became a catalyst for the conclusion of a large number of BITs. It heralded a new era of investment dispute settlement and was a sort of silent revolution in international foreign investment law. This momentum received further impetus when the Iran–US Claims Tribunal was established in the early 1980s to entertain cases submitted by US nationals, companies and businesses that were adversely affected by the Islamic revolution in Iran in the late 1970s. Following the massive political and economic changes that took place towards the end of the 1980s and the early 1990s, and the subsequent expansion of globalisation in the marketplace, new standards and values in international relations came to occupy centre stage in the conduct of international economic relations. Old values and dogmas gave way to new ones, and even countries that had traditionally rejected the idea of allowing private companies direct access to international dispute settlement mechanisms, such

---

[37] See Schreuer (n 31).

as Argentina and Mexico, concluded BITs or joined RTAs that provided for such access.

Prominent among the bundle of protections granted to foreign investors by host states is the provision for ISDS mechanisms through an independent international arbitration, whether it is under ICSID, the ICSID Additional Facility, the UNCITRAL Arbitration Rules or other comparable arrangements. As stated by an ICSID tribunal in *Gas Natural SDG v the Argentine Republic*, such a provision

> offered to foreign investors assurances that disputes that might flow from their investments would not be subject to the perceived hazards of delays and political pressures of adjudication in national courts. Correspondingly, the prospect of international arbitration was designed to offer to host States freedom from political pressures by governments of the state of which the investor is a national.[38]

The ICSID tribunal went on to highlight the significance of international arbitration in the following words: 'We remain persuaded that assurance of independent international arbitration is an important – perhaps the most important – element in investor protection.'[39]

The silent revolution in foreign investment law that took place during the 1960s by way of ICSID and other BITs gained new momentum in the late 1990s and the early 2000s as foreign investors made the most of the revolution with the help of sophisticated lawyers, legal loopholes and lacunae in the BITs negotiated, often under pressure, by the IMF and the World Bank. Messy privatisation programmes managed by often incompetent and corrupt political leaders and government officials and unsound and faulty commercial contracts concluded by governments often under the influence of corrupt officials helped the momentum towards the consolidation of the ISDS mechanism. Innovative interpretations of BIT provisions by arbitrators mostly in favour of foreign investors and the demands placed on them by the globalisation of market forces accelerated the process of consolidation of the BIT regime. The silent revolution has been in full swing until recently largely for the benefit of the foreign investor often at the expense of the host states and other societal values.

However, despite its publicly inconspicuous proceedings, ICSID has come under pressure in the recent past. It is worth noting that when calling upon all Latin American countries to denounce ICSID, Bolivian President Evo Morales was reported to have said that '[We] emphatically reject the legal, media and diplomatic pressure of some multinationals that ... resist the sovereign rulings of countries, making threats and initiating suits in international arbitration.'[40] This suggested that there was a growing unease with the manner in which this silent revolution is delivering results. However, when subscribing to the agenda against the ICSID or other ISDS mechanisms, one should be mindful that by doing away with ISDS mechanism the world may witness the revival of gunboat diplomacy and investors may be back in the foreign ministries of the home countries to enlist help rather than knocking on the doors of international

---

[38] *Gas Natural SDG v The Argentine Republic*, ICSID Case No ARB/03/10, 17 June 2005, para 29.
[39] Ibid, para 49.
[40] As cited in the *Investment Treaty News*, 9 May 2007 (www.iisd.org/investment/itn), quoting a report published in the *Washington Post*.

investment tribunals. Institutions such as ICSID are needed and should be strengthened and not abolished or side-lined. Yet, they should be reformed to make them in tune with the changing expectations of states and other stakeholders of the contemporary world and that is what ICSID appears to be trying to accomplish with its reform agenda.

The Multilateral Investment Guarantee Agency

In addition to legal certainty, potential foreign investors wish to have some sort of additional guarantee of their investment when they invest in countries with a poor legal and physical infrastructure. Indeed, many developed countries have their own internal system of investment guarantee for those investing in developing countries, and investment risks can also be covered through private insurance. However, it was thought desirable to have an additional international system of investment guarantee against non-commercial risks, such as expropriation, nationalisation and other political risks, in order to promote foreign investment in general and private foreign investment in particular in developing countries. Similarly, although protection under BITs, international law principles relating to the treatment of foreign investment, and diplomatic channels were available to foreign investors, it was considered sensible to have an additional mechanism designed to alleviate concerns related to non-commercial risks in order to promote the flow of foreign investment to developing countries. Therefore, as a measure complementary to the existing national and regional investment guarantee programmes[41] and private insurers of non-commercial risks and supplementary to the activities of the World Bank Group, the Convention Establishing the Multilateral Investment Guarantee Agency (MIGA)[42] was adopted in 1985. Specifically, Article 2 of the Convention outlines the objectives and purposes of the Agency in the following terms:

> The objective of the Agency shall be to encourage the flow of investments for productive purposes among other member countries, and in particular to developing member countries, thus supplementing the activities of the International Bank for Reconstruction and Development (hereinafter referred to as the Bank), the International Finance Corporation and other international development finance institutions.
>
> To serve its objective, the Agency shall:
>
> (a) issue guarantees, including coinsurance and reinsurance, against non-commercial risks in respect of investments in a member country which flow from other member countries;

---

[41] Many developed countries have their own agencies to provide insurance coverage to their nationals who wish to invest abroad. For a list of such schemes, see A Akinsanya, 'International Protection of Direct Foreign Investment in the Third World' (1987) 36 *ICLQ* 67.

[42] Secretary-General, International Centre for Settlement of Investment Disputes, *MIGA and Foreign Investment: Origins, Operations, Policies and Basic Documents of the Multilateral Investment Guarantee Agency* (Dordrecht, Martinus Nijhoff, 1988).

(b) carry out appropriate complementary activities to promote the flow of investments to and among developing member countries; and

(c) exercise such other incidental powers as shall be necessary or desirable in the further-ance of its objective.

Article 11 of the Convention outlines the risks that may be covered by the guarantee of the Agency. The risks covered include problems associated with currency transfer, expropriation and similar measures; breach of contract; and war and civil distur-bance. The guarantee applies to foreign investment made in a developing country by a third-country national, whether natural or juridical, or whether from a developing or developed country.

The 1992 Guidelines of the World Bank

The promotion of foreign investment has long been an area of interest for the World Bank. It was joined by the MIGA whose constituent document states that it is supposed to carry out research, to undertake activities that promote investment flows, and to disseminate information on investment opportunities in developing member countries.[43] Accordingly, the Development Committee, a joint committee of the World Bank and the IMF, requested the MIGA in 1991 to prepare a 'legal frame-work' to promote foreign direct investment. In 1992, the Development Committee adopted a set of Guidelines on the Treatment of Foreign Direct Investment. Neither the Bank nor the IMF nor the MIGA has the competence to adopt any legally binding instrument for the international community or to modify the existing rules of inter-national law on matters such as the regulation of foreign investment. Nevertheless, the Guidelines adopted as a result of the work carried out under the auspices of these three important financial organisations do carry certain weight and thus merit examination.

In his foreword to the World Bank document containing the Guidelines, the then President of the Bank stated that the 'world community' was asking the World Bank Group to prepare 'universal standards' for the legal treatment of foreign direct invest-ment, but he did not make it clear to which world community he was referring. It seems to have been more a product of an internal process within these institutions rather than the 'world community' asking them to take such a role. The world community of states was then otherwise engaged and still struggling to come up with a code of conduct to this effect within the UN CTC. Rather, it was the joint committee of the World Bank and the IMF that asked the MIGA to undertake such a task. According to the 1985 Convention establishing the MIGA, this agency was supposed to work in the interest of developing countries by promoting foreign investment into these countries.

---

[43] Art 23 MIGA Convention.

However, as will be seen later, the Guidelines seem to have been adopted primarily to protect foreign investment. Indeed, according to Rubin:

> Since the 'Legal Framework' was prepared largely after the triumph of market over centrally guided economies, and is explicitly aimed at the *encouragement* of foreign direct investment (and incidentally portfolio investment), it reflects principles which ought to be welcomed by investors of capital or technology. The introduction to the Framework makes a bow in the direction of the developing countries which argued, in the 1970s and 1980s, that criteria had to be framed and agreed to ensure that the activities of transnational enterprises – and their investments – had to be controlled to prevent abuse of TNC power, and to bring them into line with the developmental objectives of 'host' nations – especially developing countries. That firmly held belief, reinforced by a series of scandals or alleged scandals involving transnational corporation activities, had led to general rejection of the 1967 OECD Draft Convention on the Protection of Foreign Property, which almost completely ignored these developing country convictions.[44]

The Report to the Development Committee prepared under the chairmanship of the Vice-President and General Counsel of the World Bank admitted that this report was designed to afford protection to foreign investors. The past efforts made within the UN and the OECD in the 1970s and 1980s were aimed at achieving a 'balance' between the interests of investors in protection and those of the hosts in 'responsible' conduct. However, the 1992 Report containing the Guidelines admits that the work reflected in this report differs from the task being undertaken since 1977 by the UN CTC: '[T]his report covers general principles suggested to guide governmental behaviour toward foreign investors; it does not include rules of good conduct on the part of the foreign investors.' In other words, the Guidelines address the conduct of states vis-à-vis foreign investors but not the conduct of foreign investors.

Although the General Counsel of the World Bank went to great lengths to justify the approach taken in the report, stating that the principles outlined in the Guidelines were consistent with the *emerging* rules of customary international law, the Guidelines went beyond settled rules of international law on the subject matter in many respects or extended the scope of the existing rules. The provision in Part IV of the Report on the question of expropriation is an example:

Expropriation and Unilateral Alterations or Termination of Contracts

1. A State may not expropriate or otherwise take in whole or in part a foreign private investment in its territory, or take measures which have similar effects, except where this is done in accordance with applicable legal procedures, in pursuance in good faith of a public purpose, without discrimination on the basis of nationality and against the payment of appropriate compensation.
2. Compensation for a specific investment taken by the State will, according to the details provided below, be deemed 'appropriate' if it is adequate, effective and prompt.
3. Compensation will be deemed 'adequate' if it is based on the fair market value of the taken asset as such value is determined immediately before the time at which the taking occurred or the decision to take the asset became publicly known.

---

[44] SJ Rubin, 'Introductory Note' to the 'World Bank: Report to the Development Committee and Guidelines on the Treatment of Foreign Direct Investment' (1992) 31 ILM 1363.

4.   Determination of the 'fair market value' will be acceptable if conducted according to a method agreed by the State and the foreign investor (hereinafter referred to as the parties) or by a tribunal or another body designated by the parties.

...

7.   Compensation will be deemed 'effective' if it is paid in the currency brought in by the investor where it remains convertible, in another currency designated as freely usable by the International Monetary Fund or in any other currency accepted by the investor.
8.   Compensation will be deemed to be 'prompt' in normal circumstances if paid without delay.[45]

Thus, this provision makes the definition of expropriation very wide and includes situations such as unilateral termination of contracts that would not have been deemed expropriation under traditional international law. The provision in the Guidelines was drawn mainly from BITs in existence at the time rather than being based on settled rules of international law. Indeed, the following passage in the report to the Development Committee is noteworthy:

> Many national investment codes, virtually all bilateral investment treaties and most pertinent multilateral instruments contain provisions to the effect that host States may expropriate foreign investments only if the takings are done in accordance with applicable legal procedures, for a public purpose and against payment of compensation. These provisions are typically broad enough to encompass partial as well as total expropriations of foreign investments. The provisions in the bilateral investment treaties and multilateral instruments also often explicitly cover not only outright expropriations but also measures, such as excessive and repetitive tax or regulatory measures, that have a *de facto* confiscatory effect in that their combined effect results in depriving the investor in fact from his ownership, control or substantial benefits over his enterprise, even when each such measure taken separately does not have this effect (so-called 'creeping expropriations').[46]

By the time the Guidelines were adopted it was clear that the UN CTC was highly unlikely to come up with a code of conduct for TNCs. Accordingly, the Guidelines should have included provisions not only on the conduct of states vis-à-vis foreign investors, but also on the conduct of foreign investors, rather than leaving the latter matter to the CTC. Since the CTC was unable, as predicted, to get TNCs to adopt an internationally agreed code of conduct and was eventually disbanded, the 1992 World Bank Guidelines remained as an international instrument, albeit an unbalanced one, of foreign investment law.

The WTO Agreements and Foreign Investment

The idea of regulating foreign investment as part of international trade was introduced during the WTO Uruguay round of multilateral trade negotiations. At the end

---

[45] (1992) 31 ILM 1363, 1383. See also Secretary-General, International Centre for Settlement of Investment Disputes, *Legal Treatment of Foreign Investment, The World Bank Guidelines* (Dordrecht, Martinus Nijhoff, 1993).
[46] (1992) 31 ILM 1363, 1375–76.

of the negotiations the Agreement on Trade-Related Investment Measures (TRIMS) was concluded. The Agreement deals with certain trade-related aspects of foreign investment. The main objective of this Agreement was to improve economic efficiency. It forbids WTO members from applying any TRIM that is inconsistent with the principle of national treatment to be found in the General Agreement on Tariffs and Trade (GATT) Article III and with the provision concerning prohibition of quantitative restrictions in GATT Article XI. It prohibits governments from requiring foreign investors to purchase inputs locally or to sell their output domestically rather than exporting it. In other words, the TRIMS Agreement forbids states from taking measures that circumvent the principle of national treatment or the ban on quantitative measures. An Annex to the TRIMS Agreement outlines the obligations of WTO members as follows:

1. TRIMs that are inconsistent with the obligation of national treatment provided for in paragraph 4 of the Article III of GATT 1994 include those which are mandatory or enforceable under domestic law or administrative rulings, or compliance with which is necessary to obtain an advantage, and which require:

    (a) the purchase or use by an enterprise of products of domestic origin or from any domestic source, whether specified in terms of particular products, in terms of volume of value products, or in terms of a proportion of volume or value of its local production; or

    (b) that an enterprise's purchases or use of imported products be limited to an amount related to the volume or value of local products that it exports.

2. TRIMs that are inconsistent with the obligation of general elimination of quantitative restrictions provided for in paragraph 1 of Article XI of GATT 1994 include those which are mandatory or enforceable under domestic law or under administrative rulings, or compliance with which is necessary to obtain an advantage, and which restrict:

    (a) the importation by an enterprise of products used in or related to its local production, generally or to an amount related to the volume or value of local production that it exports;

    (b) the importation by an enterprise of products used in or related to its local production by restricting its access to foreign exchange to an amount related to the foreign exchange inflows attributable to the enterprise; or

    (c) the exportation or sale for export by an enterprise of products, whether specified in terms of particular products, in terms of volume or value of products, or in terms of a proportion of volume or value if its local production.[47]

As can be seen from the provisions just outlined, the TRIMS Agreement is a fairly technical agreement of narrow scope, the application of whose provisions are limited to trade in goods. Nevertheless, it is designed to promote foreign investment across international frontiers by eliminating certain trade-related barriers to such investment. The US desired the removal of TRIMs as they were both restrictive and obstructive to

---

[47] World Trade Organization, *The Legal Texts: The Results of the Uruguay Round of Multilateral Trade Negotiations* (Cambridge, Cambridge University Press, 1999) 143–46, 146.

trade and the development of the global economy. It also sought freedom for foreign investors to hire nationals of their choice in key management positions.

The view held by developing countries was that the right to permit foreign invest-ment and its regulation was an internal matter and therefore did not fall within the scope of GATT. Basically, the argument was that GATT was not the appropriate forum for the discussion of investment policy issues. The counter-argument was that the restrictions imposed on the capacity of foreign companies to invest locally were a matter of concern for international trade law. This latter argument prevailed and the TRIMs were adopted, paving the way for further regulation of foreign investment under the auspices of the WTO in the future, rather than under the auspices of the UN Conference on Trade and Development (UNCTAD), as preferred by developing countries.

Only a few cases referred to the WTO's Dispute Settlement Body (DSB) have dealt with foreign investment matters. Moreover, since the scope of the DSB is limited to interpreting the provisions of the TRIMS Agreement, the WTO cases, unlike the ICSID cases, do not deal with traditional issues relating to foreign investment. For instance, the case of *Certain Measures Affecting the Automobile Industry*,[48] referred to the DSB, concerned the compatibility of Indonesian local content requirements for the automobile industry with Indonesia's TRIMS obligations. The TRIMS Agreement is about freedom for foreign investors in a WTO member country. When the EU and the US challenged the Indonesian measures, the WTO Panel held that these measures were not consistent with Indonesia's obligations under the TRIMS Agreement.

There are other WTO agreements such as the General Agreement on Trade in Services (GATS), the Agreement on Trade-related Aspects of Intellectual Property Rights (TRIPS) and the plurilateral Agreement on Government Procurement which include provisions relating to the entry and treatment of foreign investors and the protection of their intellectual property rights. GATS deals with foreign investment issues by defining four modes of supply. One of these consists of the provision of services through an established presence in a foreign country, referred to as a 'commer-cial presence' in the Agreement. Under the most-favoured nation (MFN) rule of GATS, WTO members are committed to treating services and service providers from one member country in the same way as services and service providers from any other member country.

With regard to the relevance of the TRIPS Agreement to foreign investment, it relates to the share of TNC assets accounted for by tangible assets, such as brands, patents, trademarks, etc. These assets of TNCs are protected by the TRIPS Agreement in the same manner as any other intellectual property belonging to other entities, or to the creators, owners or innovators of such property. The plurilateral Agreement on Government Procurement requires that there can be no discrimination against foreign products and foreign suppliers or against locally established suppliers on the basis of their degree of foreign affiliation or ownership.

---

[48] WT/DS44/R, Panel Report adopted by the DSB on 23 July 1998.

The OECD Guidelines and the Multilateral Agreement on Investment

The OECD has been involved in the development of both draft conventions and guidelines on foreign investment since the 1950s. When the newly independent developing countries were gaining a majority within the UN and driving the UN agenda to further their own interests, the industrialised countries sought to adopt their own instrument of foreign investment law. The first attempt by the OECD to adopt a Convention on the Protection of Private Property was launched in the late 1950s. It resulted in a Draft Convention on the Protection of Foreign Property in 1962.

However, this Draft Convention did not go much further because of the differences of opinion among states on a number of issues, including the level or standards of compensation payable upon the nationalisation or expropriation of foreign investment. The attempt made by the OECD in 1967 also failed because it ignored the concerns of developing countries and the developments that were taking place within the UN. Nearly a decade later when the agenda of the NIEO and a code of conduct for the TNCs were high on the UN agenda, the OECD adopted its own voluntary code of conduct. The 1976 Declaration of the OECD on International Investment and Multinational Enterprises includes Guidelines for Multilateral Enterprises. Dissatisfied with this voluntary code of conduct and encouraged by the 1992 Guidelines of the Joint Development Committee of the World Bank and the IMF, the OECD sought once again to conclude a Multilateral Agreement on Investment (MAI)[49] in 1998.

An OECD report on the MAI stated that the Agreement was 'needed to respond to the dramatic growth and transformation of foreign direct investment (FDI) which has been spurred by widespread liberalization and increasing competition for investment capital'. It went on to state that:

> A multilateral agreement on investment would provide a strong and comprehensive framework for international investment and would strengthen the multilateral trading regime. It would set clear, consistent and transparent rules on liberalisation and investor protection, with dispute settlement, thereby underpinning the continued removal of barriers to market access and encouraging economic growth. ... The MAI would provide a benchmark against which potential investors would assess the openness and legal security offered by countries as investment locations. This would, in turn, act as a spur to further liberalisation.[50]

In making a case for an MAI the report made it clear that:

> Growth in FDI has been underpinned by widespread liberalisation which has swept away many formal governmental restrictions on investment and severely curtailed others.

---

[49] See WH Witherell, 'The OECD Multilateral Agreement on Investment' (1995) 4(2) *Transnational Corporations* 1.

[50] Report by the OECD Committee on International Investment and Multinational Enterprises (CIME) and the Committee on Capital Movements and Invisible Transactions (CMIT) on the MAI: DAFFE/CMIT/CIME (95)13/Final, 5 May 1995, 1.

Remaining restrictions are a source of friction not least because they are widely perceived as barriers to market access.[51]

The aim of the proposed Agreement was to ensure that the liberalisation obligations of states were complemented by provisions on investment protection and reinforced by effective dispute settlement procedures. The goal of the MAI was to 'set high standards for the treatment and protection of investment' and to 'go beyond existing commitments to achieve a high standard of liberalisation'.[52] Accordingly, Article III of the draft MAI contained the following provisions with regard to the treatment of investors and investments:

1. Each Contracting Party shall accord to investors of another Contracting party and to their investments, treatment no less favourable than the treatment it accords [in like circumstances] to its own investors and their investments with respect to the establishment, acquisition, expansion, operation, management, maintenance, use, enjoyment and sale or other disposition of investments.

2. Each Contracting Party shall accord to investors of another Contracting Party and to their investments, treatment no less favourable than the treatment it accords [in like circumstances] to investors of any other Contracting party or of a non-Contracting Party, with respect to the establishment, acquisition, expansion, operation, management, maintenance, use, enjoyment and sale or other disposition of investments.[53]

On the protection of investment, draft Article IV made a very strong provision in favour of foreign investors:

1. General Treatment

Each Contracting Party shall accord to investments in its territory of investors of another Contracting Party fair and equitable treatment and full and constant protection and security. In no case shall a Contracting Party accord treatment less favourable than that required by international law.

1.2 A Contracting Party shall not impair by [unreasonable or discriminatory] [unreasonable and discriminatory] measures the operation, management, maintenance, use, enjoyment or disposal of investments in its territory of investors of another Contracting Party.

2. Expropriation and compensation

2.1 A Contracting Party shall not expropriate or nationalise directly or indirectly an investment in its territory of an investor of another Contracting Party or take any measure or measures having equivalent effect (hereinafter referred to as 'expropriation') except:

(a) for a purpose which is in the public interest,
(b) on a non-discriminatory basis,
(c) in accordance with due process of law, and
(d) accompanied by payment of prompt, adequate and effective compensation in accordance with Articles 2.2 and 2.5 below.

2.2 Compensation shall be paid without delay.

2.3 Compensation shall be equivalent to the fair market value of the expropriated investment immediately before the expropriation occurred. The fair market value shall not reflect

---

[51] Ibid, 1–2.
[52] Ibid, 2.
[53] DAFEE/MAI (98)7/REV1 of the OECD, 22 April 1998, 13 (footnotes omitted).

any change in value occurring because the expropriation had become publicly known earlier.

2.4 Compensation shall be fully realisable and freely transferable.[54]

Thus, the MAI contained provisions much stronger than those contained in the 1992 World Bank guidelines in favour of foreign investors, yet stipulated little in terms of the conduct of foreign investors themselves. The deliberate omission of the Joint Development Committee of the World Bank and the IMF in 1992 was repeated by the OECD. This led critics to describe the draft MAI of the OECD as a 'Global Bill of Rights' for foreign investors.[55] It was seen in some quarters as an instrument 'based largely on the assumption that capital has little or no social obligation in the new global economy'.[56] It was argued that virtually all the 'rights' were given to foreign based corporations while the 'obligations' were imposed on host governments. The draft MAI was criticised as being an attempt to allow TNCs to regulate states, rather than the reverse. Consequently, the OECD had to abandon the draft MAI and adopt a revised set of guidelines in the form of a 'soft law' instrument in 2000.[57]

The new OECD Guidelines were more balanced than the draft MAI; they included, inter alia, provisions recommending TNCs to take measures designed to promote sustainable development, protect the environment, and respect human rights. When outlining the concepts and principles, the Guidelines state that:

> Governments have the right to prescribe the conditions under which multinational enterprises operate within their jurisdictions, subject to international law. The entities of a multinational enterprise located in various countries are subject to the laws applicable in these countries.[58]

The Guidelines also stated that enterprises should, inter alia, take fully into account established policies in the countries in which they operate, and should furthermore consider the views of other stakeholders; contribute to economic, social and environmental progress with goal of achieving sustainable development; respect the human rights of those affected by their activities consistent with the host government's international obligations and commitments; and abstain from any improper involvement in local political activities.[59]

Although the guidelines such as those adopted by the OECD have no legally binding effect, they do carry significant weight in developing international investment law. For instance, in August 2008, the United Kingdom's National Contact Point (UK-NCP) issued its decision on *Global Witness v Afrimex Ltd* in which Global Witness had alleged that Afrimex, a British corporation, had violated the OECD's guidelines by

---

[54] Ibid, 56–57 (footnotes omitted).

[55] Eg, see a summary of the debate in the Commission on Sustainable Development in (1998) 28(3–4) *Environmental Policy and Law* 129.

[56] Ibid.

[57] After failing in its attempt to adopt a legally binding MAI, the OECD adopted a set of revised guidelines for MNEs in 2000. See the OECD Guidelines for Multinational Enterprises of 27 June 2000 in www.oecd.org/daf/investment/guidelines/mnetext.htm; (2000) 40 ILM 237. The old OECD Guidelines can be found in, *The OECD Guidelines for Multinational Enterprises* (Paris, OECD, 1997).

[58] (2000) 40 ILM 237, 239.

[59] Ibid, 240.

paying bribes to a rebel group in the Democratic Republic of the Congo (DRC) and purchasing minerals from mines in the DRC that were alleged to have employed child and forced labour. In its decision, the UK-NCP agreed with Global Witness and found Afrimex in violation of the OECD guidelines.

The 2011 OECD Guidelines

The new OECD Guidelines for Multinational Enterprises[60] are recommendations for responsible business conduct that 43 adhering governments encourage their enterprises to observe wherever they operate. The Guidelines were updated in 2011 for the fifth time since they were first adopted in 1976. They provide non-binding principles and standards for responsible business conduct in a global context consistent with applicable laws and internationally recognised standards. The updated Guidelines and the related Decision were adopted by the 43 adhering governments on 25 May 2011 at the OECD's 50th Anniversary Ministerial Meeting. According to the OECD, changes to the Guidelines include:

(i) a new human rights chapter, which is consistent with the Guiding Principles on Business and Human Rights: Implementing the United Nations 'Protect, Respect and Remedy' Framework;

(ii) a new and comprehensive approach to due diligence and responsible supply chain management representing significant progress relative to earlier approaches;

(iii) important changes in many specialised chapters, such as on Employment and Industrial Relations; Combating Bribery, Bribe Solicitation and Extortion, Environment, Consumer Interests, Disclosure and Taxation;

(iv) clearer and reinforced procedural guidance to strengthen the role of the NCPs, improve their performance and foster functional equivalence; and

(v) a proactive implementation agenda to assist enterprises in meeting their responsibilities as new challenges arise.

The International Labour Organization's Guidelines

The momentum in the 1970s towards the adoption of guidelines or codes of conduct for TNCs or multinational enterprises (MNEs) led the International Labour Organization (ILO) to adopt its own Tripartite Declaration of Principles concerning Multinational Enterprises and Social Policy in 1977 ('the MNE Declaration'), amended in 2000. The original MNE Declaration and its amendments[61] were drafted and negotiated

---

[60] Co-operation Organisation for Economic and Development, 'Annual Report on the OECD Guidelines for Multinational Enterprises 2011: A New Agenda for the Future', http://site.ebrary.com/id/1055923.

[61] (2002) 41 ILM 184.

by consensus with the Governing Body, the executive organ of the ILO consisting of 56 persons representing the tripartite constituents of the ILO: 28 governments, 14 employers and 14 workers.

The non-binding Declaration offers guidelines to MNEs, governments, and workers' and employers' organisations in areas relating to employment, training, working and living conditions, and industrial relations. Many of the principles of the ILO's MNE Declaration are reflected in the revised Guidelines of the OECD. While the OECD's Guidelines remain as guidelines, the provisions of the ILO's MNE Declaration have been reinforced by certain legally binding international labour conventions and recommendations.

Other Voluntary Schemes

In addition to the voluntary guidelines and declarations of the ILO and the OECD, there have been a number of other private and public initiatives taken to regulate foreign investment or the activities of foreign investors, mainly TNCs. One of the more prominent of such initiatives is the UN Global Compact. This is a voluntary corporate citizenship initiative of the UN Secretary-General designed to bring together large companies, civil society organisations and various UN agencies to support ten principles derived from key international instruments in the areas of human rights, workers rights, the environment and anti-corruption. These ten principles are as follows:

Human Rights

Principle 1: Businesses should support and respect the protection of internationally proclaimed human rights; and

Principle 2: make sure that they are not complicit in human rights abuses.

Labour Standards

Principle 3: Businesses should uphold the freedom of association and the effective recognition of the right to collective bargaining;

Principle 4: the elimination of all forms of forced and compulsory labour;

Principle 5: the effective abolition of child labour; and

Principle 6: the elimination of discrimination in respect of employment and occupation.

Environment

Principle 7: Businesses should support a precautionary approach to environmental challenges;

Principle 8: undertake initiatives to promote greater environmental responsibility; and

Principle 9: encourage the development and diffusion of environmentally friendly technologies.

Anti-corruption

Principle 10: Businesses should work against all forms of corruption, including extortion and bribery.

Since these broad and general principles enjoy near-universal consensus, the UN Global Compact asks companies to embrace, support and enact, within their sphere of influence, these core values of corporate social responsibility and corporate governance. Campaigns in favour of the environment and human rights launched by various corporate social responsibility or corporate social governance organisations seem to have produced a certain impact even in the typically conservative area of commercial law. Since a company is treated as a legal entity with corresponding rights, it should also have responsibilities and duties towards others, including the society in which it conducts its business.[62] Hence, there is a growing pressure to hold companies accountable for human rights violations and degradation of the environment, and to specify in the duties of company directors a duty to respect societal values, including human rights and sustainable development.

The inclusion in the UK Companies Act 2006 of a duty to pay attention to the environment in the list of company directors' duties is an example of this trend.[63] Directors of UK companies now have a duty not only to maximise profits but also to consider the impact of their business operations on the community and the environment.[64] Although this seems to be the first time that such responsibilities have been written in national company law, the trend set by the UK is likely to have a measurable influence on the company laws of other countries. The Companies Act 2006 also puts in place a link between the reporting requirements and the directors' duties. This would make it clearer that the reports must show how directors are performing regarding their duties to society and the environment. This is quite a novelty and a remarkable trend in incorporating some elements of corporate social responsibility and corporate social governance.[65]

---

[62] See D Pelsch, 'Companies Want Power without Responsibility', *Financial Times*, 24 August 2004, 17.

[63] See 'Company Bill "First Step" of Reforms' and 'Company Law: Green and Business Lobbies Gear Up for Final Battle over Bill', *Financial Times*, 26 September 2006, 1 and 4, respectively.

[64] Clause 172 of this new Act provides as follows:

Duty to promote the success of the company

(1) A director of a company must act in the way he considers, in good faith, would be most likely to promote the success of the company for the benefit of its members as a whole, and in doing so have regard (amongst other matters) to—

    (a) the likely consequences of any decision in the long term,
    (b) the interests of the company's employees,
    (c) the need to foster the company's business relationships with suppliers, customers and others,
    (d) the impact of the company's operations on the community and the environment,
    (e) the desirability of the company maintaining a reputation for high standards of business conduct, and
    (f) the need to act fairly as between members of the company.

(2) Where or to the extent that the purposes of the company consist of or include purposes other than the benefit of its members, subsection (1) has effect as if the reference to promoting the success of the company for the benefit of its members were to achieving those purposes.

(3) The duty imposed by this section has effect subject to any enactment or rule of law requiring directors, in certain circumstances, to consider or act in the interests of creditors of the company.'

[65] See generally A Clapham, *Human Rights Obligations of Non-State Actors* (Oxford, Oxford University Press, 2006); O de Schutter (ed), *Transnational Corporations and Human Rights* (Oxford, Hart Publishing, 2006); P Alston (ed), *Non-State Actors and Human Rights* (Oxford, Oxford University Press, 2005); H Ward,

Examples of other voluntary schemes designed to promote corporate social responsibility and corporate social governance include the following:[66]

1. the Business Leaders' Initiative for Human Rights (BLIHR), which brought together ten companies to explore the ways in which human rights standards and principles can inform issues of corporate responsibility and corporate governance;

2. the Global Reporting Initiative (GRI), which was initiated in 1997 by the Coalition for Environmentally Responsible Economies (CERES), has become an official collaborating centre of the United Nations Environmental Programme (UNEP) and is designed to enable business organisations to measure and report a balanced and reasonable representation of their sustainability performance and to develop and disseminate globally applicable Sustainability Reporting Guidelines;

3. the Growing Sustainable Business (GSB) of the United Nations Development Programme (UNDP), which is designed to engage MNEs in the delivery of the Millennium Development Goals (MDGs) by facilitating the development of commercially sustainable 'bottom of the pyramid' business models that have a direct impact on the lives of the poor;

4. Voluntary Principles on Security and Human Rights for the Extractive and Energy Sectors, which were developed by the governments of the UK and the US and non-governmental organisations (NGOs) working with companies in the extractive and energy sectors;

5. Worldwide Responsible Apparel Production (WRAP), which is a certification programme requiring clothing manufacturers to comply with 12 basic principles concerning good practices in workplace relations;

6. Amnesty International's 1998 Human Rights Guidelines for Companies;

7. the Equator Principles under which the International Finance Corporation (IFC) in Washington, DC, and ten leading international banks agreed in June 2003 to use clear, responsible and consistent rules for environmental and social risk management in project finance lending;[67]

8. the UK government-led Extractive Industries Transparency Initiative (EITI), which was designed to bring together major extractive businesses and host and donor governments in a bid to improve public and private transparency about revenues paid to governments for natural resources concessions;

'Corporate Accountability in Search of Treaty? Some Insights from Foreign Direct Liability', Briefing Paper No 4, May 2002, Sustainable Development Programme of the Royal Institute of International Affairs, London.

[66] See generally on corporate social responsibility, F Calder and M Culverwell, 'Following Up the World Summit on Sustainable Development Commitments on Corporate Social Responsibility: Options for Action by Governments', Final Report of the Sustainable Development Programme of the Royal Institute of International Affairs (London, Chatham House, 2005) and United Nations Conference on Trade and Development, *Social Responsibility*, UNCTAD Series on Issues in International Investment Agreements (New York, United Nations, 2001); JA Zerk, *Multinationals and Corporate Social Responsibility: Limitations and Opportunities in International Law* (Cambridge Studies in International and Comparative Law, Cambridge University Press, 2006).

[67] The number of banks signing up to this voluntary private sector initiative has been growing. See www.equator-principles.com/ga1.shtml (accessed 15 November 2005).

9. the Kimberley Process Certification Scheme, which was adopted by 36 states and the European Union in 2002 with a view to putting an end to trade in 'conflict diamonds';
10. the Global Sullivan Principles, which were developed as a voluntary code of conduct for companies conducting business in apartheid-era South Africa towards adhering to the objectives of human rights, social justice and economic opportunity;
11. the Caux Roundtable Principles for Business, which were developed in 1994 by a network of business leaders to express a standard to measure business behaviour;
12. the Goldman Sachs Energy Environmental and Social Index, which was designed for the oil and gas industry to identify specific environmental and social issues likely to be material to a company's competitiveness and reputation.[68]

There is a plethora of other such voluntary schemes such as ISO 26000, ICMM Sustainable Development Framework, Towards Sustainable Mining (TSM), PDAC E3 Plus, AA1000 Series, Trace (Anti-Bribery Compliance, Tools, Support, Standards), APEC Codes of Conduct, Mexico City Principles for Voluntary Codes of Business Ethics in the Biopharmaceutical Sector, and the Hanoi Principles for Voluntary Codes of Business Ethics in the Construction and Engineering Sector.

It is difficult to assess the effectiveness of such voluntary and self-regulatory codes of conduct since there are virtually no credible monitoring mechanisms. While some companies such as Nestlé are reported to have disciplined managers for breaching its own regulatory code of conduct,[69] many other companies seem to do little to enforce such codes of conduct.[70] Individual states have also attempted to devise voluntary mechanisms that encourage industry or TNCs to switch their methods of production, packaging and distribution to more environmentally friendly technologies or methods. An example of this is the eco-labelling scheme whereby on the basis of a so-called 'cradle-to-grave' lifecycle analysis of the impact of a product on the environment that product could be awarded an eco-logo by a government agency to enable companies to market their products as environmentally friendly. This idea started in Germany in the late 1970s and has been emulated by some 32 countries and the EU. The German, the EU and many other national schemes were official schemes and had some measurable impact on TNCs and industry. However, when the private sector instituted its own range of eco-logo schemes, without much credible scientific or governmental scrutiny, the impact or usefulness of the whole eco-logo scheme diminished sharply.[71]

---

[68] For a detailed list of most of such voluntary and informal schemes, see Report of the UN High Commissioner on Human Rights on the Responsibilities of Transnational Corporations and related Business Enterprises with regard to Human Rights, UN Doc E/CN.4/2005/91, 15 February 2005, Annex II, 24–28. See also 'Corporate Social Responsibility and International law', in International Law Association, *Report of the Seventy-First Conference, Berlin, 2004* (London, ILA, 2004) 422–40.

[69] See an interview with the head of Nestlé, Peter Brabeck, in 'Swiss Cash Cow in Search of Richer Pastures', *Financial Times*, 8 April 2002, 12.

[70] For a survey in this regard, see 'The Good Company: A Survey of Corporate Social Responsibility' published as a special supplement by *The Economist*, 22 January 2005.

[71] See SP Subedi, 'Balancing International Trade with Environmental Protection: International Legal Aspects of Eco-labels' (1999) 25 *Brooklyn Journal of International Law* 373.

An Inconclusive End to the Twentieth Century in Foreign Investment Regulation

During the formative years of foreign investment law the notion of *laissez-faire* provided the philosophical underpinning for this area of law. This traditional notion gradually gave way to the neoliberal concept of regulating foreign investment in order to achieve the higher goals of humanity. Consequently, foreign investment law became part of the attempt to create a global order supported by international law, but this attempt gave rise in due course to a divided world where the interests of developed and developing countries conflicted. When the developed world won the argument in the late 1980s and early 1990s, foreign investors wanted to have the best of both worlds. In other words, foreign investors wished to enjoy both the freedom offered by the *laissez-faire* approach and the protection afforded by regulation through BITs and other IIAs.

The current approach seems to offer foreign investors a high level of freedom in terms of their investment decisions while asking host countries to enact foreign investment laws that provide a high level of state protection. Much of the law in existence today can be regarded as pro-investment rather than imposing corresponding duties and responsibilities on foreign investors, who are accorded a very high level of protection.

Today, just as during the industrial revolution, there is a global movement of people and capital, and investors and investor countries are now seeking ever-greater protection for all forms of investment, including capital, technology, services, know-how, licensing, etc. The law that is taking shape at present is also seeking to protect foreign investment against non-commercial risks. The law is seeking to safeguard foreign investment not only from traditional forms of political risk, but also from other forms of risk, including civil strife, war, and perhaps terrorist attacks against foreign companies and their investments. The trend in the late 1980s and much of the 1990s, supported by jurisprudence, BITs, RTAs and FTAs, was to accord maximum protection to foreign investors even if this was at the expense of other societal values and other competing principles of international law.

Thus, as far as the regulation of foreign investment is concerned, the last century ended on mixed results and with no treaty on foreign investment. When the new millennium dawned, there was an increased awareness of the need for a more balanced system. Consequently, the Ministerial Declaration of the WTO adopted at the end of the Doha Conference in November 2001 included investment on the agenda of this world trade body.

The Efforts Made at the Dawn of the Twenty-First Century

With the beginning of the twenty-first century, new attempts were made to regulate foreign investment. After the failures of the World Bank, the IMF, the OECD and the UN CTC to formulate a balanced and comprehensive set of standards on foreign investment, efforts were made by the EU, with the support of the US, at the Doha Ministerial Conference in November 2001 to put the issue of regulating foreign invest-ment on the world trade agenda. The approach pursued by the EU was a measured one and was designed primarily to initiate negotiations rather than to dictate any content to be included in the negotiations. Although efforts had been made during various rounds of GATT trade negotiations to include investment on the international trade agenda,[72] and the WTO itself had been engaged in analysis and debate about the relationship between international trade and investment since 1997, it was only at the Doha Conference that the WTO committed itself to including investment as part of its main agenda. The main decisions taken at Doha on the relationship between trade and investment read as follows:

Relationship between Trade and Investment

20. Recognizing the case for a multilateral framework to secure transparent, stable and predictable conditions for long-term cross-border investment, particularly foreign direct investment, that will contribute to the expansion of trade, and the need for enhanced techni-cal assistance and capacity building in this area as referred to in paragraph 21,[73] we agree that negotiations will take place after the Fifth Session of the Ministerial Conference on the basis of a decision to be taken, by explicit consensus, at that Session on modalities of negotiations.

22. In the period until the Fifth Session, further work in the Working Group on the Relationship Between Trade and Investment will focus on the clarification of: scope and definition; transparency; non-discrimination; modalities for pre-establishment commit-ments based on a GATS-type, positive list approach; development provisions; exceptions and balance-of-payments safeguards; consultation and the settlement of disputes between Members. Any framework should reflect in a balanced manner the interests of home and host countries, and take due account of the development policies and objectives of host governments as well as their right to regulate in the public interest. The special development, trade and financial needs of developing and least-developed countries should be taken into account as an integral part of any framework, which should enable Members to undertake obligations and commitments commensurate with their individual needs and circumstances. Due regard should be paid to other relevant WTO provisions. Account should be taken, as appropriate, of existing bilateral and regional arrangements on investment.[74]

Although many developing countries had initially opposed the idea of putting the issue of foreign investment onto the world trade agenda, they eventually came to the consensus that if there was a need for regulation of foreign investment and thereby

---

[72] In 1982 the US put the regulation of foreign investment onto the agenda at a GATT Ministerial Meeting. Investment was a major issue in the Uruguay Round as well and resulted, inter alia, in the adoption of the TRIMs Agreement.

[73] Para 21 reads as follows: 'We recognize the needs of developing and least-developed countries for enhanced support for technical assistance and capacity building in this area, including policy analysis and development so that they may better evaluate the implications of closer multilateral cooperation for their development policies and objectives, and human and institutional development. To this end, we shall work in co-operation with other relevant intergovernmental organizations, including UNCTAD, and through appropriate regional and bilateral channels, to provide strengthened and adequately resourced assistance to respond to these needs.'

[74] WT/MIN(01)/DEC/W/1, 14 November 2001.

the activities of foreign investors, the WTO, where developing countries hold a numerical majority, was a better forum for regulating foreign investment than the World Bank or the OECD. However, the WTO project was narrow in scope as it focused only on trade and investment. Although the understanding in Doha was to start negotiations from a *tabula rasa*, there existed a number of complex problems with regard to the scope of such an agreement. In particular, differences between the developed and developing countries on various important issues, such as the definition of the term 'investment', acted as an obstacle to any real progress.[75] For instance, while some countries wished to include portfolio investment in the definition of 'investment', other countries opposed this classification.

Many developing countries wished to maintain the right to regulate portfolio investment – in particular, speculative short-term capital flows – whereas the developed countries wished to exclude such investments from the definition. The developed countries seemed reluctant to agree on an open-ended commitment. Many developing countries viewed a broadening of the definition of investment as allowing the liberalisation of all forms of capital investment, and thereby increasing the risk of destabilising short-term financial flows.

However, when the WTO Member States met in July 2004 to agree on the Work Programme for the Doha Development Round, they too decided to set aside the idea of negotiating an international agreement on foreign investment under the auspices of the WTO. A decision taken by the WTO General Council on 31 July 2004, known as the 'July Package', stated that a number of issues, including the relationship between trade and investment, would not form part of the Work Programme of the Doha Development Round.[76] Thus, the idea of adopting an international treaty regulating foreign investment was, once again, effectively removed from scope of action of an intergovernmental body.

The UN Commission and Council on Human Rights

One of the UN agencies that have been recently working in the area of multinational corporations and their effects on human rights is the Commission on Human Rights. Concerned by the impact of the activities of multinational enterprises on human rights,[77] the Sub-Commission on the Promotion and Protection of Human Rights began its work in the 1990s towards developing a set of norms applicable to such entities. In 2003, it proclaimed a set of Norms on the Responsibilities of Transnational Corporations and Other Business Enterprises with Regard to Human Rights.[78]

---

[75] See Report of the Working Group on the Relationship between Trade and Investment to the General Council of the WTO, WT/WGTI/6, 9 December 2002.

[76] WT/GC/W/535(1), 31 July 2004.

[77] On human rights and multinationals, see PT Muchlinski, 'Human Rights and Multinationals: Is There a Problem?' (2001) 77 *International Affairs* 31; and by the same author, 'Corporations in International Litigation: Problems of Jurisdiction and the United Kingdom Asbestos Cases' (2001) 50 *ICLQ* 1–25.

[78] ECOSOC, UN Doc E/CN.4/Sub.2/2003/12/Rev.2, 26 August 2003.

Having acknowledged that states had the primary responsibility to promote, secure the fulfilment of, ensure respect of and protect human rights recognised in international as well as national law, the Norms went on to state that within their 'spheres of activity and influence', TNCs and other business enterprises had a legal obligation – recognised in international as well as national law – to promote, secure the fulfilment of, ensure the respect of and protect human rights, including the rights of indigenous and other vulnerable groups.

In its set of non-legally enforceable norms embodied in 23 articles, the Sub-Commission outlined a number of human rights obligations of TNCs, including the right to equal opportunity and non-discriminatory treatment, the right to security of persons, rights of workers, respect for national sovereignty and human rights, and obligations with regard to consumer protection and environmental protection. However, some international institutions of business – such as the International Chamber of Commerce (ICC) and the International Organization of Employers (IOE) – some powerful TNCs and some governments were opposed to the idea that international human rights law was applicable only to governments. The states themselves, and not the TNCs, had a responsibility to ensure the promotion and protection of human rights.

Consequently, the Commission itself declared in its resolution of 20 April 2004 that the proposed Norms were merely a draft proposal and had no legal standing. The Commission then decided to request the UN Secretary-General to appoint a special representative to clarify the human rights responsibilities of companies. The UN Special Representative on the Issues of Human Rights and Transnational Corporations and Other Business Enterprises submitted his Interim Report in February 2006 in which he appeared effectively to negate the thrust of the 2003 Norms that TNCs had a responsibility to promote and protect human rights. His approach was a rather different one: he proposed that it was the states themselves which should, through national legislation, make TNCs accountable for human rights violations and require them to respect and promote human rights. This approach effectively puts the responsibility in this regard at the door of the host states themselves.[79]

According to the report submitted by the UN Representative in February 2007, the primary duty to protect human rights rests with states themselves:

> [T]he state duty to protect against non-state abuses is part of the international human rights regime's very foundation. The duty requires states to play a key role in regulating and adjudicating abuse by business enterprises or risk breaching their international obligations.[80]

The report goes on to conclude that 'it does not seem that the international human rights instruments ... currently impose direct legal responsibilities on corporations'.[81]

In his final report to the Human Rights Council submitted in March 2011, Professor Ruggie appended a document entitled 'Guiding Principles on Business and

---

[79] Doc E/CN.4/2006/97 (2006).

[80] 'Business and Human Rights: Mapping International Standards of Responsibility and Accountability for Corporate Acts', Report of the Special Representative of the Secretary-General (SRSG) on the issue of human rights and transnational corporations and other business enterprises, A/HRC/4/035, 9 February 2007, para 18.

[81] Ibid, para 44.

Human Rights: Implementing the United Nations "Protect, Respect and Remedy" Framework'.[82] He summed up his approach in the following words:

> The Framework rests on three pillars. The first is the State duty to protect against human rights abuses by third parties, including business enterprises, through appropriate policies, regulation, and adjudication. The second is the corporate responsibility to respect human rights, which means that business enterprises should act with due diligence to avoid infringing on the rights of others and to address adverse impacts with which they are involved. The third is the need for greater access by victims to effective remedy, both judicial and non-judicial. Each pillar is an essential component in an inter-related and dynamic system of preventative and remedial measures: the State duty to protect because it lies at the very core of the international human rights regime; the corporate responsibility to respect because it is the basic expectation society has of business in relation to human rights; and access to remedy because even the most concerted efforts cannot prevent all abuse.[83]

Outlining his views on the corporate responsibility to respect human rights, he recommended that:

> 11. Business enterprises should respect human rights. This means that they should avoid infringing on the human rights of others and should address adverse human rights impacts with which they are involved.
>
> 12. The responsibility of business enterprises to respect human rights refers to internationally recognized human rights – understood, at a minimum, as those expressed in the International Bill of Human Rights and the principles concerning fundamental rights set out in the International Labour Organization's Declaration on Fundamental Principles and Rights at Work.
>
> 13. The responsibility to respect human rights requires that business enterprises:
>
> (a)   Avoid causing or contributing to adverse human rights impacts through their own activities, and address such impacts when they occur; and
>
> (b)   Seek to prevent or mitigate adverse human rights impacts that are directly linked to their operations, products or services by their business relationships, even if they have not contributed to those impacts.
>
> 14. The responsibility of business enterprises to respect human rights applies to all enterprises regardless of their size, sector, operational context, ownership and structure. Nevertheless, the scale and complexity of the means through which enterprises meet that responsibility may vary according to these factors and with the severity of the enterprise's adverse human rights impacts.
>
> 15. In order to meet their responsibility to respect human rights, business enterprises should have in place policies and processes appropriate to their size and circumstances, including:
>
> (a)   A policy commitment to meet their responsibility to respect human rights;
>
> (b)   A human rights due-diligence process to identify, prevent, mitigate and account for how they address their impacts on human rights; and
>
> (c)   Processes to enable the remediation of any adverse human rights impacts they cause or to which they contribute.

---

[82] UN Doc A/HRC/17.31, 21 March 2011.
[83] Ibid, para 6.

Elaborating on his proposal on corporate responsibility for human rights, he stated that:

> The responsibility to respect human rights is a global standard of expected conduct for all business enterprises wherever they operate. It exists independently of States' abilities and/or willingness to fulfil their own human rights obligations, and does not diminish those obligations. And it exists over and above compliance with national laws and regulations protecting human rights.[84]

Towards a Binding Instrument on Multinational Enterprises and Human Rights

While exploring the alternatives to the ISDS mechanism and IIAs and with a view to establishing a mechanism to hold foreign investors accountable for human rights violations in host countries, those states which have decided to withdraw gradually from BITs or IIAs have once again gone back to the UN with a view to adopting a binding international agreement on business and human rights. Building on its earlier work on human rights and business, the UN Human Rights Council (HRC) has started a process to create an international legal instrument on multinational enterprises. Officially entitled 'Elaboration of an International Legally Binding Instrument on Transnational Corporations and other Business Enterprises with Respect to Human Rights' (A/HRC/26/L.22), the resolution represents an attempt towards the eventual adoption of an international instrument on the subject matter. It was adopted in June 2014 at the 26th session of the HRC. It was co-sponsored by Ecuador and South Africa, and supported by Bolivia, Cuba and Venezuela. However, the HRC was divided on the resolution, reminiscent of the division within the UN during the NIEO period. A total of 20 members of the HRC supported the resolution, while 13 members abstained, and 14 members voted against it.

The resolution provides for the establishment of an open-ended intergovernmental working group (IWG) that is mandated with elaborating an international legally binding instrument to regulate, in international human rights law, the activities of transnational corporations and other business enterprises. It seeks to build on the UN Guiding Principles on Business and Human Rights developed by Professor John Ruggie.[85] While the consensus achieved by him was strong in many respects, it also was a weakness in the sense that his proposals or framework did not include any implementation mechanism. Although most of the UN treaty and charter-based human rights bodies have recommendatory powers without any real powers to have their recommendations implemented, the contribution made by these bodies to the protection and the promotion of human rights cannot be underestimated. However, the Ruggie framework does not include any mechanism for follow up. It means that nowhere in

---

[84] Commentary to Guiding Principle 11.
[85] See JG Ruggie, *Just Business: Multinational Corporations and Human Rights* (WW Norton & Company, New York, 2013).

the world can individuals, communities or civil society organisations defending their rights against the activities of foreign investors, mainly TNCs, rely on the UN Guiding Principles for protection or remedy.

Anti-Corruption Conventions

A number of conventions have been adopted under the auspices of various regional organisations and the UN to prevent and combat corruption by companies in foreign jurisdictions.[86] The primary conventions are the OECD and the UN conventions that seek to control bribery and other forms of corruption by business organisations. The OECD Convention on Combating Bribery of Foreign Public Officials in International Business Transactions was adopted in 1997.[87] It requires each state party to establish measures making the bribery of a foreign official in international business transactions a criminal offence. Article 1 of the Convention reads as follows:

Article 1 – The Offence of Bribery of Foreign Public Officials:

1. Each Party shall take such measures as may be necessary to establish that it is a criminal offence under its law for any person intentionally to offer, promise or give any undue pecuniary or other advantage, whether directly or through intermediaries, to a foreign public official, for that official or for a third party, in order that the official act or refrain from acting in relation to the performance of official duties, in order to obtain or retain business or other improper advantage in the conduct of international business.

2. Each Party shall take any measures necessary to establish that complicity in, including incitement, aiding and abetting, or authorisation of an act of bribery of a foreign public official shall be a criminal offence. Attempt and conspiracy to bribe a foreign public official shall be criminal offences to the same extent as attempt and conspiracy to bribe a public official of that Party.

Articles 2 and 3 of the Convention establish responsibility of legal persons and require the imposition of sanctions on natural and juridical persons in the case of bribery:

Article 2 – Responsibility of Legal Persons

Each Party shall take such measures as may be necessary, in accordance with its legal principles, to establish the liability of legal persons for the bribery of a foreign public official.

---

[86] These are as follows: The Inter-American Convention against Corruption, adopted by the Organization of American States on 29 March 1996; the Convention on the Fight against Corruption involving Officials of the European Communities or Officials of Member States of the European Union, adopted by the Council of the European Union on 26 May 1997; the Convention on Combating Bribery of Foreign Public Officials in International Business Transactions, adopted by the Organisation for Economic Co-operation and Development on 21 November 1997; the Criminal Law Convention on Corruption, adopted by the Committee of Ministers of the Council of Europe on 27 January 1999; the Civil Law Convention on Corruption, adopted by the Committee of Ministers of the Council of Europe on 4 November 1999; and the African Union Convention on Preventing and Combating Corruption, adopted by the Heads of State and Government of the African Union on 12 July 2003.

[87] As of May 2014, 41 countries had ratified this Convention. It entered into force on 15 February 1999.

Article 3 – Sanctions

1. The bribery of a foreign public official shall be punishable by effective, proportionate and dissuasive criminal penalties. The range of penalties shall be comparable to that applicable to the bribery of the Party's own public officials and shall, in the case of natural persons, include deprivation of liberty sufficient to enable effective mutual legal assistance and extradition.

2. In the event that, under the legal system of a Party, criminal responsibility is not applicable to legal persons, that Party shall ensure that legal persons shall be subject to effective, proportionate and dissuasive non-criminal sanctions, including monetary sanctions, for bribery of foreign public officials.

3. Each Party shall take such measures as may be necessary to provide that the bribe and the proceeds of the bribery of a foreign public official, or property the value of which corresponds to that of such proceeds, are subject to seizure and confiscation or that monetary sanctions of comparable effect are applicable.

4. Each Party shall consider the imposition of additional civil or administrative sanctions upon a person subject to sanctions for the bribery of a foreign public official.

The UN Convention against Corruption was adopted in 2003.[88] It is designed to promote and strengthen measures to prevent and combat corruption more efficiently and effectively and to require states to establish liability of juridical persons such as multinational corporations for their corrupt practices. Articles 5 and 6 of the Convention outline the obligations of states as follows:

Article 5

Preventive anti-corruption policies and practices

1. Each State Party shall, in accordance with the fundamental principles of its legal system, develop and implement or maintain effective, coordinated anticorruption policies that promote the participation of society and reflect the principles of the rule of law, proper management of public affairs and public property, integrity, transparency and accountability.

2. Each State Party shall endeavour to establish and promote effective practices aimed at the prevention of corruption.

3. Each State Party shall endeavour to periodically evaluate relevant legal instruments and administrative measures with a view to determining their adequacy to prevent and fight corruption.

4. States Parties shall, as appropriate and in accordance with the fundamental principles of their legal system, collaborate with each other and with relevant international and regional organizations in promoting and developing the measures referred to in this article. That collaboration may include participation in international programmes and projects aimed at the prevention of corruption.

Article 6

Preventive anti-corruption body or bodies

1. Each State Party shall, in accordance with the fundamental principles of its legal system, ensure the existence of a body or bodies, as appropriate, that prevent

---

[88] The UN Convention was adopted by the General Assembly of the United Nations on 31 October 2003. It entered into force on 14 December 2005. It was signed by 140 states and as of 1 December 2015 a total of 178 States were party to the Convention, making it a nearly universally accepted treaty. See for the text of the Convention, UN Doc A/58/422.

corruption by such means as: (a) Implementing the policies referred to in article 5 of this Convention and, where appropriate, overseeing and coordinating the implementation of those policies; (b) Increasing and disseminating knowledge about the prevention of corruption.

2.   Each State Party shall grant the body or bodies referred to in paragraph 1 of this article the necessary independence, in accordance with the fundamental principles of its legal system, to enable the body or bodies to carry out its or their functions effectively and free from any undue influence. The necessary material resources and specialized staff, as well as the training that such staff may require to carry out their functions, should be provided.

3.   Each State Party shall inform the Secretary-General of the United Nations of the name and address of the authority or authorities that may assist other States Parties in developing and implementing specific measures for the prevention of corruption.

Thus, this is one of those rare areas in which the work of the UN in regulating the activities of foreign investors has resulted in a binding legal instrument, and a significant number of states have ratified this Convention.

A New Transparency Convention on Investor-State Investment Arbitration

Under the initiatives taken by the United Nations Commission on International Trade Law (UNCITRAL) a new convention on transparency in treaty-based investor-state arbitration (the 'Convention on Transparency', also known as the Mauritius Convention) was adopted by the UN General Assembly in 2014. The UNCITRAL Rules on Transparency in Treaty-based Investor-State Arbitration provide a procedural framework for making information available to the public on investment arbitration cases. The purpose of the Convention on Transparency is to provide a mechanism for the application of the Rules on Transparency to arbitration cases arising under the almost 3,000 investment treaties and should serve as a powerful instrument to enhance transparency in investor-state dispute settlement. The Transparency Rules are a set of procedural rules that provide for transparent arbitral proceedings, and address in that context procedural issues such as the information to be published at an early stage of arbitral proceedings, the documents to be published once the arbitral tribunal is constituted and during the proceedings, the public access to hearings, the submissions by third parties and non-disputing parties to the investment treaty under which the dispute arises, and the exceptions to public access to information. The Rules were adopted by consensus by UNCITRAL in July 2013, and entered into effect on 1 April 2014.[89]

---

[89] 'The Mauritius Convention on Transparency – A Model for Further Reforms of ISDS?', a think-piece of the World Economic Forum, ICTSD E15 Initiative Investment Policy Task Force, June 2015. On file with the author. The Convention opened for signature in Port Louis, Mauritius, on 17 March 2015, and thereafter at the United Nations Headquarters in New York. The Convention will enter into force six months after the

UNCITRAL also adopted at the same time an amendment to the UNCITRAL Arbitration Rules in order to clarify that for investor-state arbitration initiated pursuant to a treaty providing for the protection of investments or investors, the Arbitration Rules include the Transparency Rules (Article 1(4) of the UNCITRAL Arbitration Rules, 2013). The Transparency Convention does not incorporate the content of the Transparency Rules themselves, but reflects the agreement of the Contracting Parties to apply the Rules to arbitrations under their investment treaties concluded before 1 April 2014.

International Bar Association Guidelines on Conflicts of Interest

It was also in 2014 that the International Bar Association (IBA) Council approved a revised version of its 2004 Guidelines on Conflict of Interest. The IBA seems to have reflected some of the issues with conflicts of interest around the increasing involvement of third party funders and the increasing numbers of arbitrators and counsel who are either partners in very large law firms or barristers in specialised chambers focused on international arbitration expertise.

Investment Arbitration Resolution of the Institut de Droit International

The Institut de Droit International, a Nobel Prize-winning organisation consisting of the world's leading international lawyers, established a commission to look at some of the unresolved or unsettled issues and emerging challenges within international investment law and arbitration. The commission submitted its report to the Tokyo Session of the Institut in September 2013.[90] In turn, the Institut adopted the Tokyo Resolution on Legal Aspects of Recourse to Arbitration by an Investor against the Authorities of the Host State under Inter-State Treaties in September 2013. Adopted by a body of leading international lawyers of the world, consisting of many judges of the ICJ, members of the International Law Commission, leading international investment arbitrators, and professors of international law from various prestigious universities around the globe, the Tokyo resolution of the Institut is a document of considerable significance. In the absence of a global comprehensive treaty on the regulation of foreign investment, resolutions of this nature have sought to fill the gap with regard to some of the

deposit of the third instrument of ratification, acceptance, approval or accession. As of 24 December 2015 only Mauritius had ratified it. See www.uncitral.org/uncitral/uncitral_texts/arbitration/2014Transparency_Convention.html (accessed 24 December 2015).

[90] *Annuaire de l'Institut de Droit International*, vol 75, Tokyo Session, 2013 (Paris, Editions A Pedone, 2013).

core principles of the law.[91] For instance, Article 13 of the Tokyo Resolution of the Institut included the following provisions with regard to the principle of fair and equitable treatment:

Article 13

Fair and equitable treatment, which is a key standard of investment protection, must accord investors and investments, in particular: (i) due process, (ii) non-discrimination and non-arbitrary treatment, (iii) due diligence, and (iv) respect of legitimate expectations.

The notion of legitimate expectations, as applied to the investor, shall not be construed to include mere expectations of profit, in the absence of specific engagements undertaken towards them by competent State organs.

Compensation due to an investor for violation of the FET [Fair and Equitable Treatment] standard shall be assessed without regard to compensation that could be allocated in case of an expropriation, in accordance with the damage suffered by the investor.

Similarly, Article 14 of the Tokyo Resolution of the Institut de Droit International contained the following provisions with regard to expropriation and the standards of compensation for expropriation:

Article 14

Expropriation of foreign property, whether direct or indirect, including measures tantamount to an expropriation, is subject to the following rules. Foreign property cannot be expropriated except: (i) for public purposes, (ii) on a non-discriminatory basis, (iii) in accordance with due process of law, and (iv) against compensation.

Without prejudice to the particular provisions of the applicable treaty or of the specific agreement on which the investment is based, compensation must be: (i) prompt, (ii) adequate, and (iii) effective. As to the interpretation and application of the notion of 'adequate' compensation, an appropriate balance must be assured between the interests of the investor and the public purposes of the State.

In principle, these rules are also applicable to nationalisations in the absence of specific agreed rules.

There have been concerns expressed in academic and other legal literature with regard to the lack of transparency, accountability and consistency in international investment arbitration. The Tokyo Resolution of the Institut sought to address some of these issues. For instance, with regard to the norms of interpretation of bilateral and multilateral investment treaties Article 1 reads as follows:

The interpretation and application of bilateral and multilateral international instruments for the protection of international investments shall be in accordance with the general rules of international law as reflected in the Vienna Convention on the Law of Treaties.

On the issue of consistency, the Tokyo Resolution provides as follows:

Article 2

Consistency of solutions in investment arbitration contributes to legal certainty for all actors involved. The quest for consistency does not require the mechanical application of

---

[91] The Tokyo Resolution of the Institute is available at: www.idi-iil.org/idiE/resolutionsE/2013_tokyo_en.pdf.

prior practice without regard to the particular circumstances of the case or the need for the interpretation and development of the law.

The World Economic Forum in Davos and Investment Policy

The World Economic Forum in Davos together with the International Centre for Trade and Sustainable Development (ICTSD) in Geneva established an E15 Expert Task Force on Investment Policy in January 2015 with the aim of developing global policy on investment regulation. Stating that international efforts to establish comprehensive multilateral rules on investment have proved elusive, intergovernmental institutions such as UNCTAD, the OECD, the World Bank and the G-20 were working to help states, investors and other stakeholders deal with the range of issues associated with foreign direct investment, and the international investment regime as it stands today has come under criticism, with its dispute-settlement mechanism in particular mired in controversy, the Task Force was established to discuss long-term policy options and to explore the following questions:

— What will be the main features of the future, network-based Multi-National Enterprise (including in light of the emerging digital economy)? What are the implications of these changes for the international investment regime?

— What are the old and new links between the trade and the investment regimes, keeping in mind the escalation of global value chains and the negotiation of mega-regional agreements?

— What are the strengths and weakness of the current international investment regime? Are the purposes served by the current regime still adequate?

— Do the various standards contained in IIAs require a review? Does the balance of the rights and responsibilities of the principal actors in international investment need adjustment?

— Does the current ISDS mechanism meet twenty-first-century challenges? What is the role of states in ISDS, including what we can learn from the WTO dispute-settlement mechanism and an appeals mechanism/world investment court?

— Is the institutional infrastructure of the current regime satisfactory? Is it really desirable to multilateralise the investment regime?

— Is the relationship between IIAs and other international agreements of immediate relevance to international investment clear (eg UN Guiding Principles on Business and Human Rights)?

— Special issues, eg state-owned enterprises; incentives; contracts.[92]

---

[92] From a letter of January 2015 outlining the terms of reference of the Task Force received by the author inviting him to join the Task Force; on file with the author.

The Task Force was asked to discuss principal policy options with a view towards improving the international investment regime with concrete alternatives for the international community to consider in time for the 20th anniversary of the WTO at the end of 2015, and the World Economic Forum's 2016 Davos Annual Meeting of world's political and business leaders.[93]

The Shift in Emphasis on the Need for an International Agreement

A rapid and massive growth in foreign investment, a huge expansion of economic activities followed by a large increase in the number of TNCs in the post-war period, coupled with the emergence of many independent states in Africa and Asia, gave rise to the need for the regulation of foreign investment and thereby of TNCs. Initially, the UN was seen as an appropriate forum for such regulation. However, many developed countries soon saw it as a body heavily influenced by developing countries and appeared reluctant to accept the adoption of a UN code of conduct for TNCs. In the meantime, due to the dramatic political and economic changes of the late 1980s and early 1990s, the balance was shifting in favour of developed countries and foreign investors from these countries. It was at this juncture that the World Bank intervened with its own guidelines in 1992.

The 1990s saw rapid success in the capital expansion of foreign investment, and the OECD therefore tried to adopt a new agreement designed to consolidate the provisions relating to foreign investment law into a single agreement. However, a coalition of international governmental and non-governmental organisations, interest groups and civil society mounted a challenge to the OECD. After a period of reckoning the WTO chose to enter the frame in 2001, but decided in 2004 to set aside the topic of foreign investment law. Since the practice of the WTO is to work by consensus, it was hoped that any regulation of the activities of foreign investors or those who receive foreign investment would have been a balanced one. Indeed, the recognition in the 2001 Doha Declaration that any framework 'should reflect in a balanced manner the interests of home and host countries, and take due account of the development policies and objectives of host governments as well as their right to regulate in the public interest' was an indication in a positive direction. However, this mission was not made part of the WTO negotiations in July 2004 when the WTO members adopted a Work Programme for the Doha Round.

---

[93] More information about the E15 initiative can be found at http://e15initiative.org/.

Conclusions

As can be seen in the preceding paragraphs, the idea of concluding a global treaty on foreign investment is still some way off. At present, none of the international organisations have this item on their active agenda, leaving the matter to customary international law and BITs or FTAs or other IIAs. The contributions made by the UN and other international organisations may not have led to a successful conclusion of a global comprehensive treaty on this subject, but they have helped in the development of the main principles of law governing the treatment of foreign investment under international law. Previously, it was developing countries that wished to have an international instrument regulating foreign investment under the auspices of the UN where they had a numerical majority, but now these very same states appear reluctant to implement such an instrument because of the fear that they may come under pressure to agree to a higher level of protection for foreign investors than already provided in international law.

4

Protection of Foreign Investment in Customary International Law

Introduction

There are certain minimum standards of treatment of foreign investment prescribed in customary international law. Foreign investors would be entitled to the protection of their investment under these standards even in the absence of a bilateral investment treaty. The basis for the protection of foreign investment in customary international law is the traditional notion of diplomatic protection, State responsibility, and the treatment of aliens. It is the notion of diplomatic protection of citizens and their property abroad by the home country and State responsibility that gave rise to the modern rules of foreign investment law. The idea that once admitted into the country a host state was required to extend the international minimum standard of protection to both aliens and their property under international law has been the bedrock of traditional foreign investment law.

This chapter will examine the standards of treatment of foreign investment in customary international law. The aim is to assess the nature and scope of the core principles of foreign investment law and how a shift in emphasis has taken place in response to the changing international economic and political realities of the day.

Protection under International Law and Domestic Law

Much of the regulation of foreign investment is carried out through the domestic laws of the host countries concerned. Therefore, when foreign investors attempt to ascertain the laws and regulations affecting their potential and actual investment they should in the first instance consider the domestic law provisions. For instance, a foreign investor planning to invest in China would be advised to consult the Chinese Law on Wholly

Foreign-Owned Enterprises and the Law on Chinese–Foreign Equity Joint Ventures.[1] The main objective of international foreign investment law is to outline international standards of protection, provide supplementary and complimentary protection, and assure foreign investors of access to an independent international tribunal in the event of a dispute arising between the host state and a foreign investor. International law, whether based on treaties or customary rules, is there to provide a second layer of protection to foreign investors mainly against political risks. Hence, the focus of this chapter is the protection available under international foreign investment law rather than national laws protecting foreign investment.

The Fundamental Principles of Foreign Investment Protection

The basic foundation of the main principles of modern foreign investment law is the availability of customary international law protection to aliens, including foreign investors, the notion of diplomatic protection, international human rights law, the international minimum standard, and the international law of state responsibility. When an act of a state undermines the rights guaranteed to aliens, either under customary international law or under a treaty, that act gives rise to state responsibility.[2]

---

[1] The provisions on the prohibition on nationalisation or expropriation in both of these pieces of legislation are similar. Art 5 of the Chinese Law on Wholly Foreign-Owned Enterprises of 1986 as amended in October 2000 reads as follows: 'The State shall not nationalize or requisition any foreign capital enterprise. Under special circumstances required by public interest, foreign capital enterprise may be requisitioned by legal procedures, but appropriate compensation shall be made' (a copy of this legislation in English was supplied to the author by a Chinese scholar, Michael Shen, and is on file.)

[2] The basic principles of the law of state responsibility can be found in the Draft Articles on Responsibility of States for Internationally Wrongful Acts developed and adopted by the International Law Commission in 2001. The core of the general principles of state responsibility embodied in the Draft Articles of the ILC in the context of this study is as follows:

Article 1: Every internationally wrongful act of a State entails the international responsibility of that State.

Article 2: There is an internationally wrongful act of a State when conduct consisting of an action or omission: (a) Is attributable to the State under international law; and (b) Constitutes a breach of an international obligation of the State.

Article 12: There is a breach of an international obligation by a State when an act of that State is not in conformity with what is required of it by that obligation, regardless of its origin or character.

Article 28: The international responsibility of a State which is entailed by an internationally wrongful act in accordance with the provisions of Part One involves legal consequences as set out in this Part.

Article 31: (1) The responsible State is under an obligation to make full reparation for the injury caused by the internationally wrongful act. (2) Injury includes any damage, whether material or moral, caused by the internationally wrongful act of a State.

Article 34: Full reparation for the injury caused by the internationally wrongful act shall take the form of restitution, compensation and satisfaction, either singly or in combination, in accordance with the provisions of this chapter.

The main principle that has been developed to provide protection to foreign investors is the principle of an international minimum standard of treatment, at the core of which is the principle of fair and equitable treatment.[3] In explaining the status of the minimum standards of treatment, the arbitral tribunal in *Saluka Investments BV (the Netherlands) v the Czech Republic* stated that:

> It should be kept in mind that the customary minimum standard is in any case binding upon a State and provides a minimum guarantee to foreign investors, even where the State follows a policy that is in principle opposed to foreign investment; in that context, the minimum standard of 'fair and equitable treatment' may in fact provide no more than 'minimal' protection. Consequently, in order to violate that standard, States' conduct may have to display a relatively higher degree of inappropriateness.[4]

Although these basic standards are widely regarded as settled, the meaning and scope of certain principles is the subject of intense debate in both jurisprudence and in the literature on foreign investment. For instance, what is included in the 'international minimum standard' of treatment? What constitutes 'fair and equitable treatment'? Who is entitled to 'fair and equitable treatment'? What is included in the definition of 'investment'? Questions such as these surround much of foreign investment law.

The basic standard of treatment, known as the international minimum standard, was later expanded through BITs and other bilateral treaties to include 'fair and equitable treatment' and 'full protection and security' of foreign investment by the host states, and payment of fair or just compensation against expropriation. Inherent in the principle of fair and equitable treatment are a number of principles including the principle of non-discrimination. Most friendship, commerce and navigation (FCN) treaties, BITs, RTAs and FTAs accord additional protection to foreign investors. Under these treaties foreign investors are entitled not only to fair and equitable treatment but also to MFN treatment, national treatment and other protection depending on the nature of the treaty. Each of these main issues and the principles of the law surrounding them will be examined in turn.

Article 35: A State responsible for an internationally wrongful act is under an obligation to make restitution, that is, to re-establish the situation which existed before the wrongful act was committed, provided and to the extent that restitution:

(a) Is not materially impossible;
(b) Does not involve a burden out of all proportion to the benefit deriving from restitution instead of compensation.

Article 36: 1. The State responsible for an internationally wrongful act is under an obligation to compensate for the damage caused thereby, insofar as such damage is not made good by restitution.

2. The compensation shall cover any financially assessable damage including loss of profits insofar as it is established. (UN Doc A/56/10)

[3] S Vasciannie, 'The Fair and Equitable Treatment Standard in International Investment Law and Practice' (1999) 70 *British Year Book of International Law* 99.
[4] *Saluka Investments BV (the Netherlands) v the Czech Republic*, para 292, Partial Award, IIC 210 (2006), 17 March 2006, Permanent Court of Arbitration (PCA).

The Objectives of the Principles

Ensuring non-discrimination in the conduct of international business is the underlying idea behind the principles of international foreign investment law. These principles are employed to secure a certain level of treatment for foreign investors in host countries. For instance, the purpose of the MFN principle is to grant foreign investors from a country the same favourable treatment that is accorded to foreign investors from third countries operating in the host country; whereas the object of the national treatment principle is to grant treatment comparable to that accorded to domestic investors operating in the host country itself. The principle of fair and equitable treatment brings in the elements of fairness and equity drawn from international law – especially the principle of minimum standards – and practice, as well as domestic law principles concerning the overall treatment of foreign investment in a host country.

Under the MFN principle, foreign investors are entitled to more protection than available under the customary international law principle of minimum standards. However, it does not go so far as to put the foreign investor on an equal footing with domestic investors in the host country as is the case under the principle of national treatment.

However, such protection is available only to those who are recognised as 'investors' under international law or by BITs, RTAs or FTAs, and only those economic activities that are recognised as 'investment' under international law or by such treaties are entitled to the relevant protection. Therefore, it is necessary to examine the law and practice on the definition of the terms 'investor' and 'investment'.

Definition of Investor and Investment

Most treaties define the term 'investor' to include a state, state enterprise, a foreign national or a private enterprise of a foreign state that has made an investment in the territory of another state. Traditionally, only those investors that had made an investment or were making an investment enjoyed the protection offered by BITs. ICSID itself does not provide any comprehensive definition of the term 'investment'. However, the recent trend in many BITs and FTAs seems also to include investors that are attempting to make an investment, thereby recognising the pre-establishment rights of potential investors in the host countries concerned. The definition of 'investor' in the US Model BIT of 2004 reads as follows:

> 'Investor of a Party' means a Party or state enterprise thereof, or a national or an enterprise of a Party, that attempts to make, is making, or has made an investment in the territory of the other Party; provided, however, that a natural person who is a dual national shall be deemed to be exclusively a national of the State of his or her dominant and effective nationality.

A similar formulation can be found in the 2006 Canada–Peru BIT, which reads as follows:

> **Investor of a Party** means (i) in the case of Canada: (a) Canada or a state enterprise of Canada, or (b) a national or an enterprise of Canada, that seeks to make, is making or has made an investment; a natural person who is a dual citizen shall be deemed to be exclusively a citizen of the State of his or her dominant and effective citizenship; and (ii) in the case of the Republic of Peru: (a) a state enterprise of the Republic of Peru, or (b) a national or enterprise of the Republic of Peru; that seeks to make, is making or has made an investment; a natural person who is a dual citizen shall be deemed to be exclusively a citizen of the State of his or her dominant and effective citizenship;

The words 'attempts to make' or 'seeks to make' in the provisions just cited are intended to protect the pre-establishment rights of foreign investors, including MNEs, in host countries.

With a few exceptions,[5] the trend in BITs and FTAs is to define the terms 'investor' and 'investment' as broadly as possible with open-ended definitions and indicative rather than definitive lists of investors and investments. Most treaties include in the term 'investment' 'every kind of asset' and provide a non-exhaustive list of specific forms of investment or define the terms as 'all assets, such as property, rights and interests of every nature'. For instance, the US Model BIT of 2004 defines 'investment' as

> every asset that an investor owns or controls, directly or indirectly, that has the characteristics of an investment, including such characteristics as the commitment of capital or other resources, the expectation of gain or profit, or the assumption of risk.[6]

The Model BIT then goes on to provide a non-exhaustive list of investments, including traditional forms of direct investment, portfolio investment and intellectual property rights. In addition to direct investments, definitions such as these cover all forms of indirectly controlled investments. Even when treaties such as the North American Free Trade Agreement (NAFTA) or Model BITs such as the Canadian one include closed-list definitions of 'investment', they too are couched in such a form that the definition includes every conceivable form of investment as those included in the open-ended definitions. The definition of 'investment' in Article 1139 of NAFTA is an example.[7]

---

[5] BITs concluded by Canada with other states seem to provide a complete and closed definition of both 'investor' and 'investment'. The 2006 Canada–Peru BIT is an example.

[6] Art 1 of the US Model BIT of 2004.

[7] Art 1139 of NAFTA reads as follows:

[I]nvestment means:

(a)   an enterprise;
(b)   an equity security of an enterprise;
(c)   a debt security of an enterprise (i) where the enterprise is an affiliate of the investor, or (ii) where the original maturity of the debt security is at least three years, but does not include a debt security, regardless of original maturity, of a state enterprise;
(d)   a loan to an enterprise (i) where the enterprise is an affiliate of the investor, or (ii) where the original maturity of the loan is at least three years, but does not include a loan, regardless of original maturity, to a state enterprise;
(e)   an interest in an enterprise that entitles the owner to share in income or profits of the enterprise;
(f)   an interest in an enterprise that entitles the owner to share in the assets of that enterprise on dissolution, other than a debt security or a loan excluded from subparagraph (c) or (d);

The inclusion of 'indirectly controlled investments' in the definition of 'investment' is liable to extend BIT protection to a number of intermediate holding companies not intended to be protected by the host state. As observed by Legum,

> [w]here a host state has entered into BITs that cover indirectly controlled investments, there could be between one and 20 or more layers of intermediate holding companies that separate the company the host State officials see and the company that is a covered investor under the treaty.

Indeed, '[t]he covered investor could itself, in fact, be an intermediate holding company, with the ultimate parent company publicly traded or controlled by third country nationals'. As explained by Legum, the end result could be as follows:

> Under these circumstances, the only way to comply with the treaty is for the host State to assume that *all* investors – all companies – are covered by the highest standards of any BIT in force for the State. The reality that foreign capital is highly fungible and the breadth of the definitions of investor and investment thus combine to effectively transform the facially bilateral obligations of the BIT into an obligation that the host State must consider potentially applicable to all investors.

This state of affairs has the potential to make the dispute settlement mechanism of a given BIT available to all foreign investors, which perhaps is not what a host state may have contemplated at the time of concluding the BIT concerned. Indeed, a report by UNCTAD on this subject sums up the situation as follows:

> The concept of 'investor' in the context of BITs and NAFTA has a broad scope. Consequently, foreign investors that are shareholders in an investment have been allowed to use the investor-State dispute settlement procedures and the protections in the agreement, irrespective of whether they are majority or minority shareholders. Most IIAs [International Investment Agreements] regard shareholdings or participation in a company as a form of investment. Therefore, minority shareholders are entitled to submit claims in respect of their investment. In these cases, investors have standing not because they control the enterprise but because their shares constitute the investment. In one case, the shareholding amounted to 17 per cent of the investment in the host country. No case to date is known that sets a lower limit on the value of a shareholding that would allow the investor-State dispute settlement procedures to be used, where such a requirement is not set out in the text of the treaty itself. In addition, shareholdings through indirectly owned and controlled subsidiaries can also give standing to the ultimate shareholder before a tribunal to bring a claim arising out of the terms of a BIT.[8]

(g) real estate or other property, tangible or intangible, acquired in the expectation or used for the purpose of economic benefit or other business purposes; and

(h) interests arising from the commitment of capital or other resources in the territory of a Party to economic activity in such territory, such as under (i) contracts involving the presence of an investor's property in the territory of the Party, including turnkey or construction contracts, or concessions, or (ii) contracts where remuneration depends substantially on the production, revenues or profits of an enterprise; but investment does not mean,

(i) claims to money that arise solely from (i) commercial contracts for the sale of goods or services by a national or enterprise in the territory of a Party to an enterprise in the territory of another Party, or (ii) the extension of credit in connection with a commercial transaction, such as trade financing, other than a loan covered by subparagraph (d); or

(j) any other claims to money, that do not involve the kinds of interests set out in subparagraphs (a) through (h).

[8] UNCTAD, *Investor-State Disputes Arising from Investment Treaties: A Review*, UNCTAD Series on International Investment Policies for Development (New York, United Nations, 2005) 15 (endnotes omitted).

Furthermore, under these definitions of investment and investor, there is a possibility of local business firms under foreign control claiming the status of a foreign investor and invoking the dispute settlement mechanism under a BIT. Under traditional international law, a locally incorporated affiliate of the foreign parent would not be entitled to claim diplomatic protection as a foreign investor, but, as pointed out in the above-mentioned UNCTAD report, the new rules of ICSID make it possible to do so since Article 25(2)(b) of the Convention 'allows for the treatment of a local affiliate as a foreign investor where it is agreed by the parties to the dispute that it is under foreign control and that it is in fact under such control'.[9]

The inclusion of portfolio investment in the definition of investment has the potential to bring various entities within the ambit of the protection available under a BIT and the process of expanding the protection under a BIT to various forms of economic transactions – eg sales presence; market share through trade; loan agreements and construction contracts; promissory notes and other banking instruments; and even establishing law firms – seems to be growing in both state practice and jurisprudence. For instance, in *Maffezini* the tribunal found that the BIT concerned covered capital investments. In *SD Myers v Canada* a mere sales presence by an US company in Canada was regarded as an investment in Canada.[10] In another case involving a Cypriot company (owned indirectly by Canadian business interests and Hungary), an ICSID tribunal was reluctant to 'pierce the corporate veil' to look beyond the 'formal nationality' of the company to ascertain who actually controlled it.[11] Thus, nationality-shopping is possible under a broad definition of investor.

Another consequence of such a broad, asset-based definition of investment is that multiple cases could be filed by several investors in the same business entity based on the same set of facts. Different investors having shares in the same company may initiate multiple arbitrations under different corporate or shareholder capacities. For instance, in the *Lauder* cases two different investors filed cases for arbitration under different BITs before different tribunals against the Czech government which resulted in two different results: while one investor lost the case, the other won a large monetary award.[12] In the *SGS v Pakistan* arbitration SGS, a Swiss company, was able to sue Pakistan before ICSID for a dispute arising out of a contractual undertaking because the Swiss–Pakistan BIT included in its definition of 'investment' 'every kind of asset', including 'claims to money and any performance having economic value'.[13]

The ICSID tribunal in *SGS v Pakistan* held that the definition of 'investment' in this BIT was sufficiently broad to encompass a Pre-Shipment Inspection (PSI) agreement between SGS and the government of Pakistan. It also held that the PSI agreement counted as 'a concession under public laws' falling within the BIT's definition of investment. Since the Swiss–Pakistan BIT had gone much further than many treaties

[9] Ibid, 16 (endnotes omitted).
[10] (2000) 40 ILM 1408 (NAFTA Arb).
[11] *ADC v Hungary*, ICSID Case No ARB/03/16, award of 2 October 2006.
[12] See UNCTAD (n 8) 17.
[13] *SGS Société Générale de Surveillance SA v Islamic Republic of Pakistan*, ICSID Case No ARB/01/13, award of 8 September 2003, 347.

in providing as much protection to foreign investors and including as wide a definition of investment as possible, it came as no surprise that the ICSID tribunal would interpret the BIT provisions as liberally as possible in favour of foreign investors. A similar provision was included in the Swiss–Philippines BIT and the ICSID tribunal in *SGS v Philippines* drew similar conclusions: 'By definition, investments are characteristically entered into by means of contracts or other agreements with the host State and the local investment partner (or if these are different entities, with both of them).'[14]

When considering the meaning of the term 'investment', international tribunals often look beyond the BIT definition of the term to see how international law has defined it, or even how the domestic laws of the country concerned have defined it. This is what the arbitration tribunal did in *Mihaly International v Sri Lanka*, for example.[15]

However, some RTAs concluded among developing countries exclude portfolio investment from the definition of investment. The practice of the ASEAN countries[16] and the draft agreement of June 2006 between the EU and the Pacific members of the ACP countries are examples.[17] The latter makes it clear that to qualify for protection under the investment regime of the draft agreement a business has to demonstrate a significant physical presence in the host country. It goes on to state that a 'significant physical presence would not include, for example, sales offices without other operational facilities, post office box based businesses, Internet-based businesses or other types of business with very limited physical presence in the host state'.

The draft agreement further states that an investment does not include:

> market share, whether or not it is based on foreign origin trade; claims to money deriving solely from commercial contracts for the sale of goods and services to or from the territory of a party to the territory of another country; or a loan to a party or to a State enterprise; a bank letter of credit; or the extension of credit in connection with a commercial transaction such as trade financing.

This definition seems to have been inspired by the provisions to this effect in the IISD's Model International Agreement on Investment for Sustainable Development, which reads as follows:

'investment' means:

  (i) a company;
 (ii) shares, stock and other forms of equity participation in a company, and bonds, debentures and other forms of debt interests in a company;
(iii) contractual rights, such as under turnkey, construction or management contracts, production or revenue-sharing contracts, concessions or other similar contracts;
(iv) tangible property, including real property; and intangible property, including rights, such as leases, mortgages, hypothecs, liens and pledges on real property;

---

[14] *SGS v Philippines*, ICSID Case No ARB/02/6, 29 January 2004, 50.

[15] *Mihaly International v Sri Lanka*, ICSID Case No ARB/00/2, award of 15 March 2002.

[16] See Art 2 of the Framework Agreement on the ASEAN Investment Area of 1998 and Art 1 of the Protocol to Amend the Framework Agreement on the ASEAN Investment Area of 2001.

[17] Draft Art 8.2 of the investment chapter in the context of the EU/PACP EPA negotiations, DG Trade G1(D) (2006) of 10 October 2006.

  (v)   rights conferred pursuant to law, such as licences and permits provided that

      (a)   such investments are not in the nature of portfolio investments which shall not be covered by this Agreement;

      (b)   that there is a significant physical presence of the investment in the host state;

      (c)   that the investment in the host state is made in accordance with the laws of that host state;

      (d)   the investment is part or all of a business or commercial operation; and

      (e)   the investment is made by an investor as defined herein.

For greater certainty, an investment does not include: market share, whether or not it is based on foreign origin trade; claims to money deriving solely from commercial contracts for the sale of goods and services to or from the territory of a Party to the territory of another country, or a loan to a Party or to a State enterprise; a bank letter of credit; or the extension of credit in connection with a commercial transaction, such as trade financing.[18]

Thus, it is clear that opinions are divided on the inclusion of portfolio investment in the definition of investment. However, as will be seen later, the jurisprudence of international courts and tribunals identifies certain characteristics of 'investments' and one of them is that investment should have contributed to a certain extent and in some form to the economic development of the host state concerned. Not all types of portfolio investment would automatically enjoy the protection available to an investment in international law.

Fair and Equitable Treatment in Customary International Law

The concept of fair and equitable treatment is a major, if not the most important, principle of foreign investment law, and is deeply rooted in customary international law. Violation of the fair and equitable treatment principle by the host state concerned is the most common allegation made by foreign investors before international investment tribunals. In the efforts made in the immediate aftermath of the Second World War this concept figured prominently in various multilateral instruments relating to foreign investment. When states began to conclude BITs as the principal vehicle to regulate and promote foreign investment, this principle was incorporated as a key provision. Briefly, this principle provides a basic level of protection to foreign investors and is based on the elements of fairness and equity. The problem with this principle is that it is difficult to define in concrete terms and is open to different interpretations.

    The precise meaning of the phrase 'fair and equitable treatment' has been a subject of interest and often controversy both in the literature and in the case law dealing with the treatment of foreign investment. For instance, stating that this phrase was 'particularly difficult to define', the ICSID tribunal in *Noble Ventures v Romania* held

---

[18] International Institute for Sustainable Development (IISD), 'Model International Agreement on Investment for Sustainable Development', April 2005 (footnote omitted).

that this standard of protection was a more 'general standard which finds its specific application in *inter alia* the duty to provide full protection and security, the prohibition of arbitrary and discriminatory measure and the obligation to observe contractual obligations towards the investor'.[19]

One of the early cases to deal with the notion of 'denial of justice' as an example of an unfair treatment was the *Neer* case.[20] This case is regarded as having prescribed such a high threshold for governmental treatment of foreign investors as to amount to an unfair treatment under international law. In this case it was held that the treatment of aliens, in order to constitute an international delinquency, 'should amount to an outrage, to bad faith, to willful neglect of duty, or to an insufficiency of governmental action so far short of international standards that every reasonable and impartial man would recognize its insufficiency'. However, this threshold of minimum standards has been regarded as traditional rather than contemporary; the latter is broader in scope. Referring to the provision concerning the fair and equitable treatment in Article 3(10) of a BIT between the Netherlands and the Czech Republic, an arbitral tribunal held in *Saluka Investments BV v the Czech Republic* that:

> Article 3.1 of the Treaty requires the signatory governments to treat investments of investors of the other Contracting Party according to the standards of 'fairness' and 'equity' and to avoid impairment of such investments by measures which are not in compliance with the standards of 'reasonableness' and 'non-discrimination'. It is common ground that such general standards represent principles that cannot be reduced to precise statements of rules.

The tribunal held that the 'fair and equitable treatment' standard does not create an open-ended mandate to second-guess government decision-making. The standards formulated in Article 3 of the Treaty 'are susceptible of specification through judicial practice and do in fact have sufficient legal content to allow the case to be decided on the basis of law'. Article 3, paragraphs 1 and 2 of this BIT provided that:

1. Each Contracting Party shall ensure fair and equitable treatment to the investments of investors of the other Contracting Party and shall not impair, by unreasonable or discriminatory measures, the operation, management, maintenance, use, enjoyment or disposal thereof by those investors.
2. More particularly, each Contracting Party shall accord to such investments full security and protection which in any case shall not be less than that accorded either to investments of its own investors or to investments of investors of any third States, whichever is more favourable to the investor concerned.

In *Rumeli v Kazakhstan*[21] the tribunal summarised the content of the fair and equitable treatment principle as follows:

> [T]he fair and equitable treatment standard encompasses, inter alia, the following concrete principles:
>
> > the State must act in a transparent manner;
> > the State is obliged to act in good faith;

[19] *Noble Ventures v Romania*, ICSID Case No ARB/01/11, 12 October 2005, 112.

[20] *USA (LF Neer) v United Mexican States* (1927) 21 *American Journal of International Law* 555, 556.

[21] *Rumeli Telekom AS and Telsim Mobil Telekommunikasyon Hizmetleri AS v Republic of Kazakhstan*, ICSID Case No ARB/05/16, award of 29 July 2008, at 609.

the State's conduct cannot be arbitrary, grossly unfair, unjust, idiosyncratic, discriminatory, or lacking in due process; and
the State must respect procedural propriety and due process.

The case law confirms that to comply with the standard, the state must respect the investor's reasonable and legitimate expectations.

In some more recent cases, such as *El Paso*, international investment tribunals have gone a step further in according protection to foreign investors under the principle of fair and equitable treatment. In 2011 the investment tribunal in *El Paso v Argentina*[22] introduced the concept of 'creeping' analysis in the application of the fair and equitable treatment standard, which is an analysis similar to that applied to determine a 'creeping' expropriation.

In *Genin v Estonia* the arbitration tribunal stated that a violation of the fair and equitable principle could be established by 'acts showing wilful neglect of duty, an insufficiency of action falling far below international standards, or even subjective bad faith'.[23] According to a report prepared by UNCTAD, this phrase carries at least two possible meanings:

> First, it could be given its plain meaning, so that beneficiaries are entitled to fairness and equity as these terms are understood in non-technical terms. Secondly, it would mean that beneficiaries are assured treatment in keeping with the international minimum standard for investors. In practical terms, this uncertainty may influence the policy decisions of a host country that is willing to accept a treaty clause on fair and equitable treatment, but that is not prepared to offer the international minimum standard. This may be particularly the case where the host country believes that the international minimum standard implies that foreign investors could be entitled to more favourable treatment than local investors.[24]

The UNCTAD report goes on to outline the problems related to the application of this principle in law and practice in the following words:

> Although the concept of fair and equitable treatment now features prominently in international investment agreements, different formulations are used in connection with the standard. An examination of the relevant treaties suggests at least four approaches in practice, namely:
>
> An approach that omits reference to fair and equitable treatment.
> An approach in which it is recommended that States should offer investment fair and equitable treatment, but such treatment is not required as a matter of law (the hortatory approach).
> A legal requirement for States to accord investment 'fair and equitable' treatment, 'just and equitable' treatment, or 'equitable' treatment.
> A legal requirement for States to accord investment fair and equitable treatment, together with other standards of treatment, such as most-favoured-nation (MFN) and national treatment.

---

[22] *El Paso v Argentina*, ICSID Case No ARB/03/15, award of 31 October 2011.
[23] *Genin v Estonia*, ICSID Case No ARB/99/2, award of 25 June 2001.
[24] UNCTAD, *Fair and Equitable Treatment*, UNCTAD Series on Issues in International Investment Agreements (New York and Geneva, United Nations, 1999) 1–2.

These different approaches can serve as models for future practice, though it should be noted that the approach that combines fair and equitable treatment with related standards of treatment has received most support in recent practice. Because all States would, as a matter of course, seek to treat local and foreign enterprises fairly and equitably, the inclusion of a clause on the fair and equitable standard in investment agreements does not, generally speaking, raise complex issues, except that the precise meaning of the fair and equitable standard may vary in different contexts.[25]

There is wide support in the literature in favour of according a plain meaning to the term 'fair and equitable'.[26] According to the plain or ordinary meaning approach, foreign investors have to be meted out treatment that is both 'fair' and 'equitable'. This approach would be consistent with the accepted rules of interpretation embodied in the Vienna Convention on the Law of Treaties. Although there are no judicial decisions on the precise meaning of the fair and equitable standard in particular situations, there do not seem to be significant differences of opinion as to the plain scope and meaning of this term. Accordingly, it can be submitted that the term should be understood in its plain, or literal, sense. This does not, of course, necessarily imply that there are no problems in defining the subjective concepts 'fair' and 'equitable' as states with different legal traditions may approach the issue with different assumptions. Nevertheless, the plain meaning approach is not completely devoid of content and international law offers some guidance as to how these terms must be interpreted.

According to the second approach, ie the international minimum standard approach, international law provides foreign investors with a certain level of treatment, and treatment that falls short of this level gives rise to liability on the part of the state. Hence, as stated by UNCTAD:

> If, in fact, fair and equitable treatment is the same as the international minimum standard, then some of the difficulties of interpretation inherent in the plain meaning approach may be overcome, for there is a substantial body of jurisprudence and doctrine concerning the elements of the international minimum standard.[27]

> Indeed, in most treaties and other instruments that provide for fair and equitable treatment for investments, the words 'fair' and 'equitable' are combined in the form of a reference to 'fair and equitable treatment'. This is particularly true with respect to recent investment instruments. ... [F]or instance, the model BITs prepared by Chile, China, France, Germany, the United States, and the United Kingdom, as well as regional instruments such as NAFTA, the 1993 Treaty Establishing the Common Market for Eastern and Southern Africa (COMESA) and the 1994 Energy Charter Treaty, all use the phrase 'fair and equitable treatment' apparently as part of a single concept.[28]

In jurisprudence, too, the principle of fair and equitable treatment has been defined variously and in vague terms by different tribunals. For instance, in *Waste Management v Mexico* it was held that:

> [T]he minimum standard of treatment of fair and equitable treatment is infringed by conduct attributable to the state and harmful to the claimant if the conduct is arbitrary, grossly

---

[25] Ibid, 2.
[26] S Vasciannie, 'The Fair and Equitable Treatment Standard in International Investment Law and Practice' (1999) 70 *British Year Book of International Law* 99, 104. See also M Klein Bronfman, 'Fair and Equitable Treatment: An Evolving Standard' (2006) 10 *Max Planck Yearbook of United Nations Law* 609.
[27] UNCTAD (n 24) 12.
[28] Ibid, 13–14.

unfair, unjust or idiosyncratic, is discriminatory and exposes the claimant to sectional or racial prejudice, or involves a lack of due process leading to an outcome which offends judicial propriety – as might be the case with a manifest failure of natural justice in judicial proceedings or a complete lack of transparency and candour in an administrative process. In applying this standard it is relevant that the treatment is in breach of representations made by the host State which were reasonably relied on by the claimant.[29]

The purpose of this phrase seems to be to prevent 'arbitrary' and 'discriminatory' treatment of foreign investors by a host state. The term 'arbitrary' was itself defined by the ICJ in the *ELSI* case as 'a willful disregard of due process of law, an act which shocks, or at least surprises, a sense of judicial propriety'.[30] This approach was also adopted by ICSID in *Noble Ventures v Romania* in which the tribunal stated that in order to claim protection under the phrase 'full protection and security' it was necessary to demonstrate that a certain measure was directed specifically against a certain investor by reason of his nationality.[31]

One of the regional FTAs providing as much guidance as possible on the meaning of the phrase 'minimum standard of treatment' is the CAFTA treaty. Article 10.5(1) and (2) of the treaty read as follows:

1. Each Party shall accord to covered investments treatment in accordance with customary international law, including fair and equitable treatment and full protection and security.
2. For greater certainty, paragraph 1 prescribes the customary international law minimum standard of treatment of aliens as the minimum standard of treatment to be afforded to covered investments. The concepts of 'fair and equitable treatment' and 'full protection and security' do not require treatment in addition to or beyond that which is required by that standard, and do not create additional substantive rights. The obligation in paragraph 1 to provide:
    (a) 'fair and equitable treatment' includes the obligation not to deny justice in criminal, civil, or administrative adjudicatory proceedings in accordance with the principle of due process embodied in the principal legal systems of the world; and
    (b) 'full protection and security' requires each Party to provide the level of police protection required under customary international law.

In addition to this definition of 'full protection and security', the CAFTA treaty goes on to insert an additional and interesting provision entitled, 'Treatment in Case of Strife'. Such a provision has not been common in most BITs of FTAs. Under Article 10.6, each state party to CAFTA is supposed to accord to investors of another state party, and to covered investments, non-discriminatory treatment with respect to measures it adopts or maintains relating to losses suffered by investments in its territory owing to armed conflict or civil strife. Furthermore, if a foreign investor, in such circumstances, suffers a loss resulting from: (a) requisitioning of its covered investment or part thereof by the forces or authorities of the host state; or (b) destruction of its covered investment or part thereof by them, which was not required by the necessity of the situation,

---

[29] *Waste Management Inc v Mexico*, A/F/00/3, paras 98–99 (ICSID) 2004.
[30] *Case Concerning Elettronica Sicula SpA (ELSI) (United States v Italy)*, ICJ Reports, 1989, para 128.
[31] *Noble Ventures v Romania*, ICSID Case No ARB/01/11, 12 October 2005, 111.

the host must provide the investor with restitution or compensation, which in either case shall be in accordance with customary international law.

In sum, the principle of fair and equitable treatment seems to be concerned mainly with the obligation not to deny justice in criminal, civil or administrative adjudicatory proceedings in accordance with the principle of due process embodied in the principal legal systems in use worldwide. However, in practice, various investment tribunals have accorded a wider meaning to this principle as if FET is what the arbitrators say is FET.

Full Protection and Security

The entitlement of foreign investors to 'full protection and security' is another norm to be found in many BITs and FTAs. There is no generally agreed definition of this term and different parties have claimed different levels of protection under this principle. For instance, in *Noble Ventures v Romania* it was argued that Romania was required to provide Noble Ventures with 'full protection and security', which required Romania to enforce its own laws and to provide police protection to protect the investment of foreign investors located in Romania.[32] The tribunal held that this phrase should not be understood as being wider in scope than the general duty to provide protection and security of foreign nationals found in the customary international law of aliens, which was limited to requiring due diligence to be exercised by the state. A similar approach was taken by the ICJ in the *ELSI* case in which it offered a rather restricted definition of this phrase. In other words, the phrase 'full protection and security' should be dependent on whether the state in question exercised 'due diligence' in affording protection to foreign investors.[33]

As stated by the arbitral tribunal in *Saluka Investments BV v the Czech Republic*, the 'full protection and security' standard applies essentially when the foreign investment has been affected by civil strife and physical violence. The host state must show that it has taken all measures of precaution to protect the investments of the investor in its territory. However, the guarantee of full protection and security is not absolute and does not impose strict liability upon the state that grants it. The tribunal concluded that 'the standard obliges the host State to adopt all reasonable measures to protect assets and property from threats or attacks which may target particularly foreigners or certain groups of foreigners'.[34] An ICSID tribunal in *Enron v Argentina*[35] also adopted a restrictive interpretation of the phrase 'full protection and security'. A number of BITs and FTAs also state that what is expected under 'full protection and security' is the level of police protection required under customary international law.

---

[32] Ibid, 12.

[33] *Wena Hotels Ltd v Arab Republic of Egypt*, ICSID Case No ARB/98/4, para 84.

[34] *Saluka Investments BV (the Netherlands) v the Czech Republic*, partial award of 2 March 2006: Permanent Court of Arbitration, www.pcacpa.org/ENGLISH/RPC/#Saluka (accessed 3 January 2007), paras 483 and 484.

[35] *Enron v Argentina*, award of 22 May 2007, available online at www.investmentclaims.com/decisions.

Most-Favoured-Nation Treatment

Most-favoured-nation (MFN) treatment is one of the oldest and most important principles of both foreign investment law and the law of international trade. The MFN clause seems to have found its expression in a treaty concluded as early as 1417 by King Henry IV of England with Duke John of Burgundy in Amiens granting English vessels the right to use the harbours of Flanders in the same way as 'French, Dutch, Sealanders and Scots'.[36] Although traditionally the MFN principle has been linked to trade agreements, it has come to play an important role in investment protection. The Draft Articles on Most-Favoured-Nation Clauses prepared by the ILC in 1978 provide that: 'A most-favoured-nation clause is a treaty provision whereby a State undertakes an obligation towards another State to accord most-favoured-nation treatment in an agreed sphere of relations.'[37] The reason why foreign investors seek protection under the MFN principle is to avoid any discrimination against them which would put them at a competitive disadvantage compared to other investors from third countries. The underlying idea behind the MFN principle is to ensure equality of competitive opportunities between investors from different foreign countries.

The following definition of the MFN principle by Schwarzenberger can be regarded as a traditional definition of this principle. According to Schwarzenberger, an MFN clause

> consists of forming an agency of equality. It prevents discrimination and establishes equality of opportunity on the highest possible plane: the minimum of discrimination and the maximum of favours conceded to any third State. ... It is clear that MFN clauses serve as insurance against incompetent draftsmanship and lack of imagination on the part of those who are responsible for the conclusion of international treaties. While it is thus that the standard of MFN treatment has the effect of putting the services of the shrewdest negotiator of a third country gratuitously at the disposal of one's country, another aspect of the matter is more significant. ... As long as a country is content to enjoy treatment equal to that of the most-favoured third country, and that subject matter of the treaty lends itself to such treatment, the use of the MFN standard leads to the constant self-adaptation of such treaties and greatly contributes to the rationalisation of international affairs.[38]

States often specify certain qualifications or exceptions to the MFN principle when extending MFN treatment to other states. For instance, a diplomatic note exchanged between Nepal and the UK to extend MFN treatment to goods stated that Nepal was 'willing to accord to British goods entering Nepal the treatment of the most favoured nation, save for the exceptional treatment given to India and Tibet'. Similarly, the UK

---

[36] SD Sutton, '*Emilio Augustin Maffezini v Kingdom of Spain* and the ICSID Secretary-General's Screening Power' (2005) 21(1) *Arbitration International* 113, 115.

[37] Art 4 of the Draft Articles on Most-Favoured-Nation Clauses with Commentaries adopted by the International Law Commission at its 30th session, in 1978, and submitted to the General Assembly, *Yearbook of the International Law Commission* (1978) vol II, part two.

[38] G Schwarzenberger, 'The Most Favoured Nation Standard in British State Practice' (1945) 22 *British Year Book of International Law* 96, 99.

stated that it 'will continue to accord to imports from Nepal the treatment of the most favoured nation, save for the special tariff reserved for members of the Commonwealth Preference Area and the European Free Trade Association'.[39]

As defined in an UNCTAD report, MFN treatment in the context of foreign investment means that 'a host country treats investors from one foreign country no less favourably than investors from any other foreign country'.[40] The report goes on to outline the essence of this principle in the following words:

> The MFN standard gives investors a guarantee against certain forms of discrimination by host countries, and it is crucial for the establishment of equality of competitive opportunities between investors from different foreign countries.

> The MFN standard may also have implications for host countries' room for manoeuvre in respect of future investment agreements, because it can create a so-called 'free rider' situation in that the MFN standard commits a host country to extend unilaterally to its treaty partners any additional rights that it grants to third countries in future agreements. Furthermore, as the globalization of investment activities makes corporate nationality more difficult to use as a ground for distinguishing between companies, it may become equally more difficult to identify the nation that actually benefits from MFN.[41]

MFN treatment is based on the principle of reciprocity. In general, the protection available under the MFN principle applies to all kinds of investment activities, such as the operation, maintenance, use, sale or liquidation of an investment. However, different treaties extend the protection available under this principle in different terms. Although most treaties, such as NAFTA, provide the protection for the 'establishment, acquisition, expansion, management, conduct, operation, and sale or other disposition of investments' (Article 1103), some others, such as the Energy Charter Treaty, cover all investment-related activities, 'including management, maintenance, use, enjoyment, or disposal' (Article 10, paragraph 7).[42]

An ICSID tribunal in the *Maffezini* case held that the broad definition of the MFN clause to be found in the Argentina–Spain BIT encompassed not only substantive rights but also international dispute settlement procedures.[43] Thus, such extension of the application of the MFN principle to dispute settlement provisions had allowed foreign investors to resort to dispute settlement mechanisms that were not stipulated or envisaged in the BIT between the home and host states concerned, but rather had been provided for in another BIT to which the host state was a party. The tribunal in *Maffezini* concluded that:

> Unless it appears clearly that the state parties to a BIT or the parties to a particular investment agreement settled on a different method for resolution of disputes that may arise,

---

[39] Agreement on Most Favoured Nation Treatment effected by exchange of notes signed at Kathmandu in 1965: www.tpcnepal.org.np/tagree/britain.htm (accessed 11 January 2007).

[40] UNCTAD, *Most-Favoured-Nation Treatment*, UNCTAD Series on Issues in International Investment Agreements (New York and Geneva, United Nations, 1999) 1.

[41] Ibid.

[42] See ibid, 6.

[43] *Emilio Augustin Maffezini v Kingdom of Spain*, ICSID Case No ARB/97/7, 25 January 2000. Art IV, para 2 of the Argentina–Spain BIT reads as follows: 'In all matters subject to this agreement, this treatment shall not be less favourable than that extended by each Party to the investments made in its territory by investors of a third country.'

most-favoured-nation provisions in BITs should be understood to be applicable to dispute settlement.[44]

However, in *Plama Construction v Bulgaria* an ICSID tribunal held that when the BIT was silent on this issue or the MFN definition was narrow in its scope, 'one cannot reason *a contrario* that the dispute resolution provisions must be deemed to be incorporated. ... Rather, the intention to incorporate dispute settlement provisions must be clearly and unambiguously expressed.'[45] This may be one reason why the UK Model BIT made it clear in Article 3(3) that the MFN principle included in the treaty will apply to dispute settlement procedures. Another example of a BIT that extends the application of the MFN principle to 'all matters' covered by the treaty is the Bulgaria–Cyprus BIT.[46] If a BIT has such a broad protection under the MFN principle it would seem to apply to both substantive and procedural matters. In *Gas Natural SDG v The Argentine Republic* the ICSID tribunal held that the claimant, a Spanish company, was entitled to avail itself of the dispute settlement provision in the US–Argentina BIT in reliance of the broad MFN provision to be found in the BIT between Spain and Argentina.[47]

Similarly, while the vast majority of investment treaties do not include binding provisions in relation to the admission of foreign investment, a number of treaties, especially those concluded recently, extend the MFN principle to include even pre-investment conditions. If the treaty concerned has not provided for pre-investment MFN treatment, the obligation is limited to activities only *after* an investment has been made. However, if the treaty provides for MFN treatment even with regard to the pre-establishment phase, contracting parties are expected to create non-discriminatory conditions for new foreign investors and admit their investments under conditions similar to those already in place in the country concerned. An example of a treaty which provides for MFN treatment only in relation to post-entry investment is Article 10(7) of the Energy Charter Treaty, which reads as follows:

> Each Contracting Party shall accord to Investments in its Area of Investors of other Contracting Parties, and their related activities including management, maintenance, use, enjoyment or disposal, treatment no less favourable than that which it accords to Investments of its own Investors or of the Investors of any other Contracting Party or any third state and their related activities including management, maintenance, use, enjoyment or disposal, whichever is the most favourable.[48]

However, the model followed by most US BITs and some recent Canadian treaties requires the application of the MFN standard in respect of both the establishment and subsequent treatment of investment. Article 1103 of NAFTA is an example:

1. Each Party shall accord to investors of another Party treatment no less favourable than that it accords, in like circumstances, to investors of any other Party or of a non-Party

---

[44] Ibid, para 49.

[45] *Plama Consortium v Bulgaria*, ICSID Case No ARB/03/24, 8 February 2005, paras 203 and 204.

[46] See S Fietta, 'Most Favoured Nation Treatment and Dispute Resolution under Bilateral Investment Treaties: A Turning Point?' (2005) Issue 4 *International Arbitration Law Review* 131.

[47] *Gas Natural SDG v The Argentine Republic*, ICSID Case No ARB/03/10, 17 June 2005, para 31 (Preliminary Questions on Jurisdiction).

[48] As cited in UNCTAD (n 40) 14.

with respect to the establishment, acquisition, expansion, management, conduct, operation, and sale or other disposition of investments.

2. Each Party shall accord to investments of investors of another Party treatment no less favourable than it accords, in like circumstances, to investments of investors of any other Party or of a non-Party with respect to the establishment, acquisition, expansion, management, conduct, operation, and sale or other disposition of investments.[49]

Other examples of pre- and post-entry clauses can be found in the Southern Common Market (MERCOSUR), Colonia Protocol (Article 2) and in the Asia-Pacific Economic Cooperation (APEC) Non-Binding Investment Principles.[50]

National Treatment

The objective of the national treatment principle is to address discrimination on the basis of nationality of ownership of an investment. In order to ascertain what is discrimination it is necessary to compare the treatment of the foreign investor to the treatment accorded to a domestic investor in similar circumstances. What is a 'like' situation and what is not depends on the nature of investment. The decision in the *Methanex* case is instructive.

In this case the tribunal was faced with an allegation of discriminatory treatment by the state of California against Methanex Corporation, claiming that ethanol and methanol producers were in 'like circumstances' and the Californian ban on methanol products but not on ethanol products was discriminatory. The US argued that methanol and ethanol differed chemically and these two different products had different end uses. The tribunal concluded that Methanex Corporation did not receive less favourable treatment than the domestic methanol-producing comparators. Discrimination between ethanol and methanol producers was a different matter, but the Californian measure did not discriminate between methanol producers themselves.[51] The tribunal also drew a distinction between the terms 'like products' and 'like circumstances' and held that the definition of 'like products' under GATT/WTO law could not necessarily be applied to cases of foreign investment where the term 'like circumstances' was the key in according non-discriminatory treatment to foreign investors. Thus, the principle of national treatment under foreign investment law has a slightly different meaning from the meaning accorded to this principle in international trade law. As stated in an UNCTAD report on national treatment:

[T]he national treatment standard is perhaps the single most important standard of treatment enshrined in international investment agreements (IIAs). At the same time, it is perhaps the most difficult standard to achieve as it touches upon economically (and politically) sensitive issues. In fact, no single country has so far seen itself in a position to grant

---

[49] Ibid, 14–15.
[50] Ibid, 15.
[51] *Methanex Corporation v USA*, ICSID, 3 August 2005, part IV, ch B, 10.

national treatment without qualifications, especially when it comes to the establishment of an investment.[52]

The report goes on to define this principle in the following words and to outline the nature of the difficulties involved in the implementation of these principles:

> National treatment can be defined as a principle whereby a host country extends to foreign investors treatment that is at least as favourable as the treatment that it accords to national investors in like circumstances. In this way the national treatment standard seeks to ensure a degree of competitive equality between national and foreign investors. This raises difficult questions concerning the factual situations in which national treatment applies and the precise standard of comparison by which the treatment of national and foreign investors is to be compared.

> National treatment typically extends to the post-entry treatment of foreign investors. However, some bilateral investment treaties (BITs) and other IIAs also extend the standard to pre-entry situations. This has raised the question of the proper limits of national treatment, in that such an extension is normally accompanied by a 'negative list' of excepted areas of investment activity to which national treatment does not apply, or a 'positive list' of areas of investment activity to which national treatment is granted. In addition, several types of general exceptions to national treatment exist concerning public health, safety and morals, and national security, although these may not be present in all agreements, particularly not in BITs.[53]

Outlining the rationale behind this principle, this UNCTAD report states that:

> For many countries, the standard of national treatment serves to eliminate distortions in competition and thus is seen to enhance the efficient operation of the economies involved. An extension of this argument points to the ongoing internationalization of investment and production and concludes that access to foreign markets under non-discriminatory conditions is necessary for the effective functioning of an increasingly integrated world economy.[54]

However, it also has been acknowledged in international law and practice that because of stark inequalities in economic power, technical capabilities and financial strength, a certain differentiation between national and non-national firms may be necessary precisely in order to bring about a degree of operative equality since there may be no substitute for the promotion by host countries of domestic industries to ensure economic development of developing countries. Thus, according to UNCTAD, 'national treatment is a relative standard whose content depends on the underlying state of treatment for domestic and foreign investors alike'.[55] The UNCTAD report outlines the balance to be achieved and the recent trends in the application of this principle in the following words:

> It is also a standard that has its origins primarily in trade treaties, though, as noted below, the term has also been used in a quite different context, namely in relation to the customary international law standards for the treatment of aliens and their property. A certain degree

---

[52] UNCTAD, *National Treatment*, UNCTAD Series on Issues in International Investment Agreements (New York and Geneva, United Nations, 1999) 1.
[53] Ibid.
[54] Ibid, 2.
[55] Ibid, 3.

of adaptation of the standard to the characteristics of investment is therefore required so that it may be used in an effective way in IIAs.

In the context of foreign investment relations, until relatively recently, national treatment was seen to be relevant almost exclusively to the treatment accorded to foreign investors after they had entered a host country. However, some more recent IIAs particularly the BITs entered into by Canada and the United States (apart from the FCN treaties of the United States), have extended national treatment to the pre-entry stage so as to ensure market access for foreign investors on terms equal to those enjoyed by national investors. As national treatment traditionally applied in most BITs only to the post-establishment phase of an investment, and there was little question that the pre-establishment phase was left to the sovereign right of States in terms of deciding on admission of an investment, the extension of national treatment from the post- to the pre-investment phase is a 'revolution' for many countries. This has made the discussions about the type and extent of exceptions to national treatment that may be required in order to retain a measure of host country discretion in investment matters all the more important. In particular, ... there may be a choice between granting a general right to national treatment subject to a 'negative list' of excepted industries and areas to which national treatment does not apply, and proceeding on the basis of a 'positive list' where no *a priori* general right to national treatment is granted and national treatment extends only to those industries and areas specifically included in the positive list.[56]

The principle of national treatment has two facets to it. One of them has its origins in the Calvo doctrine under which aliens and their property are entitled only to the same treatment accorded to nationals of the host country under its national laws. The other has its basis in the doctrine of state responsibility for injuries to aliens and their property under which customary international law is regarded as having established a minimum international standard of treatment to which aliens are entitled. This concept of international minimum standard would allow for more favourable treatment than that accorded to nationals where this falls below the international minimum standard. Historically, the idea based on the Calvo doctrine is favoured by developing countries and the one based on the principle of state responsibility is favoured by developed countries.

One of the main issues of contention with regard to the principle of national treatment in the recent past has been its scope and application: at what stage of the investment process does national treatment apply? In other words, the question is whether national treatment applies to both the pre- and post-entry stages of the investment process or whether the national treatment standard applies only to investments that have already been admitted to a host country. The practice varies. While the trend in the recent past, especially in NAFTA and the US and Canadian Model BITs, stresses pre- and post-entry rights, the European Model provides only for post-entry protection. There also are a number of treaties which contain no provision concerning national treatment because the host countries do not wish to extend preferential treatment enjoyed by its domestic enterprises to foreign enterprises.

There is also the question as to whether it is the investment, the investor or both that are to receive national treatment. Here too, state practice seems to vary

---

[56] Ibid, 3–4 (references omitted).

considerably. While some BITs extend national treatment to investment, others refer to 'enterprises and the activities of enterprises', thereby excluding 'investors' in the enterprise from national treatment in certain matters such as taxation. Consequently, an increasing number of IIAs seem to include separate provisions granting the investor and the investment national treatment. The BIT between Jamaica and the UK (Article 3), NAFTA (Article 1102(1) and (2)) and the Asian-African Legal Consultative Committee (AALCC) Model BITs A and B are examples. The Energy Charter Treaty is one of the more recent regional treaties containing a broader coverage of protection. Its Article 10(7) extends national treatment to the operations of foreign investments/investors after they enter the host country:

> Each Contracting Party shall accord to Investments in its Area of Investors of other Contracting Parties, and their related activities including management, maintenance, use, enjoyment or disposal, treatment no less favourable than that which it accords to Investments of its own Investors or of the Investors of any other Contracting Party or any third state and their related activities including management, maintenance, use, enjoyment or disposal, whichever is the most favourable.[57]

Thus, the trend in both bilateral BITs and regional or multilateral investment treaties seems to be to move towards a more inclusive and broader application of the principle of national treatment.

Protection against Expropriation in Customary International Law

Protection of foreign investment against expropriation is a centuries-old principle of foreign investment law. International law does provide that states as sovereign entities can expropriate the assets of foreign investors in certain situations, provided that a number of conditions outlined in international law are met. But the meaning and scope of these conditions have attracted much attention in both jurisprudence and in the foreign investment law literature. There is a large amount of literature on what constitutes expropriation and what level of compensation is required in international law against expropriation.

As a rule of thumb, foreign-owned property may not be expropriated or subjected to a measure tantamount to expropriation unless four conditions are met. They are as follows:

1. an expropriation must be for a public purpose;
2. it should be non-discriminatory;
3. it is taken in accordance with applicable laws and due process; and
4. full compensation is paid.

---

[57] Ibid, 20–21.

However, questions such as what constitutes expropriation; what is a 'public purpose';[58] what constitutes discrimination; and what is meant by full compensation have been matters of acute controversy in both jurisprudence and the literature for a long time and most international law scholars have made their own contribution to this debate. According to Higgins, the 'public purpose' principle signifies 'a means of differentiating takings for purely private gain on the part of the ruler from those for reasons related to the economic preferences of the country concerned'.[59]

Taking without due process of law would entail a taking in contravention of the principle of equality before the law, fair hearing and other principles of natural justice generally recognised by the world's principal legal systems. Similarly, a discriminatory taking would entail unlawful discrimination between domestic and foreign investors engaged in like business and in like circumstances as well as between foreigners of different nationalities. No rule of customary international law prevents a state from treating foreign investors differently from domestic investors. However, a number of international human rights treaties such as the 1966 International Covenant on Civil and Political Rights (ICCPR), BITs, FTAs and WTO agreements outline the standard of treatment to be meted out to foreign investors. A violation of such standards would be a discriminatory treatment. Similarly, the principle of national treatment would prevent a state from treating domestic and foreign investors differently over certain matters. For instance, three German farmers sued the government of Namibia for expropriating their land, stating that the seizure of their land in 2004 under a 1995 land reform act was discriminatory and thus against the national standard treatment of the Namibia–German BIT. Their allegation was that the government targeted farms owned by foreign nationals and thus failed to meet its international obligation to treat German investors the same as Namibian nationals.

Although some of the more recent FTAs such as CAFTA seek to define the terms 'expropriation', 'direct expropriation' and 'indirect expropriation', the meaning of these terms in foreign investment law remains controversial. Generally speaking, based on jurisprudence and the literature on the subject matter, the following five types of expropriations can be inferred as constituting expropriation proper:

Direct Expropriation

This constitutes the actual taking of property by the host government by direct means, including the loss of all, or almost all, useful control of property. This is the most

---

[58] Art 5 of the Italy–Pakistan BIT states that an expropriation could be for a public purpose, or national interest but does not define either the terms 'public purpose' or 'national interest'. It reads as follows:

1.   The investments to which this Agreement relates shall not be subject to any measure which might limit permanently or temporarily the right of ownership, possession, control or enjoyment, save where specifically provided by law and by judgments or orders issued by Courts or Tribunals having jurisdiction.
2.   Investments of investors of one of the Contracting Parties shall not be directly or indirectly nationalized, expropriated, requisitioned or subjected to any measures having similar effects in the territory of the other Contracting Party, except for public purposes, or national interest, against immediate full and effective compensation and on condition that these measures are taken on a non-discriminatory basis and in conformity with all legal provisions and procedures.

[59] R Higgins, 'The Taking of Property by the State' (1982-III) 176 *Recueil des Cours* 259, 371.

obvious form of outright expropriation and its definition is less controversial. For instance, CAFTA defines 'direct expropriation' as a situation where 'an investment is nationalized or otherwise directly expropriated through formal transfer of title or outright seizure'.[60] Although cases of traditional forms of direct or outright expropriations are becoming rare, certain forms of direct expropriation do still take place mainly for environmental or other developmental purposes. For instance, Peru decided to issue an expropriation decree in 2001 on the grounds of public necessity concerning environmental or ecological protection. The measures taken were basically regulatory measures designed to annul or revoke operating licences granted to foreign investors, mainly from Chile, in the Ecological Reserve of Pantanos de Ville of Peru, and to remove or close the industrial establishment in the Reserve.[61] Similarly, Namibia enacted a land reform law in 1995 giving the government permission to expropriate property in the public interest, provided just compensation was paid, and the government exercised this power and expropriated land belonging to certain German nationals in 2004.

Indirect Expropriation

This involves taking a governmental, whether administrative or legislative, measure that does not directly take property but has the same impact by depriving the owner of the substantial benefits of the property. This is one of the more controversial forms of expropriation. The definition and explanation of 'indirect expropriation' in CAFTA is an example of a recent attempt to limit the scope of this term. According to Annex 10-C (4) of this treaty, indirect expropriation is a situation 'where an action or series of actions by a Party has an effect equivalent to direct expropriation without formal transfer of title or outright seizure'. It goes on to say that:

(a) The determination of whether an action or series of actions by a Party, in a specific fact situation, constitutes an indirect expropriation, requires a case-by case, fact-based inquiry that considers, among other factors:

   (i) the economic impact of the government action, although the fact that an action or series of actions by a Party has an adverse effect on the economic value of an investment, standing alone, does not establish that an indirect expropriation has occurred;
   (ii) the extent to which the government action interferes with distinct, reasonable investment-backed expectations; and
   (iii) the character of the government action.

(b) Except in rare circumstances, non-discriminatory regulatory actions by a Party that are designed and applied to protect legitimate public welfare objectives, such as public health, safety, and the environment, do not constitute indirect expropriations.

---

[60] CAFTA: www.ustr.gov/new/fta/cafta/text; Art 10-C(3).
[61] For a summary of the content of these decrees, see *Empresas Lucchetti v Peru*, ICSID Case No ARB/03/4, 7 February 2005.

There is a growing tendency on the part of foreign companies to extend the meaning of the term 'indirect expropriation' to include a raft of governmental measures, omissions and commissions that have an impact on foreign investors. For instance, in *EnCana Corporation v Ecuador* the claimant Canadian company alleged that the denial of refunds of VAT by the government of Ecuador to two of its subsidiaries doing business in Ecuador amounted to indirect expropriation. However, the arbitral tribunal sitting under the UNCITRAL Rules at the London Court of Arbitration rejected the claim.[62]

Creeping Expropriation

Creeping expropriation is also a form of indirect expropriation and involves the use of a series of governmental measures to reduce the economic value of the investment. What is involved here is the cumulative impact of the measures rather than individual measures which on their own may not amount to expropriation.

Regulatory Expropriation

This form of expropriation has been regarded as another form of indirect expropriation. Under this type of expropriation, a measure taken by the host government for regulatory purposes has an impact on the economic value of the asset owned by the foreign investor sufficient to be deemed an expropriation. The major challenge here is to distinguish between a legitimate exercise of governmental discretion that interferes with the enjoyment of foreign-owned property and a regulatory taking that amounts to expropriation requiring compensation. In order for such a measure to constitute regulatory expropriation the measure should be a discriminatory one. A non-discriminatory regulatory measure designed to protect legitimate public welfare objectives does not necessarily constitute regulatory expropriation.[63] Indeed, a number of BITs and RTAs recognise the rights of states to adopt certain measures designed to ensure that investment activity is undertaken in a manner sensitive to environmental concerns. The provisions in Article 10.12 of the FTA between Chile and the US, Article 114(2) of NAFTA, Article 12 of the 2004 Model US BIT, Article 10.11 of CAFTA and Article 15.10 of the Singapore–US FTA are examples.[64]

The Canada–Peru BIT of 2006 goes much further in outlining the scope of regulatory measures. Annex B.13(1)(c) provides that:

> Except in rare circumstances, such as when a measure or series of measures is so severe in the light of its purpose that it cannot be reasonably viewed as having been adopted and

[62] *EnCana Corporation v Ecuador*, LCIA Case UN 3481, award of an UNCITRAL tribunal sitting at the London Court of Arbitration, 3 February 2006, para 178.

[63] Eg, see Art 10-C(3)(b) CAFTA: www.ustr.gov/new/fta/cafta/text.

[64] Art 10.12 of the Chile–US FTA reads as follows: 'Nothing in this Chapter shall be construed to prevent a Party from adopting, maintaining, or enforcing any measure otherwise consistent with this Chapter that it considers appropriate to ensure that investment activity in its territory is undertaken in a manner sensitive to environmental concerns' (www.chileusafta.com/about-agreement.html). Identical provisions can be found in a number of other BITs and FTAs.

applied in good faith, non-discriminatory measures of a Party that are designed and applied to protect legitimate public welfare objectives, such as health, safety and the environment, do not constitute indirect expropriation.

A much broader provision on regulatory measures is included in a draft article in an agreement between the EU and the Pacific members of the ACP countries of June 2006:

> Consistent with the rights of States to regulate and the customary international law principle on police powers, bona fide, non-discriminatory regulatory measures taken by a Party that are designed and applied to protect or enhance legitimate public welfare objectives, such as public health, safety and the environment, do not constitute an expropriation under this Article.[65]

This set a remarkable example and began a new trend, pointing the direction of the development of foreign investment law.

As early as 1961 the Harvard Draft Convention on the International Responsibility of States for Injuries to Aliens recognised the following categories of non-compensable takings:

> An uncompensated taking of an alien property or a deprivation of the use or enjoyment of property of an alien which results from the execution of tax laws; from a general change in the value of currency; from the action of the competent authorities of the State in the maintenance of public order, health or morality; or from the valid exercise of belligerent rights or otherwise incidental to the normal operation of the laws of the State shall not be considered wrongful.[66]

This provision was regarded as representing customary international law by an arbitral tribunal of the Permanent Court of Arbitration in *Saluka Investments BV (the Netherlands) v the Czech Republic* in March 2006.[67] The tribunal stated that the above-quoted passage in the Harvard Draft Convention is subject to four important exceptions:

> An uncompensated taking of the sort referred to shall not be considered unlawful provided that:
>
> (a) it is not a clear and discriminatory violation of the law of the State concerned;
> (b) it is not the result of a violation of any provision of Articles 6 to 8 [of the draft Convention];
> (c) it is not an unreasonable departure from the principles of justice recognised by the principal legal systems of the world;
> (d) it is not an abuse of the powers specified in this paragraph for the purpose of depriving an alien of his property.[68]

---

[65] Draft Art 8.8(I) of the investment chapter in the context of the EU/PACP EPA negotiations, DG Trade G 1(D), 10 October 2006.

[66] See LB Sohn and RR Baxter, 'Responsibility of States for Injuries to the Economic Interests of Aliens' (1961) 55 *American Journal of International Law* 515.

[67] *Saluka Investments BV (the Netherlands) v the Czech Republic*, a partial award of 2 March 2006: Permanent Court of Arbitration, www.pcacpa.org/ENGLISH/RPC/#Saluka (accessed 3 January 2007).

[68] Ibid, para 257.

The tribunal went on to add that:

> [T]hese exceptions do not, in any way, weaken the principle that certain takings or depriva-
> tions are non-compensable. They merely remind the legislator or, indeed, the adjudicator,
> that the so-called 'police power exception' is not absolute.

It is noteworthy that an accompanying note to the 1967 OECD Draft Convention on
the Protection of Foreign Property includes a broader notion of 'police power' by stating that measures taken in the pursuit of a state's 'political, social or economic ends'
do not constitute compensable expropriation.[69] A similar notion is also included in the
United States Third Restatement of the Law of Foreign Relations, according to which
bona fide regulations and 'other action[s] of the kind that is commonly accepted as
within the police power of State' are permissible regulatory measures that are lawful
and non-compensable.[70] Similarly, the tribunal in *Methanex Corporation v USA* held
recently in its final award that '[i]t is a principle of customary international law that,
where economic injury results from a *bona fide* regulation within the police powers of
a State, compensation is not required'.[71]

Consequential or De Facto Expropriation

This is yet another form of indirect expropriation and is a more recent invention of
mainly international law scholars. Although this form of expropriation is akin to regulatory expropriation, some writers have grouped certain types of activities within this
form of expropriation. For instance, Reisman and Sloane define the phrase as involving

> deprivations of the economic value of a foreign investment, which within the legal regime
> established by a BIT, must be deemed expropriatory because of their casual links to failures
> of the host state to fulfil its paramount obligations to establish and maintain an appropriate
> legal, administrative, and regulatory formative framework for foreign investment.[72]

They go on to state that this form of expropriation results from misfeasance, malfeasance and nonfeasance of the host state.

However, it is very difficult to ascertain what constitutes consequential expropriation because in this form of expropriation host states do not have an intent to
expropriate. Although *mens rea* has never been a requirement to establish a host
state's responsibility to pay compensation for expropriation, 'the manifestation of
that intent at some level of the state's government generally furnishes a tribunal with
a useful demarcation'.[73] But these forms of expropriations lack such demarcations.

---

[69] OECD Draft Convention on the Protection of Foreign Property (12 October 1967) 71 ILM 117.

[70] Restatement (Third) of Foreign Relations Law, s 712 cmt g (1987).

[71] *Methanex Corporation v USA*, ICSID, 3 August 2005, para 410, Final Award on Jurisdiction and Merits,
(2005) 44 ILM 1345, Inside US Trade, 19 August 2005, 12, IIC 167 (2005), 3 August 2005, Ad Hoc Tribunal
(UNCITRAL).

[72] W Michael Reisman and RD Sloane, 'Indirect Expropriation and its Valuation in the BIT Generation'
(2003) 74 *British Year Book of International Law* 115, 130.

[73] Ibid, 131.

Furthermore, in cases such as *Olguin v Republic of Paraguay* it was implied that omission to act on the part of a host government could not be an expropriation.[74] To constitute expropriation, a positive act on the part of the host government or a transfer of rights or the fruits of the investment had to be demonstrated. Similarly, Argentina argued in *Enron v Argentina* that in international law the introduction of an expropriatory legislative or administrative measure does not necessarily empower an international tribunal, including ICSID, to impede an expropriation that falls exclusively within the ambit of state sovereignty; such tribunals can only establish whether there has been an expropriation, its legality or illegality, and the corresponding compensation.[75] However, with reference to the *Rainbow Warrior*[76] and other cases an ICSID tribunal held that:

> [I]n addition to declaratory powers, it has the power to order measures involving performance or injunction of certain acts. Jurisdiction is therefore also affirmed on this ground. What kind of measures might or might not be justified, whether the acts complained of meet the standards set out in the *Rainbow Warrior*, and how the issue of implementation that the parties have also discussed would be handled, if appropriate, are all matters that belong to the merits.[77]

Although this ruling is broadly consistent with international jurisprudence concerning public international law matters, it is a new development in foreign investment law. It may encourage foreign investors to resort to the ICSID and other international arbitration mechanisms asking for preventative measures well before an expropriation has actually taken place.

The Standards of Compensation in Customary International Law

Traditionally, international law requires a host government to pay compensation for expropriation without specifying the nature of the compensation. It has been argued that that such compensation should be regarded as 'full' compensation and the term 'full' itself means 'prompt, adequate and effective'. Indeed, a vast majority of BITs, RTAs and FTAs require 'prompt, adequate and effective' compensation against all

---

[74] *Eudoro Armando Olguin v Republic of Paraguay*, ICSID Case No ARB/98/5 Award of 26 July 2001. See UNCTAD (n 8) 45.

[75] *Enron Corporation and Ponderosa Assets, LP v The Argentine Republic*, ICSID Case No ARB/01/3, decision on jurisdiction of 14 January 2004, para 76.

[76] In the *Rainbow Warrior* case it had been held that 'The authority to issue an order for the cessation or discontinuance of a wrongful act or omission results from the inherent powers of a competent tribunal which is confronted with the continuous breach of an international obligation which is in force and continues to be in force. The delivery of such an order requires, therefore, two essential conditions intimately linked, namely that the wrongful act has a continuing character and that the violated rule is still in force at the time in which the order is issued'. (1990) XX *Reports of International Arbitral Awards* 217, 270.

[77] *Enron Corporation and Ponderosa Assets, LP v The Argentine Republic*, ICSID Case No ARB/01/3, decision on jurisdiction of 14 January 2004, para 81.

forms of expropriation. For example, Article 13 of the Canada–Peru BIT of 2006 reads as follows:

Expropriation

1. Neither Party shall nationalize or expropriate a covered investment either directly, or indirectly through measures having an effect equivalent to nationalization or expropriation (hereinafter referred to as 'expropriation'), except for a public purpose, in accordance with due process of law, in a non-discriminatory manner and on prompt, adequate and effective compensation. [footnote omitted]

This is a typical provision on expropriation and compensation which can be found in hundreds of BITs. However, this is not to say that this standard of compensation has been universally accepted. For instance, a number of BITs, such as the UK–India BIT of 1994, speak of 'just' or 'appropriate' compensation rather than 'full' or 'prompt, adequate and effective' compensation. Another example of a BIT providing for 'just' compensation is that concluded between the Netherlands and Poland. However, the details of what Article 5 of this BIT provides with regard to just compensation are very similar to the provisions concerning 'prompt, adequate and effective' compensation.[78] Similar language can be found in the Netherlands–Czech Republic BIT.

It is worth noting that NAFTA does not speak directly of 'prompt, adequate and effective' compensation, albeit the detailed provisions included on compensation come close to this standard. Even if 'prompt, adequate and effective' compensation is accepted as the requirement under international law, there is no universally accepted meaning of the terms 'prompt' or 'adequate' or 'effective'. In some cases before ICSID tribunals it has been argued that the host state concerned was required to provide 'immediate' compensation.[79] It is interesting to note that the Fifth Amendment of the US Constitution requires 'just' compensation when the state takes private property for public use. When it comes to seeking compensation for its investors abroad, the US supports the 'prompt, adequate and effective' formula.

Access to International Arbitration

Another major protection available to foreign investors is access to international arbitration tribunals operating under both public and private international law. There is no

---

[78] Art 5 of the Treaty reads as follows:

Neither Contracting Party shall take any measures depriving, directly or indirectly, investors of the other Contracting Party of their investments unless the following conditions are complied with:

(a) the measures are taken in the public interest and under due process of law;
(b) the measures are not discriminatory or contrary to any undertaking which the former Contracting Party may have given;
(c) the measures are accompanied by provision for the payment of just compensation.

Such compensation shall represent the real value of the investments affected and shall, in order to be effective for the claimants, be paid and made transferable, without undue delay, to the country designated by the claimants concerned in any freely convertible currency accepted by the claimants.

[79] *Noble Ventures v Romania*, ICSID Case No ARB/01/11, 12 October 2005, 12.

requirement under customary international law to grant access for foreign investors to international arbitration tribunals. However, most of the BITs and other IIAs provide for an international mechanism for settlement of investment disputes. Access to international commercial arbitration has, of course, been commonplace and is a matter regulated by private contracts between an investor and the host government. However, the idea of granting access to foreign investors to treaty-based bodies operating under international law is a novelty and a post-Second World War innovation. When the practice of concluding BITs to attract foreign investment began in the late 1950s and early 1960s, host states agreed to offer additional protection to foreign investors by agreeing to international arbitration in legal disputes with investors.

The objective was to assure foreign investors that they would not suffer from any hazards of delay and political pressure in the adjudication of investment disputes in national courts. Indeed a recent report demonstrated that it normally takes 880 days to enforce a contract via local courts in Pakistan and a staggering 1,442 days in Bangladesh, whereas the average within the OECD countries is 351 days.[80] A BIT is the result of a grand bargain between an investment-exporting state and investment-receiving state. In this bargain the latter agree to refer a dispute with a foreign investor to an international investment tribunal such as ICSID in return for the flow of investment from the former. Consequently, an overwhelming majority of BITs, RTAs and FTAs provide for access to international arbitration tribunals.

Conclusion

As has been seen in the preceding paragraphs, the regime of protection for foreign investors has become as comprehensive and as robust as possible in customary international law. Most of the fundamental principles of foreign investment law are now firmly established in customary international law. Accordingly, foreign investors are entitled to the protection of such principles even in the absence of a BIT between a host and home state. Although developing countries have traditionally resisted the pressure to include in multilateral instruments provisions on foreign investment providing a higher level of protection than already available under international law, they have concluded BITs with developed countries that provide much higher levels of protection to foreign investors with a view to attracting a greater flow of foreign investment. Therefore, the standard of treatment available to foreign investors under BITs is much greater than those available under traditional international law.

---

[80] See report on 'Business and Governance', *Financial Times*, 14 March 2007, 5.

5

Protection of Foreign Investment Through Bilateral Investment Treaties

Introduction

In the absence of an international treaty on the regulation or protection of foreign investment, many states have concluded BITs or other IIAs such as FTAs (for convenience all of these agreements will be referred to as BITs in this chapter) with a view to attracting foreign investment by according these investors an additional layer of protection. The primary purpose of a BIT is to protect the property rights of foreign investors, whether natural or juridical. Although it has not been proven that concluding a BIT increases the flow of foreign investment, most developing states have in recent decades jumped on the BIT bandwagon. Nevertheless, certain states, such as Brazil, continue to attract foreign investment in spite of remaining unenthusiastic about either concluding or ratifying BITs.

However, a significant number of developing states concluded such treaties with the hope of attracting foreign investment. It is only recently that many of these countries have started regretting concluding such treaties and are taking remedial measures including terminating them. Both South Africa and Indonesia have taken a lead in this direction. For instance, Indonesia took the bold decision to terminate its BIT with its former colonial power, the Netherlands, in July 2015. Nevertheless, as things stand BITs generally play a crucial role in the regulation or protection of foreign investment. Therefore, this chapter aims to analyse the institution of BITs, the nature of the protection extended to foreign investors under BITs and the contribution BITs have made to the development of foreign investment law. It will also make reference to the investment protection provisions of the main regional trade and investment treaties as well as the recent FTAs. The objective is to demonstrate how a paradigm shift is taking place in the provision of BITs, FTAs and other IIAs with regard to the protection of foreign investors under these treaties as opposed to customary international law. In doing so, this chapter will also show how the approach of developing countries themselves to foreign investment has changed over the years.

The Origins of Bilateral Investment Treaties

States have traditionally welcomed foreign investment for a variety of reasons. Foreign investment has been regarded as, inter alia, an engine of economic growth, a source of foreign currency income, a stimulator of the local economy, and a source of foreign skills, information and know-how. Foreign investment takes place in different forms, including through committing capital resources abroad either directly or through portfolio investment and by licensing the use of technology, etc. Because of the form such investment takes, it requires special protection under the law of the country concerned. This is because foreigners who purchase land and other immovable property or invest in long-term infrastructure related projects such as building dams, roads, or railways or laying the pipelines for gas, petrochemical products or water or telecommunications or the internet or enter into joint ventures to create a new company cannot leave the host country as and when they want. Their commitment to the host country is long term, and hence there is a need for long-term protection under special laws. Such protection has traditionally been sought under international law and more recently under BITs.

Unlike local laws on foreign investment, which can also offer adequate protection and incentives to foreign investors but are liable to change with a change of government, no state can unilaterally change international law or the provisions of BITs.[1] Such treaties are of long duration, usually 10 or 20 years, with continuing coverage – normally for 20 years after termination – on investments made whilst they are in force. The formal safeguards and guarantees that BITs provide for non-commercial risks have acted as an incentive to potential investors and as a useful reassurance to those with existing investments in the signatory states. Therefore, when it comes to promoting foreign investment, states have sought additional safeguards and guarantees under international law and BITs, which are designed to set standards of protection. Although any protection provided for foreign investment is always under the law of the host country, this law has to conform to the commitments undertaken by the state concerned either under BITs, FTAs or other principles of international law.

Another distinct characteristic of BITs is that they are concluded mainly between a developed and a developing country. Among the thousands of BITs concluded thus far, only a tiny number are between two developed countries. Most developed countries are stable democracies where the right to property is protected by law, the judiciary is by and large independent, and there is little non-commercial or political risk involved in investments made there.

---

[1] See a background paper on BITs produced by the British Foreign and Commonwealth Office, Press Release on Investment Promotion and Protection Agreements, Press Release No 174 (1230) 21 October 1991.

The Content of Bilateral Investment Treaties

Although thousands of BITs have been concluded, the basic characteristics of such treaties are more or less the same. As Judge Schwebel writes, '[t]he very purpose of treaties is to constrain the freedom of States'.[2] However, the questions that have dominated the debate around BITs in recent years concern to what extent the states agreed to constrain their freedom and what their intention was when they concluded such treaties. BITs are designed to cover the following five substantive areas: (i) definition of investment and investor; (ii) admission of foreign investors; (iii) fair and equitable treatment of investors; (iv) compensation in the event of expropriation; and (v) methods of settling disputes. Although the exact nature and the content of a BIT concluded between one state and another may differ from those concluded between other states, most BITs follow a certain pattern and contain similar provisions. Most BITs are designed to extend fair and equitable treatment, full protection and security, and MFN and national treatment to investors. BITs are intended to protect such investment from expropriation without compensation and against any mistreatment and to provide a legal remedy, generally through international arbitration not only between states but also between an investor and the host state, against any violations of the provisions of the BIT concerned. Some of the more recent BITs impose a ban on performance requirements and on restrictions on the expatriation of profits and investments, etc.

The Significance of Bilateral Investment Treaties

In the view of many international tribunals and scholars, the law on foreign investment at this juncture seems to be the law supported, albeit not created, by the provisions of BITs and multilateral treaties such as NAFTA. Indeed, although the individual BITs could be regarded as *lex specialis*,[3] it is difficult to deny that the practice of states in concluding such treaties is capable of strengthening the alleged rules of customary international law on the subject. As will be seen in the next section, these treaties have been regarded by international tribunals in various cases as a source of law. Of course, doubts have been expressed in the *Aminoil* case[4] and the *Sedco* case[5] on the value of such treaties in creating rules of customary international law on expropriation and compensation. In the *Sedco* case the Iran–US Claims Tribunal stated that:

> Assessment of the present state of customary law on the subject on the basis of the conduct of States in actual practice is difficult, *inter alia*, because of the questionable evidentiary

---

[2] SM Schwebel, 'In Defense of Bilateral Investment Treaties' (2015) 31 *Arbitration International* 181, 189.
[3] See M Sornarajah, 'State Responsibility and Bilateral Investment Treaties' (1986) 20 *Journal of World Trade Law* 79, 82.
[4] *Aminoil* (1982) 21 ILM 976.
[5] *Sedco (Second Interlocutory Award)*, 10 Iran–US CTR 180, 184–85 (1986).

value for customary international law of much of the practice available ... [these] types of agreements can be so greatly inspired by non-judicial considerations – eg, resumption of diplomatic or trading relations – that it is extremely difficult to draw from them conclusions as to *opinio juris*, ie, the determination that the content of such settlements was thought by the States involved to be required by international law. ... The bilateral investment treaty practice of States, which much more often than not reflects the traditional international law standard of compensation for expropriation, more nearly constitutes an accurate measure of the High Contracting Parties' views as to customary international law, but also carries with it some of the same evidentiary limitations as lump sum agreements. Both kinds of agreements involve in some degree bargaining in a context to which *'opinio juris'* seems a stranger.

Indeed, the manner in which the US has concluded its BITs with developing countries[6] testifies to the observations made by the Tribunal. The following observation made by Alvarez, who was on the US BIT negotiating team while he was in the Legal Adviser's Office of the US Department of State, is noteworthy:

BIT partners turn to the US BIT with the equivalent of an IMF gun pointed at their heads; others may feel that, in the absence of a rival superpower, economic relations with one that remains are inevitable. For many, a BIT relationship is hardly a voluntary, unco-erced transaction. They feel that they must enter into the arrangement, or that they would be foolish not to, since they have already made the internal adjustments required for BIT participation in order to comply with demands made by, for example, the IMF. ... A BIT negotiation is not a discussion between sovereign equals. It is more like an intensive training seminar conducted by the United States, on US terms, on what it would take to comply with the US draft.[7]

In the *Barcelona Traction Case* the ICJ was not prepared to take any guidance from the BITs or the so-called 'lump sum' settlement agreements because they were sui generis in character.[8] However, as we shall see in the next section, more recent cases, especially those decided by ICSID, accord considerable weight to the content of BITs in determining the rules of customary international law on the subject. According to these tribunals, these treaties could be taken to confirm and thus enlarge the traditional rules of the international foreign investment law,[9] including the Hull formula, favoured by developed investor countries rather than those preferred and championed by developing countries within the UN. However, since so much diversity exists in the content of BITs, especially with the definition of expropriation and the standards of compensation, some caution should be exercised when stating that BITs have crystallised the rules of customary international law on the subject matter. They are essentially of contractual character rather than law-making. The sheer number of BITs per se does not automatically elevate them to treaties of law-making character.

---

[6] See on the Chinese BITs, K Qingjiang, 'Bilateral Investment Treaties: The Chinese Approach and Practice' (2003) 8 *Asian Yearbook of International Law* 105.

[7] JE Alvarez's remarks were made as chairman of a panel at the 1992 ASIL annual meeting: *Proceeding of the ASIL 86th Annual Meeting* (1992) 550–55, 552 and 553.

[8] *Barcelona Traction*, ICJ Reports 1970, 3, 40.

[9] See FA Mann, 'British Treaties for the Promotion and Protection of Investment' (1982) 52 *British Year Book of International Law* 241.

Bilateral Investment Treaties for the Promotion of Foreign Investment

BITs are premised on the assumption that they promote investment from investor countries to investor-receiving countries.[10] This is the basis on which both the World Bank and the IMF have traditionally encouraged various developing countries to conclude BITs with developed countries. The objective is not only to outline a set of standards of protection available to foreign investors but also to provide for international investor-state arbitration as a substantive incentive and protection for foreign investors. However, there is no conclusive evidence to suggest that the conclusion of a BIT between a developed country and developing country has necessarily increased substantially the flow of investment from the former to the latter.[11] For example, Brazil is often cited as an example of a country that has successfully attracted sensible foreign investment without either becoming a party to ICSID or ratifying or concluding many BITs with capital-exporting countries.

Bolivia has continued to attract foreign investment in spite of taking a series of restrictive measures designed to regulate foreign investment, including its withdrawal from ICSID. The UK keeps topping the table of countries attracting foreign investment even from those countries with which it has no BIT. Both developed and developing countries have a different motive for concluding such treaties. From the perspective of an investor country, BITs provide a significant incentive to their investors to invest abroad with a view to capturing market share and exploiting the opportunities offered in the countries concerned. Every business needs to expand and grow simply to stay in business. That is why companies are on the look-out for opportunities for safe investment in other jurisdictions in order to expand their business networks and to benefit from cheap labour and raw materials, or lax tax, environmental and human rights standards. Further, the investor countries use BITs to make the regulatory framework for foreign investment in host countries more transparent, stable, predictable and secure. The aim is to reduce obstacles to future investment flows.

---

[10] See J Tobin and S Rose-Ackerman, 'Foreign Direct Investment and the Business Environment in Developing Countries: The Impact of Bilateral Investment Treaties', William Davidson Institute Working Paper No 587, June 2003 (William Davidson Institute, the University of Michigan Business School); E Neumayer and L Spess, 'Do Bilateral Investment Treaties Increase Foreign Direct Investment to Developing Countries?' (2005) 33 *World Development* 1567.

[11] Mann and von Moltke assert that there is 'no recognizable relationship between IIAs and investment flows. Some countries that are party to no IIAs receive significant international investment and many countries that that are party to numerous IIAs receive almost none.' H Mann and K von Moltke, *A Southern Agenda on Investment? Promoting Development with Balanced Rights and Obligations for Investors, Host States and Home States* (Winnipeg, International Institute for Sustainable Development, 2005) 4.

Greater Standard of Protection under Bilateral Investment Treaties

BITs are normally concluded to extend a greater standard of protection to foreign investors than accorded under customary international law or international human rights treaties. With regard to the treatment and protection of investment, the Jordan–US treaty is illustrative of the practice of states. The provisions included in Article II of the treaty are typical of the trend of the 1990s:

Treatment and Protection of Investment

1. With respect to the establishment, acquisition, expansion, management, conduct, operation and sale of other disposition of covered investments, each Contracting Party shall accord treatment no less favourable than that it accords, in like situations, to investments in its territory of its own nationals or companies (hereinafter 'national treatment') or investments in its territory or nationals or companies of a third country (hereinafter 'most favoured nation treatment'), whichever is most favourable (hereinafter 'national and most favoured nation treatment'). Each Contracting Party shall ensure that its state enterprises, in the provision of their goods or services, accord national and most favoured nation treatment to covered investments.

    ...

    (a) Each Contracting Party shall at all times accord to covered investments fair and equitable treatment and full protection and security, and shall in no case accord treatment less favourable than that required by international law.

    (b) Neither Contracting Party shall in any way impair by unreasonable and discriminatory measures the management, conduct, operation, and sale or other disposition of covered investments.

Each Contracting Party shall provide effective means of asserting claims and enforcing rights with respect to covered investments.

Each Contracting Party shall ensure that its laws, regulations, administrative practices and procedures of general application, and adjudicatory decisions, that pertain to or affect covered investments are promptly published or otherwise made publicly available.

Articles III and IV of the Treaty deal with the question of expropriation and compensation. The provisions included in the treaty are designed to provide the strongest protection possible against any potential expropriation and provide for the best form of prompt, adequate and effective compensation:

Article III

1. Neither Contracting party shall expropriate or nationalize a covered investment either directly or indirectly through measures tantamount to expropriation or nationalization ('expropriation') except for a public purpose; in a non-discriminatory manner; upon payment of prompt, adequate and effective compensation; and in accordance with due process of law and the general principles of treatment provided for in Article II(3).[12]

---

[12](1997) 36 ILM 1498.

2. Compensation shall be paid without delay; be equivalent to the fair market value of the expropriated investment immediately before the expropriatory action was taken ('the date of expropriation'); and be fully realizable and freely transferable. The fair market value shall not reflect any change in value occurring because the expropriatory action had become known before the date of expropriation.

3. If the fair market value is denominated in a freely usable currency, the compensation paid shall be no less than the fair market value on the date of expropriation, plus interest at a commercially reasonable rate for that currency, accrued from the date of expropriation until the date of payment.

4. If the fair market value is denominated in a currency that is not freely usable, the compensation paid – converted into the currency of payment at the market rate of exchange prevailing on the date of payment – shall be no less than:

   (a) the fair market value on the date of expropriation, converted into a freely usable currency at the market rate of exchange prevailing on that date, plus

   (b) interest, at a commercially reasonable rate for that freely usable currency, accrued from that date of expropriation until the date of payment.

Article IV

1. Each Contracting Party shall accord national and most favoured nation treatment to covered investments as regards any measures relating to losses that investments suffer in its territory owing to war or other armed conflict, revolution, state of national emergency, insurrection, civil disturbance, or similar events.

2. Each Contracting Party shall accord restitution, or pay compensation in accordance with paragraphs 2 through 4 of Article III, in the event that covered investments suffer losses in its territory, owing to war or other armed conflict, revolution, state of national emergency, insurrection, civil disturbance, or similar events, that result from:

   (a) requisitioning of all or part of such investments by the Contracting Party's forces or authorities, or

   (b) destruction of all or part of such investments by the Contracting Party's forces or authorities that was not required by the necessity of the situation.

Similar provisions relating to the treatment and protection of foreign investment can be found in many BITs concluded by the US with other states, including the Russian Federation.[13] Under Article II(1) of the US–Russian Treaty each state '*shall permit and treat* investment, and activities associated therewith, on a non-discriminatory basis' (emphasis added). Article 2(a) is also of interest:

> Investment shall at all times be accorded fair and equitable treatment, shall enjoy full protection and security, and shall in no case be accorded treatment inconsistent with the norms and principles of international law.

The treaty concluded between Japan and Bangladesh in 1998 is illustrative of a tight regime of protection accorded to foreign investors. Article 5(1) and (2) read as follows:

1. Investments and returns of investors of either Contracting Party shall receive the most constant protection and security within the territory of the other Contracting Party.

2. Investments and returns of investors of either Contracting Party shall not be subjected to expropriation, nationalization or any other measure the effect of which would be

---

[13] (1992) 31 ILM 794.

tantamount to expropriation or nationalization, within the territory of the other Contracting Party unless such measures are taken for a public purpose and under due process of law, are not discriminatory, and are taken against prompt, adequate and effective compensation.[14]

This provision provides protection for foreign investment in excess of that which is accorded by traditional customary international law. It incorporates not only the Hull formula, but also additional qualifications such as 'due process of law', settlement of investment disputes under ICSID and retroactive protection of foreign investment, etc. However, a BIT concluded in 1994 between India, a leading developing country, and the UK, a leading developed country, varies slightly from other BITs.

Bilateral Investment Treaties as Insurance against Political Risks

Making investments in other countries always carries risks, especially in dangerous places with underdeveloped legal systems and unstable or dictatorial political regimes. Although the MIGA and a number of other national and multinational schemes provide some insurance to foreign investors against the risks of investing abroad, especially in developing countries with unstable democracies, a BIT provides both assurance and insurance to investors that their investment abroad will be protected against expropriation or other mistreatment. A BIT is meant to provide insurance against non-commercial risks, mainly political risks. Customary international foreign investment law has hitherto dealt mainly with outright or direct cases of expropriation with some limited cases of indirect expropriations. But since human ingenuity has the capacity to invent all sorts of methods of indirect, creeping or consequential expropriations, a BIT can regulate in detail against such eventualities. The US–Russia BIT is an example of a BIT which, in the words of Reisman and Sloane, covers

> the multiplicity of inappropriate regulatory acts, omissions, and other deleterious conduct that undermines the vital normative framework created and maintained by BITs – and by which governments can, in effect but not name, now be deemed to have expropriated a foreign national's investment.[15]

At the same time a BIT gives a capital-importing country the opportunity to convey a message to the outside world that it welcomes foreign investors and is willing to accord them the level of protection available under both international law and the BIT concerned. It can offer an enhanced level of protection, concessions, privileges and immunities to foreign investors investing in certain areas in order to attract investment. Thus, a BIT is supposed to create a win–win situation for both parties.

---

[14] Reproduced in (2000) 43 *Japanese Journal of International Law* 229.
[15] WM Reisman and RD Sloane, 'Indirect Expropriation and its Valuation in the BIT Generation' (2003) 74 *British Year Book of International Law* 118.

Bilateral Investment Treaties as a Tool for Globalisation, Economic Liberalisation and Privatisation

A BIT is in effect an individual market tool designed to open a domestic market to foreign investors. In the recent past such treaties have been concluded to facilitate privatisation programmes in developing countries or economies in transition (eg Argentina, Poland, Romania) so that foreign investors would invest in the privatised local entities. They have also been concluded when socialist countries (eg China, Vietnam and Russia) or developing countries with a mixed economy (eg India, Zambia and Indonesia) have decided to embark upon a programme of economic liberalisation, privatisation and marketisation. Reisman and Sloane have neatly summed up the utility of BITs in the following words:

> Privatization ... calls for the very 'stable and orderly framework for investment' that BITs strive to establish. In this respect BITs pursue the macrolegal side of the macroeconomic structural readjustment policies encouraged by multilateral financial institutions. BITs consciously seek to approximate in the developing, capital-importing state the minimal legal, administrative and regulatory framework that fosters and sustains investment in industrialized capital-exporting states.[16]

Indeed, BITs have been used as tools for promoting capitalism and globalisation and for stimulating local economies by various states around the globe. Both BITs and FTAs regulate the macro-legal side of the macroeconomic policies of the states that are parties to the treaties concerned. In economic terms, globalisation can be defined as a process leading to an increase in the cross-border flows of goods, services, capital and know-how. It also refers to the extent of the interlinkages between a country's economy and the rest of the world. A company contributes to the process of globalisation by, inter alia, globalising a brand, launching a brand simultaneously in several countries and unifying local brands that have been acquired by takeover. All of these complex economic activities by companies, especially TNCs, require legal underpinning, and BITs are one of the instruments that provide this, enabling investors to expand in foreign markets. Hence, the liberalisation in investment regimes in so many countries has accelerated the process of globalisation, and one of the tools for such liberalisation has been BITs.

Mechanism to Expand International Standards and to Codify the *Lex Specialis*

BITs are a mechanism to extend the scope of the standard of treatment available to foreign investors under customary international law. Most BITs provide greater protection to foreign investors than is available under international law. BITs do not confine

---

[16] Ibid, 118.

themselves to codifying the rules of customary international law. Although most of their provisions tend to be close to customary international law, certain other provisions may be at variance with it. Owing to historical, geographical, cultural, political, social or economic reasons, the nature of bilateral relations between states varies a great deal.

States may wish to accommodate this unique or special relationship in a BIT that provides a slightly different level of treatment for foreign investors from those countries than those provided in other BITs with other states. For this, they may also wish to deviate slightly from international practice and provide a more favourable treatment or include special clauses in relation to the investment coming from such states. Since the international foreign investment law provides only a framework of principles, it leaves a great deal of room for manoeuvre by individual states to fashion their relationship with a state of their choice in the manner they wish. When 'fleshing out' of the rules of international customary law on foreign investment in this way, states can codify their own *lex specialis* applicable to relations between them on matters relating to foreign investment.

Of course, the MFN principle included in other BITs limits states' freedom of action when it comes to according more favourable treatment to each other. But there are many grey areas or areas that are not covered by international law or other BITs that these states can regulate via a BIT. Since there is no global treaty on foreign investment law, states do have a great deal of room for fashioning their relations with other states and they can do this through a BIT. In so doing, they can also prescribe their own method of handling claims of expropriation. For instance, there is a requirement in international law to pay compensation against expropriation. However, international law does not spell out every detail as to the method of arriving at an amount to be paid and how and when it is to be paid. Even the 'prompt, adequate and effective' compensation formula is not universally accepted. For instance, the 1994 BIT between India and the UK does not fully subscribe to this formula.[17]

Furthermore, a country which has little to offer by way of trade or one that is very keen on making its privatisation programme a success may wish to go further than other states and may offer a higher level of protection and greater threshold of compensation against potential expropriation. Conversely, a state keen to protect its environment or the rights of its workers, or wanting to exercise a greater degree of economic sovereignty, embark on new developmental programmes or revisit concessions or other contracts with foreign companies may have valid reasons for wishing to include some cautionary provisions or a lower threshold of compensation against expropriation.

The recent attempts by states such as Bolivia, Venezuela and Ecuador to renegotiate concessions and other contracts with foreign companies are examples of this approach. A BIT is a mechanism that can accommodate all such eventualities by codifying a *lex specialis* between the states concerned. Therefore, regardless of the number of BITs embodying the same and similar provisions, such provisions cannot necessarily

---

[17] Art 5 of the 1994 India–UK BIT provides for a fair and equitable compensation against expropriation: (1995) 34 ILM 935.

be regarded as having crystallised into international law. Many of the provisions of BITs may not meet the test of *opinion juris* needed to constitute custom.

A BIT or an RTA can also stipulate that the *lex specialis* provisions outlined in such a treaty would apply exclusively to the investment matters covered by the treaty concerned. An ASEAN protocol on investment includes some provisions to this effect and such a practice can also be found in other areas of international law.[18] For instance, the 1997 UN Convention on the Use of International Watercourses provides that if there is a special agreement (basically *lex specialis*) between the states concerned with regard to the sharing, management and development of the waters of an international course, the provisions of those treaties rather than the principles outlined in the UN Convention (*lex generalis*) would apply.[19]

Effect of Bilateral Investment Treaty Provisions as Obligations *Erga Omnes?*

Although BITs are designed to create a bilateral set of obligations between the contracting parties, the risk is that these obligations can become in effect obligations *erga omnes* (ie binding against all) for a number of reasons. First, due to the broad interpretation of the MFN principle it is possible that the provisions of a BIT can be invoked by investors from any country who are entitled to MFN treatment under another BIT, RTA or even a WTO agreement to which the state concerned is also a party. Second, due to recent trends in jurisprudence it is possible not only for a foreign company registered in the contracting parties concerned but also for majority or even minority shareholders of the company who could be residing anywhere in the world to invoke such a provision. As stated by Legum:

> Where a host State has entered into BITs that cover indirectly controlled investments, there could be between one and 20 or more layers of intermediate holding companies that separate the company the host State officials see and the company that is a covered investor under the treaty. The covered investor could itself, in fact, be an intermediate holding company, with the ultimate parent company publicly traded or controlled by the third country nationals. A lower level official reviewing a permit application – just like a minister reviewing a bid proposal of national importance – will not normally have access to information concerning the nationality of intermediate holding companies in the applicant's corporate hierarchy. Under these circumstances, the only way to comply with the treaty is for the host State to assume that *all* investors – all companies – are covered by the highest standards of any BIT in force for the State. The reality that foreign capital is highly fungible and the breadth of the definitions of investors and investment thus combine to effectively transform the facially

---

[18] ASEAN Protocol on Enhanced Dispute Settlement Mechanism done in Vientiane, Laos, 29 November 2004. Available at www.aseansec.org.

[19] Art 3 of the UN Convention on the Law of the Non-Navigational Uses of International Watercourses, 1997: (1997) 36 ILM 700. See generally also SP Subedi (ed), *International Watercourses Law for the 21st Century: The Case of the River Ganges Basin* (Aldershot, Ashgate Publishing, 2005).

bilateral obligations of the BIT into an obligation that the host State must consider poten-tially applicable to all investors.[20]

Indeed, as discussed earlier, the recent trend witnessed in treaty-shopping as well as forum-shopping demonstrates that the provisions of a BIT which are meant to be *lex specialis* between the contracting parties run the risk of producing obligations *erga omnes*.

Decentralisation of the Law of Foreign Investment

One of the flexibilities that the institution of BITs offers to states is the ability to make their own local foreign investment law applicable to relations with other states. In other words, this process has the effect of decentralising international foreign investment law. When negotiating a BIT, two states (and if it is a regional FTA, the states of the region) may create within the scope of their mutual agreement bilateral and regional rules or make an exception to the rules deriving from either the autonomy of domestic law or public international law, provided that these exceptions do not undermine the peremp-tory rules of international law.

Limiting the Freedom of Action of States

Although at a superficial level BITs are supposed to create a win–win situation for both sides, such treaties serve to limit the freedom of action by states in economic matters. This is especially true with regard to BITs concluded as part of a drive by states to attract foreign investment to their privatisation programmes. For instance, Argentina concluded a BIT with the United States around the time of the former's energy priva-tisation programme in the early 1990s. When Argentina was hit by an economic crisis in the late 1990s it responded by taking new measures designed to readjust the fiscal policies of the country, including tariff readjustment. This affected foreign companies that had invested in the privatised energy sector, and these mounted a legal challenge, claiming that the aggregate impact of these measures had harmed their investment and created a cause of action by virtue of the US–Argentina BIT.

Defending its measures before an ICSID tribunal in the *CMS Gas Transmission Company v The Argentine Republic* case, Argentina argued that the measures it had taken were needed to safeguard its essential economic interests. It tried to invoke the doctrine of necessity enshrined in Article 25 of the Articles of State Responsibility developed by the ILC. However, the tribunal dismissed this argument due to Argentina's contribution to the economic crisis. Argentina also relied on Article XI, the Emergency

---

[20] B Legum, 'Defining Investment and Investor: Who Is Entitled to Claim?', paper presented at a sympo-sium co-organised by ICSID, OECD and UNCTAD, 12 December 2005, Paris, 4–5.

Clause of its BIT with the US. The tribunal also rejected this argument and upheld the claim by CMS that Argentina had violated the fair and equitable treatment provision to be found in Article II(2) of its BIT with the US.

Outlining the Conditions for Expropriation

BITs are also a step forward in terms of the standard of compensation against expropriation. Regardless of the negotiating position taken by various states on international platforms, when it comes to negotiating BITs the host states have, by and large, accepted the Hull formula as favoured by the home or investor countries. Most of the BITs concluded since the 1960s reflect the Hull formula and incorporate the concerns of the investor countries because most developed countries hold views similar to those of the United States. For instance, protesting the Libyan nationalisation of the property, rights and assets under an oil concession contract of British Petroleum in 1971 the British government stated that:

> An act of nationalisation is not legitimate in international law unless it satisfies the following requirements:
>
> (i)   it must be for a public purpose related to the internal needs of the taking state; and
> (ii) it must be followed by the payment of prompt, adequate and effective compensation.
>
> Nationalisation measures which are arbitrary or discriminatory or which are motivated by considerations of a political nature unrelated to the internal well being of the taking State are, by a reference to those principles, illegal and invalid.[21]

As the debate was taking place within the UN about the codification and progressive development of foreign investment law, the business of regulating foreign investment through BITs gathered pace outside of the UN. Those developed countries that wanted to protect investment by their nationals in foreign countries also wanted to conclude BITs of *sui generis* or *lex specialis* character rather than wait for international legislation under the auspices of the UN. Most of these treaties incorporated provisions more akin to the traditional position taken by the developed countries such as the Hull formula rather than the ideas behind UN initiatives such as the NIEO or the Charter of Economic Rights and Duties of States (CERD). When new regional trading blocs such as NAFTA were created to promote the free flow of capital, goods and services among the countries of the region, they too followed the pattern of BITs.

The practice of conforming to the Hull formula and offering as many incentives as possible to foreign investors through a BIT was confined to the treaties concluded not only between one developed country and another, but also between developed and developing countries.[22] Therefore, the law on foreign investment has been understood in many quarters to be the law as incorporated in the modern bilateral and regional

---

[21] As cited in (1974) 53 ILR 317.
[22] See generally A Akinsanya, 'International Protection of Direct Foreign Investment in the Third World' (1987) 36 *ICLQ* 58.

investment treaties and not as included in the resolutions of recommendatory character of the UN General Assembly or other international 'soft law' instruments. When the international efforts to conclude an internationally acceptable treaty or a mandatory code of conduct within the UN remained unsuccessful, increasing numbers of states, including those leading developing countries that had championed the international regulation of foreign investment, also started concluding BITs along the lines favoured by the developed countries. This is one reason why greater weight has been accorded to the content of such treaties in determining what the law is on foreign investment. Thus, the 1992 Guidelines prepared under the auspices of the World Bank and the IMF, the Draft MAI or the Guidelines of the OECD itself drew heavily on such BITs.

Deviations from the Hull Formula

Individual BITs can also allow the contracting parties to deviate from the standards of treatment accorded in customary international law such as those concerning the standard of compensation. For instance, the 1994 India–UK BIT does not subscribe to the Hull formula in respect of every type of expropriation or nationalisation. Rather, it speaks of 'fair and equitable compensation' as opposed to 'prompt, adequate and effective' compensation with regard to most forms of foreign investment and 'prompt, adequate and effective' compensation only with regard to compensation for foreign shareholders in an expropriated company. The provision concerning the nationalisation and expropriation of foreign investment admits the possibility of expropriation and nationalisation not simply for 'a public purpose', but for 'a public purpose related to the internal requirements for regulating economic activity'; it accords a wider meaning to this qualification:

Article 5: Expropriation

1. Investments of investors of either Contracting Party shall not be nationalised, expropriated or subjected to measures having effect equivalent to nationalisation or expropriation (hereinafter referred to as "expropriation") in the territory of the other Contracting Party except for a public purpose related to the internal requirements for regulating economic activity on a non-discriminatory basis and against fair and equitable compensation. Such compensation shall amount to the genuine value of the investment expropriated immediately before the expropriation or before the impending expropriation became public knowledge, whichever is the earlier, shall include interest at a fair and equitable rate until the date of payment, shall be made without unreasonable delay, be effectively realizable and be freely transferable.
2. The investor affected shall have a right, under the law of the Contracting Party making the expropriation, to review, by a judicial or other independent authority of that Party, of his or its case and of the valuation of his or its investment in accordance with the principles set out in this paragraph. The Contracting party making the expropriation shall make every endeavour to ensure that such review is carried out promptly.
3. Where a Contracting Party expropriates the assets of a company which is incorporated or constituted under the law in force in any part of its own territory, and in which investors of the other Contracting Party own shares, it shall ensure that the provisions of

paragraph (1) of this Article are applied to the extent necessary to guarantee prompt, adequate and effective compensation in respect of their investment to such investors of the other Contracting Party who are owners of those shares.[23]

A further feature of significance in the 1994 India–UK BIT is the confirmation, in Article 11(1), that 'all investments shall be governed by the laws in force in the territory of the Contracting Party in which such investments are made'. These provisions demonstrate that not all BITs conform fully to the Hull formula, and nor have they completely abandoned the Calvo doctrine.

Exhaustion of Local Remedies

The requirement to exhaust local remedies prior to resorting to international arbitration also depends on the provisions in the relevant BIT. The Convention establishing ICSID itself does not require the exhaustion of local remedies unless the state has conditioned its consent on this factor. Most BITs require amicable resolution of the disputes through either consultation or conciliation within a specified period, normally within six months, prior to referring the matter to international arbitration. Those BITs that require the exhaustion of local remedies do nonetheless often contain an 'exit' or 'opt-out' provision, allowing arbitration if a national court has not rendered its judgment within a specified period of time. A sizeable number of BITs, especially those concluded recently, do not require the exhaustion of local remedies and include the resort to national courts as one of the many options available to foreign investors for the settlement of investment disputes with the host states. In practice, a vast majority of foreign investors have opted for arbitration, rendering the option to go to national courts redundant.

If a BIT requires the exhaustion of local remedies prior to resorting to international arbitration, foreign investors will have little room for manoeuvre. For instance, the BIT between Argentina and Spain stipulated two conditions prior to the commencement of arbitration: (1) the foreign investor had to exhaust all local remedies; and (2) an 18-month period had to expire without issuance of a court decision on the merits. As will be discussed later, these requirements were a major issue in the *Maffezini* case because the foreign investor had not exhausted local remedies prior to resorting to arbitration. On this basis, the tribunal did acknowledge that a jurisdictional problem existed, but the requirement was circumvented by referring to another BIT between Spain and Chile which did not stipulate these conditions under the MFN principle.

There have been other instances – eg in the context of investment contracts – where the requirement for the exhaustion of local remedies has been circumvented. If a foreign investor investing under an investment contract, such as a concessions contract, is allowed to resort to BIT arbitration, ICSID or otherwise, for the settlement of contractual disputes, the requirement to exhaust local remedies under the

---

[23] (1995) 34 ILM 935.

investment contract would not be applicable. This was the opinion of a tribunal in the *Lanco* case where it was held that the investor could resort to ICSID arbitration under the BIT in spite of the existence of a forum-selection provision requiring claims to be referred to the local courts in the host country concerned.

Investor-State Dispute Settlement Mechanism

A major feature of a modern BIT is to allow foreign investors access to international investment tribunals, such as ICSID, for the resolution of disputes between an investor and a host state. The BITs that were concluded since the 1960s made, for the first time, investor-state dispute resolution possible. Under a typical BIT, an investor is entitled to take the host state to a binding, third-party arbitration, typically under the rules of ICSID, to settle any disputes involving the interpretation of the application of the BIT.[24] Should the host state refuse to participate, the BIT provides for an appointing authority to appoint arbitrators on behalf of the host state to enable the arbitration to proceed even without co-operation of the host state. This constituted an innovation in the history of dispute settlement at the international level.

By allowing binding, third-party arbitration for state–state as well as investor-state disputes, the BITs bade farewell to essential elements of the Calvo doctrine. What is more, most BITs do not, unlike many other international dispute settlement mechanisms, require the exhaustion of local remedies before resorting to binding, third-party arbitration. In fact, as pointed out by Vandevelde,[25] under many BITs the investor forfeits the right to binding, third-party arbitration if it invokes local remedies. It could be said that by making it possible to depoliticise investment disputes, the BITs were endorsing the very ideas that lay behind the Calvo doctrine. In other words, while the Calvo doctrine sought to depoliticise investment disputes by preventing foreign state interference, either in the form of diplomatic protection or 'gunboat diplomacy', by requiring the settlement of such disputes under the local laws of the host states, BITs seek to depoliticise investment disputes by providing for binding, third-party arbitration for both state–state and investor-state disputes.

Thus, BITs allow home or investor countries to extricate themselves from involvement in private investment disputes, without diminishing the effectiveness of the remedies available to investors. This is because, prior to the BIT era, investors had to look to the government of their own country for assistance when their investment was expropriated or unlawfully impaired by a foreign government. Since there were no binding, third-party dispute settlement mechanisms available for foreign investors and host states could invoke sovereign immunity or the 'act of state' doctrine before any domestic courts, diplomatic protection was the only avenue open to such investors.

---

[24] For a detailed commentary of the ICSID Convention, see CH Schreuer, *The ICSID Convention: A Commentary* (Cambridge, Cambridge University Press, 2001).
[25] KJ Vandevelde, 'The BIT Program: A Fifteen-Year Appraisal', *Proceedings of the ASIL 86th Annual Meeting* (1992) 532, 538.

When state machinery decides to espouse a claim and pursue a remedy on behalf of its private investors through diplomatic channels or international arbitration, or impose economic sanctions on the alleged wrongdoer, the dispute acquires a political character. When an effective dispute settlement mechanism such as ICSID is available to private foreign investors, there is no need for government intervention and the politicisation of investment disputes. Thus, one of the major positive contributions made by the BITs is, to borrow the word from Vandevelde,[26] the 'depoliticisation' of investment disputes.

When the idea of settling investment disputes through international arbitration was introduced at the beginning of the twentieth century, the world of foreign investment effectively bade farewell to the era of diplomatic protection or 'gunboat' diplomacy.[27] Prior to this, influential individuals and corporations would persuade their governments to send a small contingent of warships to moor off the coast of host states as a possible threat of forcible action until reparation was forthcoming. This was practised frequently by many major trading nations of Europe especially against South American states.[28]

In 1907 this practice of 'gunboat' diplomacy ended when the Second International Peace Conference of The Hague adopted the Convention on the Peaceful Resolution of International Disputes, which opened the possibility of state-to-state arbitration on investment disputes and more recently has provided for direct access to international tribunals by investors against host governments under modern foreign investment law. The practice of 'gunboat' diplomacy became in effect outlawed when the Kellog–Briand Pact was adopted, renouncing the use of force as a means of settling disputes with other states. This was further strengthened by the prohibition on the use of force under Article 2(4) of the Charter of the UN – a provision widely regarded as a principle of *jus cogens* character. For instance, when President Chavez of Venezuela moved to nationalise the assets of foreign companies in recent years, foreign investors went to international arbitration rather than to the governments of their home countries. The politicisation of implementing investment tribunal awards still exists, but the politicisation of the disputes themselves has become a thing of the past.

Latin American Volte-Face

Most of the BITs concluded by the US with developing countries conform to the Hull formula.[29] For instance, when the US concluded in 1991 its first ever BIT more or less

[26] Ibid.

[27] Eg, Art 27(1) of the ICSID Convention forbids states from giving diplomatic protection in respect of a dispute if the matter has been referred to the ICSID: 'No Contracting State shall give diplomatic protection, or bring an international claim, in respect of a dispute which one of its nationals and another Contracting State shall have consented to submit or shall have submitted to arbitration under this Convention, unless such other Contracting State shall have failed to abide by and comply with the award rendered in such dispute.' International Centre for Settlement of Investment Disputes, *ICSID Convention, Regulations and Rules* (Washington, DC, ICSID, 2003) 19.

[28] A Redfern et al, *Law and Practice of International Commercial Arbitration*, 4th edn (London, Sweet & Maxwell, 2004) 562–63.

[29] An example is the 1998 agreement between Japan and Bangladesh concerning the Promotion and Protection of Investment. See (2000) 43 *Japanese Annual of International Law* 229.

on its own terms with a leading Latin American state, Argentina, which had been a staunch supporter of the Calvo doctrine, this sent the message that the Calvo doctrine was going to be consigned to history. As pointed out by Propp:

> The Argentina BIT is quite important. Its most notable achievement is the first-ever unqualified right to investor-state arbitration agreed to by a Latin American country in the BIT context. This overcomes the legacy of the Calvo doctrine that foreign investors should have the same recourse as local nationals, that is, local courts.[30]

The protection accorded to foreign investors under the US–Argentine BIT of 1991 was perhaps the most comprehensive and most favourable to foreign investors at the time. The provision in Article IV of this BIT is illustrative:

Article IV

1.   Investments shall not be expropriated or nationalized either directly or indirectly through measures tantamount to expropriation or nationalization ('expropriation') except for a public purpose; in a non-discriminatory manner; upon payment of prompt, adequate, and effective compensation; and in accordance with due process of law and general principles of treatment provided for in Article II(2).[31] Compensation shall be equivalent to the fair market value of the expropriated investment immediately before the expropriatory action was taken or became known, whichever is earlier; be paid without delay; include interest at a commercially reasonable rate from the date of expropriation; be fully realizable; and be freely transferable at the prevailing market rate of exchange on the date of expropriation.

2.   A national or company of either Party that asserts that all or part of its investment has been expropriated shall have a right to prompt review by the appropriate judicial or administrative authorities of the other Party to determine whether any such expropriation has occurred and, if so, whether such expropriation, and any compensation therefore, conforms to the provisions of this Treaty and the principles of international law.

3.   Nationals or companies of either Party whose investments suffer losses in the territory of the other Party owing to war or other armed conflict, revolution, state of national emergency, insurrection, civil disturbance or other similar events shall be accorded treatment by such other Party no less favourable than that accorded to its own nationals or companies or to nationals or companies of any third country, whichever is the more favourable treatment, as regards measures it adopts in relations to such losses.[32]

Thus, the provisions just cited seek to provide the tightest protection possible to foreign investors. The US seems to have tried to incorporate all the eventualities that its nationals or companies had to deal with in Iran in the run up to and in the immediate

---

[30] KR Propp, 'Bilateral Investment Treaties: The US Experience in Eastern Europe', *Proceedings of the ASIL 86th Annual Meeting* (1992) 540, 544.

[31] Art II(2) reads as follows: '(a) Investment shall at all times be accorded fair and equitable treatment, shall enjoy full protection and security and shall in no case be accorded treatment less than that required by international law. (b) Neither Party shall in any way impair by arbitrary or discriminatory measures the management, operation, maintenance, use, enjoyment, acquisition, expansion, or disposal of investments. For the purposes of dispute resolution under Articles VII and VIII, a measure may be arbitrary or discriminatory notwithstanding the opportunity to review such measure in the courts or administrative tribunals of a party. (c) Each party shall observe any obligation it may have entered into with regard to investments.' 1991 UST LEXIS 176.

[32] 1991 UST LEXIS 176.

aftermath of the Islamic revolution in Iran in 1979. This treaty seems to provide a detailed prescription for any future dispute settlement body in deciding investment cases involving US nationals or companies. Most of the principles developed by the Iran–US Claims Tribunal in favour of US nationals or companies seem to have been incorporated into this BIT itself, leaving little room for manoeuvre for future tribunals. No wonder that the arbitration panels established in the 1990s to consider investment disputes followed closely the content of what the US had dictated through its BITs. For instance, the addition of the words expropriation 'indirectly through measures tantamount to expropriation or nationalization' seems to have been inspired by the jurisprudence developed by the Tribunal.

The dispute settlement mechanism provided for in Article VII is particularly elaborate and all-encompassing. Not only has the definition of the term 'dispute' been defined as broadly as possible, but the range of choice of methods of settling disputes available to the foreign investor is also very wide. Foreign investors are not required to exhaust local remedies before resorting to international mechanisms. Through this BIT the US completed the task of cementing and institutionalising the regime of protection available to foreign investors. One by one many Latin American states concluded similar BITs with the US, signalling a volte-face in their approach to dealing with the changed reality of the world. This process was further strengthened when Mexico agreed to NAFTA, which contained provisions similar to those included in the BITs in respect of the protection of foreign investment and the settlement of investment disputes.

However, these Latin American states have recently started to reject these BITs and appear gradually to be returning to the Calvo doctrine. For instance, a bloc of a dozen Latin American states agreed in September 2013 to take collective action to oppose the IIA-based investor-state dispute settlement (ISDS) mechanism and explore alternatives to the current ISDS mechanism. Bolivia became the first country to denounce the ICSID Convention in 2007, and some other Latin American countries have since followed suit. Ecuador has not signed any BIT since 2001, and moreover has terminated many of its existing BITs and attempted to terminate many others, including those with France, Germany and the UK.[33] The irony of history is that now it is the US too which is making a volte-face in terms of the legal regime concerning investment regulation and accepting a stricter notion of regulatory expropriation, a more rigid interpretation of the principle of fair and equitable treatment, and the notion of appeal against arbitral awards.

US Volte-Face

After long pursuing a policy of maximum investor protection, opposing policies such as the NIEO within the UN, and leading the campaign for expanding certain core investor protection standards, such as fair and equitable treatment, the US itself is retrenching and its 2012 Model BIT is an example of its changing attitude.

---

[33] C Titi, 'Investment Arbitration in Latin America: The Uncertain Veracity of Preconceived Ideas' (2014) 30 *Arbitration International* 357.

The US Model BIT, which contains a number of provisions designed to strike a balance between investment protection and public interests, has set a trend in this direction and countries such as India are in the process of following suit. It is an admission that international investment law should not exist in isolation, but rather as part of the broader international legal order, and should thus accommodate competing interests. This recent trend in state practice has been characterised by various scholars as the revival of the Calvo doctrine or the return of the NIEO, considered long dead by many. For instance, commenting on the recent trend in international investment law and especially the content of the US Model BIT of 2012 and opposition to the ISDS mechanism in its present form coming from different quarters, Brower and Melikian have stated that what we are witnessing is a 'neo-NIEO' or a 'Northern neo-NIEO'.[34]

The 2012 US Model BIT is more cautious with regard to the definition and application of the principle of minimum standard of treatment of foreign investors than older Model BITs or actual BITs, IIAs or FTAs. The provision concerning the principle of fair and equitable treatment in Article 5 of the 2012 US Model BIT is an example of the US taking a cautious approach and making an attempt to limit the scope of this principle:

Article 5: Minimum Standard of Treatment

1. Each Party shall accord to covered investments treatment in accordance with customary international law, including fair and equitable treatment and full protection and security.
2. For greater certainty, paragraph 1 prescribes the customary international law minimum standard of treatment of aliens as the minimum standard of treatment to be afforded to covered investments. The concepts of "fair and equitable treatment" and "full protection and security" do not require treatment in addition to or beyond that which is required by that standard, and do not create additional substantive rights. The obligation in paragraph 1 to provide:

    (a) "fair and equitable treatment" includes the obligation not to deny justice in criminal, civil, or administrative adjudicatory proceedings in accordance with the principle of due process embodied in the principal legal systems of the world; and
    (b) "full protection and security" requires each Party to provide the level of police protection required under customary international law. [footnote omitted]

Likewise, the provision in Article 6 on expropriation and compensation is more restrictive than the provisions in older Model BITs or other BITs or IIAs or FTAs:

Article 6: Expropriation and Compensation

1. Neither Party may expropriate or nationalize a covered investment either directly or indirectly through measures equivalent to expropriation or nationalization ("expropriation"), except:

    (a) for a public purpose;
    (b) in a non-discriminatory manner;
    (c) on payment of prompt, adequate, and effective compensation; and
    (d) in accordance with due process of law and Article 5 [Minimum Standard of Treatment](1) through (3).

---

[34] CN Brower and S Melikian, 'We Have Met the Enemy and He Is Us! Is the Industrialised North "Going South" on Investor-State Arbitration?' (2015) 31 *Arbitration International* 19, 25.

2. The compensation referred to in paragraph 1(c) shall:
    (a) be paid without delay;
    (b) be equivalent to the fair market value of the expropriated investment immediately before the expropriation took place ("the date of expropriation");
    (c) not reflect any change in value occurring because the intended expropriation had become known earlier; and
    (d) be fully realizable and freely transferable.

3. If the fair market value is denominated in a freely usable currency, the compensation referred to in paragraph 1(c) shall be no less than the fair market value on the date of expropriation, plus interest at a commercially reasonable rate for that currency, accrued from the date of expropriation until the date of payment.

4. If the fair market value is denominated in a currency that is not freely usable, the compensation referred to in paragraph 1(c) – converted into the currency of payment at the market rate of exchange prevailing on the date of payment – shall be no less than:
    (a) the fair market value on the date of expropriation, converted into a freely usable currency at the market rate of exchange prevailing on that date, plus
    (b) interest, at a commercially reasonable rate for that freely usable currency, accrued from the date of expropriation until the date of payment.

5. This Article does not apply to the issuance of compulsory licenses granted in relation to intellectual property rights in accordance with the TRIPS Agreement, or to the revocation, limitation, or creation of intellectual property rights, to the extent that such issuance, revocation, limitation, or creation is consistent with the TRIPS Agreement. [footnote omitted]

More limitations on the interpretation of expropriation and conditions under which compensation is payable are included in Annex B to the Model Treaty:

Expropriation

The Parties confirm their shared understanding that:

1. Article 6 [Expropriation and Compensation](1) is intended to reflect customary international law concerning the obligation of States with respect to expropriation.

2. An action or a series of actions by a Party cannot constitute an expropriation unless it interferes with a tangible or intangible property right or property interest in an investment.

3. Article 6 [Expropriation and Compensation](1) addresses two situations. The first is direct expropriation, where an investment is nationalized or otherwise directly expropriated through formal transfer of title or outright seizure.

4. The second situation addressed by Article 6 [Expropriation and Compensation](1) is indirect expropriation, where an action or series of actions by a Party has an effect equivalent to direct expropriation without formal transfer of title or outright seizure.
    (a) The determination of whether an action or series of actions by a Party, in a specific fact situation, constitutes an indirect expropriation, requires a case-by-case, fact-based inquiry that considers, among other factors:
        (i) the economic impact of the government action, although the fact that an action or series of actions by a Party has an adverse effect on the economic value of an investment, standing alone, does not establish that an indirect expropriation has occurred;
        (ii) the extent to which the government action interferes with distinct, reasonable investment-backed expectations; and
        (iii) the character of the government action.

(b)   Except in rare circumstances, non-discriminatory regulatory actions by a Party that are designed and applied to protect legitimate public welfare objectives, such as public health, safety, and the environment, do not constitute indirect expropriations.

As can be seen from the above provisions, the 2012 US Model BIT recognises more widely than before the notion of regulatory expropriation and makes an exception to certain measures taken in pursuance of the WTO TRIPS agreement. What is interesting is the recognition in Articles 12 and 13 of the need to reconcile investment protection with environmental protection and respect for workers rights. Articles 12(1)–(3) and (5) read as follows:

Article 12: Investment and Environment

1.   The Parties recognize that their respective environmental laws and policies, and multi-lateral environmental agreements to which they are both party, play an important role in protecting the environment.
2.   The Parties recognize that it is inappropriate to encourage investment by weakening or reducing the protections afforded in domestic environmental laws. Accordingly, each Party shall ensure that it does not waive or otherwise derogate from or offer to waive or otherwise derogate from its environmental laws in a manner that weakens or reduces the protections afforded in those laws, or fail to effectively enforce those laws through a sustained or recurring course of action or inaction, as an encouragement for the establishment, acquisition, expansion, or retention of an investment in its territory.

     For the United States, "statutes or regulations" for the purposes of this Article means an act of the United States Congress or regulations promulgated pursuant to an act of the United States Congress that is enforceable by action of the central level of government.
3.   The Parties recognize that each Party retains the right to exercise discretion with respect to regulatory, compliance, investigatory, and prosecutorial matters, and to make decisions regarding the allocation of resources to enforcement with respect to other environmental matters determined to have higher priorities. Accordingly, the Parties understand that a Party is in compliance with paragraph 2 where a course of action or inaction reflects a reasonable exercise of such discretion, or results from a *bona fide* decision regarding the allocation of resources.

     ...
5.   Nothing in this Treaty shall be construed to prevent a Party from adopting, maintaining, or enforcing any measure otherwise consistent with this Treaty that it considers appropriate to ensure that investment activity in its territory is undertaken in a manner sensitive to environmental concerns.

Likewise, Articles 13 (1) and (2) contain the following provisions with regard to the interface between investment and labour:

1.   The Parties reaffirm their respective obligations as members of the International Labor Organization ("ILO") and their commitments under the *ILO Declaration on Fundamental Principles and Rights at Work and its Follow-Up*.
2.   The Parties recognize that it is inappropriate to encourage investment by weakening or reducing the protections afforded in domestic labor laws. Accordingly, each Party shall ensure that it does not waive or otherwise derogate from or offer to waive or otherwise derogate from its labor laws where the waiver or derogation would be inconsistent with the labor rights referred to in subparagraphs (a) through (e) of paragraph 3, or fail to

effectively enforce its labor laws through a sustained or recurring course of action or inaction, as an encouragement for the establishment, acquisition, expansion, or retention of an investment in its territory.

Acceptance of a Wider Definition of Investment

When the developing countries themselves started competing with each other for foreign direct investment that was flowing from developed countries, they were in competition to offer greater incentives to foreign investors; thus, they agreed to provisions designed to strengthen the position of foreign investors. The term 'investment' itself was defined as broadly as possible so as to accord protection to all conceivable forms of investment under the treaties, including asset-based investments such as portfolio investment. For instance, a BIT concluded between Jordan and the US in July 1997 defines the term 'investment' as comprehensively as possible in Article I(d) in the following terms:

'Investment' of a national or company means every kind of investment owned or controlled directly or indirectly by that national or company, and includes investment consisting or taking the form of:

(i)   a company;
(ii) shares, stock, and other forms of equity participation, and bonds, debentures, and other forms of debt interests, in a company;
(iii) contractual rights, such as under turnkey, construction or management contracts, production of revenue-sharing contracts, concessions, or other similar contracts;
(iv) tangible property, including real property; and intangible property, including rights, such as leases, mortgages, liens, and pledges;
(v)   intellectual property rights, including; copyrights and related rights, industrial property rights, patents, rights in plant varieties, utility models, industrial designs or models, rights in semiconductor layout design, indications of origin, trade secrets, including know-how, confidential business information, trade and service marks, and trade names; and rights conferred pursuant to law, such as licenses and permits.

A typical BIT would include a definition of the terms 'investor' and 'investment' and those investments included in the definition would be accorded the privileges, concessions and protections under the BIT. The treaty would also spell out the standard or level of treatment, as well as the nature and level of compensation to be paid in the event of expropriation or nationalisation and the conditions under which such expropriation can take place. It would also include provisions concerning the choice of the means of settling disputes by investors, including international arbitration. Like customary international law, BITs also do not prohibit expropriation per se, although they do expand the scope of indirect, creeping or consequential expropriations. Reisman and Sloane have outlined a number of hypothetical examples of misfeasance, malfeasance and nonfeasance which would not necessarily be regarded as indirect expropriations under the old FCN treaties but may be regarded as consequential expropriations under the new BITs.[35]

---

[35] Reisman and Sloane (n 15) 129.

Like Circumstances

The principle of national treatment and MFN requires that a state should accord investors of another state party to a BIT, RTA or FTA treatment no less favourable than that it accords, in like circumstances, to its own investors with respect to the establishment, acquisition, expansion, management, conduct, operation, and sale or other disposition of investments. For instance, Article 10.3(1) and (2) on national treatment in the Central America–Dominican Republic–United States Agreement, popularly known as the CAFTA, reads as follows:

1. Each Party shall accord *to investors* of another Party treatment no less favourable than that it accords, in like circumstance, to its own investors with respect to the establishment, acquisition, expansion, management, conduct, operation, and sale or other disposition of investments in its territory.
2. Each Party shall accord *to covered investments* treatment no less favourable than that it accords, in like circumstance, to investments in its territory of its own investors with respect to the establishment, acquisition, expansion, management, conduct, operation, and sale or other disposition of investments. [emphasis added]

The provisions concerning the MFN treatment in Article 10.4 are couched in similar fashion. Thus, the phrase 'like circumstances' is crucial for the application of the principle of national treatment since only those investments in 'like circumstances' enjoy this treatment. What are and are not like circumstances is often a matter of controversy. The phrase 'like product' has also been the subject of interpretation in a significant number of cases decided by GATT/WTO panels.

While in *SD Myers v Canada* an ICSID tribunal was prepared to draw on this jurisprudence in deciding what types of investments were covered by the phrase 'like circumstances' under a BIT, another tribunal in *Methanex Corporation v USA* rejected the view that it was bound to apply the trade law analysis or approach, in interpreting the term 'like circumstances'.[36]

Pre-Establishment Rights

Traditionally, FCN treaties or even earlier generations of BITs did not offer any pre-establishment rights to investors from another state party to the treaty concerned. Most BITs cover only investments that are already established. However, some of the more recent BITs, especially those concluded by the US and Canada with developing countries, and RTAs such as NAFTA and NAFTA-type FTAs such as the Japan–Singapore FTA, do offer certain key protections such as national treatment and

---

[36] *Methanex Corporation v USA* (3 August 2005), part II, ch B, 2 and 3.

MFN treatment to cover the entry and establishment of investments, ie to cover the stage when an investor is attempting to make or is making its investment in the host country. Broad asset-based definitions of investment are also liable to strengthen claims for pre-establishment rights. When a BIT or RTA or an FTA includes in the definition of 'investor' a foreign national or a business entity that 'attempts to make' an investment or 'seeks to make' an investment, then they would be seeking to have certain pre-establishment rights extended to them. Thus, the RTAs go much further than the WTO in granting pre-establishment rights; none of the WTO agreements provide such rights.

Articles 43, 44, 47, 48, 56 and 58 of the Treaty of Amsterdam of the EU include provisions concerning freedom of establishment and free movement of capital.[37] Other agreements concluded between the EU and central and eastern European countries also provide national treatment with regard to the establishment and operation of companies and nationals. The Treaty Establishing the Caribbean Community (CARICOM) of 1973 (as amended by a Protocol adopted in 1997), the Treaty Establishing the African Economic Community of 1991 and the Treaty Establishing the Common Market for Eastern and Southern Africa (COMESA) of 1993 include provisions designed to impose prohibitions on restrictions relating to the right of establishment of nationals of other Member States.[38]

Definition of the Applicable Law

Since most BITs provide for ad hoc arbitration, it is particularly important to determine both the substantive and procedural law governing such arbitration. Such determination is not difficult if the BIT specifies the applicable law, which many do. When the applicable law is specified, it often is a blend of the national law of the host state concerned and the generally recognised rules and principles of international law. However, many BITs do not specify it, and even those that do refer to broad and generic principles of the international foreign investment law. Many BITs give a tribunal broad discretion to determine the law within the general framework of international law. Phrases such as 'generally recognised rules and principles of international law' are the standard words used in BITs to indicate the law applicable to disputes arising under the agreement. When the BIT concerned is silent on the matter, or when the disputing parties fail to agree on the applicable law, the determination of it varies from one dispute settlement mechanism to another. For instance, ICC Arbitration Rules provide that in the absence of an agreement by the disputing parties as to the law to be applied, the tribunal would have the discretion to apply the law it deems appropriate.

---

[37] Arts 43, 44, 47, 48, 56 and 58 of the Treaty of Amsterdam of the EU, [1997] OJ C340, 61 et seq.

[38] For a summary of provisions on pre-establishment rights in RTAs, see a report of the Working Party of the Trade Committee of the OECD, 'The Relationship between Regional Trade Agreements and the Multilateral Trading System: Investment', TD/TC/WP (2002)18/Final, 13 June 2002, 8 et seq.

However, the UNCITRAL rules state that in the absence of an agreement between the parties, the tribunal will apply the law determined by the conflict-of-law rules that the tribunal considers appropriate. ICSID, on the other hand, states that in the absence of an agreement between the parties, the tribunal 'will apply the law of the Contracting State party to the dispute (including its rules on the conflict of laws) and such rules of international law as may be applicable'.[39]

Time Limitations of a Claim

The time limitation of a claim also depends on what the BIT provides. Obviously, no claim can be filed until after the BIT has entered into force. Some BITs leave the question open as to the time by which the claim has to be filed after the alleged breach of the BIT has taken place. Several BITs, such as those recently concluded by the US, specify a three-year time limit.

Contractual Character of Bilateral Investment Treaties

Basically, BITs are contractual treaties in character (hence, binding only on the parties concerned) rather than law-making treaties. Of course, BITs are evidence of state practice and are thus capable of contributing to the formation of rules of customary international law on the subject matter, but they themselves are contractual, regulating relations between the contracting parties alone. This is one reason why those very states that seem reluctant to conclude international agreements on investment are prepared to conclude a BIT or an FTA with similar provisions, which are favourable to foreign investors. A BIT or an IIA more often than not has a limited or fixed lifespan – they are normally valid for 10 or 20 years – after which the unwilling state concerned would, strictly speaking, no longer be bound by the treaty provisions because of their contractual character, albeit they may be under an obligation to adhere to the principles enunciated in such treaties if it can be established that they have acquired customary international law character. Further, in exercise of their sovereign rights inherent in them, states can also denounce a bilateral or other contractual treaty by giving advance notice if the treaty has a provision to this effect. It also is easier to renegotiate such treaties since the number of states party to it is small. However, an agreement to conclude an international treaty would mean committing the state to the provisions of the treaty for a long time to come. They may be regarded as law-making treaties in international law, creating effects binding on all parties. It would be harder to denounce or withdraw from such treaties.

---

[39] Art 42(1) of the ICSID Convention.

Protection under Stabilisation Clauses in Investment or State Contracts

Many investment contracts – also known as concessions or state contracts or host government agreements – between a host government and a foreign investor concluded in relation to infrastructure-related projects contain a 'stabilisation clause' that seeks to insulate foreign investors from any changes in the legal regime in the host country after the investment has been made. These clauses provide additional and slightly different protection from the protections that BITs afford to foreign investors. Under a BIT a host state is not prevented from taking new legal and administrative measures in accordance with the wishes of the people in the country or in order to comply with or implement the obligations flowing from an international treaty, whether dealing with human rights or environmental matters. In such a situation a company affected by a new measure would be expected to be compensated for the loss incurred due to the new legislation, regulatory or otherwise, if it amounts to 'indirect' expropriation. As seen earlier, under customary international foreign investment law, a regulatory governmental measure taken for a public purpose and in a non-discriminatory measure does not necessarily become expropriation if the measure does not result in significant economic injury to the foreign investors. However, certain investment contracts go further and require compensation for any interference by the host state that increases the costs of a project.

These provisions – known as stabilisation clauses – in such contracts stipulate that the law prevailing at the time the decision was taken by foreign investors to invest in the host countries would be applicable to them, and such laws are not be altered to the detriment of such investors. It is well and good that foreign investors commit themselves to abiding by the laws of the host country prevailing at the time the investment was made, but such clauses have the effect of preventing host states from enacting new legislation or undertaking new international obligations which would affect the profitability of the relevant foreign investors.[40]

Protection under the Umbrella Clause

Traditionally, it has been accepted in international law that a breach of a contract by a state does not give rise to direct international responsibility on the part of that state. However, some recent BITs have included provisions characterised by various

---

[40] Examples of such restrictive provisions in investment contracts are Art 30.1–2 of the Chad–Cameroon Pipeline Contract (see COTCO–Cameroon Convention 1997), and Art 34.4 in the Consortium–Chad Convention for the Development of Oil Fields and the Host Government Agreement between Turkey and the Consortium led by the British Petroleum in 2000 as cited in S Leader, 'Human Rights, Risks, and New Strategies for Global Investment' (2006) 9 *Journal of International Economic Law* 657, 667 (fn 24) and 672–73 (fn 44).

ICSID tribunals as an 'umbrella clause', which has often been interpreted as providing a blanket protection for foreign investment, including activities under a contract with a foreign investor. Once such activities are regarded as being covered by a BIT, then certain contractual undertakings to be governed by domestic law are liable to be elevated to international law obligations or enjoy protection under international law.[41] In such a situation a breach of a contractual obligation with a foreign company may become a breach of a BIT, thereby attracting the protection available under international foreign investment law. This blurs the distinction between private law disputes and public law disputes.[42] This extension of foreign investment law to contractual disputes is a relatively recent phenomenon. Article II(2)(c) of the BIT between Romania and the US provides that 'Each party shall observe any obligations it may have entered into with regard to investments.' Another example of a BIT that includes such an umbrella clause is the one between Switzerland and Pakistan. The relevant provision reads as follows: 'Either Contracting Party shall constantly guarantee the observance of the commitments it has entered into with respect to the investments of the investors of the other Contracting Party.'

Although an ICSID tribunal in *SGS v Pakistan* held that such provisions do not automatically elevate the breaches of contract to the level of breaches of international treaty law,[43] another ICSID tribunal in *SGS v Philippines* regarded a similar umbrella clause in the Swiss–Philippines BIT as being capable of application to contractual obligations. Article X(2) of this BIT stated that: 'Each Contracting Party shall observe any obligation it has assumed with regard to specific investments in its territory by investors of the other Contracting Party.' On the basis of this umbrella clause the tribunal held that the BIT had incorporated contractual commitment and brought it within the framework of the BIT: '[A]rticle X(2) includes commitments or obligations arising under contracts entered into by the host State.'[44]

Article 2(2) of the BIT between the UK and Argentina provides that: 'Each Contracting Party shall observe any obligation it may have entered into with regard to investments of investors of the other Contracting Party.' The Energy Charter Treaty provides in Article 10(1) that: 'Each Contracting Party shall observe any obligations it has entered into with an investor or an investment of an investor of any contracting

---

[41] J Wong, 'Umbrella Clauses in Bilateral Investment Treaties: Of Breaches of Contract, Treaty Violations and the Divide between Developing and Developed Countries in Foreign Investment Disputes' (2006) 14 *George Mason Law Review* 135; AC Sinclair, 'The Origins of the Umbrella Clause in the International Law of Investment Protection' (2005) 20 *Arbitration International* 433.

[42] MD Nolan and EG Baldwin, 'The Treatment of Contract-Related Claims in Treaty-Based Arbitration' (2006) 21 *Mealey's International Arbitration Report* 1.

[43] The Tribunal stated that it did not see anything in the Swiss–Pakistan BIT that could be read as 'vesting the tribunal with jurisdiction over claims resting ex hypothesi exclusively on contract'. It went on to state that the umbrella clause in this BIT did 'not purport to state that breaches of contract alleged by an investor in relation to a contract it has concluded with a State (widely considered to he a matter of municipal rather than international law) are automatically "elevated" to the level of breaches of international treaty law'. *SGS Société Générale de Surveillance SA v Islamic Republic of Pakistan*, ICSID Case No ARB/01/13, award of 8 September 2003, 361–63.

[44] *SGS v Philippines*, ICSID Case No ARB/02/6, 29 January 2004, para 127.

party.' A slightly different 'umbrella clause' can be found in Article 2(4) of the BIT between Italy and Jordan, which reads as follows:

> Each Contracting Party shall create and maintain in its territory a legal framework apt to guarantee the investors the continuity of legal treatment, including compliance, in good faith, of all undertakings assumed with regard to each specific investor.

On the basis of this an ICSID tribunal held in *Salini v Jordan* that

> each contracting Party committed itself to create and maintain in its territory a 'legal framework' favourable to investments. This legal framework must be apt to guarantee to investors the continuity of legal treatment. It must in particular be such as to ensure compliance of all undertakings assumed under relevant contracts with respect to each specific sector.[45]

Thus, umbrella clauses such as this seek not only to require a host state to create and maintain a domestic law system on foreign investment that is favourable to foreign investors but also even to extend the protection of international foreign investment law to contractual undertakings of a foreign investor under investment contracts. The ICSID tribunal in *Noble Ventures v Romania* stated that an umbrella clause is 'usually seen as transforming domestic law obligations into obligations directly cognizable in international law'. The tribunal went on to justify the rationale of its decision in the following words:

> [I]nasmuch as a breach of contract at the municipal level creates at the same time the violation of one of the principles existing either in customary international law or in treaty law applicable between the host state and the State of the nationality of the investor, it will give rise to the international responsibility of the host state. But that responsibility will co-exist with the responsibility created in municipal law and each of them will remain valid independently of the other, a situation that further reflects the respective autonomy of the two legal systems (municipal and international) each one with regard to the other.[46]

When a BIT includes an umbrella clause, such as those included in the Swiss–Pakistan or Swiss–Philippines BITs, international tribunals are quick to jump to the conclusion that such a clause is in effect creating an exception to the general separation of states' obligations under domestic law and under international law. By relying on such an umbrella clause the ICSID tribunal in the *SGS v Philippines* case was able to apply BIT protections to a contractual dispute between a Swiss company and the government of the Philippines. The tribunal held that:

> Article X (2) makes it a breach of the BIT for the host state to fail to observe binding commitments, including contractual commitments, which it has assumed with regard to specific commitments. But it does not convert the issue of the *extent* or *content* of such obligations into an issue of international law.[47]

In reaching such conclusions the ICSID tribunals do not seem to have paid full attention to the question as to whether the states in question had the intention of creating such an 'umbrella clause' in inserting such a provision in the BIT and thereby extending

---

[45] *Salini Costruttori SpA v The Hashemite Kingdom of Jordan*, ICSID Case No ARB/02/13.
[46] *Noble Ventures v Romania*, ICSID Case No ARB/01/11, 12 October 2005, para 53.
[47] *SGS v Philippines*, ICSID Case No ARB/02/6, 29 January 2004, 49.

the BIT protection to contractual undertakings. Since there are generally few *travaux préparatoires* available concerning the conclusions of BITs which could shed some light as to the intention of the states party to such BITs, international tribunals rather easily and willing regard such provisions as umbrella clauses and thereby extend the BIT protection to contractual undertakings.

This is a significant departure from the established norms of international law, which provide that a breach of a contract by a state does not give rise to direct international responsibility on the part of the state. Indeed, as stated by the ICJ in the *ELSI* case, an important principle of international law should not be held to have been tacitly dispensed with by international agreement, in the absence of words making clear an intention to do so.[48] States are free to include a provision in a BIT stating that all breaches of each state's contracts with investors of the other state would be treated as breaches of the BIT. Unless and until this has been done, the tribunals should not infer a different conclusion. That was the conclusion of the ICSID tribunal in *SGS v Pakistan*.[49] However, the ICSID tribunal in *SGS v Philippines* disagreed with many of the conclusions reached by the *SGS v Pakistan* tribunal, stating that a later ICSID tribunal was not bound by the decisions of a previous tribunal and such decisions can only have a *res judicata* effect on later tribunals. However, in a case decided in April 2006, *El Paso Energy International v Argentina*, an ICSID tribunal delivered a more balanced decision on the question of protection under the umbrella clause.

Protection under Regional Trade and Investment Treaties

In the absence of a global treaty on foreign investment, both BITs and regional treaties have sought to fill the vacuum and lead the way. This is especially the case with NAFTA and TPP and with TTIP in the offing. At the time of adoption, the provisions of NAFTA provided far more protection to foreign investors than accorded hitherto in customary international law. Appleton rightly states that: 'Plurilateral treaties such as the NAFTA go even further than customary international law.'[50] Thus, NAFTA set the trend for much greater protection of foreign investment throughout the 1990s, whether through BITs, the TRIMS agreement of the WTO or other regional treaties. Jackson, Davey and Sykes rightly observe that:

> If global progress on investment issues has been slow, more dramatic developments are visible at the regional level. NAFTA incorporates broad rules on investment within the region, including general obligations to afford MFN and national treatment to NAFTA investors. The 'investor rights' provisions of NAFTA are particularly remarkable in that they create

---

[48] *ELSI (US v Italy)*, ICJ Reports 1989, 15, 42.

[49] *SGS Société Générale de Surveillance SA v Islamic Republic of Pakistan*, ICSID Case No ARB/01/13, award of 8 September 2003, 367.

[50] See the remarks of B Appleton under the title 'Investment Disputes and NAFTA Chapter 11', *ASIL Proceedings* (2001) fn 6, 197.

private rights of action to enforce their terms (unlike most of the provisions of NAFTA, which can only be enforced by member nations), including a private right of action for damages in the event of 'expropriation,' a concept that has proved elusive.[51]

The NAFTA provisions on the treatment of foreign investors are by far the most favourable ones for foreign investors compared to other RTAs or FTAs. They offer greater protection to foreign investment than does the TRIMS agreement. The main NAFTA provision on foreign investment protection reads, in Article 1110(1), as follows:

> No Party may directly or indirectly nationalize or expropriate an investment of an investor of another Party in its territory or take a measure tantamount to nationalization or expropriation of such investment ('expropriation') except:
>
> (a)   for a public purpose;
> (b)   on a non-discriminatory basis;
> (c)   in accordance with due process of law and Article 1105 (1);
> (d)   on payment of compensation in accordance with paragraphs 2 through 6.

Article 1105(1) provides for additional protection for foreign investors:

> Each Party shall accord to investments of investors of another Party treatment in accordance with international law, including fair and equitable treatment and full protection and security.

Thus, this provision implies that the protection of foreign investment under customary international law is as broad as that provided in NAFTA, as if the NAFTA provisions were mere codification of customary international law. It is doubtful whether the protection afforded to foreign investors under customary international law goes as far as that afforded under NAFTA. This provision of NAFTA represents an attempt to broaden the scope of customary international law and expand its reach beyond the limits generally accepted in international law.

Indeed, Articles 1110(1) and 1105(1) add the following three new concepts to the regime of protection available to foreign investors:

(a)   the due process of law,
(b)   fair and equitable treatment, and
(c)   full protection and security.

Of course, there can be little doubt that these three new elements derive from customary international law on the subject matter. The problem, however, lies in the interpretation of the meaning, nature and scope of these concepts, as there have been tendencies on the part of various NAFTA tribunals to stretch the meaning of these concepts beyond the limits generally understood in customary international law. It is doubtful whether the idea of the minimum international standard of treatment of foreign investment accepted in traditional international law encompasses all of the new elements embodied in the NAFTA regime under the heading 'Minimum Standard of Treatment'.

Traditionally, BITs were designed to extend the national, non-discriminatory and MFN treatment to foreign investors and to protect their property against acts of

---

[51] JH Jackson, WJ Davey and AO Sykes, Jr, *Legal Problems of International Economic Relations: Cases, Materials and Text*, 4th edn (St Paul, MN, West Group, 2002) 1137.

expropriation. Thus, BITs sought to accord greater protection to foreign investors than that provided under customary international law. However, the NAFTA provisions imply that the protections enjoyed by foreign investors under BITs are also available under customary international law, which is, perhaps, not the case. What is more, neither customary international law nor BITs have ever provided free and unhindered opportunities for investment in any given host country; there have always been some restrictions on foreign investment, either in terms of the areas of economic activity or geographical regions of the country concerned.

Unlike other investment treaties, NAFTA includes provisions relating to the method according to which compensation has to be paid against expropriation. It provides for the award of monetary damages with interest. It also requires that compensation must be equivalent to the fair market value of the expropriated investment immediately before the expropriation took place. The treaty goes on to outline the valuation criteria of the assets expropriated: '[T]he valuation criteria shall include going concern value, asset value including the declared tax value of tangible property, and other criteria, as appropriate, to determine fair market value.'[52]

The Energy Charter Treaty of 1994 includes equally greater protection for foreign investment than that accorded under customary international law. Article 10(1) on Promotion, Protection and Treatment of Investments provides that:

> Each Contracting Party shall, in accordance with the provisions of this Treaty, encourage and create stable, equitable and favourable and transparent conditions for investors of other Contracting Parties to make investments in its area. Such conditions shall include a commitment to accord at all times to investments of investors of other Contracting Parties fair and equitable treatment. Such investments shall also enjoy the most constant protection and security and no Contracting party shall in any way impair by unreasonable or discriminatory measures their management, maintenance, use, enjoyment or disposal. In no case shall such investments be accorded treatment less favourable than that required by international law, including treaty obligations. Each Contracting Party shall observe any obligations it has entered into with an investor or an investment of an investor of any Contracting Party.[53]

Conceived initially as the European Energy Charter, the 1994 Treaty has been ratified not only by western and eastern European states, including Russia, but also by the other members of the CIS, as well as by Japan, Mongolia and Australia.[54] The protections accorded to foreign investors are enforceable by international arbitration. The protection accorded to foreign investors under the principles of national treatment and MFN treatment is also extended to the 'related activities including management, maintenance, use, enjoyment or disposal'.[55]

---

[52] Art 1135(1)(a) of NAFTA.

[53] UNCTAD, *International Investment Instruments: A Compendium*, vols I–III (New York and Geneva, United Nations), UN Publications, Sales Nos E.96.II.A.9, 10 and 11, 555.

[54] See TW Walde (ed), *The Energy Charter Treaty: An East–West Gateway for Investment and Trade* (The Hague, Kluwer Law International, 1996); AFM Maniruzzaman, 'Towards Regional Energy Co-operation in the Asia-Pacific: Some Lessons from the Energy Charter Treaty' (2002) 3 *Journal of World Investment* 1061.

[55] Art 10 (1) of the Energy Charter Treaty.

Protection under Free Trade Agreements and Model Bilateral Investment Treaties

The newest generation of trade and investment treaties concluded by the US with other states are the so-called FTAs; those concluded with Chile and Singapore are some of the most ambitious and comprehensive bilateral treaties ever concluded in the history of international economic relations. For instance, the massive 800-page treaty concluded with Chile in June 2003 and the even longer 1,400-page treaty with Singapore in May 2003 contain detailed provisions on foreign investment, spelling out many of the key terms and phrases whose definition has dogged the debate on foreign investment law for so long. The treaty with Chile defines not only terms such as 'national treatment' and 'most-favoured-nation treatment', but also more controversial and challenging terms such as 'fair and equitable treatment' and 'full protection and security'.[56] Similarly, Article 15.1(13) of the US–Singapore FTA defines the term 'investment' as comprehensively as possible in the following words:

> Investment means every asset owned or controlled, directly or indirectly, by an investor, that has the characteristics of an investment. Forms that an investment may take include:
>
> (a) an enterprise;
> (b) shares, stock, and other forms of equity participation in an enterprise;
> (c) bonds, debentures, other debt instruments, and loans;
> (d) futures, options, and other derivatives;
> (e) turnkey, construction, management, production, concession, revenue-sharing, and other similar contracts;
> (f) intellectual property rights;
> (g) licenses, authorizations, permits, and similar rights conferred pursuant to applicable domestic law; and
> (h) other tangible and intangible, movable or immovable property, and related property rights, such as leases, mortgages, liens, and pledges.[57]

Even so, the list is not exhaustive. Article 15.5 of the Treaty outlines the minimum standard of treatment to be accorded to foreign investors in the following words:

> Article 15.5: Minimum Standard of Treatment
>
> 1. Each Party shall accord to covered investments treatment in accordance with customary international law, including fair and equitable treatment and full protection and security.
> 2. For greater certainty, paragraph 1 prescribes the customary international law minimum standard of treatment of aliens as the minimum standard of treatment to be afforded to covered investments. The concepts of 'fair and equitable treatment' and 'full protection

---

[56] Art 10.4(2)(a), (b) of the US–Chile Agreement. See text of the Treaty at www.ustr.gov/new/fta/ chile.htm.
[57] www.ustr.gov/new/fta/singapore.htm (footnotes omitted).

and security' do not require treatment in addition to or beyond that which is required by that standard, and do not create additional substantive rights.

(a)   The obligation in paragraph 1 to provide 'fair and equitable treatment' includes the obligation not to deny justice in criminal, civil, or administrative adjudicatory proceedings in accordance with the principle of due process embodied in the principle legal systems of the world; and

(b)   The obligation in paragraph 1 to provide 'full protection and security' requires each Party to provide the level of police protection required under customary international law.

Although these treaties seem to be aiming to codify certain key principles of foreign investment law, various provisions keep referring to customary international law standards, taking the debate more or less back to square one. Hence, the relevance of customary international law has not been diminished, even with the conclusion of such comprehensive trade and investment treaties. It is noteworthy that provisions such as these are somewhat more cautious and narrowly defined than the provisions of many other previous BITs in terms of the protection accorded to foreign investors. This may have been due to ICSID panel decisions, such as those in *Metalclad* where the panel sought to stretch the meaning of various terms beyond the reasonable meaning accorded to them under customary international law.

The dispute settlement mechanism of BITs is also designed to deny host states a 'home country advantage' in a case against a foreign investor. By requiring that the dispute be referred to an independent international tribunal, BITs seek to ensure fairness in the settlement of investment disputes. For instance, the 2012 US Model BIT contains rather elaborate provisions concerning the settlement of investment disputes and the options available to foreign investors. This Model BIT seems to have inspired a number of BITs concluded by the US with other states or between other states themselves. Its main provisions on dispute settlement read as follows:

Article 23: Consultation and Negotiation

In the event of an investment dispute, the claimant and the respondent should initially seek to resolve the dispute through consultation and negotiation, which may include the use of non-binding, third-party procedures.

Article 24: Submission of a Claim to Arbitration

1.   In the event that a disputing party considers that an investment dispute cannot be settled by consultation and negotiation:

(a)   the claimant, on its own behalf, may submit to arbitration under this Section a claim

(i)   that the respondent has breached

(A)   an obligation under Articles 3 through 10,
(B)   an investment authorization, or
(C)   an investment agreement; and

(ii)   that the claimant has incurred loss or damage by reason of, or arising out of, that breach; and

(b) the claimant, on behalf of an enterprise of the respondent that is a juridical person that the claimant owns or controls directly or indirectly, may submit to arbitration under this Section a claim

    (i) that the respondent has breached

        (A) an obligation under Articles 3 through 10,

        (B) an investment authorization, or

        (C) an investment agreement; and

    (ii) that the enterprise has incurred loss or damage by reason of, or arising out of, that breach, provided that a claimant may submit pursuant to subparagraph (a)(i)(C) or (b)(i)(C) a claim for breach of an investment agreement only if the subject matter of the claim and the claimed damages directly relate to the covered investment that was established or acquired, or sought to be established or acquired, in reliance on the relevant investment agreement.

2. At least 90 days before submitting any claim to arbitration under this Section, a claimant shall deliver to the respondent a written notice of its intention to submit the claim to arbitration ('notice of intent'). The notice shall specify:

    (a) the name and address of the claimant and, where a claim is submitted on behalf of an enterprise, the name, address, and place of incorporation of the enterprise;

    (b) for each claim, the provision of this Treaty, investment authorization, or investment agreement alleged to have been breached and any other relevant provisions;

    (c) the legal and factual basis for each claim; and

    (d) the relief sought and the approximate amount of damages claimed.

3. Provided that six months have elapsed since the events giving rise to the claim, a claimant may submit a claim referred to in paragraph 1:

    (a) under the ICSID Convention and the ICSID Rules of Procedure for Arbitration Proceedings, provided that both the respondent and the non-disputing Party are parties to the ICSID Convention;

    (b) under the ICSID Additional Facility Rules, provided that either the respondent or the non-disputing Party is a party to the ICSID Convention;

    (c) under the UNCITRAL Arbitration Rules; or

    (d) if the claimant and respondent agree, to any other arbitration institution or under any other arbitration rules ...

Equally interesting are the provisions in the 2004 Singapore–Jordan BIT on the settlement of investment disputes. They read as follows:

ARTICLE 13

Settlement of Disputes between a Party and an Investor of the Other Party

1. The avoidance and settlement of disputes between an investor of a Party and the other Party shall be governed by this Article.

2. In the case of a dispute between an investor of a Party and the other Party, the investor shall notify the other Party if it intends to submit the dispute for conciliation or arbitration by the Centre established by the ICSID Convention. An investor shall not submit a dispute for such conciliation or arbitration unless it provides such notification to the other Party and satisfies the other conditions that are set out under this Article.

3. When an investor of a Party has given notice to the other Party that it intends to submit a dispute for conciliation or arbitration by the Centre established by the ICSID

Convention, both parties to the dispute shall seek to resolve the dispute amicably through negotiations.

4. The Party intending to resolve such a dispute through negotiations under paragraph 3 of this Article shall give written notice to the other Party of its intention. Thereafter, the Parties shall within forty five days from the date of receipt of such notice by the other Party, convene an expert working group consisting of officials designated by both Parties which shall enter into consultations with a view to facilitating the amicable resolution of the dispute.

5. Either party to the dispute may only submit a dispute for conciliation or arbitration by the Centre established by the ICSID Convention if the dispute cannot be resolved by negotiations or consultations as provided for in paragraphs 3 and 4 of this Article, within nine months from the date of the notice given by the investor to the other Party under paragraph 2 of this Article. For this purpose, each Party hereby consents to the submission of a dispute to conciliation or arbitration pursuant to Article 25 of the ICSID Convention. Such consent shall satisfy the requirements of Article 25 of the ICSID Convention for the written consent of the parties to the dispute.

However, the old Model BIT of India takes a rather cautious approach in regards to foreign investors' access to international arbitration. The dispute settlement provision of this Model BIT reads as follows:

ARTICLE 9

Settlement of Disputes between an Investor and a Contracting Party

1. Any dispute between an investor of one Contracting Party and the other Contracting Party in relation to an investment of the former under this Agreement shall, as far as possible, be settled amicably through negotiations between the parties to the dispute.

2. Any such dispute which has not been amicably settled within a period of six months may, if both Parties agree, be submitted:

    (a) for resolution, in accordance with the law of the Contracting Party which has admitted the investment to that Contracting Party's competent judicial, arbitral or administrative bodies; or

    (b) to International conciliation under the Conciliation Rules of the United Nations Commission on International Trade Law.

3. Should the Parties fail to agree on a dispute settlement procedure provided under paragraph (2) of this Article or where a dispute is referred to conciliation but conciliation proceedings are terminated other than by signing of a settlement agreement, the dispute may be referred to Arbitration. The Arbitration procedure shall be as follows:

    (a) If the Contracting Party of the Investor and the other Contracting Party are both parties to the convention on the Settlement of Investment Disputes between States and Nationals of other States, 1965 and the investor consents in writing to submit the dispute to the International Centre for the Settlement of Investment Disputes such a dispute shall be referred to the Centre; or

    (b) If both parties to the dispute so agree, under the Additional Facility for the Administration of Conciliation, Arbitration and Fact-Finding proceedings; or

    (c) to an ad hoc arbitral tribunal by either party to the dispute in accordance with the Arbitration Rules of the United Nations Commission on International Trade Law, 1976, subject to the following modifications:

        (i) The appointing authority under Article 7 of the Rules shall be the President, the Vice-President or the next senior Judge of the International Court of

Justice, who is not a national of either Contracting Party. The third arbitrator shall not be a national of either Contracting party.

(ii)   The parties shall appoint their respective arbitrators within two months.

(iii)   The arbitral award shall be made in accordance with the provisions of this Agreement and shall be binding for the parties in dispute.

(iv)   The arbitral tribunal shall state the basis of its decision and give reasons upon the request of either party.

Thus, as can be seen from the above, foreign investors have a number of options available for the settlement of their disputes with the host states, with the most popular being the ICSID tribunals. However, the new Draft Model BIT of 2015 released by India for consultation in March 2015 has more restrictive provisions on dispute settlement that require the exhaustion of local remedies before resorting to international arbitration and that limit the scope for ICSID-style arbitrations.

The Changing Character of Bilateral Investment Treaties

In the long history of international investment law, BITs are a relatively recent phenomenon – a German invention perfected over the years by the US and other investor countries. Initially, BITs were seen as a challenge to the international efforts by developing countries to regulate foreign investment through an international instrument adopted under the auspices of the UN. The Federal Republic of Germany was the first country to conclude BITs with certain developing countries in the 1960s in order to protect German investment in these countries. As pointed out by Gunawardana, German investors, 'having lost their foreign assets in the two world wars, were particularly concerned about investment protection'.[58] Both the US and the UK were relative newcomers to this sphere; the first BIT concluded by the UK was with Egypt in 1975, and it was soon followed by the US. The ancestor of the BIT was the first generation of freedom of commerce and navigation (FCN) treaties concluded by the US with various European powers, including France, Spain, the Netherlands and the UK in the eighteenth century. The second generation of FCN treaties was concluded by the US with newly independent Latin American states in the early nineteenth century, followed by the third generation during the interwar period and the fourth generation after the Second World War.

Although the early FCN treaties were concluded primarily to establish trading relations, they did include provisions concerning the protection of alien property, including a clause prohibiting the expropriation of property of aliens without compensation.[59] The fourth generation of treaties was concluded in the aftermath of the Second World War following the failure of the Havana Charter to include foreign investment provisions favoured by the US. The main purpose of the fourth generation of FCN treaties

---

[58] A de Z Gunawardana, 'The Inception and Growth of Bilateral Investment Promotion and Protection Treaties', *Proceedings of the ASIL 86th Annual Meeting* (1992) 544, 545.
[59] Vandevelde (n 25) 533.

concluded between 1946 and 1966 was to protect US investment abroad. For instance, Article IV(2) of the Treaty of Amity between the US and Iran provided as follows:

> Property of nationals and companies of either High Contracting Party, including interests in property, shall receive the most constant protection and security within the territories of the other High Contracting party, in no case less than that required by international law. Such property shall not be taken except for a public purpose, nor shall it be taken without the prompt payment of just compensation. Such compensation shall be in an effectively realizable form and shall represent the full equivalent of the property taken; and adequate provision shall have been made at or prior to the time of taking for the determination and payment thereof.[60]

Although provisions such as this one incorporating the Hull formula were typical of American FCN treaties, in 1977 the US launched its BIT programme – the fifth generation of such treaties – with a view to countering moves led by the developing countries towards an NIEO within the UN and to strengthening the long-held view of the US that the Hull formula was part of the international minimum standard guaranteed to foreign investors under international law. The US acted thus because it was having difficulty concluding new FCN treaties with newly independent Asian and African states after 1966 and the political situation was turning against US interests within the UN. Explaining the US's motive for concluding the BITs, Kenneth Vandevelde, who was on the US negotiating team for BITs while serving in the Legal Adviser's Office at the Department of State, stated that:

> [T]he legal consideration was to build a network of treaties adopting the principle that the expropriation of foreign investment was unlawful unless accompanied by prompt, adequate and effective compensation. A strong case can be made that this was the single most important goal of the BIT program.

> Consider the context in which the decision to begin the program was launched. The 1960s and early 1970s had witnessed scores of expropriatory acts by foreign governments against US investors, beginning in 1959 with the seizure of an IT&T subsidiary in Brazil and Castro's massive expropriations in Cuba. In 1974, the UN General Assembly's adoption of the Charter of Economic Rights and Duties seemed to suggest that the world community, at least in political fora, was willing to endorse expropriations unaccompanied by payment of full compensation.

> The general hostility to property rights evident in the world community during this period from 1959 to the mid-1970s was deeply troubling to American policy makers. It is no accident that these years coincided with the enactment of the Hickenlooper Amendment, the Gonzalez Amendment, and similar provisions in the Trade Act of 1974 and the Caribbean Basin Initiative, all of which imposed sanctions on foreign states that expropriated US property without payment of full compensation.

> In the midst of these expropriations and the passage of the Charter of Economic Rights and Duties, American policy makers looked for a way to bolster the traditional American position that customary international law required payment of prompt, adequate and effective compensation for expropriation of foreign-owned property. They believed that a network of treaties embracing this principle would be one highly visible way of building state practice in support of that traditional position.[61]

---

[60] 284 UNTS 93.
[61] Vandevelde (n 25) 534.

Indeed, according to the US, 'under international law', it had 'a right to expect: that any taking of American private property will be non-discriminatory; that it will be for a public purpose; and that its citizens will receive prompt, adequate and effective compensation from the expropriating country'.[62]

At the heart of the BITs concluded by the US has been the substantive provision relating to expropriation. Bolstering state practice in support of the Hull formula was the principal reason for concluding a BIT. This was the main purpose of the US Model BIT. The sixth generation of BITs comprised those concluded in the 1990s with Asian, Eastern European and Latin American states, following the triumph of Western liberal economic philosophy over the socialist philosophy as well as over the NIEO.[63] Under this generation of treaties, Asian, Eastern European and Latin American states came around to accepting the Western concept of the international minimum standard not only in its traditional form, but also its new form, which encompasses the due process of law, fair and equitable treatment, and full protection and security. For instance, Argentina, a country that had been holding out for acceptance of the Calvo doctrine, made a volte-face and concluded a BIT with the US in 1991.[64] The US regarded this as a major achievement and a major breakthrough in its economic relations with the South American countries. As outlined in a presidential communication to Congress, the main US objectives in the conclusion of this BIT were as follows:

— investment of nationals and companies of one Party in the territory of the other Party (investments) receive the better of the treatment accorded to domestic investments in like circumstances (national treatment), or the treatment accorded to third country investments in like circumstances (most-favoured-nation (MFN) treatment), both on establishment and thereafter, subject to certain specified exceptions;
— investments are guaranteed freedom from performance requirements, such as obligations to use local products or export goods;
— companies which are investments may hire top managers of their choice, regardless of nationality;
— expropriation can occur only in accordance with international law standards: in a non-discriminatory manner; for a public purpose; and upon payment of prompt, adequate, and effective compensation;
— investment-related funds are guaranteed unrestricted transfer in a freely usable currency; and
— nationals and companies of either Party, and their investments, have access to binding international arbitration in investment disputes with the host government, without first resorting to domestic courts.[65]

After concluding a number of BITs designed to achieve the above-mentioned objectives with other South American states and with states in Asia and Africa, the US has moved to the next generation of bilateral trade and investment treaties. At the time of writing, the US seems to be busy concluding the seventh generation of BITs in the

---

[62] US Department of State, Statement on Foreign Investment and Nationalization, 30 September 1975 (1976) XV ILM 186.
[63] See K Vandevelde, 'The Political Economy of a Bilateral Investment Treaty' (1998) 92 *American Journal of International Law* 621.
[64] 1991 UST LEXIS 176.
[65] US Treaty Doc 103–02, Focus – 32 of 48 Documents, 1991 UST LEXIS 176.

form of FTAs designed to ensure not only favourable treatment of foreign investment once it is in the host countries, but also to secure free and unrestricted investment access to different areas of economic activity in such countries.

Conclusion

Although there is no credible evidence to suggest that BITs have increased the flow of foreign investment from developed countries to developing countries, they certainly have instilled a sense of security in foreign investors. These treaties have provided the assurance to foreign investors that should something go wrong within the host states due to governmental interference, then they have an international legal remedy. However, most BITs contain no provisions designed to impose any obligations on foreign investors towards the host countries. With exception of a few recent BITs, most of these treaties are silent about the preservation of the environment or the protection of human rights by foreign investors in the countries where they do their business.

6

Fleshing Out the Principles Through Jurisprudence

Introduction

Having considered treaty law and practice on investment protection in the preceding chapters, this chapter aims to analyse how the jurisprudence of international courts and tribunals has interpreted the protection available to foreign investors under both customary international law and BITs. It will explore how the decisions of international courts and tribunals have fleshed out the principles of foreign investment law pertaining to, inter alia, the meaning and scope of the principle of fair and equitable treatment, expropriation and nationalisation, and determination of the level of compensation; and how the frontiers of expropriation have been extended to deal with the issues associated with regulatory takings.

Fleshing Out the Principles of Foreign Investment Law

Although it is arguable whether international investment tribunals and especially ICSID or UNCITRAL tribunals are ideally structured to play a primary role in developing customary international law, the bulk of the jurisprudence that exists on the subject matter is the jurisprudence arising from the ICSID or UNCITRAL tribunals. This is one of the reasons why concerns have been expressed about the manner such tribunals have discharged their duties. Some of the reasons for these concerns are that states litigate their investment disputes differently from how they litigate their other international disputes; the arbitrators do not have to meet any qualification threshold; unlike the ICJ judges, they are not elected and are not accountable to anyone; they are private arbitrators appointed on a case-by-case basis; some of them may not even have a background in international law, but they apply treaty law, as interpreted by them; the procedures of the ICSID or UNCITRAL panels may not meet the tests of transparency, legitimacy and accountability; and both of these are more of a technical commercial dispute mechanisms rather than a proper court of law capable of generating high-quality and well-reasoned decisions. So much so that one commentator has remarked that a NAFTA tribunal lacked, with the exception of the dissenting member, even a basic understanding of the legal text within which the decisions it was asked to rule on were made.[1]

In the absence of a global treaty on foreign investment law, international courts, claims commissions and tribunals have tried to flesh out the main principles relating to the requirements for a lawful expropriation and the nature of compensation, damages, reparation or restitution for both lawful expropriations and the illegal or confiscatory actions of states. While the main principles are not fully settled, and state practice and efforts made within and outside of the UN point in conflicting directions, the decisions of international courts and tribunals on these matters have been relied upon to deduce the rules applicable not only to expropriation and compensation, but also to the meaning of the terms 'fair and equitable treatment', 'due process of law', and 'full protection and security'. Indeed, the decisions of international courts, claims commissions and arbitration tribunals have played a major role in articulating the international standards of treatment applicable to foreign investors. Traditionally, the treatment of aliens under international law of state responsibility has been relied upon by international courts, claims commissions and tribunals to provide legal remedy to foreign investors when their investment was expropriated or unlawfully impaired by a foreign government. As stated by Asante:

> Traditional principles of customary international law relating to investments revolve around the law of State responsibility for injury to aliens and alien property. According to this doctrine, which was developed in the nineteenth century, host States are enjoined by international law to observe an international minimum standard in the treatment of aliens and alien property.[2]

However, it was not until the period between the First and Second World Wars that the idea of submitting investment disputes to a third party was accepted by those states subscribing to the Calvo doctrine. Of course, the idea of settling disputes between states through arbitration or through the involvement of a third party had long existed in international law and the Hague Peace Conference of 1907 provided an international framework for arbitration as a means of settling international disputes. However, the requirement to accord an international minimum standard did not include the right of states, let alone of private investors, to have investment disputes with host states settled by an international tribunal or via commercial arbitration. One of the core elements of the Calvo doctrine was that the home states had to abstain from interference in disputes over the treatment of foreigners and their property rights. This meant, inter alia, abstaining from the use of 'gunboat diplomacy' or diplomatic protection by investor countries in favour of their nationals doing business abroad. Even the provisions of the modern FCN treaties concluded in the aftermath of the Second World War

---

[1] Professor M Doelle, Director, Marine and Environmental Law Institute, Dalhousie University, Canada, 'Clayton Whites Point NAFTA Challenge Troubling', 25 March 2015, circulated to the FICTA Group on 26 March 2015 and on file with the author.

[2] SKB Asante, 'International Law and Foreign Investment: A Reappraisal' (1988) 37 *ICLQ* 588, 590.

were limited to providing for adjudication before the ICJ of certain disputes between the treaty parties, ie state–state disputes. The norm was to protect national investors doing business abroad through diplomatic protection by invoking the 'international minimum standard'.

Supporting the idea behind diplomatic protection, the Permanent Court of International Justice (PCIJ) held in the *Mavrommatis Palestine Concessions* case between Greece and the UK that:

> It is an elementary principle of international law that a State is entitled to protect its subjects, when injured by acts contrary to international law committed by another State, from whom they have been unable to obtain satisfaction through the ordinary channels.[3]

Cases such as *Neer*[4] supported the notion that international law required states to treat aliens according to an international minimum standard. Indeed, the *Neer* claim decided by the Mexico–United States General Claims Commission in 1926 has been relied upon to support the doctrine of an international minimum standard of treatment of foreign investors in international law:

> [T]he propriety of governmental acts should be put to the test of international standards ... the treatment of an alien, in order to constitute an international delinquency, should amount to an outrage, to bad faith, to wilful neglect of duty, or to an insufficiency of governmental action so far short of international standards that every reasonable and impartial man would readily recognize its insufficiency.[5]

Similar views were expressed by the ICJ in the *Barcelona Traction Case*.[6] The classic and often-cited case pronouncing the standard of treatment to be accorded to foreign investors is *Chorzow Factory (Indemnity) (Merits)*[7] in which the PCIJ relied on the doctrine of state responsibility to provide legal remedy to Germany. After finding that Poland had violated the Geneva Convention of 1922 between Germany and Poland on Upper Silesia, the Court held that 'it is a principle of international law, and even a general conception of law, that any breach of an engagement involves an obligation to make reparation'. The Court held further that:

> The action of Poland which the Court has judged to be contrary to the Geneva Convention is not an expropriation – to render which lawful only the payment of fair compensation would have been wanting; it is a seizure of property, rights and interests which could not be expropriated even against compensation, save under the exceptional conditions fixed by Article 7 of the said Convention.

> It follows that the compensation due to the German Government is not necessarily limited to the value of the undertaking at the moment of dispossession, plus interest to the day of payment. This limitation would only be admissible if the Polish Government had had the right to expropriate, and if its wrongful act consisted merely in not having paid to the two Companies the just price of what was expropriated ...

---

[3] *Mavrommatis Palestine Concessions*, PCIJ Reports, Series A, No 2, 12.

[4] *LFH Neer and Pauline Neer (USA) v United Mexican States* (1926) 4 RIAA iv.60.

[5] Ibid, 61–62, as cited in I Brownlie, *Principles of Public International Law*, 6th edn (Oxford, Oxford University Press, 2003) 503.

[6] *Barcelona Traction, Light and Power Co (Belgium v Spain)*, ICJ Reports, 1970, 3, para 33.

[7] *Factory at Chorzow (Germany v Poland)* (Indemnity) (Merits), PCIJ Reports (1928), Series A, No 17, 29.

> The essential principle contained in the actual notion of an illegal act – a principle which seems to be established by international practice and in particular by decisions of arbitral tribunals – is that reparation must, as far as possible, wipe out all the consequences of the illegal act and re-establish the situation which would, in all probability, have existed if that act had not been committed.[8]

The opinion of the Court in this case has been relied upon heavily by international courts and tribunals established in later years, among which the Iran–US Claims Tribunal is a prominent example.

Definition of Investment

Since only some investments, which are covered by the definition of investment in a BIT or other IIA, enjoy treaty protection, the definition of 'investment' has been a crucial issue in international investment law. Various international investment tribunals have sought to flesh out the provisions in such treaties on this matter. The definition of 'investment' becomes more crucial in cases referred to ICSID. This is because the ICSID Convention itself does not define the term 'investment', and ICSID would have no jurisdiction in cases involving investments, which are not regarded as 'investment' for the purposes of the Convention. Several ICSID tribunals have tried to define what constitutes investment for the purposes of the ICSID Convention and one of the more prominent cases is *Salini v Morocco*. In this case, an ICSID tribunal held that to qualify as an investment under the Convention, an investment should be construed as those investments that make a contribution to the 'economic development of the host state'.[9] In this case, the tribunal defines an investment as having four elements: (1) a contribution of money or assets (2) a certain duration (3) an element of risk and (4) a contribution to the economic development of the host state. More recently, panels have begun questioning the merits of that test, particularly the validity of the fourth prong. Invoking the *Salini* test, Uruguay argued in *Philip Morris Brands Sàrl v Oriental Republic of Uruguay*[10] that the investor's activities had 'harmed and continue to harm' its economic development rather than make a contribution to the economic development of the country and that the investment of Philip Morris was not an investment for the purposes of the ICSID Convention. Uruguay also argued that the measures adopted by the country to require Philip Morris to meet its new legislative requirement were measures necessary pursuant to its obligations under the WHO Framework Convention, in particular Article 11. However, the tribunal rejected the arguments of Uruguay and found that it had jurisdiction in the case.

---

[8] Ibid, 46–48.

[9] *Salini Construttori SpA v Kingdom of Morocco*, ICSID No ARB/00/4, decision on jurisdiction, 23 July 2001, para 52; 42 ILM 609 (2003).

[10] *Philip Morris Brands Sàrl v Oriental Republic of Uruguay*, ICSID No ARB/10/7, decision on jurisdiction, 2 July 2013.

Standard Claims by Foreign Investors

In most investment disputes before international courts and tribunals, the claimants, mostly investment companies, allege that the host state did not accord a minimum standard of treatment as required by international law or by a BIT or an FTA. Such a dispute can be related to either the principle of fair and equitable treatment or full protection and security. The allegation in the vast majority of cases seems to be violation or denial of fair and equitable treatment, including intentional or consequential discrimination. Most of the time they invoke both – ie the customary international law principle of international minimum standard and the protection specified in the BITs or FTAs concerned, or whichever accords greater protection in support of their claim. The most frequently made request in such cases is a request to determine a certain measure or measures or a combination of measures, commissions and sometimes even omissions as some form of expropriation, whether direct, indirect, creeping, regulatory or consequential, and ask for the award of compensation for such an expropriation.

Definition of Expropriation

What constitutes expropriation has long been one of the most vexed issues in international law. Indeed, the US Supreme Court in *Sabbatino* observed in 1964 that 'there are few if any issues in international law today on which opinion seems to be so divided as the limitations on a State's power to expropriate the property of aliens'.[11] It should be noted at the outset that almost all disputes referred to ICSID under BITs involve an allegation of host-state responsibility for some form of expropriation without compensation. This perhaps is one reason why there is a great deal of literature on defining what constitutes a 'taking of property', commonly known as expropriation or nationalisation.[12] The meaning of these terms has also preoccupied international courts and tribunals in a number of cases referred to them. Some of the more recent cases seek to cover not only direct, express or outright cases of compulsory taking of foreign property, but also indirect, 'constructive taking', 'creeping expropriation' or 'consequential expropriation' such as that considered by the ICJ in the *ELSI* case.[13]

In simple terms, 'expropriation' means the taking of the assets of foreign companies or investors by a host state against the wishes or without the consent of the company or investor concerned. It includes deprivation of the right to property owned by foreign companies. As noted by Asante, 'the standards prescribed by traditional

---

[11] *Banco Nacional de Cuba v Sabbatino* 376 US 398, 428 (1964), as cited in SM Schwebel, 'In Defense of Bilateral Investment Treaties' (2015) 31 *Arbitration International* 181, 183.

[12] O Schachter, 'Compensation for Expropriation' (1984) 78 *American Journal of International Law* 121.

[13] *Elettronica Sicula SpA (ELSI) (United States v Italy)*, ICJ Reports, 1989, 15, para 119.

international law with respect to alien property are predicated on the basic assumptions prevalent in a liberal regime of private property, in particular the inviolability of private property and sanctity of contract'.[14] Therefore, a compulsory taking of foreign property amounts to expropriation or nationalisation, and gives rise to compensation.

There are lawful expropriations and unlawful expropriations as well as direct expropriations and indirect expropriations. Lawful expropriations are those carried out against compensation and in accordance with international foreign investment law and the provisions of a BIT. Unlawful expropriations include those carried out without compensation or those in violation of international foreign investment law or the provisions of a BIT. In international law unlawful expropriations call for *restitutio in integrum*, or, if impossible, its financial equivalent, and for a lawful expropriation there is an obligation to pay compensation.

Direct expropriations are those that involve an outright or express taking of the assets of foreign companies or investors by a government decision or decree; however, with globalisation, economic interdependence and the increasing existence of a comprehensive body of law on foreign investment, outright or direct expropriations are becoming rare in today's world. Indirect or consequential expropriations are those governmental actions that undermine the interests of the foreign companies and investors. The range of such activities is too numerous to list here, but examples include: non-payment, non-reimbursement, cancellation, denial of judicial access, actual practice to exclude, constant harassment, non-conforming treatment, inconsistent legal blocks, imposition of discriminatory taxes, and other discriminatory treatment. Any one of these activities on its own may not be enough to constitute indirect or 'creeping' expropriation, but a combination of some of them may be regarded as constituting 'creeping' or indirect expropriation. Some of these activities could be lawful activities for a government, but it is the cumulative effect of these actions that may be considered as constituting 'creeping' expropriation.

In other words, an indirect expropriation is a governmental action, whether formal or informal, that impacts the normal operation of a foreign company in a negative manner. The effect of the measures taken by the government is more important than the intention. A government may make it impossible for a foreign investor to operate at a profit, thereby forcing it to abandon its business or close down its operations.[15] The degree of interference is taken into account when determining whether such activities constitute expropriation.[16] Reisman and Sloane have defined an indirect expropriation as 'an egregious failure to create or maintain the normative "favourable conditions" in the host state'.[17] Indirect expropriations have become commonplace across the globe, and the focus of attention in the literature is on this type of expropriation.

---

[14] Asante (n 2) 595.

[15] Eg, see *Restatement (Third) of Foreign Relations* (1989), s 712, nn 6, 7.

[16] An example of which is *Metalclad Corporation v The United Mexican States*, ICSID Case No ARB(AF)/97/ in which the Mexican municipality of Guadalcazar was found to have interfered with the reasonable expectations of the Metalclad company.

[17] WM Reisman and RD Sloane, 'Indirect Expropriation and its Valuation in the BIT Generation' (2003) 74 *British Year Book of International Law* 115, 119.

The Right to Expropriate

After receiving foreign investment a host state may change its mind and wish to reverse the situation. A state can reverse the situation by requiring that the foreign investor leave the country or by expropriating the assets of such an investor in a manner as prescribed by international law. Reversal may occur because of the exploitative nature of the business of the foreign investor; degradation of the local environment or violation of the rights of the host state or of its citizens by the investor; a political or economic rift between the home and host countries; a change of government or change in the priority in the host country; political revolution or regime change; or the election of a new government with policies, economic or otherwise, fundamentally different from those of the outgoing government. International tribunals have not challenged the rights of states to expropriate the assets of foreign companies. Rather, it is the question of compensation that has been expounded by such tribunals. International law does not entertain the idea that, once admitted, a foreign investor has a right to remain in the country concerned indefinitely. A sovereign state is always entitled to ask foreign investors to leave or to expropriate the assets of foreign companies by paying compensation in a manner prescribed by international law and according to BIT provisions.

A host state may negotiate the terms and conditions of the departure of foreign companies, renegotiate the contracts or concessions signed by the government with these companies, or take over their assets against the payment of a negotiated amount. However, when asking them to leave the country, the host state must ensure that its actions are not inconsistent with the protection that foreign investors are entitled to under international law, a BIT or international human rights law. International law also requires that as long as the foreign investors are in the country, the host state must treat them decently – fairly and equitably being the legal norm – and in accordance with the international minimum standard, the provisions of a BIT, and the protection enjoyed by natural and juridical persons under the international law of human rights.

International law imposes certain restrictions on the exercise of economic sovereignty by states. By the very act of inviting and admitting foreign investors into the country the state concerned voluntarily accepts limitations on its sovereignty and subjects itself to the rules of international foreign investment law. Accordingly, any taking of the assets of a foreign company in an illegal manner is confiscation.

Direct and Indirect Expropriation

The 1961 Draft Convention on State Responsibility set the tone for defining expropriation or the taking of foreign private property in the following words:

(a)   A 'taking of property' includes not only an outright taking of property but also any such unreasonable interference, use, enjoyment, or disposal of property as to justify an inference that the owner thereof will not be able to use, enjoy, or dispose of the property within a reasonable period of time after the inception of such interference.

(b)   A 'taking of the use of property' includes not only an outright taking of property but also any unreasonable interference with the use or enjoyment of property for a limited period of time.[18]

This provision itself seems to have been inspired by the writings of publicists and some foreign investment law-related decisions of the PCIJ and other international tribunals in the pre-UN period. For instance, the PCIJ in *Certain German Interests in Polish Upper Silesia*[19] in 1926 and an arbitration tribunal in *Norwegian Shipowners' Claims*[20] in 1922 outlined the nature of indirect expropriations. According to Christie, these cases established that:

> [A] State may expropriate property, where it interferes with it, even though the State expressly disclaims any such intention [and] that even though a State may not purport to interfere with rights to property, it may, by its actions, render those rights so useless that it will be deemed to have expropriated them.[21]

Many of the decisions of international tribunals, especially those of the Iran–US Claims Tribunal, have followed the definition of taking of property outlined in these two earlier cases. For instance, in *Starrett Housing Corporation v Iran (Interlocutory Order)* the Tribunal held that since Starrett, a US company, had been deprived of the effective use, control and benefits of their property rights by the Government of Iran in the aftermath of the Islamic revolution it amounted to 'creeping' or 'constructive' expropriation:

> [I]t is recognized in international law that measures taken by a State can interfere with property rights to such an extent that these rights are rendered so useless that they must be deemed to have been expropriated, even though the State does not purport to have expropriated them and the legal title to the property formally remains with the original owner.[22]

In *Tippetts v TAMS-AFFA* the Tribunal suggested that 'constructive expropriation' occurs when 'events demonstrate that the owner was deprived of fundamental rights of ownership and it appears that this deprivation is not merely ephemeral'.[23] When employing the term 'deprivation' to describe the acts and omissions of the Iranian government, the Tribunal held in this case that '[a] deprivation or taking of property may occur under international law through interference by a State in the use of that property or with the enjoyment of its benefits, even where legal title to the property is not affected'.[24]

---

[18] Art 10(3) of the Draft Convention on the International Responsibility of States for Injury to Aliens (1961) 55 *American Journal of International Law* 545.

[19] *Germany v Poland*, PCIJ Reports, 1926, Series A, No 7.

[20] *Norway v US* (1922) 1 RIAA, 307.

[21] GC Christie, 'What Constitutes a Taking under International Law' (1962) 38 *British Year Book of International Law* 310.

[22] (1984) 23 ILM 1090; 4 Iran–USCTR 122 (1983).

[23] *Tippetts v TAMS-AFFA*, 6 Iran–USCTR 219 (29 June 1984).

[24] Ibid.

In *Amoco International Finance Corporation v Iran* the issue involved was the nationalisation of the Iranian oil industry under the Single Article Act in the aftermath of the Islamic revolution during which *Khemco*, an Iranian company jointly owned and managed by Amoco, was also nationalised. In delivering its award, the Tribunal held that:

> Expropriation, which can be defined as a compulsory transfer of property rights, may extend to any right which can be the object of a commercial transaction, ie, freely sold and bought, and thus has a monetary value. It is because Amoco's interests under the Khemco Agreement have such an economic value that the nullification of those interests by the Single Article Act can be considered as a nationalization.[25]

The Tribunal also touched on the capacity of a state to nationalise or expropriate for a public purpose:

> A precise definition of the 'public purpose' for which an expropriation may be lawfully decided has neither been agreed upon in international law nor even suggested. It is clear that, as a result of the modern acceptance of the right to nationalize, this term is broadly interpreted, and that States, in practice, are granted extensive discretion.

Accordingly, the Tribunal held that Amoco's rights and interests under the Khemco Agreement, including its shares in Khemco, had been lawfully expropriated by Iran and then went on to examine the rules to be applied in determining the level of compensation to be paid in such a circumstance.

Relying on *Chorzow Factory*, the Tribunal in *Amoco* was drawing a distinction between the unlawful confiscation of foreign property, and lawful expropriation or nationalisation. In other words, to be lawful, an expropriation should be non-discriminatory and must be for a public purpose.[26] Thus, lawful taking of foreign property is expropriation which would attract compensation, but illegal expropriation or confiscation such as that which occurred in relation to *Chorzow Factory* would give rise to state responsibility and attract reparation or restitution. According to Bowett, the principles underlying the *Chorzow Factory* judgment and the *Amoco* award are as follows:

(i) A clear distinction must be made between lawful and unlawful expropriations.

(ii) For unlawful expropriations, international law requires *restitutio in integrum*, or, if impossible, its financial equivalent.

(iii) For a lawful expropriation the obligation is to pay 'fair compensation', or 'the just price of what was expropriated.'[27]

---

[25] 15 Iran–USCTR 189.

[26] However, in *Limaco* ((1981) 20(1) ILM 58–59) the sole arbitrator held that for nationalisation to be lawful there was no separate public purpose requirement in international law. Neither the 1803 PSNR resolution nor the 1974 CERD mention non-discrimination as a requirement. There are scholars who do not agree that to be lawful nationalisations should be non-discriminatory. See RS Miller, RJ Stanger and HW Baade (eds), *Essays on Expropriations* (Columbus, Ohio State University Press, 1967) 24. However, most BITs and MITs make both public purpose and non-discrimination necessary conditions for expropriation and nationalisation.

[27] DW Bowett, 'State Contracts with Aliens: Contemporary Developments on Compensation for Termination or Breach' (1988) 59 *British Year Book of International Law* 49, 67.

Accordingly, the Tribunal concluded that Amoco was deprived by the Iranian government of its contractual rights under the Khemco Agreement, and the compensation due was related to these rights. Khemco was considered to be a going concern at the time of expropriation, and the going concern value was the measure of compensation in this case:

> Going concern value encompasses not only the physical and financial assets of the undertaking, but also the intangible valuables which contribute to its earning power, such as contractual rights (supply and delivery contracts, patent licences and so on), as well as goodwill and commercial prospects.[28]

The *Amoco* case followed the principles declared in the *Chorzow Factory* case in recognising that illegal expropriation or confiscation would attract the rules of state responsibility. As stated by Bowett:

> The dictum of the Permanent Court in the *Chorzow Factory* case suggested that, as a consequence of the *illegality* of the act, restitution would be the primary remedy, and compensation would serve as a secondary remedy if restitution were not possible.[29]

In *Texaco v Libya*[30] the sole arbitrator found the nationalisation by Libya of the properties, rights, assets and interests of two US oil companies to be in violation of the contracts made by these companies with the Libyan government. The Tribunal held that:

> The recognition by international law of the right to nationalize is not sufficient ground to empower a State to disregard its commitments, because the same law also recognizes the power of a State to commit itself internationally, especially by accepting the inclusion of stabilization clauses in a contract entered into with a foreign private party. ... Thus, in respect of international law of contracts, a nationalization cannot prevail over an internationalized contract, containing stabilization clauses, entered into between a State and a foreign private company.

In the *Aminoil* case[31] the issue was the legality of a Kuwait Decree Law terminating the concession agreement with Aminoil, a US oil company, against compensation to be assessed by a Kuwait 'Compensation Committee'. The Tribunal held that Kuwait had satisfied the international law requirements for termination of the concession agreement: '[T]he "take-over" of Aminoil's enterprise was not, in 1977, inconsistent with the contract of concession, provided always that the nationalization did not possess any confiscatory character.'

Thus, running through the literature and the decisions of international courts and tribunals is the idea that 'expropriation must be analyzed in consequential rather than formal terms'. Reisman and Sloane have summarised this idea in the following statement:

> What matters is the effect of governmental conduct – whether malfeasance, misfeasance, or nonfeasance, or some combination of the three – on foreign property rights of control over

---

[28] *Amoco International Finance Corporation v Iran* (1987) 15 Iran–USCTR 189, para 264.
[29] Bowett (n 27) 59–60.
[30] *Texaco v Libya* (1977) 53 ILR 389.
[31] *Kuwait v American Independent Oil Co* (1982) 21 ILM 976.

an investment, not whether the State promulgates a formal decree of otherwise expressly proclaims its intent to expropriate.[32]

Whether it is direct or indirect expropriation, international law makes no distinction when it comes to paying compensation or making adequate reparation. In both situations compensation will have to be paid. Only the amount of compensation remains to be determined.

Determination of the Nature and Amount of Compensation[33]

When identifying the rules of international law on the nature and amount of compensation against expropriation, one cannot escape reference to the *Chorzow Factory* case, widely regarded as the seminal international decision about compensation under international law. The classic opinion of the PCIJ in this case provides the fundamental normative principles on which other subsequent international courts and tribunals have developed, expounded and formulated their own opinions. Deciding on the consequences of the illegal or confiscatory nature of expropriation in this case, the PCIJ held that:

> The essential principle contained in the actual notion of an illegal act – a principle which seems to be established by international practice and in particular by the decisions of arbitral tribunals – is that reparation must, as far as possible, wipe out all the consequences of an illegal act and re-establish the situation which would, in all probability, have existed if that act had not been committed. Restitution in kind, or if this is not possible, payment of a sum corresponding to the value which a restitution in kind would bear; the award, if need be, of damages for loss sustained which would not be covered by restitution in kind or payment in place of it – such are the principles which should serve to determine the amount of compensation for an act contrary to international law.[34]

The opinion of the PCIJ in this case has been regarded as an endorsement of the Hull formula – prompt, adequate and effective compensation. Although most of the recent BITs and RTAs also incorporate the Hull formula for compensation, and many subsequent decisions of international courts and tribunals have lent their support to this formula, there is no universal support in jurisprudence for this position, especially in the cases decided by tribunals other than the Iran–US Claims Tribunal.[35] Rather, there seems to be some support for 'appropriate' or 'just' compensation. In *Texaco*

---

[32] Reisman and Sloane (n 17) 121.

[33] See generally O Schachter, 'Compensation for Expropriation' (1984) 78 *American Journal of International Law* 121; MH Mendelson, 'Compensation for Expropriation' (1985) 79 *American Journal of International Law* 414.

[34] *Factory at Chorzow (Germany v Poland)*, PCIJ Reports (1928), Series A, No 13, 47.

[35] In the *American International Group Inc v Iran* case the Tribunal rejected the assertion by the claimant that in the absence of prompt, adequate and effective compensation the Iranian nationalisation was unlawful. The Tribunal did agree that the claimant was entitled to compensation but not as demanded. 4 Iran–USCTR 96 (1983).

v Libya,[36] *Topco/Calasiatic*[37] and *Aminoil*,[38] the tribunals supported the view of appropriate compensation. However, whether tribunals use 'just', 'appropriate' or 'prompt, adequate and effective' compensation, these vague concepts mean little in practical terms unless they are defined in concrete terms to demonstrate the differences among them. A generally accepted rule seems to be to award an amount based on the fair market value of the assets expropriated. In the *INA Corporation* case, the Iran–US Claims Tribunal defined fair market value as

> the amount which a willing buyer would have paid to a willing seller for the shares of a going concern, disregarding any diminution of value due to the nationalization itself or the anticipation thereof, and excluding consideration of events thereafter that might have increased or decreased the value of the shares.[39]

A survey of the awards made by various tribunals demonstrates that the factors to be taken into account in awarding compensation are: (1) assets, whether tangible or physical or 'book' assets such as debts or monies due; (2) interest on the value of the assets; and (3) loss of future profits. The practice seems to include both (1) and (2) in both lawful and unlawful 'taking' of foreign property, but the third factor seems to be included in determining compensation only in cases of the unlawful taking of foreign property. When determining the interest on the value of the assets, it seems to be an accepted practice to include interest over the period between the date of the taking of the property and the date of the award or its payment.

In stating what elements would have to be taken into account in determining the amount of compensation, the Tribunal in *Aminoil* held that 'the determination of the amount of an award of 'appropriate' compensation is better carried out by means of an enquiry into all circumstances relevant to the particular concrete case, than through abstract theoretical discussion'. Accordingly, the conclusion that the Tribunal reached is illustrative and of interest:

> [The Tribunal] considers it to be just and reasonable to take some measure of account of all the elements of an undertaking. This leads to a separate appraisal of the value, on the one hand of the undertaking itself, as a source of profit, and on the other of the totality of the assets, and adding together the results obtained.

The elements taken into account by the Tribunal in determining the amount of compensation and the manner in which the Tribunal arrived at a figure of compensation are as follows:

Amounts due to Aminoil—

1. These are made up of the values of the various components of the undertaking separately considered, and of the undertaking itself considered as an organic totality – or going concern – therefore as a unified whole, the value of which is greater than that of its component parts, and which must also take account of the legitimate expectations of the owners. These principles remain good even if the undertaking was due to revert,

---

[36] *Texaco v Libya* (1977) 53 ILR 389, para 87.
[37] *Topco/Calasiatic* (1978) 17 *ILM* 3.
[38] *Kuwait v American Independent Oil Co* (1982) 21 ILM 976, paras 143, 144.
[39] 8 Iran–USCTR, 380.

free of cost, to the concessionary Authority in another 30 years, the profits having been restricted to a reasonable level.

2. As regard the evaluation of the different concrete components that constitute the undertaking, the Joint Report furnishes acceptable indications concerning the assets other than fixed assets. But as regards the fixed assets, the 'net book value' used as a basis merely gives a formal accounting figure which, in the present *case*, cannot be considered adequate.

3. For the purposes of the present *case*, and for the fixed assets, it is a depreciated replacement value that seems appropriate. In consequence, taking that basis for the fixed assets, taking the order of value indicated in the Joint Report for the non-fixed assets, and taking into account the legitimate expectations of the concessionaire, the Tribunal comes to the conclusion [of a specified figure due to Aminoil in compensation].

Another case where nationalisation was held lawful is *Liamco*.[40] In this case the arbitrator rejected the argument that international law allowed the recovery of future profits in a lawful case of nationalisation. After analysing a number of cases of the Iran–US Claims Tribunal, Bowett rightly concluded that for unlawful taking, three propositions are possible:

(i) Loss of profits is relevant only up to the date of the award (*Chorzow, Amoco International Finance*).

(ii) 'Full value' may be awarded for an ad hoc or discrete taking – but this concept, to be consistent with (i), excludes loss of future profits beyond the date of the award so that 'going concern value' based on profits after that date conflicts with *Chorzow*.

(iii) A lower value – less than 'full' – may be awarded in the case of a formal, systematic, large-scale nationalization.[41]

Indeed, invoking the pronouncements made by the PCIJ in the *Chorzow Factory* case, the *Amoco* Tribunal stated that the components enumerated by the Court as included in the value of the undertaking were of paramount interest:

They appertain to three categories: corporeal properties (lands, buildings, equipment, stocks), contractual rights (supply and delivery contracts) and other intangible valuables (processes, goodwill and 'future prospects'). Using today's vocabulary, this would mean 'going concern value', which is not a new concept after all.

Amerasinghe summed up the conclusions of both the *Chorzow* and *Amoco* findings in the following words:

What is important is that for a lawful taking only *damnum emergens* is payable as compensation, ie, the value of the property, however, established *lucrum cessans* (lost future profits) and other consequential damage not being taken into account. For an unlawful taking it is damages and not merely compensation that are payable – this includes *damnum emergens* (value of the property), *lucrum cessans* (lost profits), and any other consequential damage that may be found and is directly connected with the taking of the property.[42]

---

[40] *Libyan American Oil Co (Liamco) v Libya* (1977) 62 ILR 139.

[41] Bowett (n 27) 69.

[42] Cf Amerasinghe, 'Assessment of Compensation for Expropriated Foreign Property: Three Critical Problems', in R St John Macdonald (ed), *Essays in Honour of Wang Tieya* (London, Martinus Nijhoff, 1994) 55–65, 59.

After surveying the various awards made by the Iran–US Claims Tribunal, Bowett came to the following conclusion:

> The position towards which the US/Iran Claims Tribunal now seems to be moving (and which *Aminoil* supports) is that there are, in fact, three 'standards' of compensation, ie, (i) for an unlawful taking, (ii) for a lawful *ad hoc* taking, and (iii) for a lawful, general act of nationalization. And the clear implication is that the third standard is the lowest, which would accord with State practice and the trend in the General Assembly resolutions to move towards a concept of 'appropriate' or 'just' compensation.

> Curiously, what is lacking in the jurisprudence is a clear explanation of the reasons for a difference in standards between (ii) and (iii), between the lawful *ad hoc* taking and the lawful general nationalization.[43]

Unfortunately, since Bowett made this observation in 1988, no arbitral award made by the Iran–US Claims Tribunal seems to offer a satisfactory explanation of the reasons for a difference in standards between the two.[44] What is more, the jurisprudence of the Iran–US Claims Tribunal should be treated with some caution since most of the early cases decided by the Tribunal tended to apply the provisions of the Treaty of Amity (a *lex specialis*) between the US and Iran, which had incorporated the Hull formula, rather than the rules of customary international law (a *lex generalis*). Iran unsuccessfully argued in several cases before the Tribunal that the law to be applied by the Tribunal consisted of emerging rules of customary international law as developed by the UN instruments, including the Charter of Economic Rights and Duties of States (CERD), supporting 'appropriate' compensation rather than the Hull formula. However, the Tribunal was reluctant to accept this line of argument and appeared intent on relying either on the traditional rules of customary international law based on the pronouncements made in the *Chorzow Factory* case or on the provisions of the Treaty of Amity supporting the Hull formula.

ICSID tribunals have in recent years made their own contributions to clarifying the standard of treatment and nature of compensation available to foreign investors. For instance, in *SD Myers Inc v Canada*[45] an ICSID tribunal sitting under the NAFTA drew, citing the *Chorzow Factory* pronouncements, a clear distinction between the standard of compensation for otherwise lawful expropriation and the measure of damages for unlawful expropriation resulting from discrimination or violation of treaty obligations. The Tribunal held that the amount of expropriation in cases of otherwise lawful expropriations may not include future earnings.

However, future earnings are taken into account in cases of unlawful expropriations or denial of national treatment. In this case the Tribunal held that denial of national treatment to foreign investors would be treated as a breach of NAFTA Article 1105(1) and would thus give rise to compensation. This is an interesting development within international law that is likely to make national treatment the focal point of attention in future disputes concerning expropriation and the standards of treatment of foreign investors.

---

[43] Bowett (n 27) 73.
[44] For an analysis of the awards made by the Iran–US Claims Tribunal up to about 1993, see Amerasinghe (n 42) 55–65.
[45] www.dfait-maeci.ge.ca/tna-nac/gov-en.asp; NAFTA Chapter 11 Arbitration Tribunal, 2000–02.

In awarding one of the highest amounts of compensation in recent times, an ICSID tribunal in *Enron v Argentina* held in its ruling of May 2007 that Enron was entitled to fair market value compensation for losses suffered as a result of emergency legal and regulatory measures taken by Argentina in the wake of the latter's financial crisis. The award of US$106 million in compensation was entered against Argentina for breaching treaty obligations to provide, inter alia, fair and equitable treatment.[46] What is interesting is that this amount of compensation was for breaches of other BIT obligations such as the duty to provide a fair and equitable treatment rather than against direct expropriation.

The Rights of Shareholders

In the *Barcelona Traction* case the ICJ was not prepared to provide a legal remedy to the shareholders independently of the company. Barcelona Traction was a company established under Canadian law, doing business in Spain. The majority of shareholders were, however, Belgian nationals, on whose behalf Belgium brought legal action before the ICJ against Spain alleging that its activities had injured the company. Spain objected that since the alleged injury was to the company, not the shareholders, Belgium lacked the locus standi to bring the claim. In its judgment delivered in 1970, the ICJ upheld the Spanish objection:

> Notwithstanding the separate corporate personality, a wrong done to the company frequently causes prejudice to its shareholders. But the mere fact that damage is sustained by both company and shareholders does not imply that both are entitled to claim compensation ... whenever a shareholder's interests are harmed by an act done to the company, it is to the latter that he must look to institute appropriate action; for although two separate entities may have suffered from the same wrong, it is only one entity whose rights have been infringed.[47]

However, in its judgment in the *ELSI* case delivered in 1989 the ICJ[48] was sympathetic to the argument that the injury suffered by the US shareholder, Raytheon, in ELSI, an Italian company, deserved compensation, although the Court was relying more heavily in this case on a provision contained within the FCN treaty between Italy and the United States. According to Article 25(2)(b) of the ICSID Convention, local companies in the host state subject to foreign control qualify as an investor with a right to ICSID arbitration. Although the traditional view has been that a local company can qualify as an 'investor' under a BIT if the company is 'effectively controlled', directly or indirectly, by nationals of the home state concerned, some recent decisions of ICSID tribunals have not placed a great emphasis on 'effective control'. The phrase 'effective control' or the terms 'control' or 'effective' were discussed in some detail in *Aguas del*

---

[46] *Enron v Argentina*, award of 22 May 2007 available online at www.investmentclaims.com/decisions.
[47] *Barcelona Traction, Light and Power Co (Belgium v Spain)*, ICJ Reports, 1970, 3, para 44.
[48] *Elettronica Sicula SpA (ELSI) (United States v Italy)*, ICJ Reports, 1989, 15.

Tunari v Bolivia. The ICSID tribunal faced in this case two opposing views as to the meaning of the phrase 'controlled directly or indirectly'. The disagreement was about the difference between 'control' as requiring the legal potential to control and 'control' as requiring the actual exercise of control. The tribunal went on to define the phrase 'controlled directly or indirectly' in accordance with the rules of treaty interpretation of the Vienna Convention on the Law of Treaties and concluded that 'the ordinary meaning of 'control' would seemingly encompass both actual exercise of powers or direction and the rights arising from the ownership of shares'.[49] Accordingly,

> The phrase, 'directly or indirectly,' in modifying the term 'controlled' creates the possibility of there simultaneously being a direct controller and one or more indirect controllers. The BIT does not limit the scope of eligible claimants to only the 'ultimate controller.'[50]

Even if foreign investors do not have controlling shares in a local company, they have been regarded as qualifying for protection under a BIT and thus entitled to bring a case before an ICSID tribunal if adversely affected by the measures taken by the host state. This is because their shares are regarded as 'investment' within the meaning of the term 'investment' in most BITs, and they are thus capable of bringing a case before an ICSID tribunal as foreign investors and independently of the status of the company. In both *CMS Gas Transmission Company v The Argentine Republic*[51] and *LG&E Energy Corporation v The Argentine Republic*[52] the ICSID tribunals held that the ICSID Convention does not make control a central tenet of ICSID jurisdiction. A similar conclusion was reached by an ICSID tribunal in *Gas Natural SDG v The Argentine Republic.* The tribunal justified its conclusions in the following words:

> Indeed, the standard mode of foreign direct investment, followed in the present case and in the vast majority of transnational transfers of private capital, is that a corporation is established pursuant to the laws of the host country and the shares of that corporation are purchased by the foreign investor, or alternatively, that the shares of an existing corporation established pursuant to the laws of the host country are acquired by the foreign investor. The scheme of both the ICSID Convention and the bilateral investment treaties is that in this circumstance, the foreign investor acquires rights under the Convention and Treaty, including in particular the standing to initiate international arbitration.

Accordingly, the tribunal held that a claim asserting the impairment of the value of the shares held by the claimant as a result of measures taken by Argentina gave rise to an investment dispute within the meaning of the relevant article of the Spain–Argentina BIT, and that the investor had standing to bring that claim before an international arbitral tribunal. International law has recognised the analogous right of minority and non-controlling shareholders to claim independently of a separate corporate entity for the measures that affect their investment.[53] In *Aguas del Tunari v Bolivia* an ICSID tribunal concluded by majority that:

---

[49] *Aguas del Tunari v Bolivia*, ICSID Case No ARB/02/3, decision on respondent's objections to jurisdiction of 21 October 2005, para 227.

[50] Ibid, para 237.

[51] *CMS Gas Transmission Company v The Argentine Republic*, ICSID Case No ARB/01/8, 17 July 2003.

[52] *LG&E Energy Corporation v The Argentine Republic*, ICSID Case No ARB/02/1, 30 April 2004, para 50.

[53] Eg, see *Enron Corporation and Ponderosa Assets, LP v Argentine Republic*, ICSID Case No ARB/01/3, decision on jurisdiction of 14 January 2004.

[T]he phrase 'controlled directly or indirectly' means that one entity may be said to control another entity (either directly, that is without an intermediary entity, or indirectly) if that entity possesses the legal capacity to control the other entity. Subject to evidence of particular restrictions on the exercise of voting rights, such legal capacity is to be ascertained with reference to the percentage of shares held. In the case of a minority shareholder, the legal capacity to control an entity may exist by reason of the percentage of shares held, legal rights conveyed in instruments or agreements such as the articles of incorporation or shareholders' agreements, or a combination of these.[54]

In *International Thunderbird Gaming Corporation v The United Mexican States* the UNCITRAL tribunal stated that:

The Tribunal does not follow Mexico's proposition that Article 1117 of the NAFTA requires a showing of legal control. The term 'control' is not defined in the NAFTA. Interpreted in accordance with its ordinary meaning, control can be exercised in various manners. Therefore, a showing of effective or '*de facto*' control is, in the Tribunal's view, sufficient for the purposes of Article 1117 of the NAFTA. In the absence of legal control however, the Tribunal is of the opinion that *de facto* control must be established beyond any reasonable doubt.[55]

Accordingly, despite Thunderbird having less than 50 per cent ownership of the minority Entertainmens de México, SA de CV (EDM) entities, the tribunal stated that it had found sufficient evidence on the record establishing an unquestionable pattern of de facto control exercised by Thunderbird over the EDM entities: 'Thunderbird had the ability to exercise a significant influence on the decision-making of EDM and was, through its actions, officers, resources, and expertise, the consistent driving force behind EDM's business endeavour in Mexico.'[56]

In its justification of its conclusion the tribunal stated as follows:

It is quite common in the international corporate world to control a business activity without owning the majority voting rights in shareholders' meetings. Control can also be achieved by the power to effectively decide and implement the key decisions of the business activity of an enterprise and, under certain circumstances, control can be achieved by the existence of one or more factors such as technology, access to supplies, access to markets, access to capital, know how, and authoritative reputation. Ownership and legal control may assure that the owner or legally controlling party has the ultimate right to determine key decisions. However, if in practice a person exercises that position with an expectation to receive an economic return for its efforts and eventually be held responsible for improper decisions, one can conceive the existence of a genuine link yielding the control of the enterprise to that person.[57]

In *Maffezini* the tribunal held that individual investors who have the nationality of one of the contracting states that made a capital investment in the other contracting state were entitled to claim the protection of the BIT. In *American Manufacturing v Zaire*

---

[54] *Aguas del Tunari v Bolivia*, ICSID Case No ARB/02/3, decision on respondent's objections to jurisdiction of 21 October 2005, para 227.

[55] *International Thunderbird Gaming Corporation v The United Mexican States* (award of the NAFTA tribunal under UNCITRAL of 26 January 2006), para 106 (footnote omitted).

[56] Ibid, para 107.

[57] Ibid, para 108.

the tribunal also rejected the argument of Zaire that the company did not have standing to bring a claim under the Zaire–US BIT because it was merely a shareholder in a Zairian company. The tribunal held that the company acted in its own name and in its capacity as an US enterprise that had invested in Zaire.[58] However, as stated in *Impregilo v Pakistan*, 'there is an established principle of international law that a shareholder of a company, or one member of a partnership or joint venture, may not claim for the entire loss suffered by the corporate entity or group'.[59]

A similar conclusion was reached in *American Manufacturing & Trading Inc v Democratic Republic of the Congo*. The ICSID tribunal in this case determined that a US claimant could not claim for the total damages caused to the Zairian company SINZA, in which it had a minority interest.[60]

Exhaustion of Local Remedies

Generally speaking, disputing parties are expected to exhaust local remedies prior to resorting to international means of resolving disputes, especially in disputes between a state and a private entity, unless a BIT or other treaty provides otherwise. This is the essence of the Calvo doctrine and the principle of state sovereignty. Article 26 of the ICSID Convention provides expressly that a state may require the exhaustion of local remedies as a condition of consent to international arbitration under the Convention. However, in most of the cases considered by international claims commissions and other international tribunals, whether ad hoc or permanent, the issue of the exhaustion of local remedies has not become a major issue; this is because these dispute settlement mechanisms entertain cases by virtue either of a diplomatic agreement to refer the dispute to them or of a bilateral agreement, investment treaty or contract between the litigating parties providing for the settlement of disputes by such bodies. In the absence of such specific agreements or specific provisions in bilateral agreements, a litigating party is supposed to exhaust local remedies available in the state in question before taking the matter to international courts and tribunals. The issue of exhaustion of local remedies arose before the ICJ in two cases: *Interhandel*[61] and *ELSI*.[62] While the rule on the exhaustion of local remedies was invoked successfully by the US in the former case, Italy was unsuccessful in its defence in the latter. In the *ELSI* case, the ICJ held that:

> It is never easy to decide, in a case where there has in effect been much resort to the municipal courts, whether local remedies have been truly 'exhausted'. But in this case Italy has not been able to satisfy the Chamber that there clearly remained some remedy which Raytheon ...

---

[58] ICSID Case No ARB/93/1, award of 21 February 1997.
[59] *Impregilo v Pakistan*, ICSID Case No ARB/03/03, 22 April 2005, para 154 (decision on jurisdiction).
[60] *American Manufacturing & Trading, Inc v Democratic Republic of the Congo*, ICSID Case No ARB/93/1, 21 February 1997; 5 ICSID Reports (2002) 14–36.
[61] *Interhandel Case (Switzerland v United States)* (Preliminary Objections), ICJ Reports, 1959, 6, 26–30.
[62] *Elettronica Sicula SpA (ELSI) (United States v Italy)*, ICJ Reports, 1989, 15.

independently of ELSI, and of ELSI's trustee in bankruptcy, ought to have pursued and exhausted. Accordingly, the Chamber will now proceed to consider the merits of the case.[63]

In *Ambatielos*,[64] a case between Greece and the UK, the arbitration tribunal rejected the Greek claim against the UK made on behalf of Mr Ambatielos, a Greek national, on the ground of non-exhaustion of local remedies.

However, what is interesting is that the issue of exhaustion of local remedies has been an important issue in some of the more recent ICSID cases. Even when a BIT has required foreign investors to resort to a national court prior to resorting to an international court or tribunal specified by the BIT, foreign investors have been able to resort directly to ICSID or other international dispute settlement mechanisms on the basis of the MFN principle in the BIT if the host state has concluded another BIT not requiring foreign investors to resort to a national court prior to resorting to an international mechanism. This was the outcome, for instance, in *Gas Natural SDG v The Argentine Republic*.[65] Similarly, various ICSID tribunals have held that even if there was recourse to local courts for breach of contract, this would not prevent parties resorting to ICSID arbitration for violation of BIT rights. The decision in *Enron v Argentina* is an example.[66]

Extension of the Frontiers of the Law of Foreign Investment

Moving from the requirement under traditional international law of according 'fair and equitable treatment'[67] to foreign investors, the FCN treaties concluded by the US with some developing states after the Second World War required 'full protection and security' of foreign investment mainly due to various waves of outright and creeping expropriations of the assets of Western companies in the developing world. The introduction of the concept of 'full protection and security' in certain FCN treaties became a norm in most BITs. The NAFTA and some BITs add the qualifying words 'as required by international law' after the words 'full protection and security'; some do not. Where there is no reference to international law, the level of protection and security would be the same as that included in BITs or RTAs, which often provide a higher level of protection and security. The notions of 'indirect' expropriation and 'measures tantamount to expropriation' were introduced through the US Model BIT

---

[63] See both paras 59 and 63 of the ICJ judgment in the *ELSI* case, ibid.

[64] *Ambatielos* case *(Greece v UK)* (1956) 23 ILR 306.

[65] *Gas Natural SDG v the Argentine Republic*, ICSID Case No ARB/03/10, 17 June 2005 (preliminary questions on jurisdiction), 19–20.

[66] *Enron Corporation and Ponderosa Assets v Argentine Republic*, ICSID Case No ARB/01/3, 14 January 2004 (jurisdiction), para 97.

[67] For a detailed examination of the principle of 'fair and equitable treatment', see S Vasciannie, 'The Fair and Equitable Treatment Standard in International Investment Law and Practice' (1999) 70 *British Year Book of International Law* 99.

in the early 1980s and were later incorporated into the 1986 US–Canada FTA. They then found their way into NAFTA.

Where the words providing for 'full protection and security' and according 'fair and equitable treatment' are added, they are meant to imply that foreign investors are entitled to protection over and above their entitlement to non-discriminatory treatment under international law. These are the phrases that various ICSID tribunals have employed rather generously in favour of foreign investors in many investment cases. For instance, in *Metalclad Corporation v United Mexican States* ICSID held that the decision by a local government authority to withhold planning permission to construct a facility by Metalclad for the disposal of hazardous waste in accordance with the agreement between the company and the Mexican government was regarded as treatment that did not meet the standard of fair and just treatment under NAFTA.[68] The award made by the ICSID tribunal adjudicating under NAFTA showed a leaning away from a traditional definition of the term 'expropriation' based on the idea of 'taking foreign property' to a wider term:

> Expropriation under NAFTA includes not only open, deliberate and acknowledged takings of property, such as outright seizure or formal or obligatory transfer of title in favour of the host State, but also covert or incidental interference with the use of property which has the effect of depriving the owner, in whole or in significant part, of the use or reasonably-to-be-expected economic benefit of property even if not necessarily to the obvious benefit of the host State.[69]

These types of awards (another being the award made in the *Maffezini* case)[70] sought to push the frontiers of expropriation beyond not only the traditional definition of 'taking property', but also the so-called 'creeping expropriation' or 'constructive expropriation' or 'deprivation' advanced by the Iran–US Claims Tribunal. These types of awards have the potential to give rise to challenges to any governmental regulatory measures, whether these are related to human rights or environmental protection, by foreign investors if such measures go against their interests, notwithstanding that international foreign investment law recognises the rights of states to take regulatory measures relating to the environment and essential developmental work.

The implication of the recent trend in jurisprudence could be that the host state should do nothing that undermines the profitability of foreign business or undermines the 'favourable conditions' in the host states assured under the BITs. These are tendencies that are likely to undermine the sovereign powers of states to regulate their economy or to exploit their natural resources in accordance with their national development policies; and they may clash with other obligations of states under various international environmental or human rights treaties which require states to have more stringent regulatory regimes in favour of environmental or human rights protection. Indeed, after examining the consequences of the *Metalclad* case for host states, Lowe rightly concludes that the award by ICSID in this case could

---

[68] *Metalclad Corporation v United Mexican States* ICSID Case No ARB (AF)/97/1, 30 August 2000; (2001) 16 *ICSID Review: Foreign Investment Law Journal* 165.

[69] *Metalclad*, ibid, para 103.

[70] *Emilio Augustin Maffezini v Kingdom of Spain*, ICSID Case No ARB/97/7; (2003) 124 ILR.

encompass an enormous range of regulatory measures adopted by a State. If such measures do indeed amount to expropriation, it follows as a necessary consequence that, unless the State fully and promptly compensates affected businesses, it has no right to take such measures. That is a very significant limitation upon the right of the State.[71]

By citing another award made by ICSID not long before the *Metalclad* award, namely the award made in the *Santa Elena* case[72] where ICSID had taken a more traditional approach, Lowe goes on to state that:

> The gap, and the consequent uncertainty concerning the extent of States' obligations towards investors, is a cause of real concern. Is there, one may ask, a clear and principled approach to the determination of the limits of a State's responsibilities?[73]

The Trend in Creative Interpretation of the Law

In addition to *Metalclad* and *Maffezini*, various other awards by ICSID also demonstrate creative interpretation of foreign investment law. For instance, in *Pope & Talbot*[74] ICSID held that 'investors under NAFTA are entitled to the international law minimum, *plus* the fairness elements',[75] implying that NAFTA provided greater protection than international law. However, this interpretation was criticised by a Canadian court for being an incorrect interpretation of Article 1105 of NAFTA which requires 'treatment in accordance with international law, including fair and equitable treatment and protection and security', implying that the 'fairness elements' were part and parcel of international law.[76] Perhaps realising that the ICSID tribunals were taking things a bit too far, a declaration issued by the three states party to NAFTA, ie Canada, Mexico and the United States, endorsed the position taken by the Canadian court in the following terms:

> The concepts of 'fair and equitable treatment' and 'full protection and security' do not require treatment in addition to or beyond that which is required by the customary international law minimum standard of treatment of aliens.[77]

---

[71] V Lowe, 'Regulation or Expropriation', 6. The text of a lecture delivered by Professor Lowe at University College London in 2003, which he was so kind as to supply to the present author.

[72] *Compania Del Desarrollo de Santa Elena SA v Republic of Costa Rica* (2000); (2001) 39 ILM 1317, para 77. It reads as follows: 'There is ample authority for the proposition that a property has been expropriated when the effect of the measures taken by the State has been to deprive the owner of title, possession or access to the benefit and economic use of his property.'

[73] Lowe (n 71) 7.

[74] *Pope & Talbot Inc v Government of Canada* (2002) 122 ILR 293.

[75] Ibid, para 110. When making this pronouncement the Tribunal was relying on not only Art 1105 of NAFTA but also regarding the BITs concluded by the US and other industrialised states as a principal source of the obligations of states with respect to their treatment of foreign investment.

[76] *United Mexican States v Metalclad Corporation*, Judicial Review, Supreme Court of British Columbia (Tysoe J) (2 May 2001). See ICSID Reports (2002) 5. In this case Mexico challenged the arbitration award issued by the ICSID Tribunal of 30 August 2000 and the Canadian Court annulled in part the award of the ICSID Tribunal and revised the payment payable thereunder.

[77] Joint Statement on NAFTA Free Trade Commission, 31 July 2001, reproduced in J Jackson et al, *Legal Problems of International Economic Relations: Cases, Materials and Text*, 4th edn (St Paul, MN, West Group, 2002) 1166.

Even then it is doubtful whether the leaders of these three countries were correct in their interpretation of customary international law minimum standards.

What should be noted here is that the NAFTA provision itself goes slightly beyond what is covered by the 'international minimum standard' prescribed by classical rules of customary international law. NAFTA is not necessarily a good example of *lex generalis* on the standards of treatment of foreign investment, but an example, like other BITs, of *lex specialis* agreed among the contracting parties. Although Appleton has asserted on the basis of the pronouncements made in cases such as *Metalclad* and *Pope & Talbot* that 'a substantial part of the controversy' over the meaning of expropriation in international law 'has been settled',[78] it is difficult to agree with such an assertion. The awards made by the ICSID tribunals either under the BITs or NAFTA should be treated with some caution as far as their implications for international investment law are concerned. The message running through the awards made by the ICSID tribunals is the curtailment of the regulatory rights of sovereign states in favour of foreign investors. Lowe has summed up the situation as follows:

> The tenor of the cases [ie the ICSID cases] suggests that it is now regarded as 'unfair' or 'inequitable' for a State to make material changes in the business environment that prevailed when the investor committed itself to its investment. The impact of the 'fair and equitable treatment' obligation on the freedom of a government to regulate its economy is potentially very considerable indeed.

> These, and other, applications of the fair and equitable standard, point towards an exceptionally wide interpretation of that standard, greatly favouring investors. The same trend is evident in respect of the obligation to accord full protection and security to investments. That phrase, common in British and American BITS, but not generally found in French, German, Italian or Swiss BITS, plainly requires States to protect investments against physical destruction. It plainly requires States to maintain a legal system in which investors can obtain remedies against breaches of contract and unfair commercial practices visited upon them by third parties. All of that is implicit in the minimum international standard. It seems, however, to be coming to be applied so as to require States to intervene, and to act positively to protect investors against such practices and transactions.[79]

Indeed, the trend seen in cases such as *Metalclad* and *Maffezini*[80] goes somewhat beyond the level of protection accorded to foreign investors under customary international law. Decisions of such nature run the risk of undermining the legal weight to be accorded to ICSID jurisprudence in determining the law applicable to foreign investment. Accordingly, it becomes necessary to return to the provisions of international instruments and the pronouncements of international courts and tribunals that apply *lex generalis* rather than *lex specialis* in deciding cases submitted to them, in order to establish the status of the rules of foreign investment. Just because foreign investment law is not codified in any internationally agreed instrument, this should not mean that international tribunals are empowered to 'stretch' the law beyond a reasonable limit. Their role should be confined to interpreting and declaring the law rather than making

---

[78] B Appleton, 'Investment Disputes and NAFTA Chapter 11' [2001] *ASIL Proceedings* 198.
[79] Lowe (n 71) 21.
[80] *Emilio Augustin Maffezini v Kingdom of Spain*, ICSID Case No ARB/97/7; (2003) 124 ILR.

or rewriting it. If the trend seen in *Metalclad* and *Maffezini* were to continue, many states would not be able to adopt regulatory measures without paying compensation if such measures impaired the business of a foreign investor, even if these measures are indeed designed to protect certain human rights (eg workers' rights) or to fulfil states' environmental obligations under various regional and international treaties.

The expansive trend in the interpretation of indirect expropriation moved to a new level when an ICSID tribunal determined in *Saipem v Bangladesh*[81] that certain orders of a Bangladeshi court amounted to expropriation because they effectively removed the fruits of an arbitration award made in favour of the investor.[82] A similar pronouncement was made by a tribunal in *White Industries v India*.[83] In this case, an Australian company had brought an investment treaty claim against India on the grounds that it was unable to enforce an award made by the International Chamber of Commerce about a decade earlier. The view of the tribunal was that India was liable for failing to provide an effective means of enforcing the ICC award.[84] Likewise, in some recent cases, such as *El Paso*, international investment tribunals have gone a step further in according protection to foreign investors under the principle of fair and equitable treatment. In 2011 in *El Paso v Argentina*[85] an investment tribunal introduced the concept of 'creeping' analysis in the application of the fair and equitable treatment standard, an analysis similar to the analysis applied to determine a 'creeping' expropriation.

Controversy Raised by Inconsistency

One of the major concerns about the current investor-state dispute settlement (ISDS) mechanism is the inconsistency in its jurisprudence produced not only by various investment tribunals, but also by ICSID annulment panels. Several highly publicised decisions have demonstrated the lack of consistency in international investment arbitration; in cases where the facts are the same or very similar, different investment tribunals have managed to reach diametrically opposing decisions. Some of the most famous examples of such inconsistent decisions include *CME* and *Lauder*[86] and the *SGS* cases (*SGS Société Générale de Surveillance SA v Islamic Republic of Pakistan*[87] and *SGS Société Générale de Surveillance SA v Republic of the Philippines*).[88] Having

---

[81] *Saipem SpA v The Republic of Bangladesh*, ICSID Case No ARB/05/7, award of 30 June 2009.

[82] See S Menon, 'The Transnational Protection of Private Rights: Issues, Challenges, and Possible Solutions' (2015) 5 *Asian Journal of International Law* 219, 231.

[83] *White Industries Australia Limited v The Republic of India*, final award, 30 November 2011.

[84] Menon (n 82) 232.

[85] *El Paso v Argentina*, ICSID Case No ARB/03/15, award of 31 October 2011.

[86] *CME Czech Republic BV v Czech Republic*, Ad Hoc UNCITRAL Arbitration Rules, partial award of 13 September 2001 and IIC 62 (2003), final award of 14 March 2003 and *Lauder v Czech Republic*, Ad Hoc UNCITRAL Arbitration Rules, final award, 3 September 2001.

[87] *SGS Société Générale de Surveillance SA v Islamic Republic of Pakistan* ICSID Case No ARB/01/13; (2003) 42 ILM 1290.

[88] *SGS Société Générale de Surveillance SA v Republic of the Philippines* ICSID Case No ARB/02/6 (2004).

inconsistency in the approach of two different tribunals in similar or even the same facts is not necessarily new in the practice of courts in various jurisdictions. However, the difference between these jurisdictions and investor–state arbitration is that, in the case of the latter, there is no supreme court or appellate mechanism to harmonise jurisprudence, achieve consistency, and rationalise or reconcile the judicial approach. As stated by Schreuer, even the ad hoc annulment committees of ICSID 'have interpreted the grounds for annulment expansively or extensively'.[89]

Although the views taken by other NAFTA panels in cases before (*Pope & Talbot*) and after (*SD Myers Inc v Canada*) *Metalclad* were slightly different and much narrower in interpreting the terms 'expropriation' and 'measures tantamount to expropriation', and the panel in *Metalclad* itself was measured in its interpretation of the impact of non-discriminatory regulation on foreign investors, there is a great deal of inconsistency in the jurisprudence of the BIT and NAFTA tribunals. Referring to the regulatory measures of the Canadian government and interpreting the provisions of Article 1110 of the NAFTA Treaty, the panel in *Pope & Talbot* held that it did 'not believe that those regulatory measures constitute an interference with the Investment's business activities substantial enough to be characterized as expropriation under international law'.[90] The panel held that it did not regard the phrase 'measure tantamount to nationalization or expropriation' in Article 1110 to broaden the ordinary concept of expropriation under international law so as to require compensation.

Unlike the generous views taken in the *Metalclad* case, the panel held in this case that the export control regime of Canada did not cause an expropriation of the investor's investment, creeping or otherwise. The panel went on to state:

> While it may sometimes be uncertain whether a particular interference with business activities amounts to an expropriation, the test is whether that interference is sufficiently restrictive to support a conclusion that the property has been 'taken' from the owner.

Thus, the panel in this case was not willing to accord to the NAFTA provision a wider meaning than that provided for in customary international law. A similar view was taken in *SD Myers v Canada*.[91] The panel in this case took a clear position on the distinction between expropriation and regulatory measures:

> Expropriations tend to involve the deprivation of ownership rights; regulations a lesser interference. The distinction between expropriation and regulation screens out most potential cases of complaints concerning economic intervention by a state and reduces the risk that governments will be subject to claims as they go about their business of managing public affairs.

In *Feldman v Mexico*[92] an ICSID panel did not find that the application of certain tax laws by Mexico against the claimant was tantamount to expropriation. What the tribunal outlined in explaining the nature of consequential expropriations is noteworthy:

> The ways in which governmental authorities may force a company out of business, or significantly reduce the economic benefits of its business, are many. In the past, confiscatory

---

[89] C Schreuer, 'Remarks' [2011] *ASIL Proceedings* 196.
[90] As cited in A Lowenfeld, *International Economic Law* (Oxford, Oxford University Press, 2003) 477–78.
[91] Ibid, 479.
[92] *Feldman v Mexico* (2003) 42 *ILM* 625, 669.

taxation, denial of access to infrastructure or necessary raw materials, imposition of unreasonable regulatory regimes, among others, have been considered to be expropriatory actions. At the same time, governments must be free to act in broader public interest through protection of the environment, new or modified tax regimes, the granting or withdrawal of government subsidies, reductions or increases in tariff levels, imposition of zoning restrictions and the like. Reasonable governmental regulation of this type cannot be achieved if any business that is adversely affected may seek compensation, and it is safe to say that customary international law recognizes this.

The tribunal did, nevertheless, find that Mexico had acted inconsistently with its other obligations under NAFTA. Owing to the excess of protection provided to foreign investors in awards such as those in the *Metalclad* case, the NAFTA Free Trade Commission issued some 'clarifications' relating to certain provisions of NAFTA, mainly the nature and scope of Article 1105. The Commission defined the minimum standard of treatment in accordance with international law available to foreign investors under the NAFTA provisions in the following words:

Minimum Standard of Treatment in Accordance with International Law

1. Article 1105 (1) prescribes the customary international law minimum standard of treatment of aliens as the minimum standard of treatment to be afforded to investments of investors of another Party.
2. The concepts of 'fair and equitable treatment' and 'full protection and security' do not require treatment in addition to or beyond that which is required by the customary international law minimum standard of treatment of aliens.
3. A determination that there has been a breach of another provision of NAFTA, or of a separate international agreement, does not establish that there has been a breach of Article 1105 (1).[93]

Similarly, in *Occidental Exploration and Production Company v The Republic of Ecuador* Occidental, a US company, invoked the BIT between Ecuador and the United States over a matter involving non-reimbursement of VAT to the company by the government of Ecuador in a case decided by the London Court of Arbitration under an UNCITRAL arbitration.[94] The company alleged that by not reimbursing the VAT, Ecuador failed, inter alia, to accord its investment fair and equitable treatment and treatment no less favourable than that required by international law and expropriated, directly or indirectly, all or part of its investment in violation of the internationally accepted norms of the treatment of foreign investment. Using the narrower criterion of 'substantial deprivation' under international law identified in *Pope & Talbot*, the Tribunal dismissed Occidental's claim of expropriation.

Nevertheless, some other ICSID cases dealing with the issue of 'full protection and security' provided to foreign investors under BITs from the host state have raised controversy as to the meaning and scope of this phrase. In some cases the ICSID panels have gone on to interpret this phrase rather generously; under it governments would in effect be expected to deploy the police and the army for the protection of

---

[93] As quoted in Jackson et al (n 77) 1166.
[94] London Court of Arbitration, Final Award in the Matter of an UNCITRAL Arbitration, *Occidental Exploration and Production Company v The Republic of Ecuador*, Case No UN 3467 (1 July 2004).

foreign investors free of charge in the event of civil strife and armed insurgency within the country. As stated by Lowenfeld, 'BITs seem to require the government of the host State not only not to attack the facilities or personnel of the investor, but to defend the investor or investment against others, including, for instance, rebel forces.'[95]

Indeed, in *Asian Agricultural Products Ltd v Republic of Sri Lanka* an ICSID tribunal established Sri Lanka's state responsibility for failing to take the appropriate precautionary measures to protect the interests of Asian Agricultural Products, a British company that had its business in an area where fighting was taking place between the government and rebel forces.[96]

A more pronounced inconsistency in jurisprudence was in the *Lauder* arbitrations in which two investment tribunals came to completely contradictory conclusions concerning the important issues of expropriation and fair and equitable treatment in spite of the circumstances, parties and legal norms being almost identical.[97] However, commenting on this much publicised example of inconsistency in jurisprudence, Judge Schwebel has stated that the two decisions 'did not interpret the two concordant BITs conflictually. They rather interpreted the facts differently. Their difference was not of treaty interpretation but of factual causality.'[98]

The Trend Towards Extensive Protection

A variety of state activities have been declared by various international courts and tribunals to be measures tantamount to expropriation or creeping or indirect forms of expropriation. Sampliner has produced the following list of such activities based on the decisions of various courts and tribunals:

— Prohibition of sale or disposition of property, through measures that were reasonably believed to be permanent or of indefinite duration;
— Forced sale of property to others at grossly substandard prices, following physical harassment or threats to employees or management, government-organized boycotts, or arbitrary refusals to permit investors to operate;
— Imposition of taxation that is confiscatory in magnitude;
— Creeping expropriations (relatively minor individual actions, possibly legitimate when considered individually, that cumulatively result in a taking), eg:

    (a) harassing employees, blocking their access to a plant, taking over a key supplier and then refusing to supply the company;
    (b) government announcement of its ultimate intent to nationalize the bauxite industry, followed by a new severe bauxite tax, revision of a Mining Act to require minimum

---

[95] Lowenfeld (n 90) 476.
[96] *Asian Agricultural Products Ltd v Republic of Sri Lanka* (1991) 30 ILM 577, paras 85–86.
[97] *Lauder v Czech Republic*, Ad Hoc UNCITRAL Arbitration Rules, Final Award, 3 September 2001, 5–7. For academic commentary of inconsistencies, see, for example, S Franck, 'The Legitimacy Crisis in Investment Treaty Arbitration: Privatizing Public International Law through Inconsistent Decisions' (2005) 73 *Fordham Law Review* 1521.
[98] Schwebel (n 11) 190.

        production quotas and higher royalties, and repudiation of other contract provisions (where the contract included a stabilization clause);

(c)   imposing a 45–50% tax on rental income from property, followed by a requirement of 30% withholding for a building repair account, and controls on identity of tenants.

—   Forced appointment of a Manager, Supervisor or Receiver who deprives a company of various fundamental rights or benefits of ownership, such as collecting and remitting the proceeds of sales;

—   Deprivation of contractual rights to produce future goods and/or services;

—   Government creation of a monopoly for itself or another preferred supplier, thereby putting an established company out of business;

—   The granting of 'cultivation licenses' to Panamanian peasants for portions of a claimant's land.[99]

Given recent trends, it is conceivable that in due course foreign investors will demand full protection against terrorist activities at the expense of the host state, and in the event of terrorist attacks claim compensation against host states for failing to prevent such attacks. It is possible that the doctrine of state responsibility will be stretched to argue that the host state concerned failed in its obligation to provide '*full* protection and security' to the foreign investor. Although there have been quite a few expropriation cases in which regulatory measures of states have not been regarded as measures constituting expropriation, the tendency in some of the cases examined earlier has been to regard many regulatory measures as constituting 'creeping' expropriation. The three-part test prescribed by the US Supreme Court in the landmark case of *Penn Central Transportation Co v New York City*[100] is illustrative. In order to establish whether a regulatory measure was tantamount to expropriation, that measure had to be examined against the following three tests: (i) the economic impact of the regulation on the claimant; (ii) the extent of interference with the property owner's reasonable investment-backed expectations; and (iii) the character of the government action.[101] Although this domestic law case has not been cited openly as a source of authority by international courts and tribunals, this three-part test seems in the legal literature to have had a measure of influence. Article 114(2) of NAFTA preserves the 'police powers' of states in the following words:

> Nothing in this Chapter shall be construed to prevent a Party from adopting, maintaining or enforcing any measure otherwise consistent with this Chapter that it considers appropriate to ensure that investment activity in its territory in undertaken in a manner sensitive to environmental concerns.

It seems to be agreed that only if the regulatory measure in question interferes with the investor's legitimate and reasonable expectations in making the investment does it constitute expropriation. Regulations that impose general limitations on the activities

[99] GH Sampliner, 'Arbitration of Expropriation Cases under US Investment Treaties – A Threat to Democracy or the Dog That Didn't Bark?' (2003) 18 *ICSID Review: Foreign Investment Law Journal* 1, 8–9 (footnotes omitted).

[100] *Penn Central Transportation Co v New York City* 438 US 104, 124 (1978), as cited in Sampliner, ibid, 11.

[101] Sampliner (n 99).

of the investors to protect the general interest of the public would not be regarded as expropriation. In addition, the regulatory measures in question have to be subjected to other tests, including proportionality.

From International Minimum to Maximum Standard of Treatment[102]

As seen in the preceding paragraphs, many of the provisions of BITs and certain regional agreements such as NAFTA have gone beyond what customary international law provides in terms of protection of foreign investment; however, it is doubtful whether the BIT or NAFTA provisions are capable of modifying the rules of customary international law. Traditionally, the doctrine that underpins foreign investment law is, of course, the concept of the international minimum standard of treatment based on the rule of law in general and the traditional doctrine of state responsibility in particular. It is well established in international law that an internationally wrongful act of a state entails the responsibility of that state.[103] However, it is less straightforward to establish whether a given act of a state is an internationally wrongful act.

Before the BITs and other regional economic agreements such as NAFTA or other FTAs were concluded it was less easy to establish whether a particular act of a state against a foreign investor was an internationally wrongful act. But when there is a BIT or another agreement outlining a plethora of protections, privileges and concessions available to foreign investors, any infringement of such protections, concessions or privileges, however excessive they may be, could constitute an internationally wrongful act giving rise to state responsibility. Thus, the doctrine of state responsibility that was used to argue for an international minimum standard during the early years of foreign investment law is now being used to argue and defend the maximum international standard of treatment for foreign investors provided for in either the BITs or in other international treaties such as NAFTA or WTO agreements.

The attempts by certain ICSID tribunals to exploit this nexus between the provisions of BITs and the doctrine of state responsibility in order to provide the maximum protection possible – over and above what is accorded under customary international law to foreign investors – are seeking gradually to transform the rules from being *lex specialis* in character to *lex generalis*, thereby changing foreign investment law in accordance with the factual realities of the changing world. For instance, although it is submitted that the primary obligation under the NAFTA provisions on foreign investment is to accord treatment to foreign investors in accordance with international law in general and the minimum standard of treatment in particular, the attempts on the part of some ICSID tribunals and the Iran–US Claims Tribunal have been to expand

---

[102] See generally, V Bean, 'Does an International "Regulatory Takings" Doctrine Make Sense?' (2002) 11 *New York University Environmental Law Journal* 49.

[103] See for the Draft Articles of the ILC on State Responsibility UN Doc A/CN.4/L.602/Rev.1, 26 July 2001.

the meaning of the 'minimum standard', of which the ruling given in *Metalclad* is a classic example. However, there have been other cases in which the ICSID tribunals have taken a more balanced or traditional approach to expropriation. For instance, in *SGS v Philippines*[104] the tribunal did not regard non-payment of invoices by the Philippines as constituting expropriation. Nevertheless, in advancing the analysis made by the tribunal in this case, another ICSID tribunal in *Feldman v Mexico* found that the application of certain tax laws by Mexico to the export of tobacco products by a company owned and controlled by a US citizen amounted to a violation of NAFTA Article 1102 and awarded compensation to the company.[105]

Similarly, in *Enron v Argentina*[106] the tribunal upheld jurisdiction over Enron's claim that certain tax assessments imposed by some Argentine provinces were tantamount to expropriation and thus in violation of the Argentina–US BIT, relying on the principles of fairness and equity of the treaty. In *Azurix v Argentina* the claimant argued that by failing, inter alia, to provide transparency concerning the regulations, administrative practices and procedures, etc, that affected Azurix's investment, Argentina had breached the Argentina–US BIT. The claimant invoked the principles of fair and equitable treatment and full protection and security to argue that Argentina had failed to comply with the standards of treatment required by international law. Argentina then challenged the claim that the claimant's investment was covered by the BIT, arguing that the dispute was a contractual one related to the concession agreement. Nevertheless, the ICSID tribunal found that Azurix's investment made through its local subsidiary was covered by the BIT between the two countries.[107] There have been other bold awards made by ICSID tribunals. For instance, in *Salini v Morocco*[108] the tribunal regarded a construction contract as an investment within the meaning of the ICSID Convention and the applicable BIT. In *SGS v Pakistan* the tribunal decided to move forward with the proceedings despite a Pakistani Supreme Court decision restraining SGS from pursuing or participating in the ICSID arbitration while a Pakistani arbitrator was considering the case.[109]

Another matter for debate within international investment law is whether the minimum standard in international law encompasses the principle of fair and equitable treatment or they are two principles separate from each other. After analysing a number of cases decided by international investment tribunals Haeri concludes that: 'Investment treaty jurisprudence suggests that the fair and equitable treatment standards could be interpreted as an autonomous treaty standard which differs from the international minimum standard (despite the apparent provenance of the fair and equitable treatment in the international minimum standard), especially where treaty so allows'. He goes on to add that '"jurisprudence indicates that the fair and equitable treatment standard could be interpreted as a broader Standard than the international minimum standard'.[110]

---

[104] *SGS v Philippines*, ICSID Case No ARB/02/6, 29 January 2004.
[105] *Marvin Feldman v Mexico*, ICSID Case No ARB (AF)/99/1, 16 December 2002: (2003) 42 ILM 625.
[106] *Enron v Argentina*, ICSID Case No ARB/01/3, 14 January 2004.
[107] *Azurix v Argentina*, ICSID Case No ARB/01/12, 8 December 2003.
[108] *Salini v Morocco* (2003) 42 ILM 606.
[109] *SGS v Pakistan* (2003) 42 ILM 1285.
[110] See Hussein Haeri, 'A Tale of Two Standards: "Fair and Equitable Treatment" and the Minimum Standard in International Law', 27 (1) *Arbitration International* (2011), pp 27–45 at 45.

Jurisprudence on Regulatory Expropriation

One of the most contentious issues in international investment law is the question of regulatory expropriation. As more and more states are resorting to measures designed to protect the environment, human rights and public health, either on their own volition or with a view to implementing international treaties ratified by them, these states are being sued by foreign investors alleging, among other things, that these measures are a violation of the fair and equitable treatment principle and/or constitute indirect expropriation. As stated by Lise Johnson, Lisa Sachs and Jeffrey Sachs,[111] there have been a series of cases in which the regulatory powers of host states have been challenged, many of them successfully, by foreign investors. For instance, challenge was made against new and stronger environmental regulations in *Glamis Gold v United States*[112] and *Lone Pine v Canada*;[113] against decisions not to grant permits or not to go ahead with projects (eg *Pac Rim v El Salvador*,[114] *Bilcon v Canada*,[115] *PSEG v Turkey*,[116] *MTD v Chile*);[117] against changes to fiscal regimes (eg *Perenco v Ecuador*,[118] *Burlington v Ecuador*,[119] *Occidental v Ecuador I*);[120] against requirements to purchase local goods and services or invest in research and development (*Mobil v Canada*); against actions to change or not change tariffs for public services (*Teco v Guatemala*,[121] *Iberdola v Guatemala*);[122] against judicial interpretations of the scope of patent protections for pharmaceutical products (*Eli Lilly v Canada*);[123] phasing out of nuclear power (*Vattenfall v Germany*);[124] against health measures such as anti-tobacco legislation and regulation (*Philip Morris v Australia*,[125] *Philip Morris v Uruguay*);[126] and against attempts to restructure sovereign debt (*Abaclat v Argentina*,[127] *Ambiente Ufficio v Argentina*,[128] *Alemanni v Argentina*).[129]

---

[111] L Johnson, L Sachs and J Sachs, 'Investor-State Dispute Settlement, Public Interest and US Domestic Law', Columbia Centre on Sustainable Development, Policy Paper, May 2015, 2–3.

[112] Award, 8 June 2009 (deciding in favour of the US on the merits).

[113] This case was still pending at the time of writing.

[114] *Pac Rim v El Salvador*, ICSID Case No ARB/09/12 (dismissed on jurisdiction).

[115] *Bilcon v Canada*, PCA Case No 2009-04, award of 17 March 2015 (deciding against Canada on the merits).

[116] *PSEG v Turkey*, ICSID Case No ARB/02/5 (deciding against Turkey on the merits).

[117] *MTD v Chile*, ICSID Case No ARB/01/7, award of 25 May 2004 (deciding against Chile on the merits).

[118] *Perenco v Ecuador*, ICSID Case No ARB/08/6, award of 12 September 2014 (deciding against Ecuador on the merits).

[119] *Burlington v Ecuador*, ICSID Case No ARB/08/5, award of 14 December 2012 (deciding against Ecuador on the merits).

[120] *Occidental v Ecuador I*, LCIA Case No UN3467, award of 1 July 2004 (decided against Ecuador on the merits).

[121] *Teco v Guatemala*, ICSID Case No ARB/10/23, award of 19 December 2013 (deciding against Guatemala on the merits).

[122] *Iberdola v Guatemala*, ICSID Case No ARB/09/5, award of 17 August 2012 (deciding in favour of Guatemala).

[123] *Eli Lilly v Canada*, ICSID Case No UNCT/14/2 (case still pending at the time of writing).

[124] *Vattenfall v Germany*, ICSID Case No ARB/12/12 (case still pending at the time of writing).

[125] *Philip Morris v Australia*, PCA Case No 2012-12 (case still pending at the time of writing).

[126] *Philip Morris v Uruguay*, ICSID Case No ARB/10/7 (case still pending at the time of writing).

[127] *Abaclat v Argentina*, ICSID Case No ARB/07/5 (case still pending at the time of writing).

[128] *Ambiente Ufficio v Argentina*, ICSID Case No ARB/08/9 (case still pending at the time of writing).

[129] *Alemanni v Argentina*, ICSID Case No ARB/07/8 (case still pending at the time of writing).

In *Lone Pine v Canada*[130] the provincial government of Quebec responded in 2011 to public pressure and concerns over water pollution by implementing a moratorium on the use of hydraulic fracturing ('fracking') for oil and gas exploration under and near the St Lawrence River. In 2012 Calgary-based Lone Pine Resources Inc (via an incorporation in the US tax haven of Delaware) launched a NAFTA challenge against the fracking moratorium and a related revocation of drilling permits. The company sought C$250 million (€175.7 million) plus interest in damages. Similarly, in *Eli Lilly v Canada* the US-based pharmaceutical giant Eli Lilly launched a C$500 million (€351.5 million) NAFTA claim in 2013 disagreeing with a decision of the Federal Court of Canada's decision to reject its supplementary patent applications for two reformulated drugs (olanzapine and atomoxetine) because they were not sufficiently innovative.[131]

As stated by Perrone, the challenge to regulatory expropriation began with awards such as *Metalclad v Mexico* and *TECMED v Mexico*, where tribunals promoted the stability of the legal and business framework while seriously constraining the policy space of host states.[132] However, some of the subsequent awards tried to adjust the interpretation of certain treaty standards, such as the fair and equitable treatment, and awards such as *Saluka v Czech Republic* became landmarks in investment arbitration as a result. Nevertheless, in the absence of an appellate mechanism and the lack of an obligation on later arbitration tribunals to follow previous precedent, many of the awards made since *Saluka* have undermined the reasoning in this case.

Regulatory expropriation is a relatively new phenomenon in international investment law. Most of the older-generation BITs contained no provision on regulatory expropriation as an exception to the rules on expropriation and compensation. For instance, the India–Nepal BIT of 2011 defines in Article 5(2) the nature and scope of regulatory expropriation in the following words:

(c) Non-discriminatory regulatory measures by a Contracting Party that are designed and applied to protect legitimate public welfare objectives including the protection of health, safety and environment do not constitute expropriation or nationalization; except in rare circumstances, where those measures are so severe that they cannot be reasonably viewed as having been adopted and applied in good faith for achieving their objectives.

(d) Actions and awards by judicial bodies of a Contracting Party that are designed, applied or issued in public interest including those designed to address health, safety and environmental concerns, do not constitute expropriation or nationalization.

This is a rather generous acceptance and definition of regulatory expropriation, yet is generally in tune with changes taking place both within international investment law and other areas of international law that have an impact on the activities of foreign investors. A provision of this nature is an attempt to reconcile the law on foreign investment protection with other competing principles of international law. It respects

---

[130] *Lone Pine Resources Inc v The Government of Canada*, ICSID Case No UNCT/15/2.
[131] P Eberhardt, B Redlin and C Toubeau, 'Trading Away Democracy: How CETA's Investor Protection Rules Threaten the Public Good in Canada and the EU' (published by an alliance of civil society organisations including the Association Internationale de Techniciens, Amsterdam, November 2014) 5.
[132] NM Perrone, 'The International Investment Regime at a Crossroad: Should We Be Rethinking Foreign Investment Governance?', *Investment Treaty News*, 19 February 2015.

the sovereignty of states and enables them to fulfil their commitments flowing from other international treaties or to pursue bona fide economic, environmental, health- and safety-related policies in the greater interest of the native residents in the host countries.

However, what is missing from this definition of regulatory expropriation is any measure designed to protect human rights. Having said this, it should be noted that this BIT is not alone in omitting human rights considerations. Human rights are the latest entrants into the realm of international investment law and it will take time for them to find their way into BITs or FTAs. If the trend of accepting legitimate or bona fide governmental measures undertaken in a non-discriminatory manner for good environmental, health or safety causes as non-compensable regulatory expropriation continues, it will not be long before bona fide governmental measures to protect core human rights will also be subsumed under the definition of regulatory expropriation.

Of the cases that have dealt with the notion of regulatory expropriation, perhaps the most prominent is *Methanex Corporation v United States of America*.[133] In this landmark case the tribunal dismissed all of Methanex's claims and rejected some of the findings in the *Metalclad* case. Although two different decisions of two arbitral tribunals in similar circumstances are not new in the world of arbitration, *Methanex* has had far-reaching implications as the major findings of the tribunal are founded on various well-established principles of the law of foreign investment. The corporation's claim related to the production and sale of a methanol-based gasoline oxygenating compound (ie an additive that increases the octane rating of gasoline) known as methyl tert-butyl ether, which was banned under Californian regulations. The company, a producer of methanol, had claimed that the Californian regulations were discrimina- tory, and were in fact sham environmental regulations designed to benefit and protect the US ethanol industry, a direct competitor of the methanol industry. The company alleged, inter alia, that as a result of the regulations the United States was violating Article 1102 of NAFTA Chapter 11, and claimed that the regulations were designed to deny foreign methanol producers, including Methanex, the favourable treatment the United States accorded its domestic ethanol investors. However, the tribunal concluded that Methanex failed to meet its burden of proof for all of its claims. Rejecting the idea that regulations were tantamount to expropriations, the tribunal held that:

> [A]s a matter of general international law, a non-discriminatory regulation for a public purpose which is enacted in accordance with due process and which affects, *inter alia*, a foreign investor or investment is not deemed expropriatory and compensable unless specific commitments had been given by the regulating government to then putative foreign investor contemplating investment that the government would refrain from such regulation.[134]

Accordingly, the tribunal held that, 'From the standpoint of international law, the California ban was a lawful regulation and not an expropriation.'[135] Another

---

[133] *Methanex Corporation v United States of America*, Final Award on Jurisdiction and Merits of 3 August 2005. The text of the decision is available at: www.state.gov/documents/organization/51052.pdf.
[134] Ibid, Final Award, Part IV, Chapter D, para 7.
[135] Ibid, para 15.

noteworthy case decided by an ICSID tribunal is *Noble Ventures, Inc v Romania*.[136] In this case the tribunal dismissed the investor's claims, finding that there was no breach by Romania of the US–Romania BIT of 1992. The case concerned a dispute between a US company, Noble Ventures, and Romania arising out of a privatisation agreement concerning the acquisition, management and operation of a Romanian steel mill, Combinatul Siderugic Resita, and other associated assets. The US company claimed that Romania had failed, inter alia, to honour the terms of several agreements relating to the control of the Romanian mill, in violation of the principle of fair and equitable treatment, and tantamount to expropriation. However, the tribunal found that the substance of Noble Venture's claims were without merit. Interpreting the scope and meaning of the term 'full protection and security', the tribunal noted that the duty to provide full protection and security is not to be understood as an absolute standard providing for strict liability but as a due-diligence standard. Accordingly, the tribunal found no specific failure by Romania to exercise due diligence in protecting the investment by Noble Ventures. Referring to the provision in the 1992 BIT regarding the 'full protection and security' available to foreign investors, the tribunal stated:

> [I]t seems doubtful whether that provision can be understood as being wider in scope than the general duty to provide for protection and security of foreign nationals found in the customary international law of aliens. The latter is not a strict standard, but one requiring due diligence to be exercised by the State.[137]

The decisions in these two cases seek to reconcile the rights of foreign investors with those of the host states. Also important is the decision by an international arbitral tribunal sitting under the rules of the Permanent Court of Arbitration in The Hague in *Saluka Investments BV (the Netherlands) v the Czech Republic*.[138] In this case, the tribunal held that in interpreting the provisions of treaties such as BITs or FTAs, account has to be taken of any relevant rules of international law, including general customary international law, applicable in the relations between the parties. In elaborating upon its approach, the tribunal implied that its decision was based on a rule of the interpretation of treaties prescribed by the Vienna Convention on the Law of Treaties of 1969 under which international courts and tribunals are obliged to pay attention to the obligations of host states under other treaties, including those international treaties concerning environmental protection, human rights and the maintenance of public morals, when applying or interpreting the provisions of a BIT or an FTA.

Another noteworthy case is *Philip Morris v Uruguay*. In 2010, Philip Morris Products S.A. and related entities launched an arbitration under the 1998 Switzerland–Uruguay BIT against Uruguay's tobacco control measures. In 2011, Philip Morris Asia Limited brought claims under the 1993 Australia-Hong Kong BIT against Australia's mandatory 'plain' packaging of tobacco products. In the end Philip Morris lost both disputes. The ICSID tribunal demonstrated how international investment law

---

[136] *Noble Ventures, Inc v Romania*, ICSID Case No ARB/01/11.

[137] Ibid, para 164. The text of the decision is available at: ita.law.uvic.ca/documents/Noble.pdf.

[138] *Saluka Investments BV (the Netherlands) v The Czech Republic*, partial award of 17 March 2006, para 254. This is available at: www.pca-cpa.org/showpage.asp?pag_id=1149.

can accommodate public health and other domestic policy objectives. The award of July 2016 in *Philip Morris v Uruguay* accorded appropriate weight to sovereign regulatory objectives: 'investment tribunals should pay great deference to governmental judgments of national needs in matters such as the protection of public health'.[139] This is a landmark ruling because it supports regulatory powers of not only Uruguay but of States in general to adopt laws and regulations to protect public health.

Modification of Customary International Law?

Given the limited significance of the contractual provisions of individual BITs and the decisions of ICSID tribunals and the Iran–US Claims Tribunal reached on the basis of *lex specialis*, it is doubtful whether this kind of new practice in jurisprudence had already altered the central tenets of traditional foreign investment law. For instance, the Iran–US Claims Tribunal was required to consider cases of not only expropriation but also of 'other measures affecting property rights'. It is difficult to establish whether a particular award of this Tribunal was based on the application of the established or settled principles of international foreign investment law or on its broader jurisdiction allowing it to consider cases involving 'other measures affecting property rights'. The political background to the Tribunal, its ad hoc character resembling a factual inquiry, and the peculiar factual situation of the cases it considered, do not allow its awards to command the same authority as do the judgments of other truly independent international courts and tribunals such as the ICJ.

Regardless of the number of BITs embodying the same and similar provisions, such provisions cannot necessarily be regarded to have crystallised into rules of international law. BITs are clearly evidence of state practice, but it is not certain whether this state practice is necessarily accompanied by *opinio juris* in all of the cases. Many of the provisions of BITs may not meet the test of *opinio juris* needed to constitute custom. Until it can be established that the central tenets have been modified by new state practice, traditional customary international law, including the principles embodied in truly international legal instruments and in resolutions of declaratory character such as the Permanent Sovereignty of States over their Natural Resources (PSNR) declaration of the UN General Assembly of 1962, seem to remain valid. For instance, CAFTA provides in its 'Investment' section that the states party to that treaty confirm their shared understanding that 'customary international law' generally and as specifically referenced in certain articles of the treaty 'results from a general and consistent practice of States that they follow from a sense of legal obligation'. It goes on to state that the 'customary international law minimum standard of treatment of aliens' refers to 'all customary international law principles that protect the economic rights and interests of aliens'.

Of course, while customary international law is constantly evolving and new examples of state practice are liable to change the existing rules, such new practice should,

---

[139] *Philip Morris Brands Sàrl v Uruguay*, ICSID No ARB/10/7, Award (8 July 2016), para 399.

nevertheless, meet other criteria, including consistency, generality and uniformity, before they can alter the existing rules. Nevertheless an arbitration tribunal held recently that so far as the application of customary international law rules to NAFTA disputes was concerned the term 'customary international law' 'refers to customary international law as it stood no earlier than the time at which NAFTA came into force'.[140] However, it should be borne in mind that the law developed by NAFTA is not ipso facto capable of altering the meaning, nature and scope of general customary international law.

When the NAFTA treaty provisions and the decisions of the ICSID tribunals refer to customary international law, they should be understood to be referring to the law that evolves out of state practice and meets the tests of customary international law. There has been no single major development of truly universal significance that can be regarded as a landmark event capable of altering the character of customary international law. Resolutions such as the UN declaration on PSNR can safely be claimed to have altered some of the elements of foreign investment law. Yet the problem remains that the 1962 PSNR declaration covers only a limited aspect of foreign investment law. For guidance on the rest of the rules on foreign investment law, reference should be made to other sources, including jurisprudence, state practice and the writings of scholars.

Because of the attempts that have been made to interpret NAFTA and other BIT provisions in a manner too favourable to investors and too restrictive to sovereign states – even to the extent of limiting the so-called police powers of states – there has recently been a move to counter the excesses of NAFTA and other ICSID tribunals by stating that when interpreting the NAFTA provisions, reliance must be placed on customary international foreign investment law; the protection that NAFTA provides is not over and above what customary international law provides.[141] Indeed, in some cases decided by ICSID there has been an attempt to accord a narrow meaning to the term 'full protection and security' rather than a broad one. For instance, in the *Asian Agricultural Products* case the ICSID tribunal, held that:

> The State into which an alien has entered ... is not an insurer or a guarantor of his security. ... It does not, and could hardly be asked to, accept an absolute responsibility for all injuries to foreigners.[142]

The ICJ, too, was reluctant in the *ELSI* case to accord a broad meaning to the term 'full protection and security'.[143] These developments give an indication that international courts and tribunals are perhaps willing to accept that states can exercise their regulatory powers or 'police powers' to impose certain reasonable restrictions

---

[140] *Mondev International Ltd v United States*, ICSID Case No ARB(AF)/99/2. NAFTA Chapter 11 Arbitral Tribunal, 11 October 2002. (2003) 42 ILM 85, para 125.

[141] Eg, in a statement the government of Canada described the limits of Art 1105 in the following terms: 'Article 1105, which provides for treatment in accordance with international law, is intended to assure a minimum standard of treatment of investments of NAFTA investors ... this article provides for a minimum absolute standard of treatment, based on long-standing principles of customary international law' [1994] Part I *Canada Gazette*, 1 January, 149.

[142] *Asian Agricultural Products, Inc v Sri Lanka*, ICSID Reports 245, 4; Final award of 27 June 1990.

[143] *Elettronica Sicula SpA (ELSI) (United States v Italy)*, ICJ Reports, 1989, 15; (1989) 28 ILM 1109.

on foreign investors. This is partly due to the challenge mounted by foreign investors to the regulatory powers of those investor countries that had championed unfettered rights for foreign investors. However, the developed countries supported investors as long as they were initiating legal proceedings against the regulatory powers of developing countries, but when the investors began to challenge the regulatory powers of the developed countries themselves there was a shift in attitude in these countries. The following observations of Sampliner with regard to the shift in attitude on the part of the US and Canada in relation to the implications of the investment protection provisions of NAFTA are noteworthy:

> The right of foreign investors to proceed directly to arbitration against their host States under investment treaties for alleged expropriation has received increasing attention in recent years. Although the United States has entered into such treaties [ie BITs] for more than two decades, significant controversy about this right has only arisen since the first cases under the investment chapter of the North American Free Trade Agreement (NAFTA) were filed against the United States and Canada in the late 1990s. It was only at that point that the realization hit home in the United States and other developed countries that these investment treaties, thought necessary to address disputes with developing country governments, could be used by foreign investors in developed countries to challenge a wide variety of national and sub-national actions.[144]

Indeed, the provisions of the US Trade Act of 2002 concerning future directions with regard to the protection of foreign investment within the US are noteworthy. Providing guidance as to the future course of action on the matter, the Act goes on to read as follows:

> (3) Foreign investment – Recognizing that United States law on the whole provides a high level of protection for investment, consistent with or greater than the level required by international law, the principal negotiating objectives of the United States regarding foreign investment are to reduce or eliminate artificial or trade-distorting barriers to foreign investment, while ensuring that foreign investors in the United States are not accorded greater substantive rights with respect to investment protections that United States investors in the United States, and to secure for investors important rights comparable to those that would be available under United States legal principles and practice, by—
>
> A. reducing or eliminating exceptions to the principle of national treatment;
> B. freeing the transfer of funds relating to investment;
> C. reducing or eliminating performance requirements, forced technology transfer, and other unreasonable barriers to the establishment and operation of investments;
> D. seeking to establish standards for expropriation and compensation for expropriation, consistent with United States legal principles and practice;
> E. seeking to establish standards for fair and equitable treatment consistent with Untied States legal principles and practice, including the principle of due process;
> F. providing meaningful procedures for resolving investment disputes;
> G. seeking to improve mechanisms used to resolve disputes between an investor and a government through—
>
>> (i)   mechanism to eliminate frivolous claims and to deter the filing of frivolous claims;
>> (ii) procedures to ensure the efficient selection of arbitrators and the expeditious disposition of claims;

---

[144] Sampliner (n 99) 23.

(iii) procedures to enhance opportunities for public input into the formulation of government positions; and

(iv) providing for an appellate body or similar mechanism to provide coherence to the interpretations of investment provisions in trade agreements; and

H. ensuring the fullest measure of transparency in the dispute settlement mechanism, to the extent consistent with the need to protect information that is classified or business confidential, by—

(i) ensuring that all requests for dispute settlement are promptly made public;

(ii) ensuring that—

(I) all proceedings, submissions, findings, and decisions are promptly made public; and

(II) establishing a mechanism for acceptance of *amicus curiae* submissions from businesses, unions, and non-governmental organizations.[145]

This demonstrates that while the US will continue to seek greater protection for its investors abroad than the protection available to domestic investors in the host countries, it would not accord any protection to foreign investors in the US greater than that available to US investors in the US. In other words, the US is claiming some of its sovereignty or sovereign control back in its dealing with foreign investment. If other states were to emulate this US practice the world would in effect be witnessing the revival, to a certain extent, of the Calvo doctrine. What the US legislation is trying to do is to accord national treatment to foreign investors. One of the central elements of the Calvo doctrine was designed to do precisely this. After challenging this doctrine for so long, the US seems to be embracing the idea for different reasons. One of the reasons given was that there was a tendency on the part of certain NAFTA tribunals, or at least on the part of certain claimants before these tribunals, to interpret the term 'expropriation' too broadly so as to challenge many regulatory measures of the US.[146]

Consequently, some of the FTAs concluded by the US since the enactment of the 2002 Trade Act have sought to limit the scope of the term 'expropriation' and protect the regulatory measures or the police powers of the US. Indeed, as stated by Rubins:

> The realization that international law is a two-way street has engendered sharp political pressure in Canada and the United States to scale back the power of NAFTA tribunals – a campaign that may lead to additional challenges of NAFTA awards.[147]

Furthermore, with a view to imposing a constraint on NAFTA and ICSID tribunals, states, including the US, have introduced the idea of appealing against the awards of such tribunals.[148] For instance, the proposed Model BIT of the US and the draft CAFTA envisage an appellate system for investment disputes.[149] The US–Chile and

---

[145] Trade Act of 2002, Pub L107–210 (107th Cong, 2d Sess), s 2102(b)(3).

[146] See a statement of the Senate Committee in SRep 107–39 (107th Cong, 2d Sess) 13–5 (2002).

[147] N Rubins, 'Judicial Review of Investment Arbitration Awards', in T Weiler (ed), *NAFTA Investment Law and Arbitration: Past Issues, Current Practice and Future Prospects* (Ardsley, NY, Transnational Publishers, 2003) 359–90, 362.

[148] See WH Knull, III and ND Rubins, 'Betting the Farm on International Arbitration: Is it Time to Offer an Appeal Option?' (2000) 11 *American Review of International Arbitration* 531.

[149] Outlining the US objectives for future negotiations on investment agreements, a report of the Committee on Finance of the US Congress on the Bipartisan Trade Promotion Authority Act of 2002 states that the US

US–Singapore FTAs also allow for this possibility. Although the WTO has an appeal mechanism against the recommendations of its panels, the idea of an appeal against the awards of arbitration tribunals on investment disputes would be quite a novelty in foreign investment law. What is equally interesting is the absence of any investment dispute settlement mechanism in the US–Australia FTA.[150] This also represents an indirect revival of the Calvo doctrine under which investment disputes with foreign investors were supposed to be entertained by domestic courts.[151]

Extension of Bilateral Investment Treaty Protection to Contractual Undertakings

Many international investment tribunals sitting under BITs have begun to extend BIT protection to contractual disputes if the dispute relates to a breach of a contract that binds the state directly; they have done so on the basis of the MFN principle, 'umbrella clauses' and jurisdictional clauses found in the BIT concerned. The decision of a tribunal on jurisdiction in *Salini v Morocco* in 2001 was one of the first cases to do so on the basis of a broad jurisdictional provision in a BIT. The tendency towards the extension of the application of BITs to disputes of a contractual nature between a private foreign investor and a host state went a step forward in *SGS v Pakistan* when the tribunal was prepared to look at contractual disputes under the 'umbrella clause' in a BIT. Furthermore, in a case against Pakistan brought by Impreglio, an Italian company, the tribunal was prepared to look at the contractual disputes between the company and the host state. Although the tribunals in both *Salini* and *Impregilo* restricted themselves to the extension of their jurisdiction to contractual disputes between the investor and the state, directly stating that the jurisdiction would not be extended to contractual disputes between an investor and an autonomous corporate body that was legally and financially distinct from the host government, both of these decisions demonstrated that treaty-based tribunals could entertain cases involving contractual disputes even if the contract itself provided for another mechanism for the settlement of such disputes.

In the *Vivendi* case the ad hoc Committee established to consider a request for annulment of an arbitral award sought to distinguish the difference between the breach

---

negotiators 'should seek to establish a single appellate body to review decisions in investor-state disputes. As the United States enters into more investment agreements and the number of investor-state disputes grows, the need for consistency of interpretations of common terms – such as expropriation and fair and equitable treatment – will grow. Absent such consistency, key terms may be given different meanings depending on which arbitrators are appointed to interpret them. This will detract from the predictability of rights conferred under investment agreements. A single appellate mechanism to review the decisions of arbitral panels under various investment agreements should help to address this issue and minimize the risk of aberrant interpretation.' Calendar No 319, 107th Congress, 2d Session, Report 107–39 (2002).

[150] US–Australia FTA concluded on 18 May 2004. For the text of the agreement, see www.ustr.gov/newfta/Australia/final/final.pdf.

[151] Indeed, both Brazil and Argentina were reported to have stated that that they would not agree to the investor–state arbitration dispute settlement mechanism in the future FTA of the Americas.

of a contractual obligation and the breach of a treaty provision: 'A State may breach a treaty without breaching a contract, and *vice versa*.' Indeed, Article 3 of the ILC Draft Articles on State Responsibility makes this point clear in the following words: 'The characterization of an act of a State as internationally wrongful is governed by international law. Such characterization is not affected by the characterization of the same act as lawful by internal law.'

Citing this provision and describing this principle as a general principle declaratory of general international law, the ad hoc Committee went on to state in this case between two companies and Argentina that:

> [W]hether there has been a breach of the BIT and whether there has been a breach of contract are different questions. Each of these claims will be determined by reference to its own proper or applicable law – in the case of the BIT, by international law; in the case of the Concession Contract, by the proper law of the contract, in other words, the law of Tucumán. For example, in the case of a claim based on a treaty, international law rules of attribution apply, with the result that the state of Argentina is internationally responsible for the acts of its provincial authorities. By contrast, the state of Argentina is not liable for the performance of contracts entered into by Tucumán, which possesses separate legal personality under its own law and is responsible for the performance of its own contracts.[152]

Accordingly, the Committee held that an ICSID tribunal could entertain a case alleging the breach of a BIT provision by a company against the host state even if there is an exclusive jurisdiction clause in the contract with the state concerned providing for another mechanism for resolving disputes arising out of the interpretation or application of the provisions of the contract concerned. The *Vivendi* ruling has been endorsed by many other subsequent ICSID tribunals and the *Impregilo v Pakistan* case is an example.[153] In this case the ICSID tribunal held that:'[T]he taking of contractual rights could, potentially, constitute an expropriation or a measure having an equivalent effect.' The tribunal noted that the present case did not concern a situation of nationalisation or expropriation in the traditional sense of those terms, but behaviour that could, at least in theory, constitute an indirect expropriation or a measure having an effect equivalent to expropriation.[154]

The tribunal concluded that it had no jurisdiction *ratione materiae* over the claimant's contract claims, but the alleged breaches of the contracts may constitute breaches of the Italy–Pakistan BIT if they meet the criteria defined in the decision in which case the tribunal would have jurisdiction over such matters.[155] In *Aguas del Tunari v Bolivia* an ICSID tribunal made it clear that it did not have

> the authority under the ICSID Convention for it to abstain from exercising its jurisdiction simply because a conflicting forum selection clause exists. To the contrary, it is the

---

[152] *Compania de Aguas del Aconquija and Vivendi Universal (formerly Compagnie Generale des Eaux) v the Argentine Republic*, ICSID Case No ARB/97/3, 3 July 2002 (footnote omitted). Similar views were expressed by the ICJ in the *Reparations for Injuries* and *ELSI* cases.
[153] *Impregilo v Pakistan*, ICSID Case No ARB/03/03, 22 April 2005 (jurisdiction), para 210.
[154] Ibid, para 274.
[155] Ibid, para 291.

Tribunal's view that an ICSID tribunal has a duty to exercise its jurisdiction in such instances absent any indication that the Parties specifically intended that the conflicting clause act as a waiver or modification of an otherwise existing grant of jurisdiction to ICSID. A separate conflicting document should be held to affect the jurisdiction of an ICSID tribunal only if it clearly is intended to modify the jurisdiction otherwise granted to ICSID.[156]

Thus, the norm that seems to be evolving is that ICSID or other international arbitration tribunals would have no jurisdiction on purely contractual matters under the contract but would have jurisdiction under ICSID or the BITs concerned to address violations of contracts, which, at the same time, constitute a breach of the relevant BIT. When there is no practical way to separate the operation of a provision in a contract from the alleged breach of a BIT provision, then an ICSID or a BIT tribunal will have jurisdiction to consider the matter on its merits. This is a new development in foreign investment law that runs the risk of gradually engulfing contractual disputes by an ICSID tribunal or other international arbitration tribunals whose task is to apply international law or *lex specialis* embodied in a BIT.

This is not to say that this approach is universally adopted. A number of other tribunals have taken a rather cautious approach to this matter. For instance, in the *Waste Management* case the ICSID tribunal sitting under NAFTA held that:

> The mere non-performance of a contractual obligation is not to be equated with a taking of property, nor (unless accompanied by other elements) is it tantamount to expropriation ... [T]he normal response by an investor faced with a breach of contract by its governmental counter-party (the breach not taking the form of an exercise of governmental prerogative, such as a legislative decree) is to sue in the appropriate court to remedy the breach. It is only where such access is practically or legally foreclosed that the breach could amount to an outright denial of the right, and the protection of Article 1110 [of NAFTA] would be called into play.[157]

However, if the BIT concerned provides for a broad provision stating that 'any dispute with respect to investment' would be covered by the BIT's dispute settlement mechanism, then it would be a different matter. For instance, Article 24 of the US Model BIT expressly confers a treaty-based tribunal with jurisdiction over breaches of an investment agreement. In situations where the BIT contains an observance of undertakings clause, the contracting states are creating a treaty standard and this in turn is capable of providing a basis for the jurisdiction of a treaty-based tribunal. This was the reasoning adopted in *LESI-Dipenta v Algeria* and *Eureko v Poland*. In the latter case, the tribunal held that Poland had breached its treaty commitment to 'observe any obligations it may have entered into with regard to investments of investors'.[158]

---

[156] *Aguas del Tunari v Bolivia*, ICSID Case No ARB/02/3, decision on respondent's objections to jurisdiction of 21 October 2005, para 119.

[157] *Waste Management Inc v United Mexican States* (2004) 43 ILM 967, 1002 (para 174).

[158] See E Gaillard, 'Treaty-Based Jurisdiction: Broad Dispute Resolution Clauses' (2005) 234(68) *New York Law Journal* 3.

Extension of the Most-Favoured-Nation Clause to Establish Jurisdiction

As stated by Menon, MFN clauses

> were originally intended to ensure that host states would not discriminate in terms of the competitive opportunities offered by treaty partners. But tribunals have interpreted MFN clauses broadly, seemingly allowing investors to pick and choose from provisions present in BITs between the host state and other third-party states. This can sometimes enable an investor to construct a cause of action that might never have been in the contemplation of the contracting states.[159]

Although it is generally accepted in international law that any arbitration requires the explicit consent of the parties concerned, the recent trend in the jurisprudence of international investment tribunals has been to resort to other means of deducing such consent of a host state party to the dispute by relying on not only the BIT in question but also on other treaties concluded by the state concerned with extending the nature, meaning and scope of the MFN principle. This trend, which began with early cases such as *Ambatielos*[160] in establishing indirect consent to arbitration, was confirmed by a tribunal in *Maffezini*, and has been further developed by other tribunals in subsequent cases. In *Maffezini* an ICSID tribunal outlined the reasons for its decision in the following words:

> Notwithstanding the fact that the basic treaty containing the clause does not refer expressly to dispute settlement as covered by the most favoured nation clause, the Tribunal considers that there are good reasons to conclude that today dispute settlement arrangements are inextricably related to the protection of foreign investors, as they are also related to the protection of rights of traders under treaties of commerce. Consular jurisdiction in the past, like other forms of extraterritorial jurisdiction, were considered essential for the protection of rights of traders and, hence, were regarded not merely as procedural devices but as arrangements designed to better protect the rights of such persons abroad. It follows that such arrangements, even if not strictly a part of the material aspect of the trade and investment policy pursued by treaties of commerce and navigation, were essential for the adequate protection of the rights they sought to guarantee.

Prior to the *Maffezini* ruling, various international tribunals had been reluctant to extend the MFN principle to cover jurisdictional matters and the ruling of the ICJ in the *Anglo Iranian Oil Company* case in 1952 is an example.[161] However, the *Maffezini* tribunal went on to explain why its interpretation to extend the MFN principle to jurisdictional matters was consistent with the objective of promoting foreign investment by offering an assurance to foreign investors that any legal dispute that they may have

---

[159] Menon (n 82) 235 (footnotes omitted).

[160] *Ambatielos* case *(Greece v UK)* [1963] RIAA 107.

[161] In this case, the ICJ had held that the MFN clause in the treaties between Iran and the UK had no relation whatsoever to jurisdictional matters between the two governments. *Anglo Iranian Oil Company*, preliminary objection, judgment, 22 July 1952.

with the host state would be entertained by an international tribunal immune from political interference by the host states concerned:

> [I]t can be concluded that if a third-party treaty contains provisions for the settlement of disputes that are more favourable to the protection of the investor's rights and interests than those in the basic treaty, such provisions may be extended to the beneficiary of the most favoured nation clause as they are fully compatible with the *ejusdem generis* principle. Of course, the third-party treaty has to relate to the same subject matter as the basic treaty, be it the protection of foreign investments or the promotion of trade, since the dispute settlement provisions will operate in the context of these matters; otherwise there would be a contravention of that principle. This operation of the most favoured nation clause does, however, have some important limits arising from public policy considerations.

On the basis of the above analysis, the tribunal concluded that it could rely on the provisions included in another BIT concluded by the host state with a third state providing for better access to international arbitration to foreign investors by virtue of the expansion of the MFN clause in the BIT in question:

> In light of the above considerations, the Tribunal is satisfied that the Claimant has convincingly demonstrated that the most favoured nation clause included in the Argentine–Spain BIT embraces the dispute settlement provisions of this treaty. Therefore, relying on the more favourable arrangements contained in the Chile–Spain BIT and the legal policy adopted by Spain with regard to the treatment of its own investors abroad, the Tribunal concludes that Claimant had the right to submit the instant dispute to arbitration without first accessing the Spanish courts. In the Tribunal's view, the requirement for the prior resort to domestic courts spelled out in the Argentine–Spain BIT does not reflect a fundamental question of public policy considered in the context of the treaty, the negotiations relating to it, the other legal arrangements or the subsequent practice of the parties. Accordingly, the Tribunal affirms the jurisdiction of the Centre and its own competence in this case in respect of this aspect of the challenge made by the Kingdom of Spain.[162]

This expansion of the meaning of the MFN principle to cover even dispute settlement procedures has introduced yet another new trend towards treaty-shopping or forum-shopping among foreign investors, and has been followed by other subsequent international investment tribunals such as those in *Tecmed*[163] and especially in *Siemens v Argentina*.[164] Although some recent ICSID cases such as *Salini v Jordan*[165] and *Plama v Bulgaria*[166] seem to have put a brake on this trend, it remains to be seen whether future tribunals will follow the *Maffezini* principle or the rulings in the *Salini* and *Plama* cases.[167] Indeed, the ILC stated in Article 9.1 of its 1978 Draft Articles on State

---

[162] *Emilio Augustin Maffezini v Kingdom of Spain*, ICSID Case No ARB/97/7, 25 January, 2000 (decision on jurisdiction), paras 54–56, 64.

[163] *Tecnicas Medioambientales Tecmed SA v The United Mexican States*, ICSID Case No ARB(AF)/00/2, award of 29 May 2003.

[164] *Siemens AG v The Argentine Republic*, ICSID Case No ARB/02/8, decision of 3 August 2004.

[165] *Salini Costruttori SpA and Italstrade SpA v The Hashemite Kingdom of Jordan*, ICSID Case No ARB/02/13, decision of 15 November 2004.

[166] *Plama Consortium Ltd v Republic of Bulgaria*, ICSID Case No ARB/03/24, decision of 8 February 2005.

[167] See S Fietta, 'Most Favoured Nation Treatment and Dispute Resolution under Bilateral Investment Treaties: A Turning Point?' (2005) Issue 4 *International Arbitration Law Review* 131.

Responsibility that the MFN clauses in various trade and investment treaties confer 'only those rights which fall within the limits of the subject-matter of the clause'. The *ejusdem generis* principle (ie the same kind) implies that an MFN clause 'can only attract matters belonging to the same category of subject as that to which the clause itself relates'.[168] The ICJ stated in *Anglo-Iranian Oil Company* that the scope of application of the MFN principle depends on the basic treaty providing for this principle in the first place. It held that the basic treaty establishes the 'juridical link' between the beneficiary state and a third party and confers upon that state the rights enjoyed by the third party. The ICJ went on to pronounce that a treaty between third parties cannot produce any legal effect as between the beneficiary state and the host state since it is *res inter alios acta*.[169]

Conclusion

As seen in the foregoing analysis, more or less every area of foreign investment law has been subjected to an examination by international investment tribunals, and these tribunals have interpreted the principles of foreign investment law or the provisions of BITs and FTAs in most cases as liberally or as broadly as possible in favour of foreign investors. The jurisprudence of international investment courts and tribunals has expanded the scope and meaning of various principles of foreign investment law in as pro-investment a manner as possible. In the absence of an internationally negotiated global instrument on foreign investment law, international courts and tribunals have gone on to invoke the provisions of BITs and FTAs to strengthen and expand the standard of protection available to foreign investors under customary international law. Further, as stated by Appleton, many of the problems fundamentally arise

> from the lack of proper application of international law. Fundamental and basic concepts such as those contained in the Vienna Convention on the Law Treaties and the ILC Draft Articles on State Responsibility are often not followed in the interpretation of international economic law treaties.[170]

Thus, it is becoming increasingly necessary to find a means to ensure greater coherence within international investment case law and this will be one of the major issues discussed in the following chapters.

---

[168] For the views of the Commission of Arbitration in the *Ambatielos* case, see [1963] RIAA 107.
[169] *Anglo-Iranian Oil Company* case *(Iran v UK)*, ICJ Reports 1952, 109.
[170] B Appleton, 'The Song Is Over: Why it's Time to Stop Talking about an International Investment Arbitration Appellate Body', *Proceedings of the Annual Meeting of the American Society of International Law*, vol 107 (April 2013) 23, 25.

7

Current Issues in International Investment Law

Introduction

The purpose of this chapter is to examine current issues within foreign investment law. As stated by an international arbitral tribunal sitting under the rules of UNCITRAL in a case between Saluka Investments BV (the Netherlands) and the Czech Republic, in interpreting the provisions of treaties such as BITs or FTAs, account has to be taken of any relevant rules of international law, including general customary international law, applicable in the relations between the parties.[1] This is based on a rule of the interpretation of treaties prescribed by the Vienna Convention on the Law of Treaties of 1969.[2] Provisions such as this require international courts and tribunals to pay attention to the obligations of host states under other treaties, including those international treaties concerning environmental protection, human rights and the maintenance of public morals, when applying or interpreting the provisions of a BIT or an FTA. They reiterate the position of foreign investment law as an integral part of international law. Indeed, an ICSID tribunal sitting under NAFTA in the *Methanex* case stated that: '[A]s a matter of international constitutional law a tribunal has an independent duty to apply imperative principles of law or *jus cogens* and not give effect to parties' choices of law that are inconsistent with such principles.'[3]

However, the question remains as to whether the changes that have taken place in foreign investment law have taken into account the obligations of host states under other principles of international law when adjudicating on investment matters. To what extent has international investment law taken into account the public policy objectives of host states inherent in them as sovereign entities in adjudicating on investment disputes? These are the questions that will be examined in this chapter.

---

[1] *Saluka Investments BV (the Netherlands) v the Czech Republic*, partial award of 22 May 2006, para 254; Permanent Court of Arbitration (PCA).

[2] Art 31(3)(c) of the Vienna Convention on the Law of Treaties, 1969.

[3] *Methanex Corporation v United States of America*, Part IV, ch C, 11, final award of the tribunal on jurisdiction and merits of 3 August 2005 (2005) 44 ILM 1345.

The Law at a Crossroads

Although there is a sizeable body of customary international law as well as treaty law, whether bilateral or regional, dealing with different aspects of investment protection, the rules are scattered. Most of the customary international law on the subject matter has evolved out of diplomatic exchanges, the jurisprudence of international courts and tribunals, bilateral and regional investment treaties, and a host of 'soft law' instruments adopted under the auspices of the UN and its specialised agencies. A great deal of success has been achieved in the past 60 or so years in developing and codifying customary international law rules in a number of areas, yet no such success has been achieved in foreign investment law. Of course, there are a few international treaties dealing with certain aspects of foreign investment law. The ICSID Convention dealing with the settlement of both state–state and investor-state investment disputes has been ratified by a large number of states. Similarly, there are international or regional treaties dealing with the control of corruption by transnational businesses in host countries, and the UN Anti-Corruption Convention is an example. However, these treaties are limited in scope and deal only with one sector of the issues involved.

Attempts were made within the UN in the 1970s and 1980s to adopt a comprehensive code of conduct for TNCs, the main vehicles of foreign investment. However, when in the early 1990s political and economic events overtook the efforts, the idea was abandoned. The OECD tried in the late 1990s to conclude a multilateral agreement on investment (MAI), but it, too, resulted in failure. The WTO then decided to include foreign investment in its agenda for the Development Round of trade negotiations through the Doha Declaration of November 2001. However, in July 2004 the WTO also decided to set aside the project. It was too complex an area for the WTO as well, since an unwieldy number of differences of opinion among its members existed as to the nature, scope and desirability of the conclusion of an international treaty on such a matter under the auspices of the WTO.

Once again, an all-too-familiar traditional clash of interests between developing and developed countries on the subject matter surfaced during the Doha Round of multilateral trade negotiations. This seems to have led to the virtual abandonment of the topic by the WTO when the 'July 2004 Package' or the 'Mid-Point Deal' was reached in Geneva. The main difference between these two groups of states centred around the very purpose of an international treaty on foreign investment. While the developed or capital-exporting states wished to achieve through the treaty the free mobility of capital by minimising the authority of governments with regard to the imposition of conditions and regulations on foreign investors, the developing or capital-importing countries wished to protect the autonomy of their respective governments over both investment policy and the right to regulate the activities of foreign investors.[4]

---

[4] See Report of the Working Group on the Relationship between Trade and Investment to the General Council of the WTO, WT/WGTI/6, 9 December 2002.

One of the main points of contention within the WTO was whether an international agreement on foreign investment should encompass portfolio investment. The principles of foreign investment law have traditionally been applied to foreign direct investment – the traditional form of investment. The developed states within the WTO attempted not only to accelerate the process of liberalisation of foreign investment but also to include a broad, asset-based definition of investment, bringing both foreign direct investment and portfolio investment within the regime of protection available to foreign investors. This move was resisted by developing countries, who wished to maintain the right to regulate portfolio investment, in particular speculative short-term capital flows. The proposal was to exclude altogether these investments from the definition of 'covered investment', which would qualify for protection under the treaty.

Thus, the very definition of the term 'foreign direct investment' was a matter of controversy within the WTO and therefore no progress could be made towards the conclusion of a treaty. Although most of the recently concluded BITs between a developed and a developing country, and most of the FTAs, include portfolio investment in the definition of investment, some RTAs concluded among developing countries themselves exclude portfolio investment from the definition of investment. The practice of the ASEAN[5] and the agreement between the EU and the Pacific members of the ACP countries of June 2006 are examples of such practice.[6] States are divided on the inclusion of portfolio investment in the definition of investment. Thus, foreign investment law itself is currently at a crossroads in terms of its codification and progressive development.

Absence of Guidelines on the Standard of Compensation

Traditional international law admits the existence of (i) the 'police power' of states and (ii) regulatory expropriations that could attract either no compensation or less than full compensation, or less than what is required for other normal forms of expropriations, whether direct or indirect.[7] According to Brownlie, the following is the standard of compensation in international law:

1. Expropriation for certain public purposes, eg exercise of police power and defence measures in wartime, is lawful even if no compensation is payable.
2. Expropriation of particular items of property is unlawful unless there is provision for the payment of effective compensation.

---

[5] See Art 2 of the Framework Agreement on the ASEAN Investment Area of 1998 and Art 1 of the Protocol to Amend the Framework Agreement on the ASEAN Investment Area of 2001.

[6] Draft Art 8.2 of the investment chapter in the context of the EU/PACP EPA negotiations, DG Trade G 1(D) (2006), 10 October 2006.

[7] Eg, see Art 10(5) of the Harvard Draft on State Responsibility and the views of Sir R Jennings and Sir A Watts in *Oppenheim's International Law*, 9th edn (Harlow, Longman, 1992) vol I, parts II–IV, 911 et seq.

3. Nationalization, ie expropriation of a major industry or resource, is unlawful only if there is no provision for compensation payable on a basis compatible with the economic objectives of the nationalization, and the viability of the economy as a whole.[8]

In his view,

[E]xpropriation under (2) and (3) is unlawful, if at all, only sub modo, ie if appropriate compensation is not provided for. The controversial difference between (2) and (3) is the basis on which compensation is assessed.[9]

However, several recent decisions of arbitral tribunals have sought to narrow the scope of regulatory expropriations and award huge sums of compensation regarding regulatory expropriations as constituting a breach of a BIT or the standards of full compensation.

Under international law, examples of regulatory expropriatory measures are those resulting from a bona fide governmental action designed to protect and promote legitimate objectives of public interest, such as measures pursued as part of economic reform or liberalisation programmes or those designed to achieve greater social justice within the host country concerned. A number of BITs and RTAs recognise the rights of states to adopt certain measures designed to ensure that investment activity is undertaken in a manner sensitive to environmental concerns.[10] The idea that bona fide, non-discriminatory measures taken by a host state to comply with its international obligations under other treaties should not be regarded as constituting expropriation, whether direct, indirect, consequential or regulatory, seems to be gaining some recognition and momentum. The Canada–Peru BIT of 2006 offers an example of a provision indicating a recent trend in BIT practice whereby the nature and scope of 'indirect expropriation' is defined narrowly.

Similarly, a draft article in an agreement between the EU and the Pacific members of the ACP countries of June 2006 stipulates that certain regulatory measures do not constitute expropriation.[11]

Jurisprudence already seems to be leading the way in this direction. For instance, it was held in the *Methanex* case that, 'as a matter of general international law, a non-discriminatory regulation for a public purpose, which is enacted in accordance with due process and, which affects, *inter alios*, a foreign investor or investment is not deemed expropriatory and compensable'.[12] Leader similarly argues that when a state is taking regulatory measures in fulfilment of its human rights obligations flowing

---

[8] I Brownlie, *Principles of Public International Law*, 6th edn (Oxford, Oxford University Press, 2003) 514.
[9] Ibid.
[10] The provisions in Art 10.12 of the FTA between Chile and the US, Art 114(2) of NAFTA, Art 12 of the 2004 Model US BIT, Art 10.11 of CAFTA and Art 15.10 of the Singapore–US FTA are examples. Art 10.12 of the Chile–US FTA reads as follows: 'Nothing in this Chapter shall be construed to prevent a Party from adopting, maintaining, or enforcing any measure otherwise consistent with this Chapter that it considers appropriate to ensure that investment activity in its territory is undertaken in a manner sensitive to environmental concerns.' Identical provisions can be found in a number of other BITs and FTAs.
[11] Draft Art 8.8(I) of the investment chapter in the context of the EU/PACP EPA negotiations, DG Trade G 1(D) (2006), 10 October 2006.
[12] *Methanex Corporation v United States of America*, part IV, ch D, para 7, final award of the tribunal on jurisdiction and merits of 3 August 2005.

from international treaties, there should be no compensation payable.[13] Therefore, the trend seems to point in the direction that bona fide, non-discriminatory measures taken by a host state to comply with its international obligations under other treaties should not be regarded as constituting expropriation, whether direct, indirect, consequential or regulatory.

However, foreign investment law does not provide a clear guidance as to the balance that has to be struck between unlawful expropriations and regulatory expropriations. Neither any treaty nor the jurisprudence of international investment tribunals has developed an agreed standard of compensation or drawn a clear distinction between (i) uncompensable forms of expropriation resulting from the exercise of traditional 'police power' of states; (ii) regulatory expropriations permissible under evolving and extant international law which may call for a less than full compensation; (iii) permissible but compensable forms of expropriation warranting full compensation according to the Hull formula; and (iv) unlawful and confiscatory forms of expropriation requiring restitution or a much higher level of compensation. Thus, the search for an agreed international standard of compensation called for by Franck in 1995 continues.[14]

The Impact of Cross-Fertilisation of Competing Principles

Until recently, investment arbitration was regarded as a private commercial matter between two disputing parties. However, the proliferation of investment cases is producing much wider implications that go beyond traditional commercial considerations. This is one reason why some scholars have stated that such investment tribunals are basically a 'businessman's court' in character and are not suited to adjudicate on public policy issues.[15] Indeed, the decisions of such tribunals are having an impact on global and national public policy issues such as the environment, human rights, health and safety, etc. It was held in *Methanex* that: 'There is an undoubtedly public interest in this arbitration. The substantive issues extend far beyond those raised by the usual transnational arbitration between commercial parties.'[16]

Similar views were expressed in another recent ICSID case, *Vivendi Universal v Argentina*. In this case the tribunal held that: 'In examining the issues at stake in the present case, the tribunal finds that the present case potentially involves matters of public interest.'[17] The ICSID tribunal in *Methanex* went on to assert that: '[A]s a matter

---

[13] S Leader, 'Human Rights, Risks, and New Strategies for Global Investment' (2006) 9 *Journal of International Economic Law* 657, 690.

[14] TM Franck, *Fairness in International Law and Institutions* (Clarendon Press, Oxford, 1995) 457.

[15] G van Harten, *Investment Treaty Arbitration and Public Law* (Oxford, Oxford University Press, 2007) ch 7, 152 et seq.

[16] *Methanex Corporation v United States of America*, decision of the tribunal on petitions from third persons to intervene as 'amici curiae' of 15 January 2001, para 49.

[17] *Vivendi Universal v Argentina*, ICSID Case No ARB/03/19, order in response to a petition for transparency and participation in amicus curiae of 19 May 2002, para 19.

of international constitutional law a tribunal has an independent duty to apply imperative principles of law of *jus cogens* and not to give effect to parties' choices of law that are inconsistent with such principles.'[18]

This was a rather remarkable statement with far-reaching implications. It was also a signal that a significant change in paradigm was taking place in foreign investment law. There are quite a few principles of international human rights law, international environmental law and other branches of international law that can be regarded as being *jus cogens* in character. Furthermore, there are many rules of customary international law or universally accepted general principles of international law that are binding on all states except for those which are subsequent and persistent objectors. An investment tribunal operating within the framework of public international law would be expected to have regard for such principles when issuing its award.

In this age of globalisation, no area of law can remain uninfluenced by the developments taking place in other areas of law. There is a great degree of interconnectedness or cross-fertilisation taking place both within public international law and foreign investment law. Foreign investment law is therefore influenced by cross-fertilisation from other areas of public international law, especially those relating to human rights and environmental protection, as well as certain fundamental principles of international economic law such as the principle of economic self-determination of states, the right to develop, and the permanent sovereignty of states over their natural resources. Thanks mainly to a vigorous campaign launched by various NGOs and scholars across the globe in recent years in favour of human rights and environmental considerations in the realm of trade and investment law, both human rights and environmental issues are making inroads into the corpus of both trade and investment law, whether through BITs or FTAs or jurisprudence.[19]

Developments taking place in international trade law within the GATT/WTO framework have also had a direct impact on foreign investment law. For instance, the *Methanex* case has already demonstrated that GATT/WTO jurisprudence may be taken into account by ICSID tribunals.[20] It should be noted here that the GATT/WTO jurisprudence itself is coming out of its mercantilist straitjacket and taking into account environmental considerations in the resolution of trade disputes. The ruling of the WTO Dispute Settlement Body in the *Shrimps and Turtles*[21] case is an example. The pressure will increase on international investment tribunals to follow suit, especially since new BITs, such as that concluded between Peru and Canada in 2006, has included the promotion of sustainable development as one of its objectives.

---

[18] *Methanex Corporation v United States of America*, part IV, ch C, 11, final award of the tribunal on jurisdiction and merits of 3 August 2005.

[19] Eg, the Canada–Peru BIT of 2006 states as one of its objectives the promotion of sustainable development. The 1994 Marrakesh Agreement establishing the WTO contains similar provisions. More and more states are making human rights and the environment crucial issues to be taken into account by BITs and FTAs. Human rights considerations seem to have become a serious issue in the negotiations between the EU and India on an FTA; see 'EU–India Trade Pact Stumbles on Human Rights Rider', *Financial Times*, 5 March 2007, 9.

[20] *Methanex Corporation v United States of America*, part II, ch B, 2–3, final award of the tribunal on jurisdiction and merits of 3 August 2005.

[21] *United States: Import Prohibition of Certain Shrimp and Shrimp Products*, WTO Report of the Appellate Body, WT/DS58/AB/R (12 October 1998).

Similarly, developments taking place within foreign investment law, whether under BITs or investment contracts, have produced much wider implications, beyond the disputing parties and often beyond the ambit of foreign investment law itself, and have impinged on the very foundation of the international legal order. Indeed, the impact of many of the investment cases recently decided by international investment tribunals has gone far beyond the commercial and touched on public policy objectives such as the protection of human rights and the environment. This perhaps is one reason why another international arbitral tribunal sitting under the rules of the Permanent Court of Arbitration in The Hague held recently in the case of *Saluka Investments BV (the Netherlands) v the Czech Republic* that in interpreting the provisions of treaties such as BITs or FTAs, account has to be taken of any relevant rules of international law, including general customary international law, applicable in the relations between the parties.[22]

In elaborating upon its approach, the tribunal implied that its decision was based on a rule of the interpretation of treaties prescribed by the Vienna Convention on the Law of Treaties of 1969,[23] under which international courts and tribunals are obliged to pay attention to the obligations of host states under other treaties, including those international treaties concerning environmental protection, human rights and the maintenance of public morals, when applying or interpreting the provisions of a BIT or an FTA. This demonstrates that foreign investment law should not operate in isolation from the rest of the rules of international law; the tribunals interpreting and applying the rules of international foreign investment law should take into account other competing principles of international law. A 2006 ILC report also supported this view, stating that:

> *International law as a legal system.* International law is a legal system. Its rules and principles (ie its norms) act in relation to and should be interpreted against the background of other rules and principles. As a legal system, international law is not a random collection of such norms. There are meaningful relationships between them. Norms may thus exist at higher and lower hierarchical levels, their formulation may involve greater or lesser generality and specificity and their validity may date back to earlier or later moments in time.[24]

Indeed, an ICSID tribunal sitting under NAFTA in the *Methanex* case stated that: '[A]s a matter of international constitutional law a tribunal has an independent duty to apply imperative principles of law or *jus cogens* and not give effect to parties' choices of law that are inconsistent with such principles.'[25]

Another area of tension that is emerging is caused by the growing interconnectedness of disputes under investment contracts and BITs. As more and more disputes

---

[22] *Saluka Investments BV (the Netherlands) v the Czech Republic*, partial award of 22 May 2006, para 254.

[23] Art 31(3)(c) of the Vienna Convention on the Law of Treaties, 1969.

[24] ILC Report, 'Conclusions of the Work of the Study Group on the Fragmentation of International Law: Difficulties Arising from the Diversification and Expansion of International Law', para 1, adopted by the International Law Commission at its 58th session, in 2006, and submitted to the General Assembly as a part of the Commission's report covering the work of that session (A/61/10, para 251). The report will appear in *Yearbook of the International Law Commission* (2006) vol II, part two.

[25] *Methanex Corporation v United States of America*, part IV, ch C, 11, final award of the tribunal on jurisdiction and merits of 3 August 2005.

under investment contracts are elevated to the status of BIT disputes, the tension between public and private interests will become starker. This is because investment contracts, especially those relating to infrastructure projects, often provide far higher levels of protection to investors by insulating them from future changes in the domestic law of the host country.[26] Known as the stabilisation clauses,[27] such provisions state that the law in force in the host state at the time the contract takes effect is the law that will apply to supplement the terms of the contract, regardless of any future change in the legal regime in the country concerned. Such stabilisation clauses not only restrict the permanent sovereignty of states over their natural resources for example, but may also clash with the obligations flowing from international human rights and environmental treaties that impose obligations on states.

Problems Posed by the Expansive or Creative Trend in Interpretation

Encouraged by the opportunities presented by globalisation, multinational enterprises and other foreign investors have been taking ambitious decisions to invest in faraway countries and territories with varying degrees of legal development. These enterprises are taking both commercial and non-commercial risks when investing in countries with unstable democracies as well as countries rife with internal strife, corruption, bad governance and politicised judiciaries.[28] Therefore, they are seeking the maximum protection possible under both international law (through a BIT or an FTA) and individual investment contracts with both substantive standards of protection and broad access to international dispute settlement mechanisms should things go wrong due to actions taken by host governments.

Governments, whether home or host, have sought to respond to this demand by providing, via BITs and FTAs, as comprehensive and as watertight provisions as possible for the protection of foreign investment and by agreeing to investment contracts with elaborate provisions that often even limit the freedom of action of the host countries concerned. Some of these BITs or investment contracts contain innovative provisions providing comprehensive protection to foreign investors. On their part, international arbitral tribunals have sought to apply, interpret and expand the scope of the standard of protection enunciated in such treaties in the light of the investment environment that existed at the time the treaties were concluded or the assurances that were given to foreign investors when they were invited into the country. These tribunals

---

[26] Referring to a number of investment contracts, Leader concludes that investment contracts 'usually contain declarations of supremacy over existing law (some exclude while others include supremacy over the host state's constitution), and all future law that applies to the project for its life time.' See Leader (n 13) 667; examples of such contracts can be found in fn 24 of this article.

[27] For a concise account of this clause, see Brownlie (n 8) 526–27.

[28] See a report on 'Doing Business in Dangerous Places', *The Economist*, 14 August 2004, 9.

have made far-reaching and enterprising decisions expanding the nature and scope of certain key principles of foreign investment law. For instance, the expanded meanings of the term 'expropriation', whether direct, indirect, regulatory or consequential, or of the phrases 'fair and equitable treatment' or 'MFN principle', or the development of new notions such as the so-called 'umbrella clause', have added new dimensions to foreign investment law.

What is more, investors have begun to claim successfully BIT protection before treaty-based tribunals against breach of investment contracts concluded with host governments even when the contract has provided for another mechanism for settling disputes of a contractual nature. This trend began with foreign investors claiming breaches of traditional treaty-based protections such as expropriation without compensation or violation of the principle of fair and equitable treatment. But the trend now also seeks to encompass the breach of the contracts themselves. This inter-nationalisation of contract claims is threatening to blur the traditional distinction in jurisprudence between public law (treaties) and private law (contracts). So much so that in a case between Turkey and US investors PSEG Global Inc and its subsidiary Konya, an ICSID tribunal awarded compensation, albeit a modest sum compared to the sum claimed, to the US investors for an alleged deliberate and successful attempt to derail PSEG Global's plans under a build, operate and transfer contract to build a coal-fired power plant in Turkey. The work to build the proposed coalmine and power plant had never commenced. Nevertheless, PSEG Global had spent substantial amounts of money on an initial feasibility study and follow-up studies, etc. Although the tribunal did not find that Turkey's actions had resulted in compensable regula-tory expropriation, it did declare that a violation of the principle of fair and equitable treatment had taken place.[29]

The Notion of 'Police Powers' of States and Regulatory Expropriation

The main reason host states conclude BITs or FTAs is to attract foreign investment. Although states limit their sovereign rights when entering into international agree-ments, as sovereign states they retain the power to regulate their economic and financial activities. Furthermore, a number of BITs and RTAs now recognise the rights of states to adopt regulatory measures designed to protect the environment. However, at times these regulatory activities have a detrimental impact on foreign investors or on their profitability, at which time they challenge the regulatory measures of the host state, claiming that such measures are tantamount to 'indirect', 'consequential' or 'regula-tory' expropriation. While international law recognises the 'police powers' of states,

---

[29] *PSEG v Turkey*, ICSID Case No ARB/02/S. The final award of 19 January 2007: www. investment-claims.com/decisions/PSEGGlobal-Turky-Award.pdf, as cited and summarized in *Investment Treaty News*, 1 February 2007, www.iisd.org/investment/itn.

eg, the power to adopt regulatory measures, foreign investment law recognises the concept of 'regulatory' expropriation. Thus, the challenge for an international tribunal called upon to adjudicate on a dispute claiming 'regulatory' expropriation is to strike a balance between these competing principles of international law.

Although it is submitted that the regulatory or 'police power' of a state is inherent in its sovereign status, a state accepts certain limitations upon its sovereignty when it concludes a BIT or an FTA with another state. By doing so, the host state gives assurances to prospective foreign investors that the exercise of its 'police power' will be conditioned by the provisions of the treaty concerned. The question that arises in this context is what is permitted under general international law as well as under the BITs or FTAs. Unless clearly prohibited in a BIT or an FTA, under general international law a host state can take certain lawful regulatory measures under narrowly defined conditions which may involve expropriation without compensation. Thus, there can be differences in approach as to what is permissible under general international law and under BITs and FTAs.

A decision of an UNCITRAL tribunal in a dispute between Saluka Investments BV (the Netherlands) and the Czech Republic is illustrative of the clash between these two competing principles of international law. The case arose out of events consequent upon the reorganisation and privatisation of the Czech banking sector. The Czech government had privatised one of the country's major banks, IPB, by selling the state's shareholding to a company within the Nomura group. Nomura bought the shares in IPB and transferred them to one of its subsidiaries, Saluka Investments BV, a company incorporated under the laws of the Netherlands. While teetering on the edge of bankruptcy, due to mismanagement and its 'generous' lending policy, IPB was put under forced administration by the Czech government in June 2000. The decision by the government to sell IPB to a Czech company, Českoslovesnká obchodní banka, for the symbolic price of one crown, prompted Nomura, which then held a 46.16 per cent stake in IPB, to initiate arbitration proceedings for the loss of its investment, claiming that these measures amounted to expropriation, even though Saluka had sold its IPB shares back to Nomura after June 2000 for the same amount as it had purchased those shares.

In its defence the Czech Republic argued that the measures taken were 'permissible regulatory actions'. The arbitration tribunal was faced with the task of deciding whether these measures were lawful measures under Article 5 of the Agreement on Encouragement and Reciprocal Protection of Investments between the Kingdom of the Netherlands and the Czech and Slovak Federal Republic.[30] The tribunal held that

---

[30] Art 5 of the Treaty reads as follows:

Neither Contracting Party shall take any measures depriving, directly or indirectly, investors of the other Contracting Party of their investments unless the following conditions are complied with:

a.   the measures are taken in the public interest and under due process of law;
b.   the measures are not discriminatory;
c.   the measures are accompanied by provision for the payment of just compensation. Such compensation shall represent the genuine value of the investments affected and shall, in order to be effective for the claimants, be paid and made transferable, without undue delay, to the country designated by the claimants concerned and in any freely convertible currency accepted by the claimants.

in imposing the forced administration of IPB on 16 June 2000 the Czech Republic adopted a measure that was valid and permissible as within its regulatory powers, notwithstanding that the measure had the effect of eviscerating Saluka's investment in IPB.[31] However, the tribunal did find that the Czech Republic had violated Article 3 of this BIT dealing with fair and equitable treatment.

Explaining the permissibility of regulatory actions by governments in general international law, the arbitral tribunal stated that: 'Article 5 imports into the Treaty the customary international law notion that a deprivation can be justified if it results from the exercise of regulatory actions aimed at the maintenance of public order.' The tribunal went on to add that

> It is now established in international law that States are not liable to pay compensation to a foreign investor when, in the normal exercise of their regulatory powers, they adopt in a non-discriminatory manner *bona fide* regulations that are aimed at the general welfare.[32]

Similarly, the tribunal in *Methanex* held in its final award that: 'It is a principle of customary international law that, where economic injury results from a bona fide regulation within the police powers of a State, compensation is not required.'[33]

As early as 1961, the Harvard Draft Convention on the International Responsibility of States for Injuries to Aliens recognised the following categories of non-compensable takings:

> An uncompensated taking of an alien property or a deprivation of the use or enjoyment of property of an alien which results from the execution of tax laws; from a general change in the value of currency; from the action of the competent authorities of the State in the maintenance of public order, health or morality; or from the valid exercise of belligerent rights or otherwise incidental to the normal operation of the laws of the State shall not be considered wrongful.[34]

This provision was regarded as representing customary international law by the arbitral tribunal in *Saluka Investments*.[35] The tribunal stated that the above-quoted passage in the Harvard Draft Convention is subject to four important exceptions:

> An uncompensated taking of the sort referred to shall not be considered unlawful provided that:
>
> (a)   it is not a clear and discriminatory violation of the law of the State concerned;
> (b)   it is not the result of a violation of any provision of Articles 6 to 8 [of the draft Convention];

---

[31] *Saluka Investments BV (the Netherlands) v the Czech Republic*, partial award of 2 March 2006: Permanent Court of Arbitration, www.pcacpa.org/ENGLISH/RPC/#Saluka (accessed 3 January 2007), para 276.

[32] Ibid.

[33] *Methanex Corporation v United States of America*, part IV, para 410, final award of the tribunal on jurisdiction and merits of 3 August 2005.

[34] See LB Sohn and RR Baxter, 'Responsibility of States for Injuries to the Economic Interests of Aliens' (1961) 55 *American Journal of International Law* 515.

[35] *Saluka Investments BV (the Netherlands) v the Czech Republic*, partial award of 2 March 2006: Permanent Court of Arbitration, www.pcacpa.org/ENGLISH/RPC/#Saluka (accessed 3 January 2007).

(c)   it is not an unreasonable departure from the principles of justice recognised by the principal legal systems of the world;

(d)   it is not an abuse of the powers specified in this paragraph for the purpose of depriving an alien of his property.[36]

The tribunal went on to add that:

[T]hese exceptions do not, in any way, weaken the principle that certain takings or deprivations are non-compensable. They merely remind the legislator or, indeed, the adjudicator, that the so-called 'police power exception' is not absolute.

It is noteworthy that an accompanying note to the 1967 OECD Draft Convention on the Protection of Foreign Property includes a broader notion of 'police power' by stating that measures taken in the pursuit of a state's 'political, social or economic ends' do not constitute compensable expropriation.[37] A similar notion is also included in the *United States Third Restatement of the Law of Foreign Relations* according to which bona fide regulations and 'other action of the kind that is commonly accepted as within the police power of State' are permissible regulatory measures.[38]

The question that arises here is what is meant by the phrase 'police powers' of states? What activities of states can be included within this principle? What are permissible regulatory measures? Is this concept dynamic and thus liable to expansion in line with developments in international law? Is the above-cited description of the 'police powers' of states accepted in general international law? It is proposed in the following paragraphs to examine these questions in light of the several candidates as lawful cases of regulatory measures.

Legitimate Expectations of Foreign Investors and the Regulatory Powers of States

Every state is confronted with the challenge of addressing changing domestic political, economic and environmental situations while honouring the promises made to outside investors when they decided to invest in the country. While it is accepted in international law that indirect expropriation claims generally cannot be based on actions aimed at protecting 'legitimate public welfare objectives', it is not clear which public welfare objectives can be regarded as legitimate. However, as has been seen in the preceding chapters, the trend in jurisprudence seems to be to require the host state to honour the status quo prevailing at the time the government offered incentives and made promises to foreign investors, encouraging and inviting them into the country.

---

[36] Ibid, para 257.

[37] OECD Draft Convention on the Protection of Foreign Property (12 October 1967), 71 ILM 117.

[38] Restatement (Third) of Foreign Relations Law, s 712 cmt g (1987).

In *International Thunderbird Gaming Corporation v Mexico* a NAFTA tribunal sitting under UNCITRAL stated that:

> Having considered recent investment case law and the good faith principle of international customary law, the concept of 'legitimate expectations' relates, within the context of the NAFTA framework, to a situation where a Contracting Party's conduct creates reasonable and justifiable expectations on the part of an investor (or investment) to act in reliance on said conduct, such that a failure by the NAFTA Party to honour those expectations could cause the investor (or investment) to suffer damages.[39]

However, the arbitral tribunal in *Saluka Investments* acknowledged that circumstances do change in the host states and they would be expected to respond to changing circumstances by adopting regulatory measures. The tribunal stated that:

> No investor may reasonably expect that the circumstances prevailing at the time the investment is made remain totally unchanged. In order to determine whether frustration of the foreign investor's expectations was justified and reasonable, the host State's legitimate right subsequently to regulate domestic matters in the public interest must be taken into consideration as well.[40]

Nevertheless, the tribunal held that the host state is under an obligation not to frustrate an investor's legitimate and reasonable expectation to be treated fairly and equally.[41]

Regulatory Measures to Protect the Environment

States have an obligation to take certain measures designed to protect the environment under both customary and conventional international law. If a state takes regulatory measures designed to protect the environment or to control pollution, these will be deemed valid measures even if they have a detrimental impact on foreign investors. New international treaties may introduce new environmental standards and obligations requiring the states party to them to enact laws and take other administrative measures to implement the provisions of such treaties. Businesses, whether local or foreign-owned or -controlled, may be required to abide by such measures. Compliance with such measures involves additional costs and such costs may undermine the profitability of a foreign company doing business in the country concerned. For instance, owing to obligations imposed by new international environmental treaties or to new environmental policies adopted by the government concerned, a host state may adopt stricter standards for the control of pollution, the discharge of chemicals into the environment, and the level of emission of harmful substances into the atmosphere, etc.

---

[39] *International Thunderbird Gaming Corporation v Mexico*, award of 26 January 2006, para 147 (footnote omitted); Award, IIC 136 (2006), 26 January 2006, Ad Hoc Tribunal (UNCITRAL).

[40] *Saluka Investments BV (the Netherlands) v the Czech Republic*, partial award of 2 March 2006: Permanent Court of Arbitration, www.pcacpa.org/ENGLISH/RPC/#Saluka (accessed 3 January 2007), para 305.

[41] Ibid, para 446.

International environmental law is more progressive in holding non-state actors liable for environmental harms. In accordance with the 'polluter-pays' principle, an array of international treaties places liability directly upon polluters, including corporations. Although these environmental treaties are designed to impose obligations on private parties through the intermediary of the state, certain of these treaties go out of the way to impose obligations directly on non-state actors. For instance, as early as 1982 the World Charter for Nature imposed direct obligations on private actors with regard to the protection of nature and natural resources, and the need to conserve these resources and exploit them in a sustainable manner.[42] The Charter declares that: 'Man can alter nature and exhaust natural resources by his action or its consequences and, therefore, must fully recognize the urgency of maintaining the stability and quality of nature and of conserving natural resources.'[43]

The Draft Code of Conduct on Transnational Corporations prepared by the UN Commission on Transnational Corporations and presented to ECOSOC in 1990[44] did contain some interesting proposals vis-à-vis TNCs. For instance, paragraphs 41 and 43 of this Draft Code dealt with environmental protection in the following terms:

> 41. Transnational corporations shall carry out their activities in accordance with national laws, regulations, established administrative practices and policies relating to the preservation of the environment of the countries in which they operate and with due regard to relevant international standards. Transnational corporations should, in performing their activities, take steps to protect the environment and where damaged to rehabilitate it and should make efforts to develop and apply adequate technologies for this purpose.
>
> ...
>
> 43. Transnational corporations should be responsive to requests from Governments of the countries in which they operate and be prepared where appropriate to co-operate with international organisations in their efforts to develop and promote national and international standards for the protection of the environment.

The 2011 OECD Guidelines also contain provisions recommending that MNEs abide by the environmental standards of host states. Similarly, the Johannesburg Plan of Implementation of the World Summit on Sustainable Development (known as the Earth Summit 2002) states in paragraph 27 that: '[T]he private sector, including both large and small companies, has a duty to contribute to the evolution of equitable and sustainable communities and societies.' Paragraph 29 goes on to state that: '[T]here is a need for private sector corporations to enforce corporate accountability, which should take place within a transparent and stable regulatory environment.'[45]

The jurisprudence of international investment tribunals is also lending some support to such an approach. For instance, in the NAFTA Chapter 11 arbitration

---

[42] UNGA Res 37/7; (1983) 22 ILM 455, adopted on 28 October 1982.
[43] Preambular paragraphs to the World Charter for Nature.
[44] See UN Doc E/1990/94, 12 June 1990.
[45] For an analysis of these provisions, see F Calder and M Culverwell, 'Following Up the World Summit on Sustainable Development Commitments on Corporate Social Responsibility: Options for Action by Governments', Final Report of the Sustainable Development Programme of the Royal Institute of International Affairs (Chatham House, London, 2005) 13 et seq.

in *Methanex*[46] the tribunal was examining, inter alia, the compatibility of regulatory powers, or the so-called 'police powers', of states in favour of the environment with the minimum standards of protection guaranteed to foreign investors under NAFTA. The tribunal's final award dismissed all of Methanex's claims and rejected some of the findings in the *Metalclad* case in which regulatory measures were regarded to be expropriation and thus compensable. The company alleged, inter alia, that the United States, as a result of the regulations, violated Article 1102 of NAFTA Chapter 11, claiming that the regulations were designed to deny foreign methanol producers, including Methanex, the same standard of treatment the US accorded to domestic ethanol investors. However, rejecting the idea that the regulations were tantamount to expropriation, the tribunal held that:

> [A]s a matter of general international law, a non-discriminatory regulation for a public purpose, which is enacted in accordance with due process and, which affects, *inter alia*, a foreign investor or investment is not deemed expropriatory and compensable unless specific commitments had been given by the regulating government to then putative foreign investor contemplating investment that the government would refrain from such regulation.[47]

Accordingly, the tribunal held that: 'From the standpoint of international law, the California ban was a lawful regulation and not an expropriation.'[48] Developments within the European Court of Human Rights and the European Court of Justice are also moving in this direction.[49] In *Hatton & Others v UK* the European Court of Human Rights held that: '[E]nvironmental protection should be taken into consideration by Governments acting within their margin of appreciation and by the Court in its review of that margin.'[50]

Indeed, a number of BITs and RTAs recognise the rights of states to adopt certain measures designed to ensure that investment activity is undertaken in a manner sensitive to environmental concerns. The provisions in Article 10.12 of the FTA between Chile and the US, Article 114(2) of NAFTA, Article 12 of the 2004 Model US BIT, Article 10.11 of CAFTA and Article 15.10 of the Singapore–US FTA are examples.[51] What is more, the Canada–Peru BIT of 2006 goes much further in narrowing the scope of indirect expropriations, and a draft article in agreement between the EU and the

---

[46] *Methanex Corporation v United States of America*, final award on jurisdiction and merits of 3 August 2005, www.state.gov/documents/organization/51052.pdf.

[47] Ibid, part IV, ch D, para 7.

[48] Ibid, para 15.

[49] Indeed, Art 1 of Protocol 1 to the European Convention on Human Rights provides, inter alia, that protection of property 'shall not ... in any way impair the right of a State to enforce such laws as it deems necessary to control the use of property in accordance with the general interest' 213 UNTS 262. See also M DeMerieux, 'Deriving Environmental Rights from the European Convention for the Protection of Human Rights and Fundamental Freedoms' (2001) 21 *Oxford Journal of Legal Studies* 521, 539–42.

[50] *Hatton & Others v UK* (2003) 37 EHRR 28 (Application 36022/97), para 122. See also S Giorgetta, 'The Right to a Healthy Environment, Human Rights and Sustainable Development' (2002) 2 *International Environmental Agreements: Politics, Law and Economics* 173.

[51] Art 10.12 of the Chile–US FTA reads as follows: 'Nothing in this Chapter shall be construed to prevent a Party from adopting, maintaining, or enforcing any measure otherwise consistent with this Chapter that it considers appropriate to ensure that investment activity in its territory is undertaken in a manner sensitive to environmental concerns.' Identical provisions can be found in a number of other BITs and FTAs.

Pacific members of the ACP countries of June 2006 admits regulatory measures as non-compensable expropriations:

> Consistent with the rights of States to regulate and the customary international law principle on police powers, bona fide, non-discriminatory regulatory measures taken by a Party that are designed and applied to protect or enhance legitimate public welfare objectives, such as public health, safety and the environment, do not constitute an expropriation under this Article.[52]

It remains to be seen whether this draft article will be adopted in the final agreement. If it did, it would set a remarkable example and strengthen a new trend emerging in the development of foreign investment law.

Regulatory Measures to Protect Human Rights

Although no major international investment dispute has occurred involving a direct or formal challenge of human rights-related regulatory measures of states, there is scope for foreign investors to challenge host states over such measures. Indeed, the threat of a lawsuit against the government of South Africa in relation to its policy efforts to promote greater racial diversity in management and ownership positions in the domestic economy[53] became a reality when three Italian mining companies, Marlin Holdings, Marlin Corp and RED Graniti SA, filed an international arbitration case with the ICSID secretariat, claiming that the laws concerning positive racial discrimination of South Africa violated investment treaties with other countries.[54] However, in such cases states should be able to invoke their human rights obligations under international treaties in defence of their regulatory measures since states have an obligation to protect human rights under both customary and conventional international law.

Some human rights, such as the right to self-determination, have even been regarded as *jus cogens*, and states are under an obligation to take measures designed to protect such rights. What is more, even foreign companies have a duty to ensure that their activities do not undermine such rights. Debate exists as to their positive obligation to promote human rights in the countries where they do business,[55] but they do have an obligation not to undermine human rights wherever they conduct their business. Since a company is treated as a legal entity with corresponding rights, it should also have responsibilities and duties towards others, including the society where its business

[52] Draft Art 8.8(I) of the investment chapter in the context of the EU/PACP EPA negotiations, DG Trade G 1(D) (2006), 10 October 2006.

[53] See International Institute for Sustainable Development (IISD), 'International Human Rights in Bilateral Investment Treaties and in Investment Treaty Arbitration', a research paper prepared by the IISD for the Swiss Department of Foreign Affairs (April 2003) 2.

[54] See 'Mining Trio Mount Court Challenge to South Africa', *Financial Times*, 9 March 2007, 8.

[55] Eg, C Wells and J Elias, 'Holding Multinational Corporations Accountable for Breaches of Human Rights', Discussion Paper, published by the Cardiff Centre for Ethics, Law and Society of the University of Cardiff, www.ccels.cardiff.ac.uk/pubs/wellspaper.html (accessed 13 January 2005).

is conducted. Hence, there is a growing pressure to hold companies accountable for human rights violations and degradation of the environment, and to specify in the duties of company directors a duty to respect societal values, including human rights and sustainable development.

If a state takes regulatory measures designed to protect and promote such rights they stand to be valid measures even if they have a detrimental impact on foreign investors. New international treaties may introduce new rights requiring the states party to them to enact laws and take other administrative measures to implement the provisions of such treaties. All natural and juridical persons, including foreign investors, may be required to abide by such measures even if compliance with such measures may involve additional costs, and such costs may undermine the profitability of a foreign company doing business in the country concerned. For instance, by a vote of 122 in favour to none against, with 41 abstentions, the UN General Assembly adopted a resolution on 28 July 2011 calling on states and international organisations to provide financial resources, build capacity and transfer technology, particularly to developing countries, in scaling up efforts to provide safe, clean, accessible and affordable drinking water and sanitation for all. This resolution is likely to accord more powers to states to regulate their water industry and could be claimed as non-compensable regulatory expropriation in favour of this right. This will have an impact on the activities of foreign investors investing in the water industry. As stated by Simma: '[I]t will be economic and social rights that will occupy a prominent place in foreign investment disputes, put forward as defenses on the part of host Sates accused of BIT violations.'[56]

There are examples of cases in which foreign companies have been held accountable for human rights violations in the host countries concerned. For instance, in a case concerning oil spills from the tanker *Amoco Cadiz* off the French coast, an American court had stated in 1984 that:

> As an integrated multinational corporation which is engaged through a system of subsidiaries in the exploration, production, refining, transportation and sale of petroleum products throughout the world, Standard is responsible for the tortious acts of its wholly owned subsidiaries and instrumentalities, AIOC and Transport.[57]

Similarly, a British citizen sued the Rio Tinto Zinc (RTZ) group of companies in England for the damage to his health while working for their subsidiary in southern Africa. In a case brought by Mr Connelly against RTZ, an MNE, the House of Lords held that companies with a UK base could be sued in the UK for the wrongs committed by them or their subsidiaries abroad.[58] In another case, *Lubbe v Cape Plc*, the House of Lords held that a British-based parent MNE could be taken to court for the injurious acts of its subsidiaries abroad.[59] Thus, courts have not hesitated to 'lift the corporate veil' to dispense justice, and to pronounce that local workers working

---

[56] B Simma, 'Foreign Investment Arbitration: A Place for Human Rights?' (2011) 60 *ICLQ* 573, 586.
[57] *The Amoco Cadiz* [1984] 2 Lloyds Rep 304.
[58] *Connelly v RTZ Plc* [1998] AC 854. See also *The Times*, 10 November 1998, 30.
[59] *Lubbe v Cape* [2000] 1 WLR 1545. For a good account of the issues involved in this case, see P Muchlinski, 'Corporations in International Litigation: Problems of Jurisdiction and the United Kingdom Asbestos Cases' (2001) 50 *ICLQ* 1.

for MNEs do have certain rights under international human rights law, including the ILO conventions.[60]

The core ILO Conventions, such as the Constitution of the ILO 1946, the 1948 Convention Concerning Forced or Compulsory Labour, the 1949 Convention Concerning the Application of the Principles of the Right to Organise and to Bargain Collectively, and the 1981 Convention Concerning Occupational Safety and Health and the Working Environment, provide for basic rights for workers. These rights include the freedom to bargain collectively, freedom of association, elimination of discrimination in the workplace, elimination of workplace abuse such as forced labour and certain types of child labour, adequate wages, proper working conditions, adequate social insurance rights, no obligatory overtime, etc. Since the provisions of these conventions have to be implemented through national laws, a host state could adopt the necessary regulatory measures to this effect and such measures may have financial implications for foreign companies in terms of higher wages or better working conditions, etc.

Indeed, the revised OECD Guidelines of 2010 enshrine the provisions contained in the core ILO instruments mentioned above and, more significantly, have also created a mechanism for monitoring corporate behaviour and investigating abuses.[61] The Guidelines state that MNEs should respect 'the human rights of those affected by their activities consistent with the host government's international obligations and commitments'.[62] Serious violations of human rights by commercial entities have long been regulated by international law. For instance, banning of the slave trade together with the abolition of slavery was the one of the first instances of enforcement of human rights law against commercial entities. Unlike other initiatives, the governments of countries in which the world's major MNEs are based have supported the new OECD Guidelines. Referring to the various ILO Conventions, Ratner rightly argues that 'both the purpose of the conventions and their wording make clear that they do recognize duties on enterprises regarding their employees'.[63]

Indeed, many ILO Conventions accord rights to employees in respect of their employment against their employers, including corporations. The primary object of the ILO Conventions is to require state parties to enact laws to safeguard the rights of workers in accordance with the Conventions. These conventions also imply that the employers, including corporations, have a duty not to interfere with the enjoyment of such rights by their employees. The UN's Global Compact programme launched by the UN Secretary General in 1999 in collaboration with business leaders sets out two distinct duties of corporations relating to human rights: (i) to respect human rights within their sphere of influence; and (ii) to avoid being complicit in human

---

[60] See generally *John Doe I v Unocal Corp* WL 31063976 (9th Cir, 18 September 2002).

[61] After failing in its attempt to adopt a legally binding MAI, the OECD adopted a set of revised guidelines for MNEs in 2000. See the OECD Guidelines for Multinational Enterprises (27 June 2010) in www.oecd.org/daf/investment/guidelines/mnetext.htm. The old OECD Guidelines can be found in *The OECD Guidelines for Multinational Enterprises* (Paris, OECD, 1997).

[62] www.oecd.org/daf/investment/guidelines/mnetext.htm.

[63] SR Ratner, 'Corporations and Human Rights: A Theory of Legal Responsibility' (2001) 111 *Yale Law Journal* 443, 478.

rights abuses.[64] The tendency to hold MNEs accountable for human rights violations is gaining acceptance not only within the human rights NGOs such as Human Rights Watch[65] but also within intergovernmental organisations such as the UN[66] and the EU.[67] As stated by Muchlinski: '[W]hat is now expected is that corporations – not unlike states – can be holders of duties to observe human rights.'[68] However, it should be emphasised that this is not the same as stating that companies are responsible for protecting human rights within their sphere of operation.

Regulatory Measures in Pursuance of Social and Economic Objectives

One of the fundamental principles of international law is the economic sovereignty of states, which has found its expression in, inter alia, the principle of the permanent sovereignty of states over their natural resources and wealth, the right of states to economic self-determination, and the right to development. Mann and Moltke state that the 'most important of host State rights – the right to regulate – is not in the gift of an investment agreement'.[69] Many states have argued before international investment tribunals that they have a right to adopt regulatory measures and any foreign investor entering the country should assume the risk of being regulated by the host state. Of course, such regulatory power should be exercised within the bounds of the law, including those set by the rule of law or by the treaties to which the host state is a party.

Both the principles of economic sovereignty and the right of economic self-determination of states are serious contenders to qualify as principles of *jus cogens*, which override all other rules, whether treaty-based or otherwise. Since the principles of *jus cogens* are non-derogable, it is doubtful whether the provisions of BITs or investment contracts can limit or undermine such principles. Of course, when concluding such BITs or investment contracts, states are doing so in exercise of their sovereign rights and the right of economic self-determination; there is no rule of international law that prevents states from accepting voluntarily limitations upon their sovereignty

---

[64] www.unglobalcompact.org/un/gc/unweb.nsf/content/thenine.htm.

[65] Human Rights Watch, 'The Price of Oil: Corporate Responsibility and Human Rights Violations in Nigeria's Oil Producing Communities' (1999), www.hrw/reports/1999/nigeria.

[66] See the UN Security Council Resolution on illegal trade in diamonds in Sierra Leone, SC Res 1306, UN SCOR, 55th Sess 4168th mtg, UN Doc S/RES/1306 (2000).

[67] European Parliament's resolution on EU Standards for European Enterprises Operating in Developing Countries: Towards a European Code of Conduct, [1999] OJ C104. Through this resolution the European Parliament called upon the European Commission to develop a binding document regulating the activities of companies' operations worldwide.

[68] PT Muchlinski, 'Human Rights and Multinationals: Is There a Problem?' (2001) 77 *International Affairs* 31, 32.

[69] H Mann and K von Moltke, *A Southern Agenda on Investment? Promoting Development with Balanced Rights and Obligations for Investors, Host States and Home States* (Winnipeg, International Institute for Sustainable Development, 2005) 11.

and freedom of action. However, a treaty or a contract that prevents the state in the future from performing such tasks as required to fashion its economic and political policy in accordance with changing economic and political realities may not be allowed to prevail over other more fundamental principles of international law which underpin the very system of international order.

In a case between LG&E Energy Corp and Argentina an ICSID tribunal held that the emergency financial measures taken by Argentina under its Public Emergency and Foreign Exchange System Reform Law to address the financial crisis in the early 2000s provided valid grounds for its claim from exemption from liability for treaty violations under the doctrine of necessity. The Argentine legislation, which had eliminated the conversion of tariffs from US dollars to pesos, had undermined the investment of foreign investors invited into the country in the 1990s to invest in newly privatised public utilities. Having accepted that the Argentine measures amounted to a violation of the principle of fair and equitable treatment embodied in the US–Argentine BIT, the tribunal was, nonetheless, willing to accept the Argentine defence of its law under the doctrine of necessity.[70]

Regulatory Powers and the Protection under Investment or State Contracts

Investment contracts, especially those relating to infrastructure projects, often provide far higher levels of protection to investors than typical commercial contracts by insulating them from future changes in the domestic law of the host country.[71] Such provisions state that the law in force in the host state at the time the contract takes effect is the law that will apply to the terms of the contract, regardless of future changes in the legal regime of the host country. Such provisions are liable not only to limit the sovereignty of states but also undermine the object and purpose of future international human rights and environmental treaties that may be concluded for the greater good of the world. Under such contracts host states often accept limitations to their own sovereignty and undertake not to enact new laws or accept new obligations under international treaties that may interfere with the business activities of foreign investors.[72]

Such contracts stipulate that the law prevailing at the time the decision was taken by foreign investors to invest in the host countries would be applicable to them and such laws would not be altered to the detriment of the investors; however, if changes

---

[70] *LG & E Energy Corporation v Argentina*, ICSID Case No ARB/02/1, decision on liability of 3 October 2006, paras 238, 240 and 266.

[71] For a discussion of stabilisation clauses, see O Schachter, *International Law in Theory and Practice* (Dordrecht, Martinus Nijhoff, 1991) 314–15. See also Leader (n 13) 667.

[72] For an account of the impact of 'stabilisation' clauses in investment contracts on sustainable development, see D Ayine et al, 'Lifting the Lid on Foreign Investment Contracts: The Real Deal for Sustainable Development', International Institute for Environment and Development (IIED), Sustainable Markets Briefing Paper, No 1 (London, September 2005).

detrimental to the foreign investor do take place, then compensation would be payable. Such provisions deter states from taking regulatory measures and the provisions of investment contracts often override the power of parliament or any other authority within the host states if such regulatory measures interfere with the business activities of foreign investors. Thus, in the words of Leader, 'The contract becomes an instrument of governance.'[73]

Although such provisions of investment contracts are liable to clash with other competing principles of international law, international investment or commercial tribunals have paid little attention to this actual and potential conflict. Certain universal principles of general international law, the principles of *jus cogens*, and the principles to be found in the UN Charter (thanks to Article 103), are capable of prevailing over any provisions in investment contracts which contradict such principles.

However, due to the narrow commercial focus of international investment or commercial arbitration tribunals, adequate attention to such competing principles of international law has not been given in resolving investment disputes. For instance, the ICSID tribunal in *Enron v Argentina*[74] held in an award of US$106 million against Argentina for breaches of, inter alia, fair and equitable treatment, that the BIT between the US and Argentina obliged Argentina to maintain a stable regulatory framework for foreign investors and that the fair and equitable treatment principle provides for the protection of investors' expectations, at least those that were promised to foreign investors at the time of investment. Citing rulings by various investment tribunals in previous cases such as *LG&E v Argentina*,[75] the Enron tribunal concluded that 'a key element of fair and equitable treatment is the requirement of a "stable framework for the investment"'. It went on to add that 'this interpretation has been considered "an emerging standard of fair and equitable treatment in international law"'.[76]

The analysis in the preceding paragraphs indicates that regulatory expropriation is basically a type of indirect expropriation which may not in every case require compensation or at least full compensation. It consists of a state's regulatory act resulting in interference with foreign-owned property that could be construed as expropriation. Within the jurisprudence of the European Court of Human Rights, a state's regulatory autonomy has been expressed as 'margin of appreciation' which is a doctrine adopted by the European Court of Human Rights for determining whether a state has complied with its obligations under the European Convention on Human Rights. Regulatory autonomy basically forms a core concept of the police power of a state under which a state can exercise such powers without international legal interference, in pursuit of public purposes, such as health, safety, national security and so on. However, the test will depend on the bona fide character of the measures taken by the state. For instance, the tribunal in *Sedco* held that it was an accepted principle of international law that

---

[73] Leader (n 13) 677.

[74] *Enron v Argentina*, award of 22 May 2007, available online at: www.investmentclaims.com/decisions.

[75] *LG&E Energy Corp, LG&E Capital Corp and LG&E International Inc v Argentine Republic*, ICSID Case No ARB/02/1, decision on liability of 3 October 2006, available at www.worldbank.org/icsid/cases/pdf/ARB021_LGE-Decision-on-Liability-en.pdf, para 125.

[76] *Enron Corporation and Ponderosa, LP v Argentine Republic*, ICSID Case No ARB/01/3, award of 22 May 2007, para 260.

'a State is not liable for economic injury which is a consequence of a bona fide regulation within the accepted police power of States'.[77] Likewise, the tribunal in *Emmanuel Too* held that a state 'is not responsible for loss of property or for other economic disadvantage resulting from bona fide general taxation or any other action that is commonly accepted as within the police power of States'.[78]

This understanding in jurisprudence is reflected in treaty practice. For instance, the Investment Agreement for the COMESA Common Investment Area makes reference to bona fide regulations and the principle of the police power in differentiating an ordinary regulatory measure from an indirect expropriation:

> Consistent with the right of States to regulate and the customary international law principles on police powers, *bona fide* regulatory measures taken by a Member State that are designed and applied to protect or enhance legitimate public welfare objectives, such as public health, safety and the environment, shall not constitute an indirect expropriation under this Article.[79]

According to the *United States Third Restatement of the Law of Foreign Relations*, bona fide regulation and 'other action of the kind that is commonly accepted as within the police power of State' are permissible regulatory measures.[80] It is widely accepted that when a regulatory measure is taken in good faith and in the exercise of the police power, it does not constitute an indirect expropriation. The United States Model BIT of 2012 provides in Annex B.4(a) that the determination of an indirect expropriation should consider the following factors:

(i) the economic impact of the government action, although the fact that an action or series of actions by a Party has an adverse effect on the economic value of an investment, standing alone, does not establish that an indirect expropriation occurred;

(ii) the extent to which the government action interferes with distinct, reasonable investment-backed expectations; and

(iii) the character of the government action.[81]

The Canadian Model BIT of 2004 contains similar rules in Annex B.13(1) and other subsequent BITs or FTAs such as the United States' FTAs with Australia (2004), CAFTA-DR (2004), Morroco (2004) and Peru (2006); Canada's BITs with Peru (2007) and Romania (2009); and the Australia–Chile (2008) and India–Republic of Korea (2009) BITs.[82] The China–New Zealand FTA of 2008 recognises additional conditions for scrutinising a state's conduct, including proportionality, discrimination and breach of the state's previous written commitments to the investor. The tribunal in *Fireman's Fund Ins Co v Mexico* held that:

> To distinguish between a compensable expropriation and a non-compensable regulation by a host State, the following factors (usually in combination) may be taken into account: whether the measure is within the recognized police powers of the host State; the (public)

---

[77] *Sedco, Inc v National Iranian Oil Co*, (1985) Iran–US CTR 248, 275.

[78] *Emmanuel Too v Greater Modesto Insurance Associates and the United States of America*, award (1989) Iran–US CTR 378, vol 23, 1989-II.

[79] Art 20(8) of the Investment Agreement for the COMESA Common Investment Area of 2007.

[80] *US Third Restatement of the Law of Foreign Relations*, s 712 cmt g (1987).

[81] Annex B [Expropriation] 4(a) of the United States Model BIT of 2004.

[82] Annex B.13(1) of Canada Model BIT of 2004. See UNCTAD, Expropriation: A Sequel 58.

purpose and effect of the measure; whether the measure is discriminatory; the proportionality between the means employed and the aim sought to be realized; and *bona fide* nature of the measure.[83]

Thus, in ascertaining what constitutes regulatory expropriation, the intent of a government that takes a regulatory measure receives relatively less attention than the effect of an act of expropriation in international investment law[84] because the effect is the strongest indication that a regulatory interference with a foreign-owned property can potentially constitute an indirect expropriation. In international law, malice or *dolus*, namely an intention to cause harm, has less significance than the effect of the action in holding a state responsible for its internationally wrongful acts, whether against other states or aliens, including foreign investors. It should be noted that *mens rea* has never been relied on to oblige a state to award compensation for expropriation. The tribunal in *Azurix Corp v The Argentine Republic* acknowledged that the principle of proportionality, as adopted by the *Techmed* tribunal, would be a useful criterion serving to determine whether a state's regulatory measures could constitute an indirect expropriation where the compensation obligation could occur.[85]

Catch-All Interpretation of the Principle of Fair and Equitable Treatment

Although traditionally the principle of fair and equitable treatment is supposed to be concerned with the obligation not to deny justice in criminal, civil or administrative adjudicatory proceedings in accordance with the principle of due process embodied in the principal legal systems of the world, the scope of fair and equitable treatment has been expanded in the recent past. As can be seen from an analysis of jurisprudence of international investment tribunals, there is a trend in interpreting the principle of fair and equitable treatment – a cardinal principle of foreign investment law – in a broad manner to catch a wide variety of state activities that have detrimental consequences for foreign investors. What are the essential ingredients or characteristics of this principle? Does it include fairness in the treatment of foreign investors by the executive branch of the host state as well as fairness in the administration of justice or in other administrative systems of the state? If the system of administration of justice in a country does not measure up to the international standards, is that system a fair one so far as the foreign investors are concerned? Can the principle of fair and equitable treatment be regarded as requiring the host state to overhaul its system of administration of justice in order to bring it up to international standards?

---

[83] *Fireman's Fund Ins Co v United Mexican States*, ICSID Case No ARB(AF)/02/01, award 83 (NAFTA Arb Trib 2006), available at http://italaw.com/sites/default/files/case-documents/ita0331.pdf.

[84] *Tippetts, Abbett, McCarthy, Stratton v TAMS-AFFA Consulting Eng'rs of Iran*, (1984) 6 Iran–US CTR 219, 225–226.

[85] *Azurix Corp v The Argentine Republic*, ICSID Case No ARB/01/12 (2003), paras 311–12.

The principle of fair and equitable treatment is not a free-standing obligation. It constitutes only those obligations that are recognised in customary international law. Indeed, one of the early cases to define the nature and scope of the principle of fair and equitable treatment was *Neer*, in which Commissioner Nielsen stated, in delivering his separate concurring opinion, that:

> In deciding claims predicated on a denial of justice, the propriety of governmental acts should be put to the test of international standards. The treatment of an alien, in order to constitute an international delinquency, should amount to an outrage, to bad faith, to wilful neglect of duty, or to an insufficiency of governmental action so far short of international standards that every reasonable and impartial man would readily recognize its insufficiency. Whether the insufficiency proceeds from deficient execution of an intelligent law, or from the fact that laws of the country do not empower the authorities to measure up to international standards, is immaterial.[86]

This statement seems to require a higher threshold for an act, whether of commission or omission, to qualify as a breach of the principle of fair and equitable treatment. Generally speaking, a reasonable and impartial person would regard the terms 'fair' and 'equitable' in this context to mean a proper balance of conflicting needs, rights and demands. In a normal context they would imply an elimination of personal feelings, interests and prejudices, or freedom from favour toward either or any side. These terms should be interpreted in the manner that they have been defined in standard English dictionaries or learned companions to law. For instance, the *Oxford Companion to Law* defines the term 'equitable' as 'What is fair, reasonable and right.'[87] Since the term 'equitable' derives from the term 'equity', the definition of 'equity' is relevant here. The *Oxford Companion* defines the term 'equity' as follows:

> The basic meaning of equity is evenness, fairness, justice, and the word is used as a synonym for natural justice. In a secondary meaning the term is used as contrasted with strict rules of law, *aequitas* as against *strictum jus* or *rigor juris*; in this sense equity is the application to particular circumstances of the standard of what seems naturally just and right, as contrasted with the application to those circumstances of a rule of law, which may not provide for such circumstances or provide what seems unreasonable of unfair. A court or tribunal is a court of equity as well as of law in so far as it may do what is right and in accordance with reason and justice. The opposition between equity and law is frequently minimized by rules of law laying down flexible standards and conferring discretionary powers, but in some cases the conflict between what is fair and just and what is lawful may arise. This distinction, sometimes opposition, between law and equity was recognized in Roman law where the action of the praetors in granting remedies in situations for which the *jus civile* provided no remedy was well recognized.[88]

Thus, the principle of fair and equitable treatment calls for an adjustment of a given situation, accommodation of competing interests, and balancing of competing principles rather than a strict adherence to the letter of the law or to the rules of foreign

[86] *LFH Neer and Pauline E Neer v Mexico* (1926), see (1927) 21 *American Journal of International Law* 555.
[87] DM Walker, *The Oxford Companion to Law* (Oxford, Clarendon Press, 1980) 423.
[88] Ibid, 424–45.

investment law enunciated in the BITs. From this standpoint, the protection available to foreign investors under this principle could be lower than that resulting from a strict adherence to the principles of the rule of law. In essence, this principle requires that international tribunals balance conflicting needs, rights and demands of both the host states and the investors in deciding investment cases rather than relying on this principle to accord a higher level of protection to foreign investors. Similarly, international law provides for a reasonably narrow interpretation of the phrase 'discriminatory treatment'. For instance, in *ELSI*, the ICJ held that in order to establish when a measure is discriminatory, there must be (i) an intentional treatment, (ii) in favour of a national, (iii) against a foreign investor, (iv) that is not taken under similar circumstances against another national.[89]

Thus, general international law does not sanction a catch-all interpretation of this principle; it calls for a generally understood definition of this principle based on its plain meaning so that investment tribunals do not unduly stretch the protection under the principle to include all sorts of governmental activities, of both omission and commission. Indeed, when interpreting the equitable principle under other areas of international law, such as the law of the sea, international courts and tribunals have demonstrated flexibility in applying this principle.[90] The ICJ has taken into account geographical, geological, topographical, economic, political, strategic, demographic and scientific factors in reaching its decision on what is equitable.

However, many ICSID or UNCITRAL tribunals seem to rely increasingly on whether or not there was a breach of the principle of fair and equitable treatment in awarding compensation to foreign investors. One such example is the award of US$106 million, to Enron against Argentina by an ICSID tribunal.[91] As has been noted previously, the expansion of the principle of fair and equitable treatment was one of the reasons given by Bolivia for its withdrawal from ICSID in May 2007, along with the allegation that ICSID tribunals have tailored the principle of fair and equitable treatment in favour of foreign corporations. Bolivian President Evo Morales was reported to have called upon all Latin American countries to denounce the ICSID Convention: '[We] emphatically reject the legal, media and diplomatic pressure of some multinationals that ... resist the sovereign rulings of countries, making threats and initiating suits in international arbitration.'[92] The decision by Bolivia has been regarded in certain quarters as an expression of growing unease on the part of developing countries with the manner in which the ICSID tribunals have handled investment disputes.

Since the principle of fair and equitable treatment is a cardinal principle of foreign investment law, it is the meaning of this principle that is at the centre of disputes in a vast majority of investment cases. One of the common allegations made by foreign

---

[89] *United States of America v Italy*, ICJ Report 1989; RLA 56, 61–62.

[90] For an analysis of the principles of fairness and equitability in international law, see generally Franck (n 14) esp chs 3 and 14.

[91] *Enron v Argentina*, award of 22 May 2007, available online at www.investmentclaims.com/decisions.

[92] As cited in the *Investment Treaty News*, 9 May 2007, www.iisd.org/investment/itn, quoting a report published in the *Washington Post*.

investors against host states is the breach of this principle. In the recent past there have been more cases alleging a breach of this principle than unlawful expropriation. Although traditionally this principle is supposed to be concerned mainly with the obligation not to deny justice in criminal, civil or administrative adjudicatory proceedings in accordance with the principle of due process embodied in the principal legal system of the world, the scope of this principle has recently been expanded beyond the original intention.

The application or interpretation of this principle in international law calls for an adjustment of a given situation, accommodation of competing interests of both host states and foreign investors, and balancing of competing principles of international law. However, it is an irony that the trend in jurisprudence of international investment tribunals is to accord a much higher and stricter level of protection to foreign investors under this principle than would be the case under a traditional definition of the principle. For instance, in *Rumeli v Kazakhstan*[93] the tribunal summarised the content of the fair and equitable treatment principle as follows:

> [T]he fair and equitable treatment standard encompasses, *inter alia*, the following concrete principles:
>
> – the State must act in a transparent manner;
> – the State is obliged to act in good faith;
> – the State's conduct cannot be arbitrary, grossly unfair, unjust, idiosyncratic, discriminatory, or lacking in due process; and
> – the State must respect procedural propriety and due process.
>
> The case law confirms that to comply with the standard, the State must respect the investor's reasonable and legitimate expectations.

This is an expansive interpretation of the principle of fair and equitable treatment. Under the traditional definition of this principle foreign investors are protected mainly against any conduct of a state that is arbitrary, grossly unfair, unjust, idiosyncratic, discriminatory or lacking in due process. In some recent cases, such as *El Paso*, international investment tribunals have gone a step further in according protection to foreign investors under the principle of fair and equitable treatment. In *El Paso v Argentina*[94] an investment tribunal in 2011 introduced the concept of 'creeping' analysis in the application of the fair and equitable treatment standard, similar to the analysis applied to determine a 'creeping' expropriation.

In essence, this principle requires international tribunals to balance the conflicting needs, rights and demands of both host states and investors in deciding investment cases rather than rely on this principle to accord a higher level of protection to foreign investors.[95] Scholars such as Muchlinski have stated that investor conduct is important

---

[93] *Rumeli Telekom AS and Telsim Mobil Telekommunikasyon Hizmetleri AS v Republic of Kazakhstan*, ICSID Case No ARB/05/16, award of 29 July 2008, at 609.

[94] *El Paso v Argentina*, ICSID Case No ARB/03/15, award of 31 October 2011.

[95] For an analysis of the principles of fairness and equitability in international law, see generally Franck (n 14) esp chs 3 and 14.

in applying the fair and equitable treatment standard by investment tribunals.[96] The argument is that foreign investors have a duty to operate investments reasonably in the host countries concerned. Indeed, if international investment tribunals take such factors into account, their interpretation or application of the fair and equitable principle would be a measured one. Article 5 of the 2012 US Model BIT provides good guidance as to the nature and scope of the principle of fair and equitable treatment. The US Model BIT states that the principle of fair and equitable treatment includes the obligation not to deny justice in criminal, civil or administrative adjudicatory proceedings in accordance with the principle of due process embodied in the principle legal systems in the world.[97]

The Extent of Protection under the Most-Favoured-Nation Clause

As seen in previous chapters, there is now a trend in favour of extending the MFN principles to cover jurisdictional matters or matters relating to the administration of justice. Although this trend is not followed universally by all international investment tribunals, the divergent views taken by different tribunals have given rise to confusion. To what extent can the MFN principle be extended? Is it applicable only to procedural difficulties or can it also be invoked to create jurisdiction that would not otherwise exist? If the presumption is in favour of a liberal interpretation, foreign investors and their lawyers may engage in treaty-shopping to find the treaty most beneficial to them, and this will give rise to further uncertainty as to the law or treaty applicable to the dispute at hand. In this age of globalisation, there exists a messy morass of treaties concluded between states to regulate different areas of economic activity. Thus, a degree of harmonisation of rules and the meaning and scope of such rules is becoming more desirable than ever before in this area of law. This may be one reason why the IISD's Model International Agreement on Investment for Sustainable Development makes it clear in its definition of the MFN principle that it applies only to substantive provisions and not procedural provisions.[98]

---

[96] P Muchlinski, '"Caveat Investor"? The Relevance of the Conduct of the Investor under the Fair and Equitable Treatment Standard' (2006) 55 *ICLQ* 527.

[97] It was in February 2009 that the Obama administration initiated a review of the US Model BIT to ensure that it was consistent with the public interest and with the administration's overall economic agenda. The new Model BIT, which was published in 2012, builds on the 2004 model BIT, in particular its carefully calibrated balance between providing strong investor protections and preserving the government's ability to regulate in the public interest. Among the new elements in the 2012 Model BIT are provisions designed to improve protections for US firms, promote transparency, and strengthen the protection of labour rights and the environment. The 2012 Model BIT expands obligations in the areas of labour and environment. The text of the 2012 Model BIT is available at: http://www.state.gov/e/eb/ifd/bit/index.htm.

[98] A footnote to Art 6(A)(a) on the definition of the MFN in the IISD's Model Agreement states clearly that: 'This Article does not apply to procedural, institutional or dispute settlement provisions of other international agreements relating to investment that enter into force after this Agreement.'

Public Disputes and Private Tribunals

Although investment tribunals such as ICSID have traditionally been regarded as private international law arbitration,[99] most investment disputes these days are in effect public disputes. Of course, the definition of the term 'commercial'[100] also includes 'investment' and not only UNCITRAL but also ICSID arbitrations can thus be categorised as 'international commercial arbitrations'.[101] But these commercial or private tribunals, often lacking in transparency and accountability, entertain in effect many public disputes involving questions of public international law. Such tribunals consist of members of varying legal qualifications, standing and experience appointed by states as well as private parties.

Many of their proceedings are held in camera and the rulings are not always published. They nevertheless, as stated by Leader, 'wield enormous power – displacing local courts and making decisions about the rules that govern major portions of host country economies and, by extension, their societies'.[102] Given the degree of impact of certain awards of investment tribunals on the economic and social policy of the host states concerned, such awards or a trend in this direction have even been described as amounting to subversion of democracy. Indeed, the recent trend in jurisprudence indicates that investment tribunals, which are characterised by van Harten as the 'businessman's court', are increasingly adjudicating on matters that have implications for public policy issues to accord greater protection to foreign investors.[103]

Many of the arbitration rules such as UNCITRAL or arbitration centres were designed originally to entertain private cases between contractual parties in commercial disputes. Their decisions were meant to affect only the parties to the dispute. However, these days such tribunals give their ruling on important questions of international law affecting not only the contractual rights and obligations of states but also their sovereign rights and other rights in international law.

What is more, many such decisions often limit the regulatory powers of states even when they are intended to implement a public policy of the state concerned or comply with the international treaty obligations of that state. Although strictly speaking the decisions of such tribunals apply only to the parties, the pronouncements that these tribunals make as to the existence or non-existence of an alleged rule of international foreign investment law or the meaning and scope of a rule have wider ramifications

---

[99] Eg, Merrills puts the ICSID arbitration under private international arbitration in his book on international dispute settlement. See JG Merrills, *International Dispute Settlement*, 3rd edn (Cambridge Cambridge University Press, 1998) 111–15.

[100] Eg, the 1985 UNCITRAL Model Law on International Commercial Arbitration defines the term 'commercial' to include investment in a long list of commercial activities.

[101] See generally on international commercial arbitration, WM Reisman et al, *International Commercial Arbitration: Cases, Materials and Notes on the Resolution of International Business Disputes* (University Casebook Series, Westbury, NY, The Foundation Press, 1997) and A Redfern et al, *Law and Practice of International Commercial Arbitration*, 4th edn (London, Sweet & Maxwell, 2004).

[102] Leader (n 13) 684.

[103] Van Harten (n 15) ch 7, 152 et seq.

and implications for other states as well as for international law as a whole. In addition, international investment tribunals, which are willing to venture into private law areas by elevating contractual disputes to BIT disputes, are not necessarily prepared to take into account public international law principles and public interests in adjudicating on such matters. Thus, these tribunals can effectively engage in 'cherry-picking' in the application of rules in settling disputes. After analysing some notable arbitration cases in the public utilities sector, Tanzi, states that: 'It has long been a commonplace that international arbitral awards interpret and apply BITs in a way favourable to foreign investors and containing the regulatory power of host states, particularly with regard to investment disputes in the public utilities sector'.[104]

Difficulty in Application of Domestic Law by International Tribunals

As the distinction between public law disputes and private law disputes becomes increasingly blurred, and more and more tribunals demonstrate their willingness to entertain contractual claims under BIT regimes, the time may come when such tribunals may be called upon to enter into the domain of domestic law in deciding international law disputes. This is because investment contracts for the granting of concessions, managing privatisation programmes, overseeing engineering projects or construction of infrastructure, or the operation of public services, stipulate that the law applicable to such contracts will be the domestic law of the host state. When a tribunal finds jurisdiction over contractual disputes pursuant to an umbrella clause or to a broad jurisdictional provisions in a BIT, that tribunal may have to examine and apply domestic law governing the obligations of the host state concerned. Such an eventuality would not only change, as stated by Nolan and Baldwin, the 'international law-driven complexion'[105] of the proceedings of international investment tribunals, but would also empower arbitrators of differing calibre and legitimacy serving on such tribunals, which often lack the degree of transparency and accountability expected of a judicial mechanism, to pass judgment on domestic law issues.

Multiplication of Proceedings and Investment Tribunals

Under the internationalisation of contract-related disputes, it is possible that different bodies of law, both domestic and international, may apply to a dispute and various

[104] See Attila Tanzi, 'On Balancing Foreign Investment interests with Public Interests in Recent Arbitration Case Law in the Public Utilities Sector', in *The Law and Practice of International Courts and Tribunals* (2012), pp 47–76.
[105] MG Nolan and EG Baldwin, 'The Treatment of Contract-Related Claims in Treaty-Based Arbitration' (2006) 21(6) *Mealey's International Arbitration Report* 5.

treaties could be invoked and different dispute settlement mechanisms could be resorted to by foreign investors. The possibility of both contract-based and treaty-based arbitration may give rise to the multiplication of proceedings between different parties involved in the dispute, and some of these may not have been a party to the initial investment contract itself. There may be situations in which even noncontract domestic law issues may become attractive to treaty-based arbitration. A possible conflict between the standards of protection available to foreign investors under domestic law on the one hand and international law on the other hand may also pose problems. For instance, principles such as fair and equitable treatment may have slightly different connotations in domestic law on the one hand and international law on the other.

What is more, there have been instances where host states have had to defend two arbitration proceedings arising out of the same dispute, which were brought under two different BITs in two different arbitral forums, the *CME* case being an example. Ronald Lauder filed a claim in London against the Czech Republic under the US–Czech Republic BIT. His allegation was that by abrogating a television licence granted to his company, Central European Media (CME), the Czech Republic had violated the Czech Republic–Netherlands BIT. But CME, which was incorporated in the Netherlands, filed a separate claim against the Czech Republic in Stockholm. An interesting feature of this case was that the two proceedings produced consistent results on the issue of breach of the BIT but opposite results on compensation. While the London tribunal did not award compensation to Lauder, finding that the breach was too remote to qualify as the cause of the harm, the Stockholm tribunal awarded CME the fair market value of the company's investment in the Czech Republic, in the sum of $350 million.[106]

The rise in the number of cases concerning the treatment of foreign investment referred to international arbitral tribunals under BITs or FTAs such as NAFTA, or other regional trade and investment agreements, or under investment contracts, has led to a rapid growth in the body of jurisprudence on the subject matter. The number of cases referred to such tribunals operating under the rules of ICSID based in Washington, DC, the Permanent Court of Arbitration (PCA) based in The Hague, UNCITRAL, and other mechanisms such as the London Court of Arbitration has recently increased a great deal. In addition, both the ICJ and the WTO's Dispute Settlement Body (DSB) have also been resorted to for the settlement of investment law disputes, albeit the number of such cases is limited. There is also a growing number of cases referred to international arbitration under the rules of the International Chamber of Commerce or other regional arbitration centres under investment contracts.

More investment cases have been referred to the international courts, investment tribunals and other dispute settlement mechanisms in the past 30 or so years than the number of international law disputes referred to the ICJ since its inception in 1945. The ever-increasing new and intriguing interpretations of various extant and evolving rules, concepts and doctrines by a plethora of international tribunals are having a profound impact on the landscape of this area of law. The applicable international

---

[106] See in GM von Mehren et al, 'Navigating through Investor-State Arbitrations – An Overview of Bilateral Investment Treaty Claims' (2004) 59(1) *Dispute Resolution Journal* 69, 76.

law on investment, both customary and conventional, between any states or between a state and a foreign investor is much more specific and further reaching than ever before. What is more, the decisions of ICSID or other international arbitrations are becoming more complex; the decisions of arbitral tribunals are getting longer and the issues involved are getting more sophisticated.

The Trend in Treaty-Shopping, Forum-Shopping and Nationality-Shopping

The culture of litigation seems to have spread rapidly to the world of foreign investment law. This is especially true in relation to countries where privatisation or economic liberalisation programmes have gone wrong, whether they be Eastern European countries or South American ones. It appears that the dispute settlement mechanism in BITs is more significant for foreign investors than other substantive protection available under such treaties. Forum selection is not new to the world of foreign investment as most BITs and investment contracts include provisions designed to offer the option of resorting to either national courts or international arbitration for the settlement of investment disputes, known as the 'fork-in-the-road' provision. But different types of forum-shopping and treaty-shopping trends are also evolving within this body of law. As stated by Rogers, the BITs often represent, 'an open invitation to unhappy investors, tempted to complain that a financial or business failure was due to improper regulation, misguided macroeconomic policy or discriminatory treatment by the host government'.[107]

The current wave of arbitration began in the 1990s following the economic and political crisis and civil unrest in Latin America which paved the way for many foreign investors to seek international arbitration. Allegations of a variety of activities of a host state as being tantamount to 'regulatory' or 'indirect' expropriations have been the most innovative yet controversial claims made by foreign investors in cases recently referred to various international arbitral tribunals. While the more recent state practice reflected in FTAs such as CAFTA of 2004 and some BITs such as the Canada–Peru BIT of 2006 seeks to limit the scope of 'regulatory' or 'indirect' expropriations, much of the jurisprudence, with the exception of a few arbitral awards made in some recent cases such as *Methanex*,[108] *Saluka Investments*[109] or *Suez and Vivendi*,[110] is full of instances of enterprising or creative interpretations that stretch the scope of the law to its limits.

---

[107] WD Rogers, UNCTAD, 'Taking of Property', Issues in International Investment Agreement Series, as cited in L Peterson, 'Changing Investment Litigation, BIT by BIT' (2001) 5(4) *Bridges Between Trade and Sustainable Development* 2.

[108] *Methanex Corporation v United States*, 44 ILM 1345 (2005), 1457 (NAFTA Ch 11 Arb Trib 2005).

[109] *Saluka Investments BV (the Netherlands) v the Czech Republic*, Swiss Federal Tribunal Decision (7 September 2006).

[110] *Suez, Sociedad General de Aguas de Barcelona, SA and Vivendi Universal, SA v Argentine Republic*, ICSID Case No ARB/03/19.

Relying on sufficiently broad-language provisions on dispute settlement in BITs, some treaty-based arbitral tribunals have established their jurisdiction even over contractual claims such as the performance of a contract. Thus, the trend towards expanding the scope of public international law arbitration to adjudicate even on certain matters of private law under contractual undertakings by invoking either the so-called 'umbrella clause' in the BITs or the 'stabilisation clause' in investment contracts, or by expanding the meaning of a substantive principle such as the MFN principle to cover dispute settlement procedures, is gaining momentum.[111] One of the first known cases successfully invoking that actions taken by a state impairing contracts may violate the BIT provision was *Lanco International v Argentina* in 1998.[112] In this case, Argentina was unsuccessful in its argument that the tribunal did not have jurisdiction to hear the claims because the contract with Lanco required that such disputes be submitted to local courts. Another case deciding on treaty-based jurisdiction to contractual disputes on the basis of a broad jurisdictional clause in a BIT was *Salini v Morocco*.[113]

Similarly, *SGS v Pakistan*[114] was perhaps the first case to examine the effect of an 'umbrella clause' of a BIT, and subsequent cases such as *SGS v Philippines*[115] and *Vivendi Universal v Argentina*[116] have given a further impetus and momentum to this trend. It was held in *Vivendi* that since the tribunal could not separate out the 'contract claims' from the BIT claims, the contract claims had to be decided by the local courts applying domestic law.[117] However, by interpreting the 'umbrella' clause also to cover access to international tribunals by foreign investors in certain matters of contractual undertakings, even if there exists a separate or exclusive dispute settlement provision under the contracts concluded between the host state and the foreign investors concerned, the *Vivendi* Annulment Committee opened up the way towards the admission of contractual claims under BITs if the alleged breaches were also breaches under BITs. The reasoning given by the Annulment Committee was that a 'state may breach a treaty without breaching a contract and *vice versa*'.[118]

The expansion of the meaning of the MFN principle to cover even dispute settlement procedures has introduced yet another new trend towards treaty-shopping or forum-shopping among foreign investors. Although it is generally accepted that any arbitration requires the explicit consent of the parties concerned, the trend in jurisprudence has been to resort to other means of deducing such consent of a host state party to the dispute by relying on not only the BIT in question but also on other treaties concluded by the state concerned by extending the nature, meaning and scope

---

[111] See Ayine et al (n 72).

[112] *Lanco International, Inc v Argentine Republic*, ICSID Case No ARB/97/6.

[113] The tribunal was relying on a broad language in allowing for international arbitration with respect to '[a]ll disputes or differences ... between a Contracting party and an investor of the other Contracting Party concerning an investment' (2003) 42 ILM 606, para 59.

[114] *SGS Société Générale de Surveillance SA v Islamic Republic of Pakistan*, ICSID Case No ARB/01/13, award of 8 September 2003.

[115] *SGS v Republic of the Philippines*, Case No ARB/02/6 (29 January 2004).

[116] *Vivendi Universal v Argentina*, ICSID Case No ARB/97/3, award of 21 November 2000.

[117] Ibid.

[118] *Vivendi Universal v Argentina*, ICSID Case No ARB/97/3, decision on annulment, 3 July 2002.

of the MFN principle. This trend in establishing indirect consent to arbitration was confirmed by a tribunal in *Maffezini*[119] and has been further developed by other tribunals in subsequent cases such as *Tecmed*[120] and especially in *Siemens v Argentina*.[121] In the latter case, the tribunal seemed in effect to support the 'cherry-picking' tendency on the part of foreign investors. This may become a disruptive development for foreign investment law if investors are allowed to invoke other BITs and possibly even investment contracts providing for a more favourable dispute settlement mechanism. Indeed, a possible disruptive impact of such developments was envisaged by the *Maffezini* tribunal itself. Although recent ICSID cases such as *Salini v Jordan*,[122] *Plama v Bulgaria*[123] and *El Paso Energy v Argentina* seem to have put a brake on this trend, it remains to be seen whether future tribunals will follow the *Maffezini* principle or the rulings in *Salini*, *Plama* and *El Paso*.[124]

Since the nationality of the foreign investor is a crucial factor in making a valid claim under a BIT, and most BITs require companies to have their seat in the home country concerned to extend the BIT protection, there have been instances in which companies have relocated to another jurisdiction in order to avail themselves of such protection. For instance, Bechtel Corporation shifted its registration from the Cayman Islands to the Netherlands to sue the government of Bolivia for the losses it incurred in Bolivia because the Cayman Islands did not have a BIT with Bolivia, whereas the Netherlands did.[125] This practice of shifting registration to acquire the flag or nationality of convenience without having 'effective economic activities' in the home country concerned may encourage nationality-shopping or the establishment of 'mailbox' operations to take advantage of the most investor-friendly BIT in existence if the laws of such home countries are lax in this regard. Furthermore, in a more recent case it was alleged that two Egyptian nationals had changed their nationality in order to bring a claim as foreign investors against Egypt before ICSID under the Italy–Egypt BIT.[126]

At present there is a complex network of thousands of BITs and FTAs containing mostly similar investment provisions. With the increased trend in forum-shopping, treaty-shopping and nationality-shopping, the picture is likely to get more complex with different lawsuits filed on the same dispute in several forums or by several parties within the same business organisation. This may become a disruptive development for foreign investment law if investors are allowed to invoke other BITs and possibly even

---

[119] *Maffezini v Kingdom of Spain*, ICSID Case No ARB/97/7, 25 January, 2000.

[120] *Tecnicas Medioambientales Tecmed SA v The United Mexican States*, ICSID Case No ARB(AF)/00/2, award of 29 May 2003.

[121] *Siemens AG v The Argentine Republic*, ICSID Case No ARB/02/8, decision of 3 August 2004.

[122] *Salini Costruttori SpA and Italstrade SpA v the Hashemite Kingdom of Jordan*, ICSID Case No ARB/02/13, decision of 15 November 2004.

[123] *Plama Consortium Ltd v Republic of Bulgaria*, ICSID Case No ARB/03/24, decision of 8 February 2005.

[124] *El Paso Energy International v Argentina*, ICSID Case No ARB/03/15, decision on jurisdiction of 27 April 2006. See also S Fietta, 'Most Favoured Nation Treatment and Dispute Resolution under Bilateral Investment treaties: A Turning Point?' (2005) Issue 4, *International Arbitration Law Rewiew* 131.

[125] *Aguas del Tunari SA v Republic of Bolivia*, ICSID Case No ARB/02/3. See von Mehren et al (n 105) 72.

[126] International Institute for Sustainable Development, *Investment Treaty News*, 27 May 2007, www.investmenttreatynews.com.

investment contracts. Indeed, a possible disruptive impact of such developments was envisaged by the *Maffezini* tribunal itself. It sought to draw a distinction between the 'legitimate extension of rights and benefits by means of the operation of the [MFN] clause, on the one hand, and disruptive treaty-shopping that would play havoc with the policy objectives of underlying specific treaty provisions, on the other hand'.[127] However, many other tribunals, such as *Tecmed*[128] and *Siemens v Argentina*,[129] followed the *Maffezini* tribunal. In *Siemens v Argentina* the tribunal seemed in effect to support the 'cherry-picking' tendency on the part of foreign investors.

As argued by Fietta, if a tribunal is willing to import the advantageous aspects of the dispute resolution provisions of a third BIT, then it should also import the disadvantageous aspects of such a treaty.[130] The *Plama* tribunal observed that the adaptation of the MFN principle from a third treaty would allow the investor to pick and choose provisions from the various BITs. If this were to be allowed,

> a host State which has not specifically agreed thereto can be confronted with a large number of permutations of dispute settlement provisions from the various BITs which it has concluded. Such a chaotic situation – naturally counterproductive to harmonization – cannot be the presumed intent of Contracting Parties.[131]

Reverse Discrimination between Domestic and Foreign Investors

Much of traditional foreign investment law is founded on the principle of non-discrimination. It is premised on the notion that there should be no unfair or undue discrimination against foreign investors doing business in a host country. Yet, this very body of law is giving rise to discrimination against domestic investors. As stated in a concept paper submitted by the EU to the WTO's Working Group on trade and investment, many countries that are keen to attract foreign investment are 'creating a sort of reverse discrimination against their own local companies'.[132] Thanks to the international law of human rights, both domestic and foreign investors enjoy the protection available under human rights instruments, including the right to property.

However, foreign investors have additional protection under customary international law, BITs, investment contracts, WTO agreements, and other regional and international instruments. They have direct access to international investment tribunals and they stand to get compensation according to international standards against

---

[127] *Maffezini v Kingdom of Spain*, ICSID Case No ARB/97/7, 25 January 2000, para 63.
[128] *Tecnicas Medioambientales Tecmed SA v The United Mexican States*, ICSID Case No ARB(AF)/00/2, award of 29 May 2003.
[129] *Siemens AG v The Argentine Republic*, ICSID Case No ARB/02/8, decision of 3 August 2004.
[130] Fietta (n 123) 134.
[131] *Plama Construction v Bulgaria*, ICSID Case No ARB/03/24, decision on jurisdiction of 8 February 2005, para 219.
[132] WTO Doc WT/WGTI/W/122, 27 June 2002.

expropriation, whether traditional direct expropriation or relatively recent forms of indirect, regulatory or consequential expropriation. Therefore, it is better to do business in many countries as a foreign investor than as a domestic investor. This may be one reason why domestic investors are increasingly looking into ways of bringing themselves under the umbrella or parentage of international business organisations. As seen in a case brought before ICSID by two Egyptian nationals, the practice of changing nationality in order to bring a claim as foreign investors against their previous home state is coming to the fore.[133]

If the object of the international law of trade and investment is to ensure a level playing-field[134] and equality before the law, the challenge for foreign investment law is to take into account the underlying ideas behind the principle of non-discrimination and treat domestic and foreign investors alike in these respects. Of course, when it comes to extending the protection under the principle of national treatment to foreign investors, it is extended on the basis of like domestic circumstances, but many other protections available to foreign investors are not available to domestic investors.

A strict application of the principle of equality before the law would mean subjecting foreign investors to the laws of host states that are also applicable to domestic investors. This would also mean requiring foreign investors to submit their disputes to national courts rather than taking the matter to international tribunals. This can happen if the national legal system of the countries concerned is up to international standards and if the independence of the judiciary is assured not only on paper but in every practical sense of the term. As and when states achieve this level of legal development, then a revival of the Calvo doctrine, whereby national courts are supposed to be resorted to prior to taking an investment dispute to an international tribunal, would be possible.

Anti-Corruption Law and Investment Disputes

Since international investment tribunals are willing to venture into private law areas by elevating contractual disputes to BIT disputes, they should also be prepared, at the same time, to look into credible claims of corruption by foreign investors, especially MNEs, regarding either securing lop-sided investment contracts from corrupt politicians and senior civil servants or other corrupt business practices. This is because international treaties such as the UN anti-corruption convention, the OECD's anti-bribery convention and other soft law instruments such as the UN Global Compact and other guidelines outlaw corrupt business practices by TNCs.

It can be argued that such anti-corruption laws are now becoming part of the corpus of international foreign investment law. In the *Enron* case the ICSID

---

[133] International Institute for Sustainable Development, *Investment Treaty News*, 27 May 2007, www.investmenttreatynews.com.

[134] SP Subedi, 'The Notion of Free Trade and the First Ten Years of the World Trade Organization: How Level Is the "Level Playing Field"?' (2006) 53 *The Netherlands International Law Review* 273.

tribunal held that it had broad powers to adjudicate on the matters before it.[135] If such tribunals can claim such broad powers, there is no reason why they should not take into account the background leading to the conclusion of investment contracts including corruption on the part of state and company officials in concluding such contracts.

Article 34 of the 1985 Model Law of UNCITRAL on International Commercial Arbitration states that a national court of the seat of arbitration can set aside an arbitral award made by an arbitral tribunal sitting under the UNCITRAL rules if the award is in conflict with the public policy of the state concerned. Although there is no internationally agreed definition of the phrase 'public policy', it would cover, as stated by Redfern and others, 'the possibility of setting aside an award if the arbitral tribunal has been corrupted in some way, or if it has been misled by corrupt evidence'.[136]

In a case decided by an ICSID tribunal it was held that investment contracts concluded through corrupt practices stand to be rejected by such tribunals. In *World Duty Free Company v Kenya* the ICSID tribunal held that a payment made by the company to the president of Kenya, Daniel arap Moi, to obtain a contract was a bribe. Since such a contract secured by using bribe was voidable in law, the ICSID tribunal would not enforce it, stating that bribery was contrary to international public policy.[137] Although the Vienna Convention on the Law of Treaties would not apply to investment contracts between a state and a foreign company, it applies to BITs. Under the Convention, fraud and corruption are valid reasons to declare a treaty null and void.[138] By applying this analogy, it would be logical to deny protection under such treaties for companies engaged in fraudulent and corrupt practices.

In another case, *Inceysa Vallisoletana v El Salvador*, an ICSID tribunal declined jurisdiction over a fraudulently or illegally made investment. No matter what protection is available to foreign investors under customary international law, or BITs or FTAs, an investment has to be made in accordance with the law of the host state to enjoy such protection. The Spanish company in this case had made various misrepresentations to secure a contract from the government of El Salvador and the ICSID tribunal was not willing to exercise jurisdiction over the matters related to such fraudulently made investment.[139]

However, in a case between Siemens and Argentina an ICSID tribunal was reluctant to investigate the allegations of corruption against Siemens even though there were serious allegations of corrupt business practice by Siemens to secure contracts in Argentina, and some officials of the company were being investigated by German law enforcement authorities. Indeed, some senior officials at Siemens seem to have

---

[135] *Enron Corporation and Ponderosa Assets, LP v Argentine Republic*, ICSID Case No ARB/01/3, decision on jurisdiction of 14 January 2004, 32–34.
[136] Redfern et al (n 101) 489.
[137] *World Duty Free Company v Kenya*, ICSID Case No ARB/00/7, award of 4 October 2006.
[138] Arts 49 and 50 of the Vienna Convention on the Law of Treaties of 1969.
[139] *Inceysa Vallisoletana v El Salvador*, ICSID Case No ARB/03/26, award of 2 August 2006.

admitted that bribery was a normal business practice, not just at Siemens but also at other competitors.[140] Some other ICSID tribunals have also been reluctant to get involved in allegations of corruption by the companies concerned when adjudicating on investment matters; examples include *Empress Lucchetti*,[141] *SGS v Pakistan*[142] and *Methanex*.[143]

The Institution of Exceptions and the Law of Foreign Investment

The regime of exceptions to be found in GATT/WTO law is being replicated or imported into some recently concluded BITs. Article XX of GATT includes a provision whereby the contracting parties can deviate from the normal trading rules if necessary to protect human, animal or plant life or health, or to conserve exhaustible natural resources. This exception was subject to the condition that such measures did not discriminate between sources of imports or constitute a disguised restriction on international trade. Furthermore, the Agreement Establishing the World Trade Organization itself embraces the idea of promoting sustainable development. It states that the contracting parties recognise that

> their relations in the field of trade and economic endeavour should be conducted with a view to raising standards of living, ensuring full employment and a large and steadily growing volume of real income and effective demand, and expanding the production of and trade in goods and services, while allowing for the optimal use of the world's resources in accordance with the *objective of sustainable development*, seeking both *to protect and preserve the environment* and to enhance the means for doing so in a manner consistent with their respective needs and concerns at different levels of economic development.[144]

The WTO Dispute Settlement Body has demonstrated in cases such as *Shrimps and Turtles*[145] that it can be more sympathetic in its attitude towards environmental concerns than the pre-WTO decisions such as the one in the *Tuna-Dolphin* cases[146] under GATT. In the *Shrimps* case, the WTO Appellate Body stated that the above-mentioned

---

[140] See a report on the statements made at an ongoing trial of Siemens officials on corruption charges at a court in Germany, 'Siemens "Had a System for Paying Bribes"', *Financial Times*, 14 March 2007, 27 and 'Results Awaited: Investors Are Stoical as Siemens Seeks to Shake Off its Past', ibid, 15.

[141] *Empresas Lucchetti*, award of 7 February 2005, 17 and 19; ICSID Case No ARB/03/4.

[142] *SGS Société Générale de Surveillance SA v Islamic Republic of Pakistan*, ICSID Case No ARB/01/13, award of 8 September 2003, 330, 350.

[143] *Methanex Corporation v United States of America*, final award on jurisdiction and merits of 3 August 2005, www.state.gov/documents/organization/51052.pdf.

[144] Marrakesh Agreement Establishing the World Trade Organization, 1994 (emphasis added).

[145] *United States – Import Prohibition of Certain Shrimp and Shrimp Products*, Report of the Appellate Body, AB-1998-4, WTO Doc WT/DS58/AB/R, 12 October 1998, (1999) 38 ILM 118.

[146] *United States – Restrictions on the Imports of Tuna*, Report of the Panel, submitted to the parties on 20 May 1994, (1994) 33 ILM 839.

preambular paragraph of the WTO Agreement was relevant to the interpretation of provisions contained in the various WTO agreements including Article XX of GATT. Pointing to the provisions of this preambular paragraph, the Appellate Body held that the contracting parties 'were, in 1994, fully aware of the importance and legitimacy of environmental protection as a goal of national and international policy'. It went on to state that the language of the Preamble

> demonstrates a recognition by WTO negotiators that optimal use of the world's resources should be made in accordance with the objective of sustainable development. As this preambular language reflects the intentions of negotiators of the WTO Agreement, we believe that it must add colour, texture and shading to our interpretation of the agreements annexed to the WTO Agreement, in this case the GATT 1994.[147]

The regime of general exceptions applied to trade in goods can also apply to the protection available to foreign investors under international law and BITs. Indeed, several recent BITs have started to spell out the exceptions to national treatment and MFN treatment under such treaties. The Mexico–UK BIT of 2006 is an example.[148] Another example is the Jordan–Singapore BIT of 2004, the provisions of which on general and security exceptions read as follows:

ARTICLE 18

General Exceptions

Subject to the requirement that such measures are not applied in a manner which would constitute a means of arbitrary or unjustifiable discrimination, between the Parties where like conditions prevail, or a disguised restriction on investments in the territory of a Party by investors of the other Party, nothing in this Treaty shall be construed to prevent the adoption or enforcement by a Party of measures:

(a) necessary to protect public morals or to maintain public order;
(b) necessary to protect human, animal or plant life or health;
(c) necessary to secure compliance with laws or regulations which are not inconsistent with the provisions of this Treaty including those relating to:

    (i) the prevention of deceptive and fraudulent practices or to deal with the effects of fraud on a default of contract;
    (ii) the protection of the privacy of individuals in relation to the processing and dissemination of personal data and the protection of confidentiality of individual records and accounts;
    (iii) safety;

(d) imposed for the protection of national treasures of artistic, historic or archaeological value;
(e) relating to the conservation of exhaustible natural resources if such measures are made effective in conjunction with restrictions on domestic production or consumption. (footnote omitted.)

---

[147] *United States – Import Prohibition of Certain Shrimp and Shrimp Products*, Report of the Appellate Body, AB-1998-4, WTO Doc WT/DS58/AB/R, 12 October 1998, (1999) 38 ILM 118, paras 129 and 152.
[148] Art 5 of this BIT spells out the exceptions and include the obligations resulting from any existing or future customs union and common market free trade area, etc.

ARTICLE 19

Security Exceptions

Nothing in this Treaty shall be construed:

(a) to require a Party to furnish any information, the disclosure of which it considers contrary to its essential security interests; or

(b) to prevent a Party from taking any action which it considers necessary for the protection of its essential security interests:

   (i)   relating to fissionable and fusionable materials or the materials from which they are derived;
   (ii) taken in time of war or other emergency in international relations;
   (iii) relating to the production or supply of arms and ammunition.

(c) to prevent a Party from taking any action in pursuance of its obligations under the United Nations Charter for the maintenance of international peace and security. [footnote omitted]

The practice of including such exceptions in a BIT is a relatively recent phenomenon and was inspired by the US Model BIT which introduced the concept. However, some investment tribunals have already had to deal with matters covered by such exceptions. For instance, in *International Thunderbird v Mexico* the tribunal stated in its decision that it would take into account the need to protect public morals.[149] The law and practice in the area of international trade law is likely to influence the application of the notion of exceptions in foreign investment law too.

States Seeking to Restrain Tribunals Rather than vice versa

Normally speaking, it is the judicial mechanism that seeks to restrain states when state machinery seeks to exceed the bounds of the law or the powers granted to the government by law, whether constitutional or otherwise. However, it is intriguing that in foreign investment law it is the states which have taken a number of measures to restrict the tribunals from exceeding the powers granted to them by the law. For instance, when tribunals in cases such as *Metalclad*[150] went out of their way to expand the meaning and scope of the term 'expropriation', the NAFTA Free Trade Commission decided to issue an interpretative statement defining what was covered by the NAFTA provisions on expropriation in an attempt to restrict reactions to the interpretations offered by such tribunals. Similarly, when tribunals in cases such as *Maffezini* and especially *Siemens* interpreted the MFN principle to extend its application to cover even jurisdictional or dispute settlement matters, states had to react to this trend by deciding

---

[149] *International Thunderbird Gaming Corporation v Mexico*, award of 26 January 2006; IIC 136 (2006), 26 January 2006, Ad Hoc Tribunal (UNCITRAL).
[150] *Metalclad Corporation v United Mexican States*, ICSID Case No ARB (AF)/97/1, 30 August 2000.

to exclude explicitly the application of the MFN principle to jurisdictional or dispute settlement matters.

As noted by the tribunal in the *Plama* case, the provisions in NAFTA and the draft FTA of 21 November 2003 to this effect were in reaction to the rulings in cases such as *Maffezini* and *Siemens*.[151] Even when states have decided explicitly to include jurisdictional or dispute settlement matters within the scope of the MFN principle in actual or Model BITs, they may have done so with a view to bringing to an end the uncertainty in jurisprudence in this regard as different tribunals began to make differing pronouncements.[152] This seems to have been one of the reasons for an interpretative statement or a shared understanding issued by the US Trade Representative of the US and the Minister for Trade and Industry of Singapore through an exchange of letters during the conclusion of the US–Singapore FTA of 2003. The exchange of letters sought to restrain future investment tribunals by outlining a shared understanding as to the nature and scope of non-discriminatory regulatory actions of the host governments.

The Principle of *Tabula Rasa* and Investment Treaties and Contracts

Although the principle of *tabula rasa* (or the 'clean slate' principle) does not have much support in international law especially with regard to the unilateral abrogation of investment treaties or commercial contracts with foreign investors, the possibility of states invoking this principle after a major political upheaval or a revolution in order to negate the BITs or investment contracts concluded by previous regimes, whether dictatorial or corrupt, cannot be discounted. According to the *tabula rasa* principle, any newly independent state is not bound to maintain in force, or to become a party to, any treaty of its predecessor state, but may establish its status as a party to any such treaty by way of a unilateral declaration.[153] Treaties that had been in force with respect to a predecessor state would not automatically become applicable to the successor state, which would come into existence free of all treaty rights and obligations applicable to the predecessor state. Such states may also invoke the principle of economic sovereignty or the right of economic self-determination to support their claim. Indeed, at the height of people's movement for democracy in Cambodia, the main opposition party in Cambodia leading the campaign, the Cambodian National Rescue Party (CNRP), announced in an open letter of 29 October 2013 concerning

---

[151] *Plama Consortium Ltd v Republic of Bulgaria*, ICSID Case No ARB/03/24, decision of 8 February 2005, para 203.
[152] Eg, the UK Model BIT clearly states in its Art 3(3) that: 'For avoidance of doubt it is confirmed that the treatment provided for in paragraphs (1) and (2) above shall apply to the provisions of Articles 1 to 11 of this Agreement.' Arts 8 and 9 of the UK Model BIT provide for a dispute settlement mechanism.
[153] A Zimmermann, 'State Succession in Treaties', in *Max Planck Encyclopaedia of Public International Law* (Oxford, Oxford Univeristy Press, 2006) para 12.

loans and investments its stance not to recognise or to review later the loan contracts, investment licences, ie the buying, selling, swapping or renting of the state private real property that were concluded by the autocratic Cambodian government.[154] The spokesman for Press and Quick Reaction Unit of the Council of Ministers reacted stating that the government 'elected' by the people and headed by Prime Minister Hun Sen had the rights to do everything within the legal framework.[155] However, given the process of the globalisation of ideas and of production, marketing and distribution networks, it is very difficult for any state in this interdependent world to invoke the principle of *tabula rasa* to escape from its international obligations. It was possible to do so to a certain extent after the agrarian revolution in Mexico or the Bolshevik revolution in Russia, but these states too had ultimately to recognise and respect the basic tenets of foreign investment law, including the right to property of foreign investors. The Litvinov agreement[156] between the US and the Soviet Union is an example.

The Notion of International Public Policy and Investment Protection

The idea that a state can adopt measures to implement or safeguard its 'public policy' or *ordre public* finds its recognition and expression in different forms. An extension of this national policy can become 'international public policy'. For instance, Article 34 of the 1985 Model Law of UNCITRAL on International Commercial Arbitration states that a national court of the seat of arbitration can set aside an arbitral award made by an arbitral tribunal sitting under the UNCITRAL rules if the award is in conflict with the public policy of the state concerned. Although there is no internationally agreed definition of the phrase 'public policy', the basic elements that are covered by this phrase would be common in most countries. The Swiss Federal Supreme Court stated that public policy denotes fundamental legal principles.[157] The Supreme Court of Justice of Ontario stated that this phrase denotes the most basic and explicit principles of justice and fairness.[158] The accumulation of the elements of domestic public policy could provide the basis for an international public policy. The French Code of

---

[154] Cambodian National Rescue Party, Open Letter on 'Loan and Investment' No 0131/13.CNRP, 29 October 2013. A copy of the letter is on file with the author.

[155] 'Opposition Warns Foreign Countries Not to Invest; Govt Reacts', *Rasmei Kampuchea*, News Roundup, Cambodia Office of the UN High Commissioner for Human Rights, 30 October 2013.

[156] It is actually known as the Litvinov assignment as the content of the Soviet undertaking came in the form of a letter to the President of the US from Litvinov, People's Commissar for Foreign Affairs. It is reproduced in *United States v Pink*, 315 US 203 at 212 (1942), as cited in A Lowenfeld, *International Economic Law* (Oxford, Oxford University Press, 2003) 393.

[157] Eg, the decision of the Swiss Federal Supreme Court of 18 September 2001 (2002) *Bull ASA* 311, as cited in Redfern et al (n 101) 497.

[158] *United Mexican States v Marvin Roy Feldman Karpa*, File No 03-CV-23500, Ontario Superior Court of Justice, 3 December 2003, para 87. See www.naftalaw.org.

Civil Procedures makes it possible to set aside an arbitral award if the recognition or execution of it 'is contrary to international public policy'.[159]

The ILA Committee on International Commercial Arbitration included in its definition of 'international public policy' the 'principles of universal application – comprising fundamental rules of natural law, principles of universal justice, *jus cogens* in public international law, and the general principles of morality accepted by what are referred to as "'civilised nations"'.[160] Thus, this definition has the possibility of including all peremptory norms of international law in the definition of 'international public policy'.[161] Consequently, the principles of economic sovereignty of states, the principle of permanent sovereignty of states over their natural resources, the right of self-determination and the principle of sustainable development may qualify for inclusion in 'international public policy' since they all are serious candidates for *jus cogens*. If this analogy is accepted, an award of an international arbitration tribunal that undermines these principles of international law could be set aside or annulled. This analogy strengthens the legitimacy of the regulatory measures of states designed to assert, strengthen or implement their legitimate public interests, including vital economic and social objectives.[162]

The Doctrine of Necessity in International Investment Law

General international law admits, under narrowly defined conditions, the possibility for states to escape from their international obligations, including those undertaken under BITs or FTAs regarding the protection of foreign investment under the doctrine of necessity or 'state of emergency'. If the claim of the doctrine of necessity is accepted by an international investment court or tribunal, the state concerned will not be required to pay compensation against any adverse consequences faced by foreign investors due to measures, whether economic, security or other, taken by the host state in order to

---

[159] French Decree Law No 81-500 of 12 May 1981, Art 1502.5, as cited in Redfern et al (n 101) 498 and sources therein.

[160] International Law Association (ILA), *Report of the Sixty-Ninth Conference, London, 2000* (London, ILA, 2000) 345–46.

[161] For a comprehensive study of the principle of *jus cogens*, see A Orakhelashvili, *Peremptory Norms in International Law* (Oxford, Oxford University Press, 2006). See also the latest position of the ILC on *jus cogens* in 'Conclusions of the Work of the Study Group on the Fragmentation of International Law: Difficulties Arising from the Diversification and Expansion of International Law', adopted by the International Law Commission at its 58th session, in 2006, and submitted to the General Assembly as a part of the Commission's report covering the work of that session (A/61/10, para 251). The report will appear in the *Yearbook of the International Law Commission* (2006) vol II, part two. Para 33 of this report reads as follows: '*The content of jus cogens*. The most frequently cited examples of *jus cogens* norms are the prohibition of aggression, slavery and the slave trade, genocide, racial discrimination apartheid and torture, as well as basic rules of international humanitarian law applicable in armed conflict, and the right to self-determination. Also other rules may have a *jus cogens* character inasmuch as they are accepted and recognized by the international community of States as a whole as norms from which no derogation is permitted' (footnote omitted).

[162] See generally on this issue, van Harten (n 15).

address a grave economic, security or other situation prevailing in the country. The power of states to take such measures is not limited to military action and war. Other emergency situations such as the impending collapse of the economy may also qualify under the doctrine of necessity. Indeed, in *LG&E v Argentina* an ICSID tribunal was prepared to admit Argentina's claim that the drastic measures that it had taken were necessary to stop the country's economic decline. The tribunal held that:

> To conclude that such a severe economic crisis could not constitute an essential security interest is to diminish the havoc that the economy can wreak on the lives of an entire population and the ability of the Government to lead. When a State's economic foundation is under siege, the severity of the problem can equal that of any military invasion.[163]

Indeed, Draft Article 25 of the ILC's Draft Articles on State Responsibility provides that a state can invoke necessity as a ground for precluding the wrongfulness of an act not in conformity with an international obligation of that state if it:

> (a) Is the only way for the State to safeguard an essential interest against a grave and imminent peril; and (b) Does not seriously impair an essential interest of the State or States towards which the obligation exists, or of the international community as a whole.[164]

However, in *Enron Corporation and Ponderosa, LP v Argentine Republic* the ICSID tribunal was not prepared to accept the argument of Argentina based on the doctrine of necessity even though the situations invoked were similar. After acknowledging that 'a major crisis indeed there was', the *Enron* tribunal held that 'these unfortunate events do not in themselves amount to a legal excuse'.[165] It went to add that:

> The Tribunal has no doubt that there was a severe crisis and that in such context it was unlikely that business could have continued as usual. Yet, the argument that such a situation compromised the very existence of the State and its independence so as to qualify as involving an essential interest of the State is not convincing. Questions of public order and social unrest could be handled as in fact they were, just as questions of political stabilization were handled under the constitutional arrangements in force.[166]

> The Tribunal must note in addition that ... the various conditions discussed above must be cumulatively met, which brings the standard governing the invocation of state of necessity to a still higher echelon. In light of the various elements that have been examined, the Tribunal concludes that the requirements of the state of necessity under customary international law have not been fully met in this case.[167]

Thus, two ICSID tribunals considering a similar set of situations reached two different conclusions with regard to the application of the doctrine of necessity. What is also ironic is that one individual arbitrator sat on both of these three-member tribunals. Similarly, in *CMS v Argentina* an ICSID annulment committee criticised the reasoning of the original arbitration on its treatment of the doctrine of necessity and went on to state that if it were 'acting as a court of appeal, it would have to reconsider

---

[163] ICSID Case No ARB/02/1, decision on liability of 3 October 2006, para 238.
[164] UN Doc A/RES/56/83.
[165] *Enron Corporation and Ponderosa, LP v Argentine Republic*, ICSID Case No ARB/01/3, award of 22 May 2007, para 232.
[166] Ibid, para 306.
[167] Ibid, para 313.

the [original] Award on this ground'. However, another example of an interesting annulment of an ICSID award was in *Sempra Energy International v Argentina*. A new jurisprudential trend was set by an ad hoc committee of ICSID in this case when this committee annulled the arbitral award previously made by an ICSID tribunal. The tribunal had found that the violations by Argentina of its investment obligations were not excused by reasons of necessity under customary international law or the US–Argentina BIT. However, the ad hoc committee held that the tribunal had manifestly exceeded its powers by committing a manifest error of law. This is a landmark decision which is likely to have far-reaching implications for international investment arbitration in the years to come.[168]

The so-called Non-Precluded Measures (NPM) clause, also known as the 'essential interest' clause,[169] provided for by international investment agreements has also been invoked in support of the application of the doctrine of necessity by international investment tribunals. The NPM clause can be found, for example, in Article XI of the US–Argentine BIT, which reads as follows:

> This Treaty shall not preclude the application by either Party of measures necessary for the maintenance of public order, the fulfillment of its obligations with respect to the maintenance or restoration of international peace and security, or the protection of its own essential security interests.[170]

Likewise, Article 18(2) of the US Model BIT provides for such a clause for essential security:

> Nothing in this Treaty shall be construed to preclude a Party from applying measures that it considers necessary for the fulfillment of its obligations with respect to the maintenance or restoration of international peace or security, or the protection of its own essential security interests.[171]

The basic objective of such clauses is to exclude the application of a treaty from certain measures taken in pursuit of the protection of public order or security. Both the customary principle of necessity and the NPM clause of necessity work to the effect that they relieve a state of responsibility for violations of international obligation. Both the customary principle of necessity and the NPM clause were invoked by Argentina in investment disputes that arose in the context of Argentine economic crisis of 2001. As stated above, the notion 'necessity' also appears in WTO law, in particular, the WTO General Exceptions (GATT Article XX and GATS Article XIV) which operate the necessity exception test for the protection of certain public purposes. The necessity exception can be invoked by a state in order to justify or defend its derogation or deviation from its obligations under WTO law.

Although the WTO-type necessity exception test may not be immediately available for application to investment cases, the potential utility of the necessity defence for the operation of international investment law demands careful reconsideration

---

[168] *Sempra Energy International v Argentina*, ICSID No ARB/02/16, 29 June 2010.
[169] G Sacerdoti, 'BIT Protection and Economic Crises: Limits to their Coverage, the Impact of Multilateral Financial Regulation and the Defence of Necessity' (2013) 28 *ICSID Review* 351, 356.
[170] Art XI of the US–Argentine BIT.
[171] Art 18(2) of the US Model BIT of 2012.

because it is possible that the necessity exception test can provide useful legal guidance in scrutinising a state's necessity plea. It has often been argued that economic necessity is covered by the principle of necessity. In both the *CMS* and *LG&E* cases, the arbitration tribunals concerned examined the concept of necessity but reached contrasting conclusions. While the former tribunal did not accept the plea of necessity of Argentina,[172] the latter tribunal accepted the plea on the grounds that Argentina's essential interests were threatened.[173] Whatever the outcome will be in these cases, it is generally accepted that the necessity defence can be relied on by a state temporarily as long as the situation of necessity lasts, and when such a situation ceases to exist, the original obligation will restore.

The Notion of *Force Majeure* in Foreign Investment Law

One of the arguments that has been advanced in some cases by host states in defence of their regulatory or emergency measures has been the notion of *force majeure*. Indeed, the emergence of extraordinary and unforeseeable events has long provided grounds for parties to a contract to request its termination on the grounds that the contract has become excessively onerous. The underlying idea behind it is to allow for an opportunity for rebalancing the contractual benefits and obligations between the parties concerned through renegotiations. Draft Article 23 on State Responsibility prepared by the ILC recognises the concept of *force majeure*, according to which the situation should not only be extraordinary and unforeseeable but it also should be as a result of occurrence of an irresistible force, beyond the control of the state, making it materially impossible in the circumstances to perform the obligation. However, as stated in the commentary to this Draft Article: '*Force majeure* does not include circumstances in which performance of an obligation has become more difficult, for example due to some political or economic crisis.'[174]

Resource Nationalism and the Revival of the Calvo Doctrine

There appears to be some movement in a number of Latin American countries towards the revival in a different form of some of the tenets of the Calvo doctrine. Resource

---

[172] *CMS Gas Transmission Company v The Republic of Argentina*, ICSID Case No ARB/01/8, paras 320–21.
[173] *LG&E Energy Corp, LG&E Capital Cor., and LG&E International, Inc v Argentine Republic*, ICSID Case No ARB/02/1, – para 257.
[174] J Crawford (ed), *The International Law Commission's Articles on State Responsibility: Introduction, Text and Commentaries* (Cambridge, Cambridge University Press, 2002) 171.

nationalism has resurfaced in some South American countries against foreign investors, initially driven primarily by President Hugo Chavez of Venezuela and President Evo Morales of Bolivia. Both of these states have sought either to renationalise foreign-controlled businesses in certain sectors[175] or to renegotiate investment contracts with foreign investors in the hydrocarbon sector.[176] Other countries, such as Ecuador, have also attempted to change their oil contracts with foreign companies. Bolivia has even denounced the ICSID Convention, making it the first country publicly to take action against the international regime for the settlement of investment disputes, stating that the ICSID dispute settlement mechanism is not in its national interests.[177] Following the failure of the government of Venezuela and Conoco Phillips and Exxon Mobil to agree the terms of a handover of operations in the oil-rich Orinoco belt to the state-owned oil company PdVSA, the government decided in June 2007 to take over the multibillion dollar projects owned by these companies.[178]

Although the Bolivian and Venezuelan campaigns for resource nationalisation have not been outright expropriations, as was the case with some other countries in the past, some MNEs affected by these measures have decided to resort to ICSID, alleging that such requirements to renegotiate existing contracts amount to a breach of international law on foreign investment. Although settlement was agreed by the parties and proceeding discontinued at the request of the company, this case did raise some interesting issues in this regard. The drive to renegotiate investment contracts seems to be designed to persuade foreign companies to renegotiate their contracts with the government, which would result in more revenue for the state and transfer of commercialisation rights.[179] Of course, sovereign states such as Bolivia and Venezuela have a right, in principle, to renegotiate investment contracts with foreign companies so long as they stay within the rule of law. They can carry out their decisions by mutual consent with affected foreign companies. They may also go ahead and expropriate the assets of foreign companies with compensation, provided that such expropriations meet the others tests of international law.

Countries such as Argentina whose privatisation programmes have encountered problems have also sought to renegotiate investment contracts by mutual consent with foreign investors as an alternative to settling disputes through international courts and tribunals. During the 1990s, a period that saw privatisation programmes, economic liberalisation and deregulation, Argentina was one of the major destinations for foreign investment in the developing world. Much of the foreign investment Argentina was receiving was in the service sector, geared to serving the domestic market, and in the exploitation of natural resources, which was geared to exporting products to the world market.

---

[175] See 'Chavez in Push to Nationalise Key Industries', *Financial Times*, 9 January 2007, 1 and 'Morales Seizes Swiss Tin Smelter', *Financial Times*, 10 February 2007, 6.

[176] See M Cali, 'Why Evo Morales Is Not Going to Be the Next Hugo Chavez', Opinion Paper, Overseas Development Institute, London, February 2007, www.odi.org.uk (accessed 23 February 2007).

[177] As reported in the *Investment Treaty News*, 9 May 2007, www.iisd.org/investment/itn. See *Eni Dación v Venezuela Eni Dación BV v Bolivarian Republic of Venezuela* (ICSID Case No ARB/07/4).

[178] 'Venezuela Takes Over Orinoco Oil Projects', *Financial Times*, 27 June 2007, 7.

[179] See 'Energy and Nationalisation: Barking Louder, Biting Less', *The Economist*, 10 March 2007, 71.

However, events such as the collapse of the currency board and the ensuing financial meltdown required Argentina to take emergency measures to protect its legitimate national interests. Foreign companies adversely affected by such measures began to resort to international investment arbitration, seeking compensation against existing losses and loss of future earnings. While cases against Argentina brought by some companies were progressing before ICSID and other arbitration tribunals, the government of Argentina was able to persuade many responsible and longer-term foreign investors to renegotiate investment contracts to reflect the new reality of the country. In order perhaps to pre-empt possible legal action by foreign companies such as those witnessed against Argentina, Bolivia expressed its intention to pursue revisions to its 24 BITs with various countries in the following three areas: the definition of investment; performance requirements; and dispute resolution.

The Attempt to Seek Protection against Commercial Risks

The main objectives of foreign investment law are to provide protection against political risks in the host country concerned, to increase economic efficiency, and to ensure legal certainty and predictability to foreign investors. However, the foregoing analysis of the recent trends in jurisprudence and the practice of foreign investors demonstrates that many foreign investors are seeking protection against business or commercial risks under various rules of foreign investment law by trying to come up with creative interpretations of such rules. As stated by the PCIJ in the Oscar Chinn affair of 1934:

> No enterprise ... can escape from the chances and hazards resulting from general economic conditions. Some industries may be able to make large profits during a period of general prosperity, or else by taking advantages of a treaty of commerce or of an alteration in customs duties; but they are also exposed to the danger of ruin or extinction if circumstances change. Where this is the case, no vested rights are violated by the State.[180]

However, the claims made by many foreign investors against host states before international courts and tribunals allege a wide range of governmental activity that may produce negative consequences for foreign investment as measures tantamount to indirect expropriation or violation of the fair and equitable treatment principle, and some investment tribunals have been persuaded by this. In view of the decisions handed down in the past by ICSID and other tribunals, which appear to give a very broad meaning to the notion of 'indirect' or 'consequential' expropriation or make an error in the interpretation or application of international foreign investment law, there was a fear that erroneous decisions of such tribunals could become the law of tomorrow. However, some of the more recent cases have demonstrated that the ICSID system can hand out more balanced awards. Nevertheless, future tribunals are under no obligation to follow such rulings and they can always change the direction.

---

[180] *Oscar Chinn*, PCIJ, 1934, Ser A/B, Case No 63.

The Investor-State Dispute Settlement Mechanism

In the absence of an international investment court, states hosting foreign investment or investor states have opted for an ad hoc investor-state dispute settlement (ISDS) mechanism through arbitration under such treaties for settling investment disputes, whether it is under ICSID, UNCITRAL or other ad hoc arbitrations. This ad hoc mechanism has brought its own challenges to the international law of foreign investment due to inconsistencies in the application and interpretation of the key principles of international investment law by such arbitration tribunals. Furthermore, there is no appellate mechanism to bring about some cohesion and consistency in jurisprudence. The investment treaties enable foreign investors to sue host governments but not vice versa, albeit under narrowly defined conditions the host governments can bring counterclaims.[181] Therefore, there are currently various proposals mooted by various scholars to address these challenges and they range from tweaks to BITs and IIAs, creation of an appellate mechanism and the negotiation of a multilateral treaty to proposals for reform of ISDS only.

In August 2010 a group of prominent international law academics issued a Public Statement on the International Investment Regime in which they said that they

> shared concern for the harm done to the public welfare by the international investment regime, as currently structured, especially its hampering of the ability of governments to act for their people in response to the concerns of human development and environmental sustainability.[182]

Accordingly, they stated that:

> States have a fundamental right to regulate on behalf of the public welfare and this right must not be subordinated to the interests of investors where the right to regulate is exercised in good faith and for a legitimate purpose.

> Awards issued by international arbitrators against states have in numerous cases incorporated overly expansive interpretations of language in investment treaties. These interpretations have prioritized the protection of the property and economic interests of transnational corporations over the right to regulate of states and the right to self-determination of peoples. This is especially evident in the approach adopted by many arbitration tribunals to investment treaty concepts of corporate nationality, expropriation, most-favoured-nation treatment, non-discrimination, and fair and equitable treatment, all of which have been given unduly pro-investor interpretations at the expense of states, their governments, and those on whose behalf they act. This has constituted a major reorientation of the balance between investor protection and public regulation in international law.

---

[181] T Kendra, 'State Counterclaims in Investment Arbitration – A New Lease of Life?' (2013) 29 *Arbitration International* 575.
[182] This public statement, initiated by a group of international law academics in Canada and supported by many other academics, is available at: www.osgoode.yorku.ca/public-statement-international-investment-regime-31-august-2010/.

> The award of damages as a remedy of first resort in investment arbitration poses a serious threat to democratic choice and the capacity of governments to act in the public interest by way of innovative policy-making in response to changing social, economic, and environmental conditions.

They went on to state that:

> Investment treaty arbitration as currently constituted is not a fair, independent, and balanced method for the resolution of investment disputes and therefore should not be relied on for this purpose. There is a strong moral as well as policy case for governments to withdraw from investment treaties and to oppose investor-state arbitration, including by refusal to pay arbitration awards against them where an award for compensation has followed from a good faith measure that was introduced for a legitimate purpose.

The ISDS mechanism has been criticised in many other quarters for producing inconsistency and confusion in jurisprudence resulting in a public backlash against this mechanism. The mechanism was initially designed primarily for settling narrow commercial law disputes of private law character, but is now often called upon to adjudicate upon public law and public international law matters affecting the rights of the public in many countries. Many commentators[183] are of the opinion that the current system is simply not working, as evidenced by the fact that a number of states are terminating their BITs and others are publicly retreating from investment arbitration. South Africa, for example, is in the midst of withdrawing from the ISDS regime provided for in various investment protection treaties. The South African government is systematically terminating all of its BITs with the ultimate aim of introducing domestic legislation, which will govern the treatment of foreign investors in its territory.[184]

There is some clear evidence that other states may follow suit, with Indonesia having already discontinued 17 out of 64 IIAs and intending to discontinue more in

---

[183] See eg, UNCTAD, 'Reforming the International Investment Regime: An Action Menu' (June 2015), http://unctad.org/en/PublicationChapters/wir2015ch4_en.pdf (accessed 28 June 2015); UNCTAD, 'World Investment Report 2015', available at http://unctad.org/en/PublicationsLibrary/wir2015_en.pdf (accessed 20 July 2015); M Waibel, A Kaushal, K Chung and C Balchin (eds), *The Backlash against Investment Treaty Arbitration: Perceptions and Reality* (Alphen aan den Rijn, Kluwer, 2010); G Van Harten, 'A Case for an International Investment Court', presentation at Society of International Economic Law Conference, 2008 available at http://papers.ssrn.com/sol3/papers.cfm?abstract_id=1153424 (accessed 23 June 2015); J Kalicki and A Joubin-Bret (eds), *Reshaping the Investor-State Dispute Settlement System* (Leiden, Brill, 2015); N Hachez and J Wouters, 'International Investment Dispute Settlement in the 21st Century: Does the Preservation of the Public Interest Require an Alternative to the Arbitral Model', Leuven Centre for Global Governance Studies, Working Paper No 81 (2012), available online https://ghum.kuleuven.be/ggs/publications/working_papers/new_series/wp81-90/wp-81-hachez-wouters-iil-arbitration-and-the.pdf (accessed 20 July 2015); and S Schill, 'Editorial: Towards a Normative Framework for Investment Law Reform' (2014) 15 *Journal of World Investment and Trade* 795.

[184] See UNCTAD IIA Navigator, South Africa has very few BITs and IIAs currently in force; many have been terminated recently, http://investmentpolicyhub.unctad.org/IIA/CountryBits/195#iiaInnerMenu (accessed 23 June 2015) and see also Norton Rose Fulbright, 'South Africa's Changing Approach to Investment Protection: What Does it Mean for Investors?' April 2015, www.nortonrosefulbright.com/knowledge/publications/127737/south-africas-changing-approach-to-investment-protection (accessed 23 June 2015).

the years ahead.[185] Nicaragua and Venezuela have also signaled a similar intention.[186] Bolivia,[187] Ecuador[188] and Venezuela[189] have all already denounced the ICSID Convention. Furthermore, there have been rumours swirling for some time that Argentina might be the next state to announce its withdrawal from ICSID.[190] Interestingly, in 2008, more than 50% of registered ICSID cases were pending against Latin American countries. Moreover, in 2012, around 25% of new ICSID disputes involved a Latin American respondent.[191] Thus, the most frequent respondents in ICSID arbitration are the ones who appear to have lost faith in the system.[192]

However, South American states are not the only ones to signal retreat from the ISDS regime. In April 2011 the Australian Labour government issued a trade policy statement asserting that Australia should avoid signing agreements containing ISDS provisions:

> [T]here are considerable policy and financial risks arising from ISDS provisions [and therefore] ... Australia should seek to avoid accepting ISDS provisions in trade agreements that confer additional substantive or procedural rights on foreign investors over and above those already provided by the Australian legal system.[193]

Although subsequent Australian governments have indicated that they may not take such a hostile approach to ISDS, the Australian approach seems to be to review the inclusion of ISDS clauses in future Australian FTAs on a 'case by case basis'.[194] Interestingly in 2012 UNCTAD also recommended 'limiting resort to ISDS and increasing the role of domestic judicial systems ... or even refraining from

---

[185] A Jailani, 'Indonesia's Perspective on Review of International Investment Agreements', Investment Policy Brief, South Centre, No 1 (July 2015).

[186] S Appleton, *Latin American Arbitration: The Story Behind the Headlines* (International Bar Association), available at http://ibanet.org/Article/Detail.aspx?ArticleUid=78296258-3B37-4608-A5EE-3C92D5D0B979> as cited in L Trakman, 'Australia's Rejection of Investor-State Arbitration' in L Trakman and N Ranieri (eds), *Regionalism in International Investment Law* (Oxford, Oxford University Press, 2013) 344.

[187] S Manciaux, 'Bolivia's Withdrawal from ICSID' (2007) 5 *Transnational Dispute Management*.

[188] ICSID News Release, 9 July 2009, https://icsid.worldbank.org/ICSID/FrontServlet?requestType=Case sRH&actionVal=OpenPage&PageType=AnnouncementsFrame&FromPage=NewsReleases&pageName=Announcement20 (accessed 30 May 2015).

[189] ICSID News Release, 26 July 2010, https://icsid.worldbank.org/ICSID/FrontServlet?requestType=CasesRH&actionVal=OpenPage&PageType=AnnouncementsFrame&FromPage=Announcements&pageName=Announcement100 (accessed 30 May 2015).

[190] Hogan Lovells News, http://www.hoganlovells.com/newsmedia/newspubs/pubDetail.aspx? publication=8717 (accessed 30 May 2014) and see also R Dalmaso Marques, 'Notes on the Persistent Latin American Countries' Attitude towards Investment Arbitration and ICSID', fn 5, Kluwer Arbitration Blog, 23 July 2014, http://kluwerarbitrationblog.com/blog/2014/07/24/some-notes-on-the-latin-american-countries- attitude-towards-investment-arbitration-and-icsid/ (accessed 28 June 2015).

[191] C Titi, 'Investment Arbitration in Latin America: The Uncertain Veracity of Preconceived Ideas' (2014) 30 *Arbitration International* 357.

[192] Ibid, where Titi argues that, 'the overall Latin American approach does not amount to a rejection of investment arbitration, nor should it necessarily be perceived as particularly hostile to it'.

[193] Australian Government Trade Policy Statement, 12 April 2011 www.acci.asn.au/getattachment/b9d3cfa e-fc0c-4c2a-a3df-3f58228daf6d/Gillard-Government-Trade-Policy-Statement.aspx (accessed 30 May 2015).

[194] See Australian Government Department of Foreign Affairs and Trade, ISDS FAQs, www.dfat.gov.au/fta/isds-faq.html (accessed 22 December 2014) and L Nottage 'The Anti-ISDS Bill before the Australian Parliament', http://blogs.usyd.edu.au/japaneselaw/2014/09/anti-isds_bill.html (accessed 28 June 2015).

offering ISDS'.[195] Additionally, the potential inclusion of ISDS in the proposed TTIP caused public outcry in Europe, causing the European Commission to issue a public consultation on investment protection in the proposed TTIP agreement in spring 2014. The Commission received 150,000 (largely negative) responses, causing it to reconsider its position, and to issue a concept paper entitled 'Investment in TTIP and Beyond – The Path for Reform'.[196] It is clear that there are fundamental, deep-rooted problems with the regulation of foreign investment. Khor states that the ISDS system

> has come under heavy criticism, including that the tribunal decisions are arbitrary and can contradict decisions of other tribunals in similar cases. There is often a conflict of interest situation. A few lawyers monopolise the international investment arbitration business; they act as lawyers in one case and as arbitrators in other cases. In a few cases, an arbitrator was on the Board of Directors of the parent company of the investor that took up the case. There is a pro-investor bias in many cases, with decisions or arguments that are quite clearly unfair to the governments being sued. However there is no appeal possible.[197]

He goes on to add that:

> [T]he ISDS system must be the world's most problematic and outrageous judicial system. Its decisions can cost a country billions of dollars. It is riddled with conflicts of interest involving the judges, the lawyers and the proponents of the case. Yet its hearings and decisions are shrouded in secrecy and even the very existence of the cases are often not public information.[198]

A report by two European groups, Transnational Institute and Corporate Europe Observatory, has alleged that:

> A small group of lawyers, working either for investors, or as arbitrators, and who are based in Europe and North America, have been benefitting from the boom in litigation linked to investment agreements, and they also encourage big companies to sue governments.

The report, 'Profiting from Injustice', revealed that:

— Only 15 arbitrators, nearly all from Europe, the US or Canada, have decided 55% of all known investment-treaty disputes. This small group sits on the same panels, acts as both arbitrators and counsels and call on each other as witnesses.

— Many arbitrators show a clear bias towards investors. Several prominent arbitrators have been members of the board of major multinational companies, including those who filed cases against developing countries.

— A few law firms have been encouraging investors to sue governments, as a weapon to weaken or prevent laws on public health or the environment. These investment lawyers are the new 'ambulance chasers' and have fuelled an increase in cases from 38 in 1996 to 450 known cases in 2011.

---

[195] UNCTAD, *Investment Policy Framework for Sustainable Development* (UN, New York, 2012) 43–44.
[196] EU Commission Concept Paper, 'Investment in TTIP and Beyond – The Path for Reform' (5 May 2015), available at http://trade.ec.europa.eu/doclib/docs/2015/may/tradoc_153408.PDF (accessed 11 May 2015).
[197] M Khor, 'When Foreign Investors Sue the State', *South Views*, No 100, 8 January 2014.
[198] M Kohr, 'The World's Worst Judicial System?', *South Views*, No 36, 30 July 2013.

— Countries have to pay exorbitant legal and arbitration costs averaging over US$8 million per dispute, and exceeding US$30 million in some cases.

— Lobbying by arbitration law firms and arbitrators succeeded in stopping reform of investment agreements in the EU and US in the four years prior to the report.

— Fairness and independence of investment arbitration is an illusion.[199]

Indeed, frustrated with BITs and their arbitration, a growing number of governments have started to retreat from the system. For instance, India started a review of its existing BITs and suspended all BIT negotiations to protect its interests. As noted above, South Africa has decided to stop negotiating new BITs and to renegotiate existing ones; and Bolivia, Ecuador and Venezuela have terminated several treaties and withdrawn from ICSID. However, the problem these countries encounter is that under a 'survival clause' in many BITs even if a country withdraws, or if a treaty expires, the provisions will remain in force for some time to come, typically 10–15 years. Nevertheless, there is growing dissatisfaction with the unfairness of the ISDS system and calls for reform are being made by more countries.

Adding its concern about the impact of international investment treaties in general and the ISDS system in particular, UNCTAD stated in 2015 that:

> IIA reform should address five main challenges. It should aim at (i) preserving the right to regulate in the public interest so as to ensure that IIAs' limits on the sovereignty of States do not unduly constrain public policymaking; (ii) reforming investment dispute settlement to address the legitimacy crisis of the current system; (iii) expanding the effective investment promotion and facilitation dimension in IIAs; (iv) ensuring responsible investment to maximize the positive impact of foreign investment and minimize its potential negative effects; and (v) enhancing the consistency of the global IIA regime so as to overcome the gaps, overlaps and inconsistencies of the current system and establish coherence in investment relationships.

Accordingly, UNCTAD went on to propose a variety of policy options for meeting these challenges while examining their pros and cons:

— *Preserving the right to regulate*: Options include clarifying or circumscribing provisions such as most favoured-nation (MFN) treatment, fair and equitable treatment (FET), and indirect expropriation, as well as including exceptions, eg for public policies or national security.

— *Reforming investment dispute settlement:* Options include (i) reforming the existing mechanism of ad hoc investment arbitration while keeping its basic structure (eg improving the arbitral process, avoiding frivolous claims), (ii) adding new elements (eg building in alternative dispute resolution or introducing an appeals facility), or (iii) replacing existing ad hoc investment arbitration systems (eg establishing a standing international investment court, or relying on State–State dispute resolution).[200]

---

[199] P Eberhardt, B Redlin, C Toubeau, 'Trading Away Democracy: How CETA's Investor Protection Rules Threaten the Public Good in Canada and the EU' (published by an alliance of civil society organisations including Association Internationale de Techniciens, Amsterdam, November 2014) 5.

[200] UNCTAD, *World Investment Report 2015: Reforming the World Investment Regime* (UNCTAD, Geneva, 2015).

Although one of the reasons for opposition to the ISDS mechanism is inconsistency in jurisprudence by tribunals against whose decisions no appeal is possible, the main reason seems to be the growing concern of states that investment tribunals have started to encroach upon the public policy space of sovereign states.

Stabilisation and Umbrella Clauses

Stabilisation and umbrella clauses in IIAs have turned out to be some of the most controversial provisions as they have been invoked and sometimes misapplied or misinterpreted by international investment tribunals. Stabilisation clauses were introduced in the 1930s to satisfy oil companies investing in long-term infrastructure projects in developing countries. They were designed to respect the sanctity of technical commercial contracts. Such clauses were included in investment contracts. However, when states began to conclude BITs stabilisation clauses began to be included in such treaties too. Consequently, these clauses have been invoked to argue against the actions of host states to pursue their public policy. Likewise, umbrella clauses have been invoked in international investment arbitrations to seek remedy under treaties other than those specifically negotiated between the states concerned.[201] Once an umbrella clause is included in a BIT or an IIA it has been interpreted as if it was meant to provide protection under any kind of treaty concluded by the host state with any other states for any purpose.

Conclusions

In spite of the massive growth in the number of BITs and FTAs and the trends in the jurisprudence of international investment courts and tribunals there remain many issues within foreign investment law that are not fully resolved. In the absence of a comprehensive international treaty codifying the rules of foreign investment law, many issues within the area remain open to differing interpretations by such tribunals as well as by states. Therefore, there is a need to address these issues within foreign investment law in order to bring consistency for the benefit of host states and foreign investors alike.

---

[201] J Antony, 'Umbrella Clauses since SGS v Pakistan and SGS v Philippines – A Developing Consensus' (2013) 29 *Arbitration International* 607.

8

Addressing Current Challenges in International Investment Law

Introduction

As seen in the preceding chapters, various developments within international investment law are pointing in different directions, adding to the existing confusion and inconsistency. Various proposals are currently being mooted by a number of scholars to address these challenges; these proposals range from tweaks to BITs and IIAs, the creation of an appellate mechanism, and the negotiation of a multilateral treaty to proposals for exclusive reform of the investor-state dispute settlement (ISDS) mechanism. The actions that states are pursuing to address these challenges include clarifying the meaning of core treaty provisions (through authoritative interpretations) such as the meaning of the terms 'investment', 'fair and equitable treatment', and 'regulatory expropriation'; revising treaties (through amendments); replacing older treaties (through renegotiation); or terminating/consolidating treaties (either unilaterally when the term of the treaty is about to expire or by mutual consent). The aim of this chapter is to explore various ways and means of addressing the current challenges within international investment law outlined in the previous chapter.

A Global Comprehensive Treaty on Foreign Investment

Experience within the Doha Round of the WTO and elsewhere demonstrates that states are reluctant to commit themselves to an international treaty unless they are fully satisfied with the provisions of such a treaty. Those very states that conclude a BIT or an FTA with provisions favourable to foreign investors seem reluctant to do the same in the case of a multilateral international agreement with similar provisions. One reason for this could be that a BIT or an IIA has a limited or fixed lifespan – they are normally valid for 10 or 20 years – after which the unwilling state concerned would no longer be bound by the provisions of such a contractual treaty, albeit the state would continue to be bound by the general principles enunciated in the treaty. States can also easily denounce a bilateral or other contractual treaty by giving advance notice. It is also easier to renegotiate such treaties since the number of states party to them are small.

However, an agreement to conclude an international treaty would mean committing the state to the provisions of the treaty for a long time to come, and it would be harder to denounce or withdraw from such treaties. This is especially so in the case of a WTO agreement since the WTO system does not allow participants to pick and choose. If a state wishes to withdraw from a WTO agreement it will have to withdraw from the WTO itself. What is more, unlike BITs, many international treaties could be regarded as law-making treaties. Thus, by agreeing to conclude an international treaty the state(s) concerned would be contributing to the making of general international law on the subject matter which would be binding on all. Once agreed, it would be much harder to renegotiate an international treaty involving a large number of states.

However, an ideal solution to address many of the problems in foreign investment law would, of course, be to have a comprehensive global investment treaty. It would be the preferred way of harmonising the rules, trends and practices in foreign investment law, and it would bring about some consistency and uniformity in protecting foreign investors. Such a treaty would, in principle, eliminate the need for individual BITs between two state parties, as do various WTO agreements on international trade law. At present there is a complex network of thousands of BITs, FTAs and other IIAs containing investment provisions, most of which contain a similar set of provisions. With the increased trend in forum-shopping, treaty-shopping and nationality-shopping the picture is likely to get more complex. However, the negotiation of a global treaty on foreign investment law is not currently on the agenda of any international organisation. Thus, it looks unlikely that a global comprehensive treaty on foreign investment law will be concluded in the near future.

Nevertheless, the case for the conclusion of such a treaty is more compelling today than ever before. Much of the ICSID and UNCITRAL jurisprudence arising out of the interpretation of the provisions of the BITs or NAFTA has a limited scope, due partly to the inconsistent approach taken by various panels and partly to the application of *lex specialis* rather than *lex generalis* by these panels. Although it has often been asserted by NAFTA parties before the ICSID and UNCITRAL tribunals that the NAFTA provisions were not intended to create a 'new' interpretation of expropriation, the survey of the evolution of foreign investment law in the preceding chapters demonstrates that the ICSID and UNCITRAL tribunals have in some cases gone beyond the norms of pre-existing customary international law while deciding on NAFTA or other BIT cases. Much of the focus of jurisprudence has been on the legality of governmental action affecting foreign investment. Neither BITs, FTAs, IIAs nor jurisprudence provide clear guidance with regard to the level of remedy or compensation available to foreign investors against breaches of obligations other than those relating to expropriation. Furthermore, it is by no means unknown for arbitral tribunals faced with similar circumstances to reach different decisions.

In the absence of both a global treaty and a hierarchy of international tribunals required to follow precedent, foreign investment law has remained controversial and the various tribunals seem to be free to interpret the law in a manner they deem appropriate. Some of the core principles relating to expropriation and the meaning and scope of terms such as 'just', 'adequate', 'full', 'prompt', 'effective' and 'fair', as well as the concepts of the 'due process of law', 'fair and equitable treatment' and 'full protection and security', have been applied to varying degrees by international courts and tribunals since there is still no internationally agreed definition of these terms. Furthermore, neither BITs nor jurisprudence provides clear guidance as to the distinction between legitimate non-compensable regulations that have an effect on the economic value of investments, on the one hand, and so-called 'regulatory takings' requiring compensation on the other. In the absence of clarity, some of the ICSID and UNCITRAL panels have often muddied the water and compounded the problems rather than clarifying the scope of certain key principles of foreign investment law. Therefore, it has become imperative to draw a distinction between legitimate non-compensable regulations and 'regulatory takings' which are akin to 'creeping' or 'disguised' expropriation.

What is needed is a balancing act that will preserve the regulatory authority of sovereign states under clearly and narrowly defined conditions when protecting foreign investors. As seen earlier, the new breed of FTAs and BITs seek to limit the excessive protection claimed by foreign investors by outlining the characteristics of direct or indirect, or outright or creeping, expropriations and spelling out the nature and scope of the customary international foreign investment law with a view to protecting the legitimate regulatory or police powers of states. However, these attempts have yet to be translated into an instrument of global or international character. In the absence of an international instrument aimed at achieving a balancing act it will be open to various tribunals, such as ICSID or UNCITRAL, to make awards based on an expansive interpretation of terms such as 'fair and equitable treatment' or 'full protection and security', or emerging notions such as 'regulatory takings', thereby undermining the sovereignty of states to take measures in exercise of their so-called 'police powers' for the global or national public good.

In the absence of a concerted effort to balance foreign investment law with other competing principles of international law, such as the protection and preservation of the environment and human rights, the world may witness further chaos and confusion in this area of law in the years to come. The irony is that even private disputes between a state and an investor on a variety of investment matters are having massive impacts on public matters. What is actually happening in many cases, such as *Azanian v Mexico*,[1] before ICSID or other arbitration tribunals is that public international law arbitration is taking place in the name of private law arbitration. Therefore, a comprehensive international treaty on foreign investment prescribing uniform standards of treatment of foreign investors in the host countries and the creation of an international court of foreign investment, modelled perhaps on the WTO's dispute settlement mechanism, are needed.

A global treaty could bring together generally accepted principles and norms on the regulation of foreign investment such as the notions of corporate social responsibility

---

[1] *Azanian v Mexico*, ICSID Case No ARB (AF)/97/2, 1 November 1999. In this case the termination of a contractual concession to supply solid refuse collection and disposal services to a local authority in Mexico was claimed to be an expropriation. UNCTAD, *World Investment Report 2003: FDI Policies for Development: National and International Perspectives* (New York, UN, 2003) 117 (UN Sales No E.03.II.D.8).

and corporate social governance to be found in 'soft law' instruments such as the UN Global Compact or the OECD Guidelines. It could harmonise different trends in state practice, balancing environmental and human rights protection with investment protection. This is partly what the IISD's Model International Agreement on Investment for Sustainable Development of 2005 seems to have tried to achieve. There are many other plausible reasons in favour of the conclusion of a comprehensive international treaty on foreign investment.

Whether by design or by default, the liberalisation of trade in goods and services is being followed by the liberalisation of investment. It is better to adopt an international instrument to manage this change either through the UN or the WTO or the World Bank rather than leave it entirely to market forces or ad hoc tribunals of ICSID or other arbitration fora. Many developing countries that have opposed the adoption of an international treaty on investment within the WTO have been forced through the decisions of ICSID and other investment tribunals to accept pro-investment standards. It would be better for the developing countries to have an internationally negotiated treaty than for them to accept the often unbalanced and controversial dicta of such tribunals.

The WTO itself could be asked to revive the negotiations for such a treaty on foreign investment. Alternatively, the matter could be referred back to the UN, after which either the International Law Commission (ILC), ECOSOC or UNCTAD or UNCITRAL which negotiated the Mauritius Convention on Transparency in 2014, or even the UN Commission on Sustainable Development, could be entrusted with the task of developing and negotiating such a treaty. The World Bank itself or even the World Economic Forum in Davos could be entrusted with the task of facilitating negotiations among states to conclude a global investment treaty.

A Global Model Treaty

In the absence of a legally binding global treaty, a widely respected model treaty could be adopted as a 'soft law' instrument. This could greatly influence the development of the law in the desired direction. For instance, the IISD's Model International Agreement on Investment for Sustainable Development is already having some impact on state practice. While certain BITs, such as the one concluded between Canada and Peru in 2006 and the Nigeria–Morocco BIT of 2016, have incorporated the provisions enshrined in this Model Agreement, negotiations of certain other treaties also seem to have been influenced by it. In the absence of a legally binding treaty, a UN body such as the ILC, the Commission on Sustainable Development, ECOSOC, UNCTAD or UNCITRAL, or the World Bank or the WTO or the World Economic Forum could negotiate and recommend a model treaty on investment. This is already the case with UNCITRAL, which adopted a Model Law of International Commercial Arbitration in 1985, which has been enacted by a sizeable number of states.

Campaigns in favour of the environment and human rights launched by various corporate social responsibility or corporate social governance organisations seem to have had some impact even on certain hard-core areas of commercial law. The inclusion in the UK's Companies Act 2006 of a duty to pay attention to the environment in the list of a company director's duties is an example. Under this law, directors of UK companies now have a duty not only to maximise profits but also to consider the impacts of their business operations on the community and the environment. Although this seems to be the first time that such responsibilities have been written in national company law, the trend set by the UK is likely to have a measurable influence on the company laws of other countries around the globe. The UK Companies Act 2006 also puts in place a link between reporting requirements and directors' duties. This makes it clearer that the reports must show how directors are performing in terms of their duties to society and the environment. This is quite a novelty and a remarkable trend in incorporating some of the elements of corporate social responsibility and corporate social governance.

A Set of Interpretative Statements or Draft Articles by the International Law Commission

Like the 2001 Draft Articles on State Responsibility or the 1978 Draft Articles on MFN clauses,[2] the ILC could be entrusted with the task of formulating or developing draft articles on the main principles of foreign investment law. Such draft articles could define the scope of application of the core principles of foreign investment law. These articles could also take the form of an interpretative statement similar to the statement issued by the NAFTA Trade Commission which sought to define the nature and scope of some of the principles of foreign investment law embodied in NAFTA. Similarly, CAFTA provides for the acceptance of interpretative statements by the CAFTA Trade Commission. In the world of international law and investment tribunals, such draft articles would carry a significant weight. Having a set of draft articles is better than having none at all. Indeed, modest efforts have been made within the UN Human Rights Council to come up with a set of human rights principles[3] governing the activities of MNEs, the main agents of foreign investment.[4] This perhaps represents a modest revival within the UN of an attempt to adopt a set of rules to regulate foreign investment at least in the area of human rights.

Prominent candidates for such an interpretative statement or draft articles are (i) the definition, meaning and scope of the principle of 'fair and equitable treatment'; (ii) the definition of 'indirect expropriation'; (iii) the nature and scope of both 'legitimate

---

[2] Text adopted by the International Law Commission at its 30th session, in 1978, and submitted to the General Assembly as a part of the Commission's report covering the work of that session (para 74). The report, which also contains commentaries on the draft articles, appears in the *Yearbook of the International Law Commission* (1978) vol II, part two.

[3] See 'Human Rights Principles and Responsibilities for Transnational Corporations and Other Business Enterprises', UN Doc E/CN.4/Sub.2/2002/XX; E/CN.4/Sub.2/2002/WG.2/WP.1.

[4] D Vasella, 'Business Must Help Frame New Human Rights Rules', *Financial Times*, 8 April 2004, 19.

regulatory' powers or the 'police powers' of states; (iv) 'legitimate expectations' and (v) the 'umbrella clause' as these are becoming more controversial and complex issues both in the literature and in the jurisprudence of international courts and tribunals. For instance, in defining the meaning, nature and scope of the principle of 'fair and equitable treatment' a number of factors could be taken into account, and one of these is the overall conduct of both investors and host states. As stated by Muchlinski,[5] if investor conduct is taken into account in applying the fair and equitable treatment standard by investment tribunals, their decisions would be more balanced. He argues that:

> It is necessary for investment tribunals to give attention to the underlying 'bargain' between investor and host country and to ask whether each side is keeping to it. In essence that is what fair and equitable treatment is about: is the host country acting in accordance with the legitimate expectations created for the investor at the time the investment was entered into, thereby allowing the investor a reasonable opportunity to profit, and is the investor delivering, to the best standard of care and due diligence, the reasonably anticipated economic and other benefits of the investment? That would appear to encapsulate the true aims and purposes of investment treaties as they are currently drafted.[6]

If proposals such as this are incorporated into an international instrument they would go a long way to providing guidance to international investment tribunals. There are a number of other candidates suitable for definition through a draft article of the ILC or an interpretative statement.

Balanced Free Trade Agreements and Bilateral Investment Treaties

The FTAs are a new breed of ambitious bilateral treaties that seek not only to regulate in as much detail as possible the rules governing trade and investment relations between the parties concerned but also to influence the development of the law at the international level through their practice. They also seek to provide guidance to future investment dispute settlement tribunals as to how some of the key principles of foreign investment law should be interpreted. Indeed, a report produced by a committee of the US Congress points out the need for clarity regarding the various principles and key terms of foreign investment law. This report also instructs US negotiators to seek, inter alia, to establish in future negotiations on foreign investment agreements standards for expropriation and for fair and equitable treatment consistent with US legal principles and practice, including the principle of due process.[7] Accordingly, the FTA agreement concluded by the US with Singapore provides in an

---

[5] P Muchlinski, '"Caveat Investor"? The Relevance of the Conduct of the Investor under the Fair and Equitable Treatment Standard' (2006) 55 *ICLQ* 527.
[6] Ibid, 556.
[7] S Rep 107–39 (107th Cong, 2d Sess) 13–15 (2002).

Annex that: 'An action or a series of actions by a Party cannot constitute an expropriation unless it interferes with a tangible or intangible property right or property interest in an investment.'[8] The agreement speaks of two types of expropriations, direct and indirect. An indirect expropriation is an action or series of actions by a party that have an effect equivalent to direct expropriation without formal transfer of title or outright seizure. The agreement goes on to outline the nature of indirect expropriation:

(a) The determination of whether an action or series of actions by a Party, in a specific fact situation, constitutes an indirect expropriation, requires a case-by-case, fact-based enquiry that considers, among other factors:

   (i) the economic impact of the government action, although the fact that an action or series of actions by a Party has an adverse effect on the economic value of an investment, standing alone, does not establish that an indirect expropriation has occurred;

   (ii) the extent to which the government action interferes with distinct, reasonable investment-backed expectations; and

   (iii) the character of the government action.

(b) Except in rare circumstances, non-discriminatory regulatory actions by a Party that are designed and applied to protect legitimate public welfare objectives, such as public health, safety, and the environment, do not constitute indirect expropriation.[9]

Thus, such provisions were designed to provide additional guidance on the manner in which the term 'expropriation' should be interpreted in the future. They limit the freedom of ICSID or other tribunals to interpret the term 'expropriation' broadly, and therefore any regulation that reduces corporate profits or value could not be interpreted as a creeping or other form of expropriation.[10] The US–Singapore FTA goes on to spell out the understanding of the parties about the nature and scope of customary international law applicable to foreign investment. It reads: '[C]ustomary international law results from a general and consistent practice of States that they follow from a sense of legal obligation.'[11] There is nothing much new or exciting about this statement, as international lawyers know that is how customary international law is formed. However, the statement with regard to the Minimum Standard of Treatment is more interesting. It states that: '[T]he customary international law minimum standard of treatment of aliens refers to all customary international law principles that protect the economic rights and interests of aliens.'[12]

Although the provisions of agreements such as these are likely to have a tremendous impact on the future development and interpretation of customary international foreign investment law, it is difficult, at least at this stage, to maintain that what the

---

[8] Side letter of 6 May 2003 on expropriation exchanged between the US and Singapore as an integral part of the FTA between the two countries: www.ustr.gov/new/fta/singapore.htm.
[9] Ibid.
[10] See V Been and J Beauvais, 'The Global Fifth Amendment? NAFTA's Investment Protections and the Misguided Quest for an International "Regulatory Takings" Doctrine' (2003) 78 *New York University Law Review* 30.
[11] Side letter of 6 May 2003 on customary international law exchanged between the US and Singapore as an integral part of the FTA between the two countries: www.ustr.gov/new/fta/singapore.htm.
[12] Ibid.

US has agreed with Chile and Singapore is an accurate reflection of the status of customary international law. The BITs and the FTAs are also *lex specialis* in character. Of course, examples of *lex specialis* may in due course transform themselves into *lex generalis*, yet there is no convincing evidence to suggest at this stage that this has already taken place. In both the *Enron* and *CMS* cases the tribunals concerned sought to imply that the *lex specialis* contained in certain BITs had become the general rule in connection with international claims.[13] However, such an approach was rejected by Argentina in its arguments presented to the tribunal in *Sempra Energy v Argentina*.[14]

A more balanced BIT could also address the problem of multiplication of disputes or conflict-of-laws issues by requiring a potential investor to choose between the BIT dispute settlement mechanism and the mechanism stipulated in the investment contract itself. It could also address the problem with regulatory expropriations. For instance, after concluding a more balanced BIT with Peru in favour of environmental and human rights protection in 2006, Canada seems to have proposed a similar provision in a Canada–India Foreign Investment Protection Agreement. However, India was reported to have opposed the proposal since India and other developing countries have been resisting attempts by developed countries to introduce human rights issues into the world of trade and investment.[15]

However, if there were enough pressure on governments, or political will on the part of governments, provisions such as those included in the Peru–Canada BIT or in the agreement between the EU and ACP countries or in the Nigeria–Morocco BIT[16] could be inserted into existing BITs and investment contracts by concluding protocols to amend them in order to bring about some order and consistency in the interpretation of the term 'expropriation'. Ejims states that: 'There is no doubt that the trend to create a balanced investment treaty through the Morocco–Nigeria BIT has been achieved, at least by empowering the host State to regulate in relation to legitimate welfare matters and counter-balancing investor protection with a series of obligations on conduct of investment'.[17] Similarly, it should also be noted that environmental impact assessment of developmental projects has become a standard requirement for the granting of planning permission or the approval of development projects above a certain threshold in most jurisdictions. Investment contracts and possibly BITs could extend this notion to require that foreign investors must subject their major investment projects to environmental, human rights and other social impact assessments in the host country. Since certain core principles of corporate social responsibility have generally been accepted by the business community, they could be included in investment contracts, BITs and other IIAs.

---

[13] *Enron Corporation and Ponderosa Assets v Argentine Republic*, ICSID Case No ARB/01/3, 14 January 2004 (jurisdiction), and *CMS Gas Transmission Co v Argentine Republic*, ICSID Case No ARB/01/8, 17 July 2003.

[14] *Sempra Energy v Argentine Republic*, ICSID Case No ARB/02/16, 11 May 2005, para 135 (jurisdiction).

[15] International Institute for Sustainable Development, *Investment Treaty News*, 13 June 2007, www.investmenttreatynews.com.

[16] Okechukwu Ejims, 'The 2016 Morocco–Nigeria Bilateral Investment Treaty: More Practical Reality in Providing a Balanced Investment Treaty?' (2019), *ICSID Review* 34, no 1, pp 62–84.

[17] Ibid, p 84.

Enhancing the Balancing Role of Investment Tribunals and Courts

International investment tribunals cannot play the role of a legislative body. However, like all systems based on the rule of law, international investment tribunals can become self-correcting mechanisms in terms of the interpretation and development of the rules of international law, leading the way in achieving a balance between the competing principles of international law and avoiding excesses. According to Article 38 of the Statute of the ICJ, decisions of international courts and tribunals are a subsidiary source of international law. Thus, even in the absence of a global comprehensive treaty on foreign investment law, it is possible for international courts and tribunals to balance competing principles and interests. Since these courts and tribunals apply international law, operate within international legal framework and are regarded as institutions of public international law, they have a duty, as stated in *Saluka*, to pay attention to all competing principles of international law and interests when making an arbitral award or deciding on cases referred to them.

It is submitted that such tribunals have, as a matter of international constitutional law, a 'duty to apply imperative principles of law or *jus cogens* and not to give effect to parties' choices of law that are inconsistent with such principles'.[18] It could also be argued that in deciding investment disputes they have a duty to uphold the fundamental principles of international law, such as the universal principles of human rights and the core principles of international environmental law, including the principle of sustainable development, intergenerational equity, sustainable exploitation of natural resources, etc. For instance, relying basically on a preambular provision concerning the principle of sustainable development, the WTO Dispute Settlement Body was able to pay adequate attention to environmental considerations in the *Shrimps and Turtles* case when deciding a trade law dispute.[19]

Investment tribunals could be expected to do the same in resolving investment disputes by invoking the generally or universally accepted norms of international environmental law and human rights principles. Indeed, the decision in *Methanex* has already demonstrated that an investment tribunal can lead the way in striking a balance between competing principles within foreign investment law. Rejecting the wider interpretation of the term 'expropriation' in *Metalclad*, the ICSID tribunal sitting under NAFTA stated in *Methanex* that regulatory measures could not be regarded as expropriatory measures.[20]

---

[18] *Methanex Corporation v United States of America*, ICSID Case, part IV, ch C, 11, final award of the tribunal on jurisdiction and merits of 3 August 2005, www.state.gov/documents/organization/51052.pdf.

[19] *United States – Import Prohibition of Certain Shrimp and Shrimp Products*, Report of the Appellate Body, AB-1998-4, WTO Doc WT/DS58/AB/R, 12 October 1998, (1999) 38 ILM 118.

[20] *Methanex Corporation v United States of America*, ICSID Case, part IV, ch C, 11, final award on jurisdiction and merits of 3 August 2005, www.state.gov/documents/organization/51052.pdf.

Methanex Corporation relied on the interpretation of expropriation in *Metalclad* as well as the pronouncements made in the *Pope & Talbot* and *SD Myers* cases. However, the tribunal in *Methanex* rejected the arguments of creeping or regulatory expropriations advanced by Methanex Corporation and offered a narrow and more balanced interpretation of expropriation. It held that:

> In this case, there is no expropriation decree or a creeping expropriation. Nor was there a 'taking' in the sense of any property of Methanex being seized and transferred, in a single or a series of actions, to California or its designees.

The tribunal cited and endorsed the ruling in *Waste Management v Mexico*; the tribunal in that case had held that in applying the minimum standard of fair and equitable treatment it is relevant that the treatment is 'in breach of representations made by the host State which were reasonably relied upon by the claimant'.[21] By applying this standard the tribunal in *Methanex* concluded that no such commitments were given to Methanex Corporation: '[T]he California ban was made for a public purpose, was non-discriminatory and was accomplished with due process. ... From the standpoint of international law, the California ban was a lawful regulation and not an expropriation.'[22]

This ruling also draws support from *Feldman v Mexico* in which the regulatory action taken by Mexico was not regarded as having deprived the claimant of control of his company. The claimant was free to pursue other continuing lines of business activity. Thus, the main criterion in determining whether a regulatory measure was tantamount to expropriation was dependent on whether the measure resulted in the deprivation of control of the company by the foreign investor. This is a narrower interpretation of the so-called regulatory expropriation and is consistent with traditional international law standards.

Similarly, in *Noble Ventures, Inc v Romania*[23] an ICSID tribunal dismissed the investor's claims, finding that there was no breach by Romania of the US–Romania BIT of 1992. The case involved a dispute between a US company, Noble Ventures, Inc, and Romania arising out of a privatisation agreement concerning the acquisition, management and operation of a Romanian steel mill, Combinatul Siderugic Resita, and other associated assets. The US company claimed that Romania had failed, inter alia, to honour the terms of several agreements related to the control of the mill in violation of the principle of fair and equitable treatment, and that its behaviour was tantamount to expropriation.

However, the tribunal found that the substance of Noble Venture's claims was without merit. Interpreting the scope and meaning of the term 'full protection and security', the tribunal noted that the duty to provide full protection and security is not to be understood as an absolute standard providing for strict liability but as a due diligence standard. Accordingly, the tribunal found no specific failure by Romania to exercise due diligence in protecting the investment by Noble Ventures. Referring to the

---

[21] Ibid, part IV, ch D, 4.
[22] Ibid, part IV, ch D, 7.
[23] *Noble Ventures v Romania*, ICSID Case No ARB/01/11, 12 October 2005.

provision in the 1992 BIT regarding 'full protection and security' available to foreign investors, the tribunal stated as follows:

> [I]t seems doubtful whether that provision can be understood as being wider in scope than the general duty to provide for protection and security of foreign nationals found in the customary international law of aliens. The latter is not a strict standard, but one requiring due diligence to be exercised by the State.[24]

Similarly, with regard to the broader application of the MFN principle to cover even jurisdictional matters, more recent ICSID cases such as *Salini v Jordan*[25] and *Plama v Bulgaria*[26] have sought to reverse the trend introduced in *Maffezini*. It remains to be seen whether future tribunals will follow the *Maffezini* principle or the rulings in the *Salini* and *Plama* cases.[27] Although most such decisions are based on a *lex specialis* created by the states concerned though a BIT or an FTA, the tribunals may draw on *lex generalis* when interpreting and applying the principles of *lex specialis*.

There is a tendency both in the literature and subsequent arbitrations to regard certain decisions of ad hoc arbitration tribunals applying *lex specialis* as a subsidiary source of *lex generalis*. Although the common law principle of precedent does not apply in international arbitrations, it does not prevent a later tribunal from drawing on the decisions of an earlier tribunal when convenient. In fact, in practice most arbitration tribunals refer to the decisions of earlier tribunals as a guide when interpreting certain principles of *lex specialis* to be found in BITs or FTAs or *lex generalis*. For instance, not only cases such as *Chorzow Factory*, *Barcelona Traction* and *ELSI* decided by the PCIJ and its successor ICJ, respectively, but also *SGS v Philippines*, *Vivendi*, *Metalclad*, *Methanex*, *Starrett Housing* and *Methanex* decided by ad hoc tribunals have been widely referred to in subsequent arbitration decisions.

However, since there is no obligation to respect an earlier precedent, each and every arbitration tribunal in a network of tribunals is independent of each other and thus free to come up with its own interpretations of various principles of foreign investment law. It is not uncommon for one tribunal to disagree with the opinions of another tribunal or even to criticise the reasoning in a decision of another tribunal. For instance, the tribunal in *Plama* stated that it was 'puzzled' by the reasoning of the tribunal in *Maffezini* as to the extension of the MFN principle to cover jurisdictional or dispute settlement matters.[28] It would have been more puzzled had it had the time to consider the reasoning or the ruling in *Siemens* on the same matter. As stated by Fietta, the *Plama* tribunal 'stopped short of denouncing the conclusion reached in *Maffezini*, which it described as being a case where "extraordinary circumstances" had been present'.[29]

---

[24] Ibid, para 164.

[25] *Salini Costruttori SpA and Italstrade SpA v the Hashemite Kingdom of Jordan*, ICSID Case No ARB/02/13, decision of 15 November 2004.

[26] *Plama Consortium Ltd v Republic of Bulgaria*, ICSID Case No ARB/03/24, decision of 8 February 2005.

[27] See S Fietta, 'Most Favoured Nation Treatment and Dispute Resolution under Bilateral Investment treaties: A Turning Point?' (2005) Issue 4 *International Arbitration Law Review* 131.

[28] *Plama Consortium Ltd v Republic of Bulgaria*, ICSID Case No ARB/03/24, decision of 8 February 2005, para 221.

[29] Fietta (n 25) 137.

In 2010, Philip Morris Products S.A. and related entities launched an arbitration under the 1998 Switzerland–Uruguay BIT against Uruguay's tobacco control measures. In 2011, Philip Morris Asia Limited brought claims under the 1993 Australia–Hong Kong BIT against Australia's mandatory 'plain' packaging of tobacco products. In the end Philip Morris lost both disputes. The ICSID tribunal demonstrated how international investment law can accommodate public health and other domestic policy objectives. The award of July 2016 in *Philip Morris v. Uruguay* accorded appropriate weight to sovereign regulatory objectives: 'investment tribunals should pay great deference to governmental judgments of national needs in matters such as the protection of public health'.[30] This is a landmark ruling because it supports regulatory powers of not only Uruguay but of States in general to adopt laws and regulations to protect public health.

Creating an Appeal Mechanism against Arbitral Awards

The idea of creating an appeal mechanism against the arbitral awards of ICSID and other tribunals has existed for some time. It has been widely held that an appeal mechanism would bring about more cohesion and more legal certainty to this body of law. The idea received more support in 2007 when an ICSID annulment committee found an error in the application of law by a previous tribunal but expressed its inability to do much about it. Although the ICSID annulment committee in *CMS* v *Argentina* overturned a portion of an arbitration ruling, it concluded that it lacked the power to overturn certain other portions of that award which the committee had found to contain significant legal errors. After criticising the reasoning of the original arbitration in its treatment of the doctrine of necessity, the annulment committee went on to state that if it were 'acting as a court of appeal, it would have to reconsider the [original] Award on this ground'. Some tribunals assert some self-claimed importance of the pronouncements that they make in their decisions, whether or not other tribunals or publicists agree with such assertions.[31]

It has been widely held that one possible way of addressing the anomaly that exists in the current system of international investment tribunals would be to allow for an appeal against certain decisions of arbitral awards under narrowly defined conditions. This could be built into the internal mechanisms of existing international instruments such as the ICSID or UNCITRAL rules. Indeed, the ICSID Secretariat itself initiated a discussion in 2004 into the possible creation of an appeal mechanism against the decisions of ICSID tribunals by issuing a Discussion Paper on 22 October 2004,[32] and

---

[30] *Philip Morris Brands Sàrl v Uruguay*, ICSID No ARB/10/7, Award (8 July 2016), para 399.

[31] An example of this is the case between Bolivia and Aguas del Tunari. See *Aguas del Tunari v Bolivia*, ICSID Case No ARB/02/3, decision on respondent's objections to jurisdiction of 21 October 2005, para 328.

[32] ICSID, 'Possible Improvements of the Framework for ICSID Arbitration', Discussion Paper, ICSID Secretariat, 22 October 2004.

a Working Paper on 12 May 2005 containing a summary of the comments received on the discussion paper. According to the Working Paper, there seems to have been a general agreement that, if international appellate procedures were to be introduced for investment treaty arbitrations, this might best be done through a single ICSID mechanism rather than by different mechanisms established under each treaty concerned. However, there appeared to be at the same time a general agreement that it would be premature to attempt to establish such an ICSID mechanism at that stage as the concern of many developing countries seems to have been with the potential costs involved in such an appeal process.[33] It should also be noted here that any amendment to the ICSID Convention requires the support of all states party to the Convention, which is not an easy undertaking. It should also be noted that another reason given by Bolivia for its withdrawal from ICSID in May 2007 was the absence of an appeal mechanism against the decisions of ICSID tribunals. The Bolivian government alleged that such tribunals were biased towards foreign corporations and it was unsatisfactory that there was no provision for any appeal against their decisions.

The notion of appeal against arbitral awards is not new as it is already a possibility in many maritime and commodity arbitration systems.[34] Moreover, it appears that more than 20 states may have signed treaties with provisions for an appeal mechanism against arbitral awards. The issue of such an appeal mechanism against decisions of arbitration tribunals was also discussed during the OECD-sponsored negotiations on Multilateral Agreement on Investment (MAI). Furthermore, as pointed out by Redfern and others, the law of the seat of arbitration already provides some way of challenging, whether 'setting aside' or 'annulling', an arbitral award in many countries,[35] and the ICSID mechanism already has a 'quasi-appeal' provision for annulment of an arbitral award under certain conditions. It is possible to challenge in national courts under narrowly defined, basically technical, conditions the awards of arbitration tribunals sitting under the UNCITRAL or other arbitration rules, but it is not possible to do so for awards made under ICSID rules because of the special status that such awards enjoy under the ICSID Convention.[36] Article 34 of the 1985 Model Law of UNCITRAL on International Commercial Arbitration states that a national court of the seat of arbitration can set aside an arbitral award made by an arbitral tribunal sitting under the UNCITRAL rules if the award is in conflict with the public policy of the state concerned or the subject matter of the dispute is not capable of settlement by arbitration under the law of the state concerned.

Scholars and practitioners alike continue to debate whether the existing jurisprudence of international investment tribunals and courts is tilted towards the

---

[33] See a report of the South Centre, 'Developments on Discussion for the Improvement of the Framework for ICSID Arbitration and the Participation of Developing Countries', South Centre Analytical Note, February 2005, SC/TADP/AN/INV/1.

[34] A Redfern et al, *Law and Practice of International Commercial Arbitration*, 4th edn (London, Sweet & Maxwell, 2004) 479.

[35] Ibid.

[36] See S Choi, 'Judicial Enforcement of Arbitration Awards under ICSID and New York Conventions' (1993) 28 *New York University Journal of International Law and Politics* 175.

'sole-effect' doctrine[37] or the 'police-powers' doctrine.[38] An appeal mechanism would be helpful in harmonising different trends in interpreting the rules of foreign investment law and the somewhat divergent views of various investment tribunals.[39] As seen earlier, two tribunals could reach two different conclusions, giving rise to legal uncertainty. Each tribunal is at liberty to cite or not to cite previous decisions of other tribunals on similar questions of law.[40] In practice, tribunals seem to be citing the decisions of previous tribunals only when convenient. Examples of two tribunals giving somewhat different rulings on similar questions of law are *SGS v Pakistan* and *SGS v Philippines*. These tribunals reached two different conclusions as to the application of the BIT protection to contractual disputes. The tribunal in *SGS v Philippines* regarded the decision in *SGS v Pakistan* as having only a *res judicata* effect rather than providing a precedent for future tribunals. The tribunal reasoned that:

> [A]lthough different tribunals constituted under the ICSID system should in general seek to act consistently with each other, in the end it must be for each tribunal to exercise its competence in accordance with the applicable law, which will by definition be different for each BIT and each Respondent State.[41]

Another example of two tribunals giving somewhat different rulings on similar issues are the rulings in *LG&E v Argentina* and *Enron v Argentina*.[42] In the former case an ICSID tribunal had accepted to an extent the plea of necessity by Argentina in adopting regulatory emergency measures in the face of a financial crisis in the country.

---

[37] According to this doctrine, as coined by authors such as Dolzer and Bloch and as summed up by Brunetti, 'the crucial factor in determining whether an indirect expropriation has occurred is solely the effect of the governmental measure on the property owner; the purpose of the governmental measure is irrelevant in making that determination'. M Brunetti, 'Indirect Expropriation in International Law' (2003) 5 *International Law Forum du droit international* 150, 151; R Dolzer and F Bloch, 'Indirect Expropriation: Conceptual Realignments?' (2003) 5 *International Law Forum du droit international* 155, 158. Cases such as *Tippetts* decided by the Iran–US Claims Tribunal and *Metalclad* decided by an ICSID tribunal are cited to support this doctrine.

[38] As summed up by Brunetti (n 34), the 'police power' doctrine too considers the purpose and context of the governmental measure in establishing whether a regulatory measure amounts to an expropriation. Cases such as *Sedco* before the Iran–US Claims Tribunal give impetus to the 'police power' doctrine. In the *Sedco* case the Tribunal held that it is 'an accepted principle of international law that a State is not liable for economic injury which is a consequence of a bona fide "regulation" within the accepted police power of States'. *Sedco, Inc v National Iranian Oil Co*, 9 Iran–US Claims Trib Rep (1985) 248, 275. Indeed, the *Restatement (Third) of the Foreign Relations Law of the US* (s 712, cmt g, 201) (1986) states that a state need not compensate foreign property owners for interference with property interests that results from 'bona fide general taxation, regulation, forfeiture for crime, or other action of the kind that is commonly accepted as within the police powers of State'. Among the authors who believe that the 'police powers' of the state are gaining predominance today is Allen S Weiner. For his analysis of this doctrine, see AS Weiner, 'Indirect Expropriations: The Need for a Taxonomy of "Legitimate" Regulatory Purposes' (2003) 5 *International Law Forum du droit international* 166, 168.

[39] WH Knull and ND Rubins, 'Betting the Farm on International Arbitration: Is it Time to Offer an Appeal Mechanism?' (2000) 11 *American Review of International Arbitration* 531; N Rubins, 'Judicial Review of Investment Arbitration Awards', in T Weiler (ed), *NAFTA: Investment Law and Arbitration: Past Issues, Current Practice, Future Prospects* (New York, Transnational, 2004) 359–90.

[40] See C Brown, 'The Use of Precedents of other International Courts and Tribunals in Investment Treaty Arbitration', paper presented at the Annual Conference of the British Institute of International and Comparative Law, 10 June 2005.

[41] *SGS v Philippines*, ICSID Case No ARB/02/6, 29 January 2004, para 97.

[42] *Enron v Argentina*, award of 22 May 2007, available online at www.investmentclaims.com/decisions.

However, in the latter case another ICSID tribunal was not prepared to do so. The irony is that one individual was sitting in both tribunals as an arbitrator. The latter tribunal remained silent as to the earlier finding of a state of necessity in the former case.

Similarly, the *Vivendi* Annulment Committee disagreed with the initial ruling of the *Vivendi* tribunal on this issue. The annulment mechanism is not an appeal mechanism. As in *Plama v Bulgaria*,[43] one ICSID tribunal may misinterpret the decision of another tribunal but there is no provision for appeal against such decisions. Even when a later tribunal finds that the award of a former tribunal contained some errors of law, it has no powers to overturn the erroneous portion of the award. For instance, although an ICSID annulment committee in *CMS v Argentina* overturned a portion of an arbitration ruling, it concluded that it lacked the power to overturn certain other portions of that award which the committee had found to contain significant legal errors. After criticising the reasoning of the original arbitration on its treatment of the doctrine of necessity, the annulment committee went on to state that if it were 'acting as a court of appeal, it would have to reconsider the [original] Award on this ground'.

Another example of an interesting annulment of an ICSID award was in *Sempra Energy International v Argentina*. A new jurisprudential trend was set in this case by an ad hoc ICSID committee, which annulled the arbitral award previously made by an ICSID tribunal. The tribunal had found that the violations by Argentina of its investment obligations were not excused by reasons of necessity under customary international law or the US–Argentina BIT. However, the ad hoc committee held that the tribunal had clearly exceeded its powers by committing a manifest error of law. This is a landmark decision that is likely to have far-reaching implications for international investment arbitration in the years to come.[44]

Some tribunals have asserted some self-proclaimed importance of the pronouncements that they are making in their decisions whether or not other tribunals or publicists agree with such assertions.[45] If there were an appeal mechanism, it would bring about more cohesion and more legal certainty to this body of law. The rulings of the appellate body would then command higher authority and respect amongst various international investment tribunals. This is the case within the WTO dispute settlement mechanism on international trade law matters and a similar approach could be adopted for foreign investment law. In a proposal made by the European Commission in relation to the draft TTIP with the US, the Commission suggested the creation of an investment court with an appellate mechanism.[46]

---

[43] *Plama Consortium Ltd v Republic of Bulgaria*, ICSID Case No ARB/03/24, decision of 8 February 2005, 69, para 217.

[44] *Sempra Energy International v Argentina*, ICSID No ARB/02/16, 29 June 2010.

[45] An example of this is the case between Bolivia and Aguas del Tunari. See *Aguas del Tunari v Bolivia*, ICSID Case No ARB/02/3, decision on respondent's objections to jurisdiction of 21 October 2005, para 328.

[46] European Commission press release, 16 September 2015, available at: http://europa.eu/rapid/press-release_IP-15-5651_en.htm (accessed 24 September 2015). The draft of the Commission of Chapter II on Investment is available at: http://trade.ec.europa.eu/doclib/docs/2015/september/tradoc_153807.pdf (accessed 24 September 2015).

Creation of an International Investment Court

The new developments within foreign investment law outlined in the preceding chapters call for a balancing act on the part of investment dispute settlement mechanisms in order to reconcile competing interests and principles. However, are the mechanisms such as ICSID or UNCITRAL capable of rising to the challenge? Are they suitable mechanisms to undertake a balancing of private rights and public interests? As argued by Mann and Moltke, existing investment dispute settlement institutions 'were not designed to address complex issues of public policy that now routinely come into play in investor–State disputes'.[47] Perhaps what the world of foreign investment needs is at least a WTO DSB-styled quasi-judicial international investment court[48] that could balance competing interests as has, to certain extent, the WTO DSB, in spite of it being primarily a trade dispute settlement mechanism. A strict timetable-bound, efficient and speedy international investment court may prove popular with investors too as they seem to be becoming increasingly frustrated with the length of time taken by international investment tribunals to settle a dispute. For instance, the average time taken by an ICSID arbitration tribunal under NAFTA is three years. This is one year longer than the average time taken to resolve a trade dispute by a WTO DSB.

After all, the WTO DSB is a blend of diplomacy, negotiation, conciliation and arbitration designed to ensure an amicable and speedy resolution of trade disputes. The proposal made in this regard in the IISD's Model International Agreement on Investment for Sustainable Development offers a good model for the settlement of investment disputes. An international investment court would also have more legitimacy, accountability and transparency than would an ad hoc arbitration tribunal. Concern has often been raised as to the competence, though not the personal integrity, of the arbitrators appointed to serve in private, commercial dispute panels; in particular there is concern as to their ability to strike a balance between public and private interests. Even if arbitrators wish to do so, would they be right to do so while adjudicating on a private dispute between a foreign investor and a host state? To ensure that the old maxim 'justice must be blind' is followed as much as possible and to increase accountability, transparency and legitimacy, there ought to be some public scrutiny in the selection of arbitrators to sit on arbitration tribunals whose decisions produce implications beyond the disputing parties and impact on national and global public policy issues.

Indeed, the European Commission seems to be moving in this direction. It released in September 2015 a revised draft Chapter II of the TTIP containing a proposal for a new and transparent system for resolving disputes between investors and

---

[47] H Mann and K von Moltke, *A Southern Agenda on Investment? Promoting Development with Balanced Rights and Obligations for Investors, Host States and Home States* (Winnipeg, International Institute for Sustainable Development, 2005) 17.

[48] Gus Van Harten also supports this idea: G Van Harten, *Investment Treaty Arbitration and Public Law* (Oxford, Oxford University Press, 2007) 180 et seq.

states – the Investment Court System. If the Commission's proposals are accepted, the new Investment Court System would replace the existing ISDS mechanism in all ongoing and future EU investment negotiations, including the TTIP.[49] What the Commission has proposed is modelled very much on the WTO's DSB and contains mechanisms for mediation, consultation, and adjudication. The Investment Court System will have a court of first instance and an appellate court.

Settlement of Investment Disputes by the WTO DSB

It is also possible to entrust the WTO DSB to settle, along with trade and investment disputes under the WTO agreements, disputes arising out of the application and interpretation of the provisions of BITs, FTAs and other IIAs. This could be done by inserting a provision to this effect in such treaties through amendment or by concluding a new protocol or through a global treaty dealing solely with the resolution of investment disputes. If it proves impossible to conclude a comprehensive global treaty on foreign investment, it should be easier to conclude an international treaty dealing solely with the settlement of investment disputes. Indeed, such a possibility was discussed within the Working Group on the Relationship between Trade and Investment of the WTO in the early 2000s.[50] This Working Group suggested, inter alia, that to secure a 'transparent, stable and predictable framework' for investment it would be desirable to entrust the DSB to settle all investment disputes since the DSB provisions were already applicable to investment disputes arising out of interpretation and application of WTO agreements, including the TRIMs. Thus, a plausible argument was advanced in favour of integrating the settlement of investment disputes into the WTO DSB in order to ensure greater coherence in the treatment of investment-related policies.

Indeed, if the WTO had intended to conclude an agreement on investment it would perhaps have included a provision for the settlement of investment disputes by its DSB. In fact, as stated earlier, the WTO system of dispute settlement allows for settlement of disputes through a process of consultation before the disputes reach the adjudication stage. The WTO system is a good blend of conciliation, mediation, arbitration and appeal within one system.[51] But the dispute settlement provisions of most BITs, FTAs and other IIAs lack some of these characteristics and are more rigid than the WTO system. Of course, the current legal, institutional and physical infrastructure of the DSB may not be able to cope with the possible flood of investment disputes

---

[49] European Commission press release, 16 September 2015, available at: http://europa.eu/rapid/press-release_IP-15-5651_en.htm (accessed 24 September 2015). The draft of the Commission of Chapter II on Investment is available at: http://trade.ec.europa.eu/doclib/docs/2015/september/tradoc_153807.pdf (accessed 24 September 2015).

[50] See Report of the Working Group on the Relationship between Trade and Investment to the General Council of the WTO, WT/WGTI/6, 9 December 2002.

[51] See SP Subedi, 'WTO Dispute Settlement Mechanism as a New Technique for Settling Disputes in International Law', in D French, M Saul and ND White (eds), *International Law and Dispute Settlement: New Problems and Techniques* (Oxford, Hart Publishing, 2010) 173–90.

if private investors are given access to the DSB since this mechanism is designed to entertain state–state trade law disputes.

In addition, if private investors are given access to the DSB in investment cases they would in no time also demand such access in trade law disputes too, and it would be difficult to resist such pressure. In that case, the international community or the WTO would have to make the DSB a mammoth organisation. This may also require substantial increases in the budget of the DSB and the developing country members may oppose such a move on the grounds of the costs involved. This was one of the concerns expressed by many developing countries when an appeal mechanism was discussed within the ICSID Convention. Furthermore, since private investors already pay the costs of international arbitration they could be required to pay the costs of the DSB too. Even then the costs of litigation for states would grow as and when more and more private actors resort to the DSB against the host states, not only in investment but also in trade disputes.

However, problems associated with costs could be addressed by creating an 'access to international justice' fund to ease the financial pressure on the least-developed and other low-income developing countries. After all, such countries can always be sued by private actors before international investment tribunals in investment disputes under the existing BITs and other IIAs, and such countries have been forced to accept the rulings of such tribunals which are less transparent, less accountable, and by and large pro-investor. Thus, it would be better for all groups of countries, whether developed or developing, to have a more transparent and better organised permanent international dispute settlement system than the ad hoc ones that currently exist.

The idea of granting access to the DSB, an intergovernmental mechanism, for private actors for both trade and investment disputes may sound like quite a bold move at this point in time,[52] but it will become increasingly difficult to resist pressure in this direction in the future. This is because at present MNEs and other trading business organisations have to rely on their home state to pursue cases on their behalf before the DSB. After all, the real victims of any trade-distorting mechanism would be MNEs and business organisations and they may grow increasingly frustrated with a system that does not allow the real victims direct access to the dispute settlement mechanism. If the evolution of the international investment dispute settlement system is any guide, the WTO DSB will have to move in this direction one day. Originally, 'gunboat' diplomacy was used to assist foreign investors. This policy gave way in due course to the notion of 'diplomatic' protection under which the home state took the matter up and pursued the case on behalf of the investor. Ultimately, diplomatic protection in turn gave way to an ISDS system under which investors have direct access to international tribunals.

At present, the system used to settle international trade disputes is akin to 'diplomatic protection'. In other words, it has evolved to the point that the system of investment dispute resolution reached some 50 or 80 years ago. Just as the system

---

[52] In fact, a provision for settlement of an international trade law dispute between a private party and a government is already in place under the Pre-shipment Inspection (PSI) Agreement.

for the settlement of investment disputes grew into a fully fledged ISDS mechanism, there will be increased pressure in the years to come for some form of 'trader–state' dispute settlement mechanism. The private actors in the arena of international trade can claim that the current WTO system offers them no real justice, and the world may witness the promotion of new slogans such as 'no litigation without representation', 'no justice without access' or 'real victims for real justice', etc.

Revision of Investment Contracts

The investment legal landscape is dominated not only by BITs or IIAs, but also by state–investor contracts. Therefore, without ensuring a balance in the state–investor contracts, any of the reform of the BIT or IIA regime will not bring about the desired results in full. Responsible contracting will in the future entail dispensing with traditional contract templates or standard form contracts and incorporating human rights and environmental protection into such contracts. The Ruggie Principles, or the UN's Guiding Principles on Business and Human Rights, do offer certain guidelines for responsible contracts. As seen earlier, since the BIT protection has been extended to some disputes under investment or state contracts, it can be argued that such contracts should fall under the purview of international law. If there was general consensus on the part of the investment-exporting and investment-receiving states to harmonise the law and practice, they could revise the investment or state contracts that exist among themselves to reflect the changes that have been taking place in this area. Similarly, if foreign investors and the host states concerned were to come to the view that both of these sides have a duty to uphold human rights and environmental values, they have a number of options to achieve this including: amending the investment contracts; inserting provisions to this effect into the contracts; concluding supplementary contracts to complement the original contracts; or amending the relevant provisions in the original contracts.

Indeed, there are a few examples in which some new understandings have been reached between investors and host states to soften the negative impact of investment contracts on human rights. Examples are ExxonMobil's statement concerning its operations in Chad and Cameroon[53] and British Petroleum's declaration on the Baku–Tibilisi–Ceyhan pipeline project.[54] After all, whether it is through the Global Compact or the Equator Principles or other self-regulatory codes of conduct, various responsible MNEs have already accepted their responsibility to maintain human rights and environmental standards in the countries where they conduct their business. Several developing countries, notably Bolivia, Venezuela and Nigeria, have stated that they will be looking to renegotiate certain investment contracts with foreign investors especially in the non-renewable energy sector.

---

[53] See S Leader, 'Human Rights, Risks, and New Strategies for Global Investment' (2006) 9 *Journal of International Economic Law* 657, 659.

[54] As cited in Leader, ibid, 659.

Investment contracts could extend this notion to require that foreign investors must subject their major investment projects to environmental, human rights and other social impact assessment in the host country concerned. In addition, an international agency could be entrusted with the task of verifying the content of an investment agreement or contract below a certain threshold and certifying that it meets the international human rights or environmental standards applicable to such an agreement. What is more, a system similar to the Inspection Panel of the World Bank could be created to receive complaints against serious violations of human rights or international environmental standards by foreign investors in the countries where they conduct their business.

Revision of Bilateral Investment Treaties Through a Protocol

As stated earlier, a clause in a draft article in the agreement between the EU and the Pacific members of the ACP countries of June 2006 included an interesting and more balanced provision with regard to regulatory measures. Most of the BITs concluded in the BIT-rush period of the 1990s will be expiring soon. Provisions such as those just suggested could be inserted when renewing such treaties. Again, an intergovernmental organisation could take the lead towards the conclusion of a framework treaty or protocol to this effect, requiring all parties to it to insert such provisions in both existing and future agreements.

In 2007, Bolivia stated that it would pursue revisions to its 24 BITs in order to accommodate a new definition of investment and new provisions on performance requirements and dispute resolution. It is well within the sovereign rights of any country to seek revisions to its BITs with other states by consent at any time or at the time of renewal of the treaty concerned if there is a provision to this effect in the treaties.

Revision of ICSID, UNCITRAL and Other Arbitration Rules

Whether or not a major overhaul of the substantive rules of foreign investment law is possible, some improvements could be made to the institutional framework and procedural rules concerning the operation of the investment tribunals constituted under ICSID or UNCITRAL, or other regional or international arbitration centres, in order to increase legitimacy, transparency, impartiality, accountability and consistency in the practices of such tribunals. Critics argue that the current system of investment dispute settlement 'assigns dispute panels an active role in implementation and interpretation without any of the institutions of good governance that are essential to such an undertaking in other jurisdictions'.[55]

A revision of these rules will go some way to addressing the problems concerning the operation of foreign investment law. Indeed, moves to amend the UNCITRAL rules[56] and the Stockholm rules[57] began some time ago. Accordingly, the 1976 UNCITRAL Arbitration Rules were revised in 2010 to provide a comprehensive set of procedural rules upon which parties may agree for the conduct of arbitral proceedings arising out of their commercial relationship. The revision seems to be designed to enhance the efficiency of arbitration under the Rules without altering the original structure of the text.[58] However, in 2014 a new UNCITRAL Convention on Transparency, known as the Mauritius Convention, was adopted by the UN General Assembly; this Convention provides for a mechanism for the application of the UNCITRAL Rules on Transparency in Treaty-based Investor–State Arbitration to arbitrations arising under investment treaties concluded before 1 April 2014. ICSID too amended its Rules of Procedure for Arbitration Proceedings (the 'ICSID Arbitration Rules'), and its Arbitration (Additional Facility) Rules (the 'Additional Facility Arbitration Rules') in 2006 in order to address some of the concerns raised by critics of ICSID; these amendments focused on (i) the ability of non-parties to intervene in arbitration proceedings and attend hearings, (ii) the public disclosure of ICSID awards and (iii) the independence of arbitrators.

ICSID has come under heavy public scrutiny about its institutional set up and procedural standards. Some commentators have gone further to allege that the institution itself has a corporate bias.[59] Whether it has a corporate bias or not, ICSID should introduce certain reforms of its own to make the system work better. For instance, it could inject more diversity into the selection or appointment of arbitrators to serve on arbitration panels or on annulment committees, avoid repeat appointments of the same arbitrators from a small pool of individuals, and reduce costs by reducing, for instance, the fees paid to arbitrators for their service. Since the ICSID rate for arbitrators is a hefty c. US$3,000 per day, larger law firms compete fiercely and often aggressively to get the business and to have persons from within a small group people appointed as arbitrators. Some commentators have accused such arbitrators of profiting from injustice or crisis.[60] As noted by Appleton, other

---

[55] Mann and von Moltke (n 44) 16.

[56] The UNCITRAL Working Group II (Arbitration) began work on revising the rules in September 2006 in Vienna.

[57] For an IISD report on this issue, see F Marshall and H Mann, 'Revision of the UNCITRAL Arbitration Rules; Good Governance and the Rule of Law: Express Rules for Investor–State Arbitration Required', International Institute for Sustainable Development, International Investment and Sustainable Development Team, September 2006.

[58] See for full text: www.uncitral.org/uncitral/uncitral_texts/arbitration/2010Arbitration_rules.html.

[59] R Broad, 'Corporate Bias in the World Bank Group's International Centre for Settlement of Investment Disputes: A Case Study of a Global Mining Corporation Suing El Salvador', Working Paper Series, Paper No 2015-3, School of International Service, American University, Washington DC, 25 March 2015.

[60] C Olivet and P Eberhardt, 'Profiting from Crisis: How Corporations and Lawyers Are Scavenging Profits from Europe's Crisis Countries' (Transnational Institute and Corporate Europe Observatory, Amsterdam/Brussels, March 2014).

procedural reforms could be borrowed from domestic procedures that exist in many countries such as a requirement of mandatory certification before an arbitrator can be appointed to sit on a tribunal. As in domestic procedures, ICSID could demand that a person cannot be named as an arbitrator until there is a demonstrated certification of competency. Appleton goes on to argue that for international economic law arbitration:

> [A] potential arbitrator should be able to demonstrate knowledge of the rules of international law and international arbitration procedure that is sufficient to establish the issuance of a proper decision. Simple mechanisms could be put into place for an arbitrator to demonstrate the achievement of these basic standards, and disputing parties appointing arbitrators could look for this certification before making appointments.[61]

In October 2019, over 60 governments held a meeting at UNCITRAL to work on reforming international investment treaties' ISDS provisions. At the time of writing, the reform process was ongoing. The items on the agenda included various reform options, such as the establishment of an advisory centre, selection and appointment of adjudicators, and possible solutions regarding third-party funding. Likewise, in August 2019, the ICSID secretariat also released the third working paper dealing with matters such as expedited arbitration, time limits to which tribunals would be subject, the ability for tribunals to name independent experts and security for costs, among others. The proposal was devoted mainly to revisions of procedural rules and regulations and the ICSID Convention itself was not subject to change under this process. However, it remains to be seen how the negotiations will develop within ICSID and UNCITRAL and whether the reforms will go far enough and develop solutions that will address the concerns of different actors or results in a cosmetic change that maintains the problematic status quo.

Access for Victims to International Courts and Tribunals

Since the emerging trend in the jurisprudence of international investment tribunals is to extend BIT protection to companies adversely affected by investment contracts, albeit under narrowly defined conditions, it could be argued that the real victims of the activities of foreign investors which undermine human rights and the environment should also be given access to international investment tribunals to present their cases under narrowly defined conditions and especially in cases of gross violations of human rights and massive degradation of the local environment. A few attempts have been made to sue foreign companies in domestic courts for polluting the local environment and a lawsuit by thousands of residents of the Amazon against Chevron International before a court in Ecuador is one example.

---

[61] B Appleton, 'The Song Is Over: Why it's Time to Stop Talking about an International Investment Arbitration Appellate Body', in *Proceedings of the Annual Meeting of the American Society of International Law* (April 2013) vol 107, 23, 25.

However, under the existing international legal framework the real victims of the violations of human rights and the degradation of the local environment have no effective legal remedy before international courts and tribunals against the perpetrators of such violations. The victims of the Bhopal gas disaster did not have any legal remedy against Union Carbide before any international tribunal. They were at the mercy of the federal Indian government to pursue the case on their behalf against the company. However, if Union Carbide had been severely negatively affected by the activities of the people or the government of India, the company could have brought a claim before an international tribunal.

The domestic laws of certain countries provide some legal remedy for the real foreign victims of the violations of human rights by national companies doing business abroad, and the US Alien Tort Claims Act of 1789 is an example of this.[62] For instance, in *Sarei v Rio Tinto* the US Court of Appeals of the Ninth Circuit held in a decision delivered in August 2006 that most of the claims of a group of people of Papua New Guinea against Rio Tinto plc concerning numerous violations of international law as a result of this company's mining operations in the country could be tried in the US under the Alien Tort Claims Act even in the absence of the exhaustion of local remedies by the people of Papua.[63] Similarly, certain English courts too have begun to entertain cases against British MNEs for their wrongdoing abroad. *Lubbe et al v Cape Plc* and *Connelly v RTZ plc* are examples.[64] But these examples are isolated cases and the trend in such cases could always be reversed if there is no clear law to this effect.

Defining the Standard or Conditions of Compensation

One of the principal reasons why foreign investors prefer international arbitration to domestic courts in the host state is the likelihood of securing much larger amounts of compensation from international arbitration tribunals. Given the concern expressed about the huge amounts of compensation claimed by investors against both regulatory and other traditional forms of expropriation, and the amount of compensation awarded by international investment tribunals against states, it is becoming imperative to develop or agree on some sort of standard or guidelines for the award of such

---

[62] 28 USC s 1350. This law allows foreign victims of human rights abuse abroad to sue the perpetrators in US courts. The Act, which was enacted in 1789 as part of the original Judiciary Act, is a one-sentence law and reads as follows: 'The district courts shall have original jurisdiction of any civil action by an alien for a tort only, committed in violation of the law of nations or a treaty of the United States.' For a critique of the recent trend in this direction, see P Waldmeir, 'Imperialism and the US Courts: The Counter-Revolution', *Financial Times*, 22 September 2003, 14.

[63] *Alexis Holyweek Sarei and others v Rio Tinto, PLC and Rio Tinted Limited*, Case No 02-56256, DC No CV-00-11695-MMM.

[64] *Lubbe et al v Cape Plc* (CA 30 July 1998) [1998] CLC 1559 and *Connelly v RTZ plc* [1998] AC 854, [1997] 4 All ER 335 (HL). For an analysis of this trend before the English courts, see PT Muchlinski, 'Corporations in International Litigation: Problems of Jurisdiction and the United Kingdom Asbestos Case' (2001) 50 *ICLQ* 1.

compensation. There is not much disagreement as to the acceptability of the Hull formula for compensation; prompt, adequate and effective compensation is generally accepted in most BITs and FTAs as well as in jurisprudence. Even when a BIT speaks of just or appropriate compensation, if the whole article or provision on compensation is taken together, the overall intention is in effect prompt, adequate and effective compensation. The days of differences of opinion over the applicability of the Hull formula or 'just or appropriate' compensation are more or less of over.

However, the Hull formula is applicable only to compensable forms of expropriations. There are several uncompensable forms of expropriations and the law is not clear whether foreign companies affected by such expropriations would be entitled to any compensation, and if so what would be the standard of compensation in such cases. Uncompensable regulatory forms of expropriation would not cause much financial distress if the companies concerned are large MNEs, but if they are small or medium-sized companies, it would be harsh to argue that they would not be entitled to any compensation in the case of permissible regulatory expropriations. Therefore, the time has come to develop in foreign investment law certain principles to provide some lower-level compensation in the cases of regulatory expropriations, especially for small and medium-sized companies; and compensation would only be denied in the rare situations of the exercise of traditional police powers of states.

Although expropriations resulting from the exercise of 'police power' of states, which may remain uncompensatable or regulatory expropriations not warranting full compensation, have always been admitted in traditional international law,[65] several recent decisions of arbitral tribunals have sought to narrow the scope of such expropriation and award huge sums of compensation even against regulatory expropriations, regarding them as constituting a breach of a BIT or the standards of expropriation. As observed by Sir Robert Jennings and Sir Arthur Watts:

> [A] balance has to be struck between the legitimate interests of the territorial State and the need to protect from arbitrary action by that State those who provide for the foreign capital, particularly since such capital is essential to the full development of the natural resources of many States and will not be forthcoming unless assured of reasonable protection.[66]

---

[65] Eg, the Harvard Draft on State Responsibility reads in Art 10 (5) as follows:

> An uncompensated taking of property of an alien or a deprivation of the use or enjoyment of property of an alien which results from the execution of tax laws; from a general change in the value of currency; from the action of the competent authorities of the State in the maintenance of public order, health, or morality; or from valid exercise of belligerent rights; or is otherwise incidental to the normal operation of the laws of the State shall not be considered wrongful, provided: (a) it is not a clear and discriminatory violation of the law of the State concerned; (b) it is not the result of a violation of any provision of Articles 6 to 8 of this Convention [these articles contain provisions concerning denial of access to a tribunal or an administrative authority, denial of a fair hearing, and adverse decision and judgments of a tribunal or an administrative authority on unfair and discriminatory basis]; (c) it is not an unreasonable departure from the principles of justice recognized by the principal legal systems of the world; and (d) it is not an abuse of the powers specified in the paragraph for the purpose of depriving an alien of his property.

[66] Sir R Jennings and Sir A Watts, *Oppenheim's International Law*, 9th edn (Harlow, Longman, 1992) vol I, parts II–IV, 915.

While endorsing the Hull formula for compensation in normal cases of expropriations, they acknowledge 'a considerable margin of appreciation in the light of the circumstances in each case'.[67] After analysing the practice of investment tribunals, they go on to conclude that:

> The prevailing practice of those tribunals makes it probable that if alien-owned property is subject to measures of expropriation which are not arbitrary or discriminatory, and which are adopted in furtherance of the public interest and accompanied by genuine and realistic provisions for payment of compensation, the state will be held not to have acted in breach of its customary international law obligations.[68]

Franck also acknowledges the right of host states to take regulatory measures to achieve social and political objectives. He sums up the situation in the following beautiful and balanced words:

> The agreed rules increasingly allow governments to take actions which promote distributive justice within their societies, providing these are bona fide, that they mitigate harm to aliens acting in good faith, are not in violation of specific international obligations assumed by these governments to attract foreign investors, and are not discriminatory. The mature democratic State, with an independent judiciary, may expect international law and process to give due deference to its political and judicial decisions. Others ought to be grateful that international law and processes stand ready to reassure the potential investor by acting as the residual guarantors of fairness.[69]

Thus, it is highly desirable to achieve a balance by having a set of guidelines designed to draw a distinction between: (i) uncompensable forms of expropriation resulting from the exercise of traditional 'police power' of states; (ii) regulatory expropriations permissible under evolving and extant international law which may call for a less than full compensation; (iii) permissible but compensable forms of expropriation warranting full compensation according to the Hull formula; and (iv) unlawful and confiscatory forms expropriations requiring restitution or much higher levels of compensation.

Some state practice is already gearing up to drawing a distinction between these different forms of compensation. For instance, a piece of South African legislation designed to implement the country's black economic empowerment policy provides for a lower amount of compensation for foreign investors whose assets are expropriated to pursue social clauses such as land reform or more equitable access to natural resources by black people.[70] A draft treaty establishing an Economic Partnership between the Pacific Members of the African, Caribbean and Pacific Group of Countries and the EU and its Member States provides that: 'Bona fide, non-discriminatory, measures taken by a Party to comply with its international obligations under other treaties shall not constitute a breach of this Chapter [ie, Chapter 8 on Investment Protection and Promotion].'

In addition, if it is permissible for states to engage in some regulatory expropriations, it should also be permissible for host states to prevail on foreign investors to

---

[67] Ibid.
[68] Ibid, 926.
[69] TM Franck, *Fairness in International Law and Institutions* (Oxford, Clarendon Press, 1995) 473.
[70] See 'Mining Trio Mount Court Challenge to South Africa', *Financial Times*, 9 March 2007, 8.

renegotiate existing investment contracts for similar 'public purpose' objectives with no compensation or a lower level of compensation. As argued by Muchlinski, '[I]n a market economy, a degree of independent judgment as to the scope of an investment risk will be expected of the investor. Not all investment risks can, or should, be protected against.'[71]

In the case of regulatory expropriations or renegotiations of investment contracts, the standards for compensation could be set at a lower limit if the loss has resulted from a bona fide governmental action designed to protect and promote legitimate objectives of public interest such as measures pursued as part of economic reform or liberalisation programmes or those designed to achieve greater social justice within the host country. In such circumstances the amount of compensation could be lower than full compensation even if the expropriatory measure is deemed to be a compensable one.[72] If the same lower threshold were to be applied to require host states to compensate foreign investors even against governmental measures traditionally regarded as permissible expropriations, many responsible MNEs would not pursue a case alleging regulatory expropriations and claiming excessive amounts of compensation. A distinction could be made between foreseeable and unforeseeable situations under which the host state has taken regulatory measures. If the state concerned has adopted regulatory measures to address some unforeseeable situations, the standard of compensation could be much lower even if the measure taken is against an investment contract, BIT or FTA. Similarly, factors such the conduct of an investor, the need to maintain public order or to promote international public policy or general welfare could be taken into account.

Most investors, and especially responsible MNEs, could be persuaded to agree on such guidelines, thus developing a distinction between different levels of compensation which could then be presented to the arbitral tribunal concerned by a party to the dispute. Even if it is quite an uphill task to adopt a broader or more comprehensive set of norms or guidelines for MNEs when dealing with issues associated with human rights violations or environmental harm, a UN agency such as ILC, ECOSOC, UNCTAD or UNCITRAL, or the World Bank, the WTO or the World Economic Forum could facilitate the adoption of an understanding on drawing a distinction between different levels of compensation among states and business organisations in the same manner in which the UN Secretary-General was able to facilitate the adoption of the Global Compact. This would bring some discipline to the world of international investment tribunals and discourage frivolous, speculative and overambitious cases.

Defining the Limits of the Amount of Compensation

One of the concerns that host states, national and international NGOs, and some intergovernmental organisations have about the trend in jurisprudence of international

---

[71] Muchlinski (n 5) 534.

[72] A case in which both the European Commission and Court of Human Rights dealt with similar issues was *Lithgow v UK* (ser A), 8 EHRR 329 (1986), as cited in Franck (n 66) 456.

investment tribunals is the excessive claims of compensation by foreign investors in disputes with foreign investors and the awarding of excessive amounts of compensation by some tribunals. Organisations such as the World Bank or the WTO or the OECD, or a credible UN agency such as the ILC, UNCITRAL or UNCTAD, could negotiate a set of guidelines or a code of conduct to this effect so that both the investors and the international investment tribunals could take these into account in arbitration proceedings. Such instruments may not have a legally binding effect, but would exert moral pressure and bring about the award of reasonable amounts of compensation. This is especially true with regard to the nature and amount of compensation payable against regulatory measures taken by host states. Concerned by the demands for excessive amounts of compensation demanded by the US business community in cases before US courts, the US Supreme Court has decided to impose new constitutional limits on some court-awarded damages.[73] There is no reason why international investment tribunals could not be required to act similarly.

One of the principal reasons why foreign investors have recently preferred international arbitration to domestic courts in the host state is the likelihood of securing much larger amounts of compensation from international arbitration tribunals. This trend should not in itself be regarded as a negative development because, thanks to the existence of this mechanism, more and more companies are demonstrating their willingness to take risks and invest, knowing that they have the right ultimately to resort to such tribunals. However, the award of compensation should be based on some generally understood guidelines.

Provision for Remedies Other than Monetary Compensation

Most investment disputes in which the investors have been victorious have resulted in monetary compensation, whether in small or large amounts. Monetary compensation seems to be the main objective of most investors when referring a dispute with a host state to an international investment tribunal; but international law also contemplates other forms of satisfaction or remedy against a violation of international law. For instance, international foreign investment law provides for restitution in cases of severe forms expropriation or unlawful confiscation of foreign assets.

As outlined in the Draft Articles on State Responsibility adopted by the ILC,[74] there are different forms of remedy against an internationally wrongful act committed by states, including cessation and non-repetition. Even when speaking of reparation, the Draft Articles include three forms of reparation: restitution, compensation and satisfaction. Similarly, the main remedy contemplated in the DSB of the WTO is not the award of compensation. Whether it is panel reports or Appellate Body reports,

---

[73] See 'US Court Restricts Damages Payouts to the Plaintiff', *Financial Times*, 21 February 2007, 6.
[74] UN Doc A/56/10, November 2001.

they recommend states found to be taking measures inconsistent with their WTO obligations revoke or modify the relevant measure or policy.

However, this flexibility does not exist in BITs, FTAs or other IIAs. In many situations, especially when privatisation or other economic liberalisation programmes have gone wrong or when the host state has had to resort to emergency measures to safeguard vital and legitimate national interests, there should be adequate scope for consultation, negotiation, mediation or the use of good offices before the matter is referred to adjudication. Of course, many such treaties provide for a period of amicable settlement of disputes through consultation before the disputes are referred to international investment tribunals, but there is not much scope or practice for resort to conciliation, mediation and consultation by such investment tribunals themselves.

It is conceivable that in many cases the foreign investors concerned, especially large MNEs or those taking a longer-term approach to investment in the development of the infrastructure or the exploitation of natural resources, would be quite satisfied with a promise of cessation, non-repetition, revocation or modification of the wrongful measures concerned on the part of the host state rather than the payment of monetary damages as such. It would be welcome if the law and practice of international investment tribunals could contribute to the exercise of such flexible methods of providing remedy to investors. This would be particularly helpful if the issues contested before such tribunals had wider implications, whether for the environment or health and safety standards at work or human or workers' rights.

Discouraging 'Cherry-Picking' in the Application of Rules

There is no formal hierarchy of investment rules or of the international courts and tribunals entrusted with the task of settling investment disputes, nor is there any scrutiny of the arbitrators appointed to sit on such tribunals, or any requirement that these arbitrators have specific qualifications. Therefore, the task of adjudicating on matters involving public international law has been shifting gradually into the hands of individuals of differing calibre and qualifications appointed by private parties and states. The arbitrators are not necessarily drawn from a permanent roster, but mostly from the international commercial bar. They are not accountable to any higher judicial authority or public or elective authority. Nor are the proceedings of all arbitrations transparent. Most importantly there is no appeal against their decisions. Consequently, it appears that different tribunals are leading the way in different directions.

As stated earlier, since BIT protection has been extended to some disputes under investment or state contracts, it can be argued that such contracts should fall under the purview of international law. What ought to be ensured is that if international investment tribunals are willing to venture into private law areas by elevating contractual disputes to BIT disputes, they should also be prepared, at the same time, to take into account public international law principles and public interest in adjudicating on such matters. Such tribunals should not be entitled to engage in 'cherry-picking' in the application of rules in settling investment disputes.

National Investment Courts

One way to address the anomaly that exists in the practice of international investment tribunals would be, of course, to revive the Calvo doctrine. In other words, this would mean requiring foreign investors to submit their disputes to national courts prior to taking them to international tribunals. This can happen if the national legal system of the countries concerned is up to international standards and if the independence of the judiciary is assured not only on paper but in every practical sense of the term. As and when states achieve this level of legal development, then a revival of the Calvo doctrine will be possible. Those countries with a more or less fully fledged democracy and independent judiciary would be justified in requiring adjudication of investment disputes by their own national courts. This may be one reason why the FTA between Australia and the US does not contain a separate international dispute settlement mechanism. In fact, most BITs are concluded between a developing country and a developed country, and it is these treaties that provide for the settlement of investment disputes by international tribunals. This is in effect a vote of no confidence by the investor countries in the national legal system and the judiciary of the host countries.

Resort to national courts in the first place for the settlement of such disputes would address some of the deficiencies in legitimacy, transparency, and accountability that exist in systems such as those under ICSID or UNCITRAL. Established democracies with an independent judiciary that, nonetheless, has a reputation of being slow, inefficient and clumsy in practice could adopt laws to establish separate investment courts or investment chambers within the supreme courts or high courts with a speedy mechanism for the settlement of investment disputes. This could win the confidence of foreign investors and ensure swift dispensation of justice.

Indeed, this should be the long-term aim of the international community in this age of globalisation of values, ideas and principles. Since it is widely acknowledged that international law has a role as a gentle civiliser of states, its aim should be to encourage states to develop legal systems that conform to international standards. In that case, these countries would not be subjected to the dicta of unpredictable rulings of international investment tribunals operating under unpredictable sets of rules and awarding excessive amounts of compensation to foreign investors for alleged breaches of the rules of foreign investment. There is already momentum in this direction especially in Latin American countries, South Africa and Indonesia. As stated by the Ecuadorian Minister of Knowledge and Human Talent:

> Ecuador has established a domestic law to protect investments. Ecuador now signs investment contracts with regional (ie Latin American) arbitration allowed, so long as it is based on national laws and regulations, excludes regulatory and tax policy space from the ambit

of arbitration, and requires that domestic jurisdiction be exhausted. These contracts also include performance requirements for the investors and are balanced. They include rights and duties for both parties – unlike BITs that are blank checks for the investor.[75]

It may only be a matter of time before India, the largest democracy in the world, follows suit. Indeed, foreign investors in India seem to be resorting to national courts to sue the government of India on many investment matters and are getting speedy and effective remedy from the Indian courts. For instance, in a dispute with the government of India concerning a ban on Nestle's Maggi noodles on the basis of the claim that it contained lead, the Swiss company managed to have the ban lifted by the Bombay High Court in August 2015. The Court held that the ban by the country's food safety regulator in June 2015 was arbitrary and went against the principles of natural justice. It was a speedy decision by the Court by any standards.[76] Another example of the use of the Bombay High Court by a leading foreign investor was a case brought by Royal Dutch Shell in which the company won a significant victory in its long-running $3 billion battle with India's tax authorities.[77] The ruling of the Bombay High Court in favour of the Anglo-Dutch energy group was seen by some observers as a boost to India's investment standing.

This demonstrates that national courts can be used by foreign investors for all sorts of BIT- or non-BIT-related matters if the judiciary is robust, independent and capable of dispensing speedy, impartial and effective justice. Therefore, the focus could be on reforming the judiciary in host countries rather than on the ISDS mechanism. Indeed, that is what the present author did in his capacity as the UN Special Rapporteur for Human Rights in Cambodia; his recommendations to enact three fundamental laws on the reform of the judiciary was acted upon by the government and the new laws were enacted by parliament.[78] Foreign investors take matters to an international tribunal only for BIT- or IIA-related matters such as expropriation. They resort to local courts for other disputes such as those relating to employment. If foreign investors can have faith in the executive arm of the host state and decide to invest in the country, there is no reason why they should not have faith in the judiciary of the country.

China has established an 'international commercial court' of its own to resolve commercial disputes, including investment disputes. In 2018, the Supreme People's Court issued the 'Supreme People's Court Regulations on Certain Issues in Establishing an International Commercial Court' (Regulations). Under these Regulations three such tribunals – in Shenzhen, Beijing and Xi'an were being established. The core concept behind these tribunals appear to create a 'one stop shop' for international commercial dispute resolution services, including mediation, arbitration and litigation that are

---

[75] A Arauz, 'Ecuador's Experience with International Investment Arbitration', *Investment Policy Brief* No 5 (August 2015) 4.

[76] BBC News, 'India Court Says Maggi Noodle Ban "Legally Untenable"', 13 August 2015, available at http://www.bbc.co.uk/news/world-asia-india-33901999 (accessed 16 August 2015).

[77] 'Shell's $3bn India Tax Case Victory Raises Hopes for Other Companies', *Financial Times*, 19 November 2014, 1.

[78] SP Subedi, 'The Situation of Human Rights in Cambodia in 2010', UN Doc A/HRC/15/46 and 'The Situation of Human Rights in Cambodia in 2013', UN Doc A/HRC/27/70.

'organically integrated'.[79] Another example is South Africa where the Protection of Investment Act of 2015 provides all investors, foreign and local, access to the national courts. Stating that reliance on domestic legislation can address concerns over the lack of consistency, coherence, predictability and correctness of arbitral decisions Kelsey goes on to assert that 'Precedent-based interpretation of investor protection rules through domestic courts increases the predictability of interpretations, with opportunities for appeal'.[80] This is especially so in common law countries.

Defining Responsibilties of Foreign Investors

Most IIAs impose obligations on states, define their responsibilities and provide protection to foreign investors. This is basically one-way traffic. In this age of interdependence, IIAs could be expanded to include responsibilities of foreign investors, whether in relation to the protection of the environment or human rights or other global societal values.

Alternative Dispute Settlement Mechanisms and an Independent Ombudsman

Adjudication and arbitration are not the only means of settling disputes between host states and foreign investors. Other non-judicial mechanisms such as alternative dispute resolution approaches (including mediation) could have a role to play in resolving investment disputes if such mechanisms are included as possible means of dispute resolution in IIAs, BITs and FTAs. Indeed, a group of leading experts in international investment law and arbitration offered at a meeting in Montreux in October 2014 a number of alternatives to the current ISDS mechanism, one of which was to establish an international investment mediation service (IIMS).[81] Since due to the high costs involved in investment arbitration the ISDS mechanism is accessed mainly by large companies, a mediation service of this nature would be helpful in resolving disputes between medium and smaller companies and host governments. Another possibility for states would be to create a powerful and independent statutory, commercial or investment ombudsman to receive complaints from private individuals or civil society organisations about malpractice by foreign investors,

---

[79] Matthew Erie, 'The China International Commercial Court: Prospects for Dispute Resolution for the "Belt and Road Initiative"', *ASIL Insight*, 22(11), 31 August 2018.

[80] Jane Kelsey, 'UNCITRAL Working Group III: Promoting alternatives to investor-state arbitration as ISDS reform', *Investment Treaty News*, 2 October 2019.

[81] 'Investment-Related Dispute Settlement: Reflections on a New Beginning', Results of an IISD Expert Meeting held in Montreux, Switzerland, 17–18 October 2014, International Institute for Sustainable Development, Canada. A copy of the report is on file with the author.

whether this is to do with breach of rules or guidelines for foreign investors concerning environmental or human rights protection or health and safety at work issues. Such a mechanism could be used by governments if they have concerns about non-compliance or breach of contractual or other obligations by foreign investors or by the foreign investors themselves if they have complaints about any conduct by the government that is detrimental to them. The institution of an independent commercial ombudsman could be used as an informal first step mechanism to deal with the issues before they become disputes in law.

Enabling Governments to Sue Companies

One of the anomalies of the current ISDS mechanism is that only investors enjoy a private right to action when seeking redress under the majority of IIAs, BITs and FTAs. Host countries do not enjoy such a choice; only investors can initiate the ISDS mechanism when disputes between investors and host countries arise. Further, under the current ISDS system, states are seldom able to file international claims against investors – thus, states can never 'win', they can only 'not lose', but foreign investors can never lose cases; they do not have to pay compensation to the host government or to the victims of violation of environmental or human rights standards. The worst that can happen to foreign investors is that they have to pay the costs of the government if the award does not go in their favour.

Of course, one could argue that states as sovereign entities can always ensure the accountability of both natural and juridical persons, including multinational companies, operating within their jurisdiction for wrongs committed by them. As Judge Schwebel has stated: '[T]hough the international investment process is indeed asymmetrical, states can, and have, brought counterclaims against investors. Arbitral rules, such as those of ICSID and UNCITRAL, expressly authorize counterclaims.'[82] Arguing in defence of BITs, he goes on to state that:

> [S]tates not only have police powers, but the police; their means of exerting pressure upon foreign investors are multiple. The ability of the investor to initiate arbitration only mitigates that imbalance ... the very purpose of treaties is to constrain the freedom of States. Notwithstanding this inherent constraint, states that enter into BITs are free to confirm and specify their rights to regulate within their borders.

However, it is widely recognised that due to the complex nature of the operation of MNEs, their institutional structure, and the immense power and influence that they wield, it is not always easy for national institutions to hold multinationals to account for the violations or non-compliance with their obligations under either national or international law. Therefore, a new provision could be added in IIAs to give governments the right to initiate arbitrations before international investment tribunals

---

[82] S Schwebel, 'In Defense of Bilateral Investment Treaties', *Columbia FDI Perspectives*, No 135 (24 November 2014).

alleging violation of the provisions of investment contracts or IIAs. Another possibility would be to reserve certain areas, such as those relating to the environment, for state-to-state dispute settlement.

Enabling Civil Society Organisations and Individuals to Sue Foreign Investors

The role of civil society organisations or other non-state actors in developing international law, especially in areas relating to environmental and human rights protection, is widely recognised. They play an important role in ensuring that states comply with international human rights and environmental standards. Under public interest litigation provisions they can petition the courts in the country of their registration alleging violations of laws involving matters of public interest. They can also petition the Inspection Panel of the World Bank and certain UN human rights treaty bodies under narrowly defined conditions. Under the Alien Tort Claims Act of the US, they can bring a claim against foreign investors to US courts for wrongs committed by US investors abroad. The can also lodge a petition in the context of the implementation of the voluntary OECD Guidelines for Multinational Enterprises.

Although the OECD's Investment Committee cannot itself pronounce on the behaviour of individual enterprises, it can take cases from individuals or civil society representatives as illustrative of issues that require clarification of the meaning of the Guidelines. During the 2011 review of the OECD Guidelines the consultative status of the Investment Committee was extended to OECD Watch (the OECD Investment Committee's recognised representative of civil society organisations). Consequently, civil society organisations can now bring cases to the attention of the OECD's committee structure, for the purpose of clarifying the Guidelines.[83] For instance, a group of 680 villagers displaced by a sugar plantation in Kampong Speu (Cambodia) filed a complaint with the OECD against the banking giant ANZ, which had partially financed the sugar plantation project. The villagers alleged that ANZ was complicit in the sugar company's violations of their rights.[84] After considering complaints by the Bahrain Centre for Human Rights, Bahrain Watch, the European Centre for Constitutional and Human Rights, Privacy International, and Reporters Without Borders in 2013 that British–German surveillance technology provider Gamma International shared responsibility for the arrest, imprisonment and torture of opposition members, journalists and dissidents in Bahrain by supplying surveillance technology and technical support, the UK's OECD National Contact Point concluded that Gamma International had infringed its human rights obligations with its products, including the 'state trojan' FinFisher software. The British OECD National Contact Point criticised Gamma International for not putting in place a due-diligence

---

[83] OECD, *OECD Guidelines for Multinational Enterprises, 2011 edition* (Paris, OECD, 2011).
[84] D de Careret, 'ANZ Complaint Taken to the OECD', *Phnom Penh Post*, 9 October 2014, 8.

process and for not committing to any binding standards for the observance of human rights.[85]

By going one step further, a provision could be included in IIAs to enable civil society organisations to sue foreign investors that violate international norms or do not comply with their responsibilities under national or international law under narrowly defined conditions. Of course, such an extension of the investment regime's dispute settlement mechanism would raise many questions that would have to be examined carefully. Such a move would profoundly change the nature of the investment dispute settlement process by turning it from an ISDS mechanism into an international investment dispute settlement mechanism. But a step in this direction is something that could be considered seriously if the ISDS system were to maintain and enhance its legitimacy, fairness, transparency and equality of arms. This would be to build on what has already been established.

If foreign investors can sue governments, there is no reason why individuals whose rights are violated by foreign investors cannot sue them for compensation under private action or tort law. International investment law seeks to protect the right to property of aliens against the excesses of host states whether in the form of expropriation or nationalisation or other forms of interference in the conduct of trade and business. The law is designed to protect the rights of persons, both natural and juridical, doing business abroad. This same body of law should take into account the rights and interests of other fellow individuals and allow them to sue foreign investors for wrongs committed by them in the countries where they do business. After all, international economic law, whether it is WTO law or international investment law, is designed to empower and benefit persons, both natural and juridical. These laws have taken a people-centred approach in the recent past by moving away from the state-centred approach designed to empower governments.[86] Just as local individuals do, foreign investors should compete on a free-world level playing field and be prepared to sue and be sued by other actors in that free world. They should not expect to be protected by laws favourable to them or by privileges not available to domestic investors or other ordinary citizens. The time has come to democratise international investment law and to create a level playing field for all. Therefore, this body of law should embrace the idea of a level playing field or equality of arms and empower individuals to sue foreign investors under private action or tort law for any business activities of such investors that violate the rights of individuals.

Of course, the tort law or private action remedy is always available to individuals under domestic law against another wrongdoer, whether it is a private individual or juridical entity. Indeed, in several cases, such as *Kiobel v Royal Dutch Petroleum*[87]

---

[85] 'UK Rebukes German–British Software Company Gamma', European Centre for Constitutional and Human Rights, Berlin, available at: http://www.ecchr.eu/en/our_work/business-and-human-rights/surveillance-technology.html.

[86] SP Subedi, 'A Shift in Paradigm in International Economic Law: From State-centric Principles to People-centric Policies' (2013) 10 *Manchester Journal of International Economic Law* 314.

[87] *Kiobel v Royal Dutch Petroleum*, 133 SCt1659 (2013). This was a putative class action brought by Esther Kiobel, the widow of a member of the 'Ogoni Nine' who was executed by hanging in 1995 along with Nigerian author and environmentalist Ken Saro-Wiwa.

and *Sosa v Alvarez-Machain*,[88] aliens have sued American investors in the US courts under the Alien Tort Statute. However, in the absence of an internationally agreed set of rules to this effect, it would be very difficult for an ordinary private individual to sue powerful MNEs with their complex business structures spread across different jurisdictions with their headquarters in their home countries or to expect domestic courts to have a proper appreciation of the rules of international law. The final ruling of the US Supreme Court in *Kiobel* is an example of the lack of a proper understanding by a domestic judge of the rules of international law or the significance of international human rights law. The US Supreme Court addressed only the question of 'whether and under what circumstances the Alien Tort Statute ... allows courts to recognise a cause of action for violations of the law of nations occurring within the territory of a sovereign other than the United States' and not the issue of corporate liability.[89] The Supreme Court applied the presumption against extraterritoriality to the creation of a cause of action under the Alien Tort Statute and dismissed the claim. As noted by Keitner, after the *Kiobel* ruling some lower courts in the US have interpreted the Supreme Court's opinion as a categorical bar to the claims under the Statute claims involving overseas conduct. The Supreme Court judgment has been interpreted to mean that claims should generally not be allowed under the Statute. However, in July 2015 a judge in Washington DC allowed a group of Indonesian villagers from Aceh province to persist in their claims of human rights abuses against the Texas oil giant Exxon Mobil Corporation, a case that may revive attempts to use US courts or any domestic courts in other countries for international corporate accountability.[90]

Recalibrating the Interpretative Authority of Governments

As sovereign entities, there is nothing in international law that prevents governments from asserting interpretative powers through IIAs or some other international legal instruments if they believe that international investment tribunals have gone beyond the intentions of the treaty parties. The older generation of IIAs were highly protective of the rights of investors and much of the jurisprudence reflects that approach. This is because the older-generation treaties were brief and outlined the principles of investment protection without spelling out what these principles were meant to cover. Consequently, international investment tribunals had huge latitude in interpreting these principles, and they did do so in the spirit of the treaties themselves, which was to protect the interests of foreign investors rather than the interests of host states.

---

[88] *Sosa v Alvarez-Machain*, 542 US 692 (2004).

[89] CI Keitner, 'Introductory Note to Kiobel v Royal Dutch Petroleum Co (US Sup CT)' (2013) 52 *ILM* 966.

[90] See D Gillision, 'Exxon Human Rights Case Survives – On Claim that Execs Knew All', 100 Reporters, available at https://100r.org/tag/courts/ (accessed 22 July 2015).

Rather than blaming international investment tribunals for their pro-investor stance, host countries could restrict the powers of such tribunals by spelling out in more detail what various principles of investment protection are meant to cover within the scope of the treaty concerned. Many states signed up to various IIAs without realising the significance of them or their longer-term consequences. However, many of the newer generation of IIAs do contain provisions designed to safeguard the regulatory policy space of host states and define the nature and scope of the various principles in the treaty concerned. The Malaysia–New Zealand FTA, the Singapore–US FTA and the EU–Canada CETA include such a provision. The EU–Canada CETA allows the parties to the treaty to issue binding interpretations on what they originally meant in the agreement and to participate in arbitration in relation to questions of interpretation, thereby restricting the latitude of investment tribunals. It is through IIAs themselves that governments can exercise their interpretative powers rather than leaving the matter to investment tribunals of dubious character. Indeed, as stated in a policy paper written by Lise Johnson and Merim Razbaeva for the Columbia Centre on Sustainable Investment, state control over interpretation of investment treaties 'is a relatively efficient tool to achieve the objectives of adding clarity to and reducing exposure under existing treaties'.[91]

Use of General Exceptions to Protect the Policy Space of States

Most rules, whether national or international, have certain exceptions and international investment law is no exception. Many states are beginning to introduce general exception clauses in BITs that are partially modelled on Article XX of GATT or Article XIV of GATS. A draft investment treaty between Canada and China is an example. It includes a 'General Exceptions' clause, which reads as follows:

> 2. Provided that such measures are not applied in an arbitrary or unjustifiable manner, or do not constitute a disguised restriction on international trade or investment, nothing in this Agreement shall be construed to prevent a Contracting Party from adopting or maintaining measures, including environmental measures:
>
> (a) necessary to ensure compliance with laws and regulations that are not inconsistent with the provisions of this Agreement;
> (b) necessary to protect human, animal or plant life or health; or
> (c) relating to the conservation of living or non-living exhaustible natural resources if such measures are made effective in conjunction with restrictions on domestic production or consumption.[92]

---

[91] L Johnson and M Razbaeva, 'State Control over Interpretation of Investment Treaties', Columbia Centre on Sustainable Investment, April 2014.

[92] As quoted in A Roberts, 'Clash of Paradigms: Actors and Analogies Shaping the Investment Treaty System' (2013) 107 *American Journal of International Law* 45, 81.

This is how states can safeguard their regulatory policy space, and as long as such measures are non-discriminatory regulatory actions that are designed and applied to protect legitimate public welfare objectives, such as public health, safety and the environment, they will not constitute indirect expropriation. Another example of how states can narrow down the scope of the various principles of investment protection in IIAs can be found in the 2004 and 2012 US Model BITs which set out three factors that should be considered in determining whether there has been an indirect expropriation: (1) the economic impact of the government action; (2) the extent to which the government action interferes with distinct, reasonable, investment-backed expectations; and (3) the character of the government action. If such a provision were to be included in a new generation of IIAs it would go a long way to addressing the concerns raised by expansive interpretations of the notion of expropriation by international investment tribunals.

Greater Protection Through National Law

Initially, BITs were concluded by developed countries with developing countries as an additional layer of protection for the protection of investors from developed countries investing in developing countries, and such treaties signified a lack of confidence on the part of developed countries in the system of governance in the developing countries. Most of the BITs provided for resolution of investment disputes between a foreign investor and the host government by an international investment tribunal rather than by the judiciary in the host country. This was a vote of no confidence in the judiciary in the developing countries by the developed countries. Developing countries were developing not only in terms of economic development but also in terms of the state of the rule of law, democracy and human rights. However, today's situation is different. The judiciary in many leading democracies in the developing world is much more independent than before, many of these states have ratified a number of core international human rights treaties and the rule of law seems to be getting strong in these countries. Therefore, the national legal system itself in many of these countries is capable of providing a high degree of protection to foreign investors and the judiciary in these countries should be able to provide legal redress to foreign investors when they have a reasonable case against the host government.

As an additional layer of protection and as a means of additional assurance, what the governments in such countries can do is to strengthen their national legal system and make the judiciary more robust and efficient so that it can dispense speedy justice. That should go a long way to satisfying existing and prospective foreign investors and dispense with the need to conclude a BIT or any other IIA for this purpose. Indeed, South Africa has already taken a lead in this direction, and the government there concluded in April 2010 that South Africa should, in the words of the country's ambassador to the WTO in Geneva:

> First, refrain from entering into BITs in the future, except in cases of compelling economic and political circumstances. Second, Cabinet instructed that all 'first generation' BITs that

South Africa signed shortly after the democratic transition in 1994, many of which have reached their termination date, should be reviewed with a view to termination, and possible renegotiation on the basis of a new Model BIT to be developed. Third, Cabinet decided that South Africa should strengthen its domestic legislation in respect of the protection offered to foreign investors. In this regard, key considerations would be to codify BIT-type protection into South African law and clarify their meaning in line with the South African Constitution. South Africa would also seek to incorporate legitimate exceptions to investor protection where warranted by public policy considerations, such as national security, health, environ-mental reasons or for measures to address historical injustice and/or promote development. Fourth, Cabinet elevated all decision-making in respect of BITs to an Inter-Ministerial Committee tasked with oversight of investment, international relations and economic development matters.[93]

It was in June 2015 that a new Promotion and Protection of Investment Bill 2015 was presented to parliament for adoption; this draft Bill seems to clarify the non-discriminatory protections offered to all investors from all countries and to provide effective protection while preserving the sovereign right of the government to pursue legitimate public policy objectives. The standards of protection for investors – both foreign and domestic – offered under the draft Bill seem to be similar to those found in BITs but accord more concrete definition to 'investment' to be protected as 'enterprise-based' requiring 'material economic investment' and, thus, not covering short-term portfolio investments. With regard to provisions on 'expropriation' and 'compensation', the draft Bill states that property may only be expropriated in terms of a law of general application for a public purpose or in the public interest. Departing from the Hull formula, the Bill calls for 'just and equitable' compensation, adding that government measures that have an incidental adverse impact on investment, where the measure is to protect legitimate public welfare objectives such as public health or safety, environmental protection or state security, would not be considered expropriation. Concerning 'dispute settlement', the Bill provides that should a foreign investor seek to challenge a government measure, the jurisdiction for the settlement of disputes will be with a competent South African court, statutory body or independent tribunal, with arbitration following the terms of South Africa's Arbitration Act of 1965. Thus, the South African initiative is a laudable one and other democratic countries in the developing world could follow suit and strengthen their own legal system to satisfy the existing and prospective investors and phase out BITs or other IIAs altogether.

China also seems to be in the process of enacting more robust laws with provisions for protection of foreign investors within a domestic context. The Draft Foreign Investment Law of the People's Republic of China released for consultation in January 2015 by the Ministry of Commerce of China speaks of 'protecting the legitimate rights and interests of foreign investors' while 'safeguarding national security and public interests'.[94] Article 3 of the Draft Law provides that 'The State protects the legitimate

---

[93] X Carim, 'International Investment Agreements and Africa's Structural Transformation: A Perspective from South Africa', *Investment Policy Brief*, no 4 (August 2015), 4.

[94] Draft Art 1 of the Draft Foreign Investment Law of the People's Republic of China of January 2015. A copy of this draft law was kindly supplied to the present author by Professor Yuwen Li of the University of Rotterdam School of Law and is on file with the author.

rights and interests of foreign investors and foreign-invested enterprises according to law', without making any explicit reference to international law. On expropriation, Article 111 provides that 'Except under special circumstances, the State will not expropriate foreign investments. In the event of expropriating foreign investments in light of the needs of public interests, the expropriation shall proceed in compliance with the statutory procedure and compensations shall be made in accordance with the law', without making any reference to international law.

The Government of Ivory Coast adopted an investment code in August 2018 that includes a series of innovations in ISDS and on promoting productive and socially responsible investment, including the withdrawal of direct consent to international arbitration, the inclusion of a fork-in-the-road clause and the promotion of institutional arbitration in Africa. It requires investor to abide by improved environmental obligations and regulatory frameworks at the domestic level and under international law. Likewise, South Africa's Protection of Investment Act of 2015 provides all investors, both local and foreign, with protections and access to national courts. In doing so, the law seeks to ensure that the protections accorded to investors are consistent with the constitution of the country and other fundamental legal instruments.

National Arbitration as Opposed to International Arbitration

If foreign investors do not have full confidence in the ability of the judiciary in the host country to dispense independent, speedy and impartial justice, they could be offered an alternative in the form of arbitration in the host country itself instead of expensive international arbitration in far-away locations by unelected arbitrators accountable to no one. For this, host countries could look into enacting a robust arbitration law in a manner that can command the trust and respect of foreign investors. This is what South Africa has done, and other states could follow suit. Another example of a domestic, yet highly respected, dispute settlement mechanism is the Cambodian Arbitration Council. It is an independent, national institution with quasi-judicial authority derived from the Labour Law of Cambodia. The Council is empowered to assist parties in resolving collective labour disputes in Cambodia. Guided by the principles of good governance – integrity, independence and neutrality, equity, participation, transparency, predictability and responsiveness – the Council is able to differentiate its strategy and operations from many other legal institutions in Cambodia.[95]

---

[95] See for more information about this Arbitration Council: http://www.arbitrationcouncil.org/en (accessed 16 September 2015).

National Commercial Courts or Hybrid Courts

One possible way of commanding the trust and confidence of foreign investors in the national legal and judicial system of the host country would be to establish specialist commercial courts with procedural rules conducive to dealing with cases related to international investment law in a speedy, efficient and independent manner. States such as Qatar and Singapore have established or are in the process of establishing commercial courts either as separate agencies or as part of the national judicial systems. Other models have been adopted to resolve disputes or to dispense justice. For instance, the Extraordinary Chambers in the Courts of Cambodia, known as the Khmer Rouge Tribunal, is a hybrid court consisting of international judges appointed by the international community, ie the UN in this case, on the one hand, and national judges appointed by the national appointing authority on the other hand.[96] The UN High Commissioner for Human Rights called for the creation of a similar hybrid criminal court to deal with cases of alleged war crimes during the civil war in Sri Lanka in a report released in September 2015.[97] It is conceivable to constitute such hybrid commercial courts involving national and international elements to deal with disputes between foreign investors and host governments or between foreign investors and other private parties in the country concerned.

Other National Dispute Avoidance and Dispute Settlement Mechanisms

Governments could consider developing national alternative dispute settlement mechanisms to address the issues and concerns raised by foreign investors before they escalate into disputes. The ISDS mechanism is basically the result of a mind-set based on the protection of the rights of foreign investors which does not take into account the duties and responsibilities of such investors towards the societies in which they operate. It is a Western concept in its origin, which overtook the traditional Asian and African conceptions of dispute avoidance or resolving disputes by resorting to alternative dispute settlement mechanisms such as conciliation, mediation and good offices. Formal or judicial dispute settlement mechanisms should be the last resort for foreign investors and they should be required to exhaust or consider other options to

---

[96] The Extraordinary Chambers in the Courts of Cambodia (ECCC) is a special Cambodian court that receives international assistance through the United Nations Assistance to the Khmer Rouge Trials (UNAKRT). The court is more commonly referred to by the more informal name the Khmer Rouge Tribunal or the Cambodia Tribunal. See for more information about this hybrid court: http://www.eccc.gov.kh/en.

[97] Report of the Office of the United Nations High Commissioner for Human Rights on Promoting Reconciliation, Accountability and Human Rights in Sri Lanka; A/HRC/30/61, 16 September 2015.

have their grievances addressed. For instance, after assessing the nature of disputes relating to land-grabbing and several forms of economic land concessions between national and foreign investors and the local, often indigenous, people, the present author working in his capacity as the UN Special Rapporteur for human rights in Cambodia proposed in 2010 to the government the creation of an informal national mechanism to amicably resolve land disputes consisting of the representatives of the government, civil society, the business community, UN human rights agencies and other major stakeholders.[98] The proposal was not to create a parallel body to substitute the judiciary or the national cadastral commission, but to create an administrative mechanism with a view to screening outstanding land disputes and proposing recommendations for resolving them in a legal and fair manner. The government was receptive to the idea, but the civil society organisations were not enthusiastic about the proposal because they thought it would be a government-dominated mechanism. If a truly independent national administrative mechanism of this nature could be created it would be able to command the trust and confidence of the business community and other stakeholders including civil society organisations.

Protection of Foreign Investment by Promoting Human Rights

One of the principal objectives of early international human rights treaties was to protect the right to property of natural and juridical persons investing their capital abroad. When people speak of business and human rights, the business community often gets jittery about it, believing that the agenda is to lay blame at the doors of the business organisations for violations of human rights. The coin of the agenda of business and human rights has two sides to it. The other side of the coin is to promote human rights in such a manner that the regime of protection of foreign investors becomes more robust. For instance, as the UN Special Rapporteur for human rights for Cambodia, the present author focused his first report on the reform of the judiciary in the country with a view to enhancing the independence and capacity of the judiciary to dispense impartial, speedy and efficient justice to all.[99] He went to great lengths to persuade the government to buy the idea that the more robust the judiciary was and the more robust the judiciary was seen to be, the more the confidence the international community would have in investing serious money in Cambodia. The government finally heeded the message and enacted three fundamental laws to reform the judiciary in order to make it more independent and robust and to provide more resources.[100] Therefore, a way forward would be to locate IIAs and investment

---

[98] SP Subedi, 'Report of the UN Special Rapporteur for Human Rights in Cambodia', UN Doc A/HRC/15/46, 16 September 2010.

[99] Ibid.

[100] SP Subedi, 'Report of the UN Special Rapporteur for Human Rights in Cambodia', UN Doc A/HRC/27/70, August 2014.

protection within a broader human rights framework underpinned by international human rights treaties adopted under the auspices of the UN. The better the human rights situation in a given country, the better the protection that foreign investors would have in the country regardless of the existence of an IIA or BIT. For instance, the traditional notion of denial of justice, which is an integral part of fair and equitable treatment, gives foreign investors a legitimate cause of action against host governments. When deciding what constitutes denial of justice[101] any court of law, whether national or international, or any international investment arbitration tribunal, may validly rely upon the provisions concerning fair trials in the near universally ratified 1966 Covenant on Civil and Political Rights. The Covenant offers a relevant vehicle to measure a host government's conformity to international standards on due process. Therefore, the promotion and protection of human rights stands to serve the longer-term interests of business community, including foreign investors.[102] For instance, expropriation of the assets of foreign investors by the host state is a denial of the right to property. Thus, international human rights treaties that protect human rights and make legal remedy against human rights violations robust would be directly and indirectly protecting the rights of foreign investors, including their right to property in all forms. Even if there was no BIT, IIA or FTA providing access to international investment tribunals for foreign investors, they can go to international or regional courts of human rights to seek compensation or other remedy against the measures taken by the host states by invoking the rights guaranteed under national laws, constitutional or statutory and international human rights treaties.

Even if the current regime of investment protection through BITs, IIAs or FTAs were to be phased out, international human rights standards would remain applicable and concepts such as the denial of justice[103] under regional and international human rights treaties and the rule of law in its broadest sense[104] can be invoked by foreign investors to sue host governments for compensation for their failure to protect foreign investors under these human rights standards. Even if ICSID were to cease to exist, there is nothing to prevent foreign investors from suing host governments before other human rights mechanisms such as the European Court of Human Rights or in national courts in the host countries. The award made by an UNCITRAL tribunal in *White Industries v India* is an example of how the denial of justice could be interpreted, invoked and applied in favour of a foreign investor.[105]

---

[101] See on the notion of denial of justice, C Focarelli, 'Denial of Justice', in *Max Planck Encyclopedia of Public International Law* (Oxford, Oxford University Press, 2013).

[102] See generally, UE Ofodile, 'Foreign Investment in Land and the Clash of Regimes: Mapping the Role of International Law and International Human Rights Law' (2013) 7(1) *Human Rights and International Legal Discourse* 56.

[103] J Paulsson, *Denial of Justice in International Law* (Cambridge, Cambridge University Press, 2005).

[104] For example, see The Bingham Centre for the Rule of Law and Investment Treaty Forum, 'Risk and Return: Foreign Direct Investment and the Rule of Law (London, British Institute of International and Comparative Law, 2015) 17, and SP Subedi, 'The Universality of Human Rights and the UN Human Rights Agenda: The Impact of the Shift of Power to the East and the Resurgence of the BRICS' (2015) 55(2) *Indian Journal of International Law* 177–207.

[105] See P Ranjan, 'Can BIT Claims Be Made against India for the Actions of the Indian Judiciary?' (2013) 1(1) *National Law University, Jodhpur Law Review* 87.

Requirement to Exhaust Domestic Remedies

Generally speaking, international legal remedies should be available to private parties only when they have exhausted domestic remedies. That is the case with regard to cases alleging a violation of human rights. Individuals should first seek remedy under domestic law before resorting to international or regional human rights mechanisms. However, in the case of investor-state disputes, the investors are in a privileged position as they are not required to exhaust the domestic options before suing the government before an international investment tribunal. States could require exhaustion of domestic remedies in future IIAs before a foreign investor can take the case before an international investment tribunal. Indeed, the second generation of IIAs concluded by China requires foreign investors to exhaust local administrative review procedures, though not judicial procedures, before resorting to an international investment tribunal.[106] According to the relevant Chinese laws, such an administrative review must not exceed two months in general cases.[107] Of course, since China is a communist country and the judiciary is under the control of the Communist Party[108] it would be rather absurd to require foreign investors to exhaust domestic judicial procedures before suing the Chinese government before an international investment tribunal. But there is no reason why democratic countries such as India or South Africa cannot require foreign investors to have faith in the judicial system in the country if they have the confidence to invest in the country, and demand they exhaust domestic procedures, whether administrative or judicial, before resorting to an international investment tribunal.

Indeed, under the 2011 Bilateral Investment Promotion and Protection Agreement between India and Nepal (BIPPA) some sort of exhaustion of domestic remedies is required before taking the matter to an international investment tribunal.[109] The preference is clearly on a negotiated settlement of disputes. Only when negotiations do not produce a mutually satisfactory outcome within six months do the other options, including referring the matter by mutual agreement of the parties to the competent national judicial, arbitral or administrative bodies in the host country or an international conciliation under UNCITRAL, arise. In other words, it is very much up to the parties to agree which of the above two approaches would be best for them. Thus, what is interesting about this BIPPA is that even when negotiations do not result in a mutually satisfactory outcome, the recourse to an international arbitration

---

[106] M Chi, 'Privileging Domestic Remedies in International Investment Dispute Settlement', *Proceedings of the Annual Meeting of the American Society of International Law* (April 2013) vol 107, 26, 29.

[107] Law on Administrative Review of the People's Republic of China, Art 31, adopted at the 9th meeting of the Standing Committee of the 9th National People's Congress of the People's Republic of China on 29 April 1999 (effective 1 October 1999), as cited in Chi (n 101) 29.

[108] See generally, SP Subedi, 'China's Approach to Human Rights and the UN Human Rights Agenda' (2015) 14 *Chinese Journal of International Law* 437.

[109] SP Subedi, 'India's New Bilateral Investment Promotion and Protection Treaty with Nepal: A New Trend in State Practice' (2013) 28 *ICSID Review: Foreign Investment Law Journal* 384.

mechanism such as ICSID or an ad hoc arbitration operating under UNCITRAL is not automatic.

The disputing parties have the option of referring the matter either to competent national judicial, arbitral or administrative bodies of the host country in accordance with the law prevailing in the country concerned, or to an international conciliation body, operating under the rules of UNCITRAL. Only when the disputing parties fail to agree as to which of these two options would be acceptable to them or when the international conciliation proceedings are terminated other than by signing of a settlement agreement can a dispute be referred to an international arbitration. Even then, it is not mandatory to refer the matter to permanent arbitration mechanisms such as ICSID. The matter can be referred to ICSID or to another arbitration operating under the rules of UNCITRAL. However, two conditions have to be met before a dispute can be referred to ICSID: first, both of the contracting parties must be parties to the ICSID Convention; and second, both parties to the dispute, ie the investor and the host government, must consent in writing to submit the dispute to ICSID. Furthermore, the parties to the dispute themselves can agree to refer to an additional facility for the administration of conciliation, arbitration and fact-finding proceedings. However, no second condition of consent of both parties is required to refer the matter to an UNCITRAL tribunal. Any disputing party can refer the matter to an UNCITRAL tribunal.[110]

New state practice reflected in new BITs such as the one between India and Belarus concluded in 2018 requires the investor State to pursue domestic judicial or administrative remedies related to the measure for at least five years when it became aware of the measure. Only when the investor finds no satisfactory resolution, it can resort to ISDS mechanism either under ICSID or UNCITRAL rules. Since the India-Belarus BIT closely follows the Indian Model BIT of 2015, it has one more innovative provision

---

[110] Art 9 of BIPPA reads as follows:

Settlement of Disputes between an Investor and a Contracting Party:

1.   Any dispute between an investor of one Contracting Party and the other Contracting Party in relation to an investment of the former under this Agreement shall, as far as possible, be settled amicably through negotiations between the parties to the dispute.
2.   Any such dispute which has not been amicably settled within a period of six months may, if both parties agree, be submitted: (i) for resolution, in accordance with the law of the Contracting Party which has admitted the investment to that Contracting Party's competent judicial, arbitral or administrative bodies; or (ii) to international conciliation under the Conciliation Rules of the United Nations Commission on International Trade Law.
3.   Should the parties fail to agree on a dispute settlement procedure provided under paragraph (2) of this Article or where a dispute is referred to conciliation but conciliation proceedings are terminated other than by signing of a settlement agreement, the dispute may be referred to Arbitration. The Arbitration procedure shall be as follows: (i) If the Contracting Party of the Investor and the other Contracting Party are both parties to the Convention on the Settlement of Investment Disputes between States and Nationals of other States, 1965 and both parties to the dispute consent in writing to submit the dispute to the International Centre for the Settlement of Investment Disputes such a dispute shall be referred to the Centre; or (ii) If both parties to the dispute so agree, under the Additional Facility for the Administration of Conciliation, Arbitration and Fact-Finding proceedings; or (iii) to an ad hoc arbitral tribunal by either party to the dispute in accordance with the Arbitration Rules of the United Nations Commission on International Trade Law, 1976.

As quoted in Subedi, ibid.

and that is to prohibit an ISDS tribunal from reviewing the merits of a decision of a domestic judicial authority.[111]

Conclusions

There is a growing interplay between foreign investment law and other competing principles of international law impacting on the economic relations between investment-exporting and investment-receiving countries. There is a need to deal with this interplay in a more comprehensive manner. If foreign investment law was harmonised and a greater consistency was achieved in this area, the law could support the objectives of the international community, including promoting international economic justice, sustainable development, protection of human rights and preservation of the environment.

---

[111] Jane Kelsey, 'UNCITRAL Working Group III: Promoting alternatives to investor-state arbitration as ISDS reform', *Investment Treaty News*, 2 October 2019.

Concluding Observations

International Investment Law: Past, Present and Future

International investment law has evolved over the centuries in response to changing political and economic realities. During the formative years of foreign investment law, the notion of laissez-faire provided the philosophical underpinnings. This traditional notion gradually gave way to the neoliberal concept of regulation of foreign investment in order to achieve the higher goals of the international community, such as raising the standards of living for all as outlined in the UN Charter. Consequently, foreign investment law became a part of the attempt to create a global order supported by international law.

It was the developing countries that sought in the 1960s, 1970s and 1980s to regulate foreign investment through an international instrument rather than leaving the matter to customary international law.[1] The idea was to impose certain conditions on foreign investors, including MNEs, by requiring them to use local raw material, to employ local people and to refrain from interfering in the internal affairs of the host states, among other duties. However, in the 1990s these developing countries became reluctant to support the regulation of foreign investment under the auspices of the WTO. When developing countries sought to regulate foreign investment under the auspices of the UN, many developed countries resisted the attempt, perhaps fearing that such an international instrument would work more in the interests of host states.

When an attempt was made through the OECD to adopt an international agreement on foreign investment in the late 1990s, developing countries opposed this move for fear that the instrument would serve the greater interest of home states. This is also the reason why many developing countries were opposed to the regulation of foreign investment under the auspices of the WTO. Thus, at present there is no single international organisation actively facilitating the conclusion of a global treaty on foreign investment law.

However, foreign investment law is confronting various challenges engendered by other developments in the international arena, including developments in international environmental law, international human rights law, corporate social responsibility and good corporate governance. The current challenge for this body of law is to balance the competing principles of international law and to further the objectives of the international community in terms of, for example, making a

---

[1] See N Schrijver, 'Developments in International Investment Law', in R St J Macdonald (ed), *Essays in Honour of Wang Tieya* (Dordrecht, Martinus Nijhoff, 1994) 703–20.

contribution to global issues such as promoting sustainable development and human rights. These challenges can be addressed by fashioning relations between foreign investors and host countries in such a way that foreign investment law is better equipped to balance public and private interests and to pay adequate attention to other competing principles of international law and the overall policy objectives of the international community. As stated in the Stern Report of 2006,[2] the task of achieving the environmental objectives of the world requires a partnership between public and private sectors and the development of international frameworks that support the achievement of shared goals.[3]

However, it is ironic that whether it is BITs, FTAs, WTO agreements or customary international law, the overall objective of all of these instruments is to impose obligations on states. There is no single, legally binding, international instrument which imposes corresponding obligations on foreign investors or powerful MNEs. This has been left to the governments themselves of the countries concerned. In the absence of internationally agreed rules on holding MNEs accountable for human rights violations or harm to the environment, it has been up to willing courts in different jurisdictions to give their ruling by relying often on emerging or soft law principles or the tenets of other areas of law.

Traditionally, foreign investment law was designed to regulate economic relations in the sphere of investment activities among states. When it began to take shape, it was a body of law for use by states to protect their citizens abroad. Now, however, the character of this body of law has changed, and it is invoked directly by private companies against states before international arbitration tribunals. Since the principle vehicles of foreign investment are MNEs, foreign investment law has become, by implication, the law that governs the activities of these entities. Their activities have a profound impact on the global environment as well as on the human rights situation in the countries where they conduct their business.

The main objectives of foreign investment law are to protect foreign investors against political risks in the host country concerned, to increase economic efficiency and stimulate the economy in the host countries, to increase the flow of foreign investment into such countries to enable them to develop their natural resources, and to ensure legal certainty and predictability to foreign investors.

Foreign investment has played a crucial role in the economic development of many developing countries and this process has been facilitated by international foreign investment law, which outlines the international standard for the treatment of foreign investors in a host country and provides additional protection, such as access to independent international tribunals, to investors who take huge risks in investing in such countries with inadequate physical as well as legal structures. This is because foreign investors that commit capital abroad for the development of infrastructure-related

---

[2] HM Treasury, *Stern Review on the Economics of Climate Change* (London, HMSO, 2006) xxvii.

[3] Indeed, Julio Barboza includes the measures designed to arrest a serious threat against the conservation of the ecology of a state in his definition of the doctrine of necessity which a state can invoke as a ground for precluding the wrongfulness of an act not in conformity with an international obligation of that state. See UN Report A/CN.4/SER.A/1980, 174.

projects cannot leave the country overnight if the government of that state turns hostile. They can be subjected to different types of unfair and discriminatory activities designed to undermine their existence. A major remedy they have against such actions of states is the ability to take matters to an independent international tribunal. The threat of a large sum of compensation against the offending government is a credible deterrent for any government.

However, there is a growing realisation that the current state of affairs is not satisfactory. The focus of most of the treaties, whether bilateral such as BITs or multilateral such as WTO agreements, has become investment protection at the expense of many other societal values and international norms. Consequently, the law has come not only to undermine the public policy space of developing countries, but also the overall objectives of the international community itself, including a fairer, more just and equitable international order. The recent trend in the jurisprudence of international investment tribunals seems to pose a challenge even to some of the well-established or well-settled principles of international economic law such as the PSNR or the economic self-determination or economic sovereignty of states. This has created an unhealthy situation for the international legal order and an unfair outcome for developing countries.

In the absence of a global treaty on the subject, many of the rules concerning foreign investment law are still based on customary international law, and different tribunals have been at liberty to declare the existence of an alleged rule of customary international law or interpret the rules in a manner they deem appropriate. This in itself is not a major problem, provided that when making decisions these tribunals are able to heed the need to balance private interests with public interests. However, most tribunals have a tendency to focus on commercial issues in deciding cases. Therefore, it has become highly desirable to ensure that international investment courts and tribunals are able to pay adequate attention to other competing principles of international law in adjudicating matters concerning foreign investment law.

The existing and evolving inconsistencies in the application or interpretation of certain key principles of foreign investment law are not helpful either to host governments or to foreign companies, including MNEs themselves. Like host states, MNEs would also benefit in their decision-making by having clarity, uniformity, predictability and consistency in the application of the rules on the treatment due to foreign citizens, traders and investors. For instance, MNEs and other investors would appreciate a clearer definition in international law of the term 'indirect expropriation'; such a definition needs to take into account the legitimate right of the state to regulate in the public interest in good faith as well as the need to protect foreign owners of property and investors from arbitrary state action. Therefore, fair play on the basis of a known and predictable set of rules and within the overall framework of international law should be the objective of foreign investment law. This would ensure predictability in the relations between host governments and foreign investors and enhance the role of international law in the management of international economic relations.

Similarly, constant moving of the goalposts makes it difficult for everybody to operate in this already complex world of investment and undermines the higher objectives of the international legal system that seeks to bring order and provide stability and predictability for all. Like the WTO system for international trade, foreign investment law should also be a rules-based system, and that system should be transparent.

International investment courts and tribunals too will have to demonstrate a greater willingness to recognise the rights of host states to take regulatory or other measures designed to ensure that the activities of foreign investors in their territory are consistent with the purposes and principles of the social, environmental and economic policy objectives of the host states concerned. The law of foreign investment is not supposed to be interpreted as providing protection for companies against all risks. Indeed, it was as long ago as the *Oscar Chinn* case that the PCIJ had held that 'favourable business conditions and good-will are transient circumstances, subject to inevitable changes',[4] and there can be no protection against such changes.

The economic, political and social conditions in a host country do change with time and any sensible investor is expected to take this into account before deciding to invest in that country. In a democracy, a new government elected to power has to implement its election manifesto. Every democratic government has to be responsive to the wishes of the people and that wish could very well be to bring about fundamental change in the economic structure of the country, improve the tax system, raise health and safety standards at work, close down environmentally hazardous industries or impose a minimum wage to raise the quality of life of low-paid workers. For instance, most of the demands these days for change in investment contracts or BITs or the adoption of certain regulatory measures are due to heavy public pressure on governments rather than due to the wishes of the people in power. Any new attempt at restructuring the economy of the country concerned or any new initiatives designed to achieve any of the objectives just outlined may have an adverse economic impact on foreign investors.

If such changes are designed to promote general welfare, in good faith, and are implemented in a non-discriminatory manner and without undermining the basic tenets of law, then such regulatory measures should be permissible. Since human rights have been accepted as universal by developed and developing states, and by investor-exporting and host states, and the need to protect the environment has been accepted as a global responsibility, regulatory measures to enhance such public welfare objectives should be accepted as a permissible exercise of state sovereignty if the measure concerned is not protectionist or discriminatory. What is more, even developed countries, which once championed a high degree of protection for foreign investors, have come to realise that they have let things go too far. Therefore, the time has come to take appropriate measures to reconcile the principles of foreign investment law with other competing principles of international law along the lines suggested in this book, and especially in Chapter 8. Such action will ensure that foreign investment law does not operate in isolation but as an integral part of the wider body of international law and in harmony with the overall policy objectives of the international community.

---

[4] *Oscar Chinn*, PCIJ Reports, Series A/B, No 63 (1934) 65.

Convergence of Views

There is a paradigm shift taking place within international law in general and international investment law in particular. Those states which were more protective of foreign investors, such as the US, have now become more protective of sovereignty, while those, such as China, which were more protective of state sovereignty are now becoming more protective of foreign investment because of the rapid expansion of their investment abroad. While states such as Bolivia and Venezuela have decided to withdraw altogether from ICSID, some others seem to be returning to the Calvo doctrine, under which an investment dispute is settled through the domestic courts. For instance, it was reported that 'India is likely to exclude in bilateral trade pacts a clause that permits investor to sue the host country at an international dispute settlement agency.'[5] Australia is also reported to be considering moving in this direction.

The manner in which international investment arbitration, especially between states and investors under the auspices of ICSID or UNCITRAL, is conducted does not look sustainable in the longer term in its present form. Unless more account is taken of transparency, diversity, accountability, legitimacy and geographical representation in their procedures and the choice of arbitrators, ICSID and other similar mechanisms will come under pressure not only from pressure groups but also from states and other actors, including academics. Indeed, in a public statement on the international investment regime, a group of scholars concerned about the manner in which some of the arbitration proceedings have been conducted expressed the view that it is difficult to accept that investment disputes having public law elements can be settled by one-off appointed arbitrators instead of standing courts, which are able to review government acts and render decisions that have a direct impact on public policy of the states concerned.[6] Schill also argues that: '[I]nternational investment law will continue to face calls for increased transparency and for leaving states sufficient policy space – precisely because of the impact of investment treaties on domestic public law.'[7]

Since many of the disputes pending before such tribunals have a direct impact on the lives of people in different countries, people from various walks of life are likely to become highly organised to scrutinise the work of such tribunals. The demonstrations outside the ICSID/World Bank offices in Washington, DC by a group of people concerned about an investment case brought against El Salvador by the Pacific Rim Mining Corporation may be an indication of things to come in the future. John Cavanagh, Director of the Institute for Policy Studies and a rally organiser, was reported to have said that: 'This tribunal is illegitimate and it shouldn't exist. ... It's an

---

[5] 'India May Exclude Clause on Lawsuits from Trade Pacts', available at http://justinvestment. org/2012/01/2049 (accessed 17 January 2012), citing Livemint.com.

[6] 'Public Statement on the International Investment Regime', 31 August 2010, available at http://www. osgoode.yorku.ca/public_statement (accessed 12 November 2011).

[7] SW Schill, 'The Public Law Challenge: Killing or Rethinking International Investment Law?', *Columbia FDI Perspectives*, no 58, 30 January 2012.

attack on democracy.'[8] What demonstrators were stating some time ago is now being said by some lawyers and a growing number of legal academics. They have criticised the investor-state dispute settlement (ISDS) mechanism itself, especially in relation to the proposed TTIP. For instance, Steven Powles has highlighted the possible threats to democracy and the rule of law posed by the TTIP in an article published in *Counsel*, a flagship magazine for British barristers.[9] It is not implied here that tribunals such as ICSID should be influenced by such demonstrations or depart from their obligation to apply and interpret the rules of international investment law as fairly, freely and robustly as possible because a group of people demonstrate against their work on a given dispute. The point is that the time has come to look at the challenges that these investment dispute settlement mechanisms, which were initially conceived, designed and developed to handle a small number of cases mostly in private by a group of mainly commercial lawyers, now face.

Of course, that is not to say that ICSID or any other international investment dispute settlement mechanism should abandon the traditional characteristics of a flexible, speedy and impartial arbitration, but they should operate more within a broader framework of international law. This is especially true since what they do these days has wider ramifications, and international investment law itself constitutes in terms of its content a marriage between public and private international law. The template of a traditional commercial arbitration for international investment dispute resolution has to give way to new developments within international law. A standing tribunal or an international investment court with a strict timeframe such as the one that exists for the WTO DSB for international trade disputes could be a possible solution to many of the problems generated by ad hoc investment tribunals, whether operating under ICSID or other arbitration schemes. The European Commission seems to be moving in this direction. It released in September 2015 a revised draft Chapter II of the TTIP containing a proposal for a new WTO-style and transparent system for resolving disputes between investors and states – the Investment Court System. If the Commission's proposals are accepted, the new Investment Court System will replace the existing ISDS mechanism in all ongoing and future EU investment negotiations.[10] What the Commission has proposed is modelled very much on the WTO's DSB, and contains mechanisms for mediation, consultation and adjudication. The Investment Court System will have a court of first instance and an appellate court.

The approach taken by the European Commission is an attempt to salvage the ISDS mechanism via certain reforms. The draft proposal of the Commission goes a long way to addressing the concerns associated with the current ISDS mechanism, which is based primarily on arbitration. What the Commission, in a significant

---

[8] Report by J Kneen, Communications and Outreach Coordinator, MiningWatch Canada, available at http://www.miningwatch.ca (accessed 26 January 2012).

[9] S Powles, 'TTIP: An Objectionable Agreement?', *Counsel*, September 2015, 28.

[10] European Commission press release 16 September 2015, available at: http://europa.eu/rapid/press-release_IP-15-5651_en.htm (accessed 24 September 2015). The draft of the Commission of Chapter II on Investment is available at: http://trade.ec.europa.eu/doclib/docs/2015/september/tradoc_153807.pdf (accessed 24 September 2015).

departure, has proposed is a formal court system rather than arbitration for settlement of investor–state disputes. It remains to be seen whether other states will follow suit. The indications from some of the developing countries are that they will not accept the ISDS mechanism in any form, whether involving arbitration or a court system, in future BITs or other bilateral IIAs. Having said this, it is apparent from the conclusion of the negotiations on the Transpacific Partnership (TPP) agreement in October 2015 that many of the developing countries in the Pacific Rim, such as Mexico, Chile and Vietnam, have accepted the ISDS mechanism with certain reforms.

The traditional distinction between developed and developing countries seems no longer to be valid when it comes to admitting the need for improving the regime regulating foreign investment. There seems to be a gradual convergence of views among all groupings of states about the need to address the issues surrounding investment protection and especially the ISDS mechanism. Companies in an increasing number of emerging markets, such as BRICs, are becoming important and dynamic outward investors. Equally, developed countries themselves have realised that that they are also important host countries, including for investors headquartered in emerging markets, and that they are increasingly respondents to international arbitration claims. Therefore, the developed countries themselves have sought to narrow down the scope of investment protection to maintain their national interests including regulatory policy space. The change of approach by the US when revising its model BIT of 2012 is an example; it narrowed protections afforded to foreign investors – a significant shift in policy for a country that had long led efforts to provide full protection to investors and facilitate their operations. As stated by Roberts:

> When capital-exporting states originally drafted investment treaties, they viewed them as exclusively or primarily aimed at protecting the rights of their investors abroad and thus demonstrated little concern about the breadth of interpretative authority being delegated to investment tribunals or the absence of clear language protecting regulatory powers. However, a number of early or notorious cases have been brought against developed States, including the United States, Canada, Australia, and Germany, increasing appreciation of the need to protect the regulatory freedom of host States and limit arbitral discretion.[11]

This convergence of policy interests between home and host countries, as well as between developed countries and a growing number of developing countries, is conducive to concluding a comprehensive international convention on the regulation of foreign investment. Of course, negotiating a universal framework treaty would face a range of challenges, as reflected in abortive past efforts to do so. One should not underestimate the challenges of reconciling competing principles and interests and articulating the rights and responsibilities that various stakeholder groups might wish to see in such a framework treaty. However, it has been widely recognised that the current regime of international investment law, especially the ISDS mechanism, is in

---

[11] A Roberts, 'Clash of Paradigms: Actors and Analogies Shaping the Investment Treaty System' (2013) 107 *American Journal of International Law* 45, 78. As she says, 'High-profile regulatory disputes, like Germany being sued over its decision to phase out nuclear power and Australia being sued over its tobacco packaging regulations, will increase the field's notoriety and galvanize NGO opposition. Battles over the scope of annulment and enforcement of awards are also leading investors to question whether the system is living up to its promise from their perspective' (91).

need of reform, and an international approach is needed to ensure consistency, transparency, fairness, legitimacy and predictability in the relations between international investors and governments. It can be hoped that such an international framework will build not only on old IIAs between and among developed and developing countries, but also on IIAs between and among developing countries themselves.

In the absence of an international treaty on the regulation of foreign investment, a carefully drafted new generation of IIAs or revised IIAs could address the challenges facing international investment law by defining the nature and scope of the various principles of investment protection, by protecting regulatory freedom of host states and spelling out under which conditions foreign investors can sue host governments before international courts and tribunals. Indeed, as pointed out by Roberts:

> [A]n increasing number of investment treaties are including provisions in their preambles that make clear that investment promotion and protection are not to be achieved at the expense of other key values, such as protection of health, safety, labour standards and the environment. In terms of substantive provisions, an increasing number of investment treaties now provide that, except in rare circumstances, non-discriminatory regulatory actions that are designed and applied to protect legitimate public welfare objectives, such as public health, safety and the environment, will not constitute indirect expropriation.[12]

Change in State Practice

The world is changing and with it the norms of international investment law. The older generation of IIAs are being replaced by a newer generation, and states are becoming more careful and cognisant of the implications of what they include in such treaties. While leading developing countries such as India, Indonesia and South Africa have embarked on the process of reviewing their existing IIAs with other states, the developed countries themselves have come under pressure from within to address the issues of legitimacy, fairness and transparency surrounding the ISDS mechanism whether it is in the context of the TTIP or TPP. Law itself is an organic concept, and international investment is no exception. Not being able to conclude a global comprehensive treaty does not mean that other means of addressing the weaknesses within the system, such as the conclusion of new IIAs, cannot do the job. For instance, as an exception to the rules on expropriation and compensation, the India–Nepal BIT defines in Article 5(2) the nature and scope of regulatory expropriation.[13]

A provision of this nature is an attempt to reconcile the law on foreign investment protection with other competing principles of international law. It respects the sovereignty of states and enables them to fulfil commitments flowing from other international treaties or to pursue bona fide economic, environmental, health- and safety-related policies in the greater interest of the native residents of the host countries.

---

[12] Roberts, ibid, 80 (footnotes omitted).
[13] See SP Subedi, 'India's New Bilateral Investment Promotion and Protection Treaty with Nepal: A New Trend in State Practice' (2013) 28 *ICSID Review: Foreign Investment Law Journal* 384.

However, what is missing in this definition of regulatory expropriation is any measure designed to protect human rights. Having said this, it should be noted that this treaty is not alone in omitting human rights considerations. Human rights are the latest entrants into the realm of international investment law, and it will take time for them to find their way into BITs or FTAs. If the trend of accepting legitimate or bona fide governmental measures undertaken in a non-discriminatory manner for good environmental, health or safety causes as non-compensable regulatory expropriation continues, it will not be long before bona fide governmental measures to protect core human rights are also subsumed under the definition of regulatory expropriation.

Many new IIAs seem to be geared to addressing the shortcomings in previous BITs and incorporating provisions designed to strengthen the right of governments to regulate in the public interest, including for environmental and human rights protection. Of course, an overarching global treaty is a desirable approach, but until there is political will for such a global treaty, greater corporate accountability for human rights, environmental protection and other global societal values could be pursued in different ways via a range of institutions and instruments. For instance, the Model BIT released by India in March 2015 aims to achieve most of what would be achieved through a global treaty. It goes a great deal further than other model BITs in narrowing down the definition of investment by excluding portfolio investment and intellectual property, omitting altogether the troublesome principles of fair and equitable treatment and MFN treatment, incorporating the notion of non-compensable regulatory expropriation, and requiring exhaustion of local remedies before resorting to international arbitration, and limiting the scope for ICSID-style arbitrations.[14] This model treaty requires foreign investors to contribute to the development of the host country and to operate by recognising the rights, traditions and customs of local communities in order to benefit from treaty provisions on investor protection; gives host countries the right to initiate counterclaims in international arbitration; makes it possible to bring civil action against foreign investors in their home countries for wrongs committed abroad; and places restrictions on their discretion when interpreting substantive obligations in the treaty.[15] It remains to be seen whether other states would follow suit.

The Future Direction

It is now widely accepted that the current state of affairs within international investment law is not satisfactory. The law is in a state of flux, and something ought to be done about it. The views of states and scholars differ on the best way forward. While some of them would like to overhaul the system, others wish to bring about

---

[14] Model Text for the Indian BIT, available at https://mygov.in/group-issue/draft-indian-model-bilateral-investment-treaty-text/ (accessed 17 August 2015).

[15] S Jandhyala, 'Bringing the State Back In: India's 2015 Model BIT', *Columbia FDI Perspectives*, no 154, 17 August 2015.

incremental change. The international legal system is based on settlement of disputes through peaceful means and through the intervention of third parties, whether it is in the form of arbitration or by resorting to international courts. Therefore, maintaining the integrity of international investment dispute settlement mechanisms such as ICSID or UNCITRAL is important to maintain the integrity of the rule of law at the international level. The criticisms against ICSID and other ISDS mechanisms could be countered by reforming the institutions such as ICSID and by introducing changes in the law governing foreign investment in a manner that reflects the demands of the public and meets the challenges of today's world. The process of reform is underway within the framework of both the ICSID and UNCITRAL. However, most of the proposals on the table for discussion do not seem to be designed to make fundamental changes in the current ISDS system. Therefore, it remains to be seen whether the current process of reform will go some way to satisfy those who have called for a major reform of the system. It is crucial at this juncture to reform the ISDS system in a more meaningful manner to keep ICSID relevant for all stakeholders. If major reform is carried out, the backlash that the world has witnessed of the ISDS system (and thereby the ICSID) would be muted to a large extent. Whether it is ICSID or another institution, there has to be an international dispute settlement mechanism to settle investment disputes between States and foreign investors. Therefore, keeping the ICSID relevant is in the interests of all and in the interests of the international rule of law.

Even if ICSID were to cease to exist there is nothing to prevent foreign investors from suing host governments before other human rights mechanisms such as the European Court of Human Rights or before national courts themselves in the host countries: international human rights standards will remain applicable and concepts such as the denial of justice[16] under regional and international human rights treaties and the rule of law in its broadest sense[17] are likely to be invoked by foreign investors to sue host governments for compensation for their failings in protecting foreign investors under these human rights standards. Abolishing ICSID or other investment treaty arbitration mechanisms will not help those who wish to deny foreign investors the right to sue host governments before national or international courts or tribunals. The award made by an UNCITRAL tribunal in *White Industries v India* is an example of how the denial of justice could be interpreted, invoked and applied in favour of a foreign investor. Therefore, the sensible way forward is to reform ICSID and other international investment dispute settlement mechanisms which are well equipped to dispense fair and impartial justice in a balanced and transparent manner. Even if BITs or other IIAs or FTAs were phased out, the issues associated with business and human rights are likely to be growth areas in the future, heralding a new phase of interesting development in international investment law.

---

[16] J Paulsson, *Denial of Justice in International Law* (Cambridge, Cambridge University Press, 2005).

[17] For example, see The Bingham Centre for the Rule of Law and Investment Treaty Forum, 'Risk and Return: Foreign Direct Investment and the Rule of Law (London, The British Institute of International and Comparative Law, 2015) 17, and SP Subedi, 'The Universality of Human Rights and the UN Human Rights Agenda: The Impact of the Shift of Power to the East and the Resurgence of the BRICS' (2015) 55(2) *Indian Journal of International Law* 177–207.

Judge Schwebel writes that:

> International lawyers have been long and rightly concerned with the progressive develop-
> ment of international law. Substitution of national adjudication for international investment
> arbitration would be a regressive development that is to be resisted rather than furthered.
> International investment law is a profoundly progressive development of international law
> which should be nurtured rather than restricted and denounced.[18]

The present author is in complete agreement with this. However, a sizeable number
of sovereign states have grown dissatisfied with certain recent developments within
international investment law – and especially the manner in which some international
investment tribunals have encroached on the public policy space of states – and have
started to assert themselves and to introduce changes in this body of law through new
state practice, whether terminating unbalanced BITs or issuing new Model BITs or
deciding to accord protection to foreign investors through domestic legislation rather
than through treaties. International lawyers have a duty to contribute by making sure
that any change being made is well informed and is in tune with the changes taking
place within the broader family of public international law and with the overall policy
objectives of the international community and this study is an endeavour to that effect.

To conclude, unlike in international human rights law or international environmental law, where there is a group of core treaties that constitutes the corpus of the
relevant law, there is no single global treaty on international investment law. Therefore,
international investment law itself is not clear, a situation that has created a 'goldmine'
for international investment lawyers. Third party funding, in particular, has fuelled the
temptation to use international investment arbitration to sue governments for alleged
breaches of all sorts of trade and investment law rules. Since many of the arbitrators
have interpreted the law according to their understanding of the law, they have been
creative and expansive in the interpretation of the principles concerning the standards
of investment protection in many cases in deciding cases before them. If no consistency
and coherence is brought to international investment arbitration, the expansive trend
may know no limits and eventually tempt business organisations to use international
investment arbitration to sue host governments for violations of WTO law.[19] Therefore,
this study has endeavoured to argue that it has become imperative to bring consistency
and coherence to international investment arbitration system and reform the institutions and mechanisms designed for the development and enforcement of international
investment law within the broader framework of international law. Indeed, it is gratifying that many of the ideas that were advanced in the first edition of this book way
back in 2008 are now being implemented by governments and international organisations. While this book witnessed positive reviews in nine leading international law
journals, there was no absence of criticism from those who were resistance to change.
International investment law has come full circle and change is coming, slowly but
surely, in one form or another.

---

[18] SM Schwebel, 'In Defense of Bilateral Investment Treaties' (2015) 31 *Arbitration International* 181, 192.
[19] SP Subedi, 'WTO Dispute Settlement Mechanism as a New Technique for Settling Disputes in
International Law', in D French, M Saul and ND White (eds), *International Law and Dispute Settlement:
New Problems and Techniques* (Oxford, Hart Publishing, 2010) 173–90.

Index